The Resources of Merseyside

The Resources of Merseyside

Edited by William T.S. Gould
and Alan G. Hodgkiss

Liverpool University Press

Published by
LIVERPOOL UNIVERSITY PRESS
123 Grove Street, Liverpool L7 7AF

First published 1982

British Library Cataloguing in Publication Data
The Resources of Merseyside.
1. Merseyside—History
I. Gould, William T. S. II. Hodgkiss, Alan G.
942.7′5 DA670. M5/

ISBN 0-85323-384-5

The preparation and publication
of this book were made possible
with the assistance of a generous
grant from Granada Television

Set in Linotron 202 Times by Wilmaset,
Birkenhead, Merseyside
Printed by Eaton Press, Wallasey, Merseyside

FOREWORD

by The Right Honourable the Viscount Leverhulme, T.D., J.P., B.A., LL.D., *Chancellor of the University of Liverpool and Chairman of the Organizing Committee of the British Association for the Liverpool Meeting*

I am delighted that on the occasion of the 144th Annual Meeting of the British Association for the Advancement of Science to be held in Liverpool in September 1982 the University is publishing *The Resources of Merseyside*, and it gives me great pleasure to write this short Foreword.

The meeting of the British Association in Liverpool is being held at a time of intense public interest in the economic and social problems of Merseyside. Those of us who live and work in the County and feel an individual and corporate commitment to it, welcome the opportunity to share that commitment with the wider scientific community through the meeting of the British Association. The advancement of science in its various aspects can contribute to the understanding of the problems of Merseyside and to their alleviation.

As part of this contribution the editors of this book have brought together an informative and well-illustrated analysis of the contemporary physical, economic and social resources of Merseyside, to indicate how these resources have been and can be used. The fund of ideas and suggestions for future development which are contained in the essays is to be welcomed. Each individual chapter and the book as a whole provide much food for thought for both the public and private sectors of society.

The Resources of Merseyside may be commended not only to those attending the Liverpool meeting of the British Association but to those who are concerned to further the development and improve the well-being of Merseyside.

CONTENTS

*Contributors marked with an asterisk are public officials, but they write in a personal capacity. The opinions expressed in their chapters do not necessarily reflect the views of their employers.

ENVIRONMENTAL RESOURCES

HUMAN RESOURCES

*Contributors marked with an asterisk are public officials, but they write in a personal capacity. The opinions expressed in their chapters do not necessarily reflect the views of their employers.

ACKNOWLEDGEMENTS

The Editors of any collection of essays are indebted to a large number of people, but principally to the contributors of the individual chapters. In the case of *The Resources of Merseyside* our indebtedness to them is particularly great, since a tight schedule was necessary to meet the successive editorial and printers' deadlines that would allow the book to be available at the Annual Meeting of the British Association for the Advancement of Science. Sandra Mather and Julie Isaac of the Drawing Office, Department of Geography, drew some of the maps, and Ian Qualtrough of the Faculty of Arts/Social and Environmental Studies Photographic Service provided some of the photographs. Mrs. B. W. Thomson typed most of the revised text. The editorial work was greatly helped by Robin Bloxsidge of the Department of Civic Design, who, together with Rosalind Campbell of Liverpool University Press, also supervised the production and publication of the book under the imprint of the University Press. At an early stage, Mr. Christopher Kerr of Granada Television was instrumental in arranging a grant towards the cost of producing the book. Without the assistance of the generous grant from Granada Television, the preparation and publication of this book would not have been possible. To all of them we are most grateful.

W. T. S. GOULD
A. G. HODGKISS

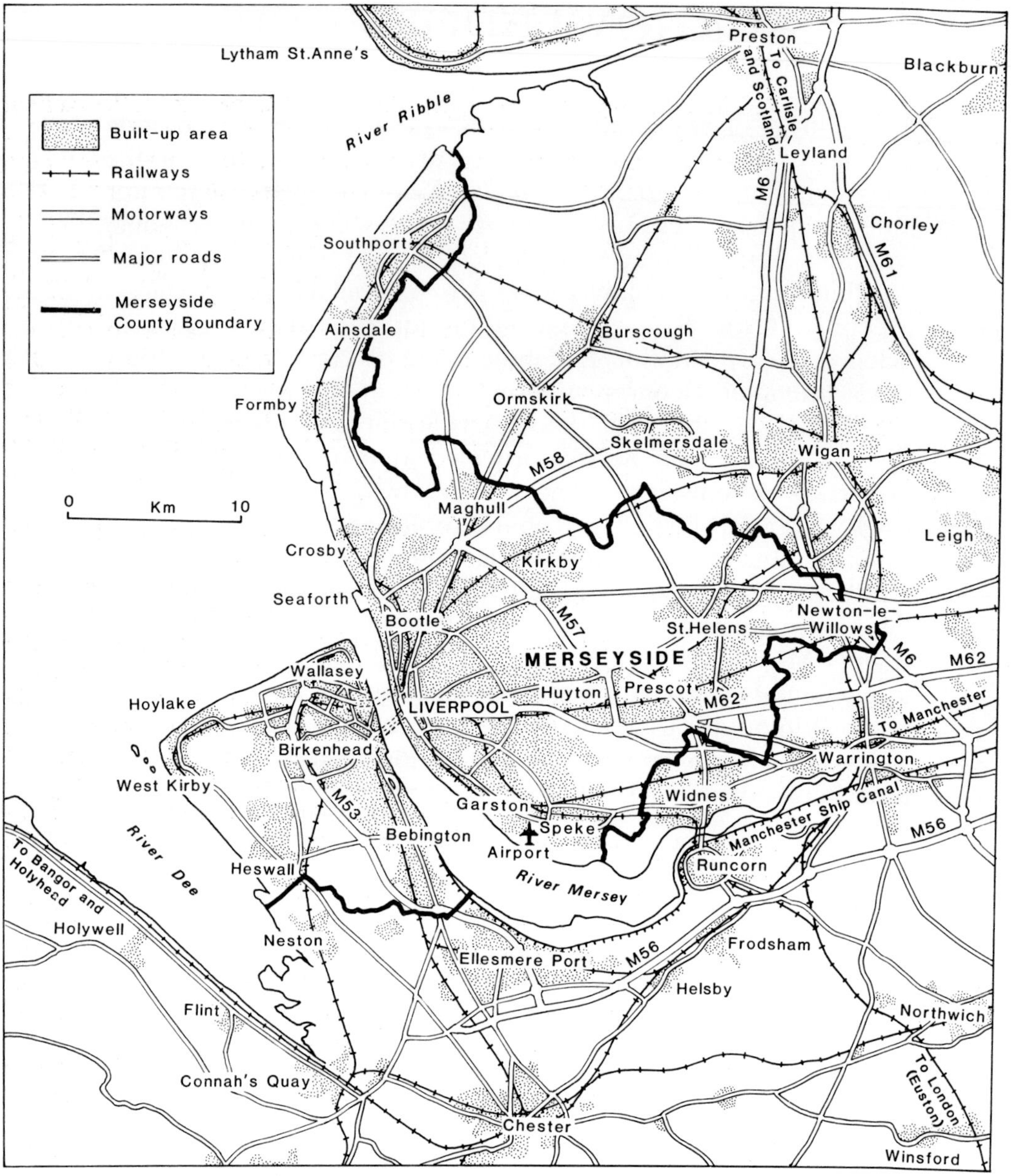

Based upon the Ordnance Survey map with the permission of the Controller of Her Majesty's Stationery Office, Crown Copyright reserved

PROLOGUE

In 1953 Wilfred Smith edited *Merseyside: a scientific survey* as a Handbook for the Annual Meeting in Liverpool of the British Association for the Advancement of Science. He introduced it thus: "Merseyside is built and founded on commerce. Without the port there would be no Merseyside" (Smith, 1953B, p. 1). This was written at a time when the area, indeed the whole of the United Kingdom and Western Europe, was still recovering from the effects of the Second World War, and Merseyside was still uncertain of its place, both nationally and internationally, in the post-war order. Economic diversification had begun, but had not progressed far; the port still dominated the life and work and also the psyche of Merseyside. Twenty-nine years later the Annual Meeting of the British Association is again held in Liverpool, but Merseyside in 1982 is a very different place from that described by Wilfred Smith and contributors to the 1953 Handbook. The intervening period has seen greater diversification of the economic base than Smith could have envisaged, but it has not brought Merseyside to a stronger position in the country. Merseyside in the early 1980s is still an economically depressed and problem-ridden part of Great Britain.

The trend has not been consistently downward. Until the early 1970s the development of new industries brought a mood of optimism. Nationally the 1950s and 1960s were decades of general economic and population growth, with Merseyside sharing in that growth. The urban area grew, mostly at the periphery of a rapidly expanding built-up area, to accommodate new industries and their workers. David Smith's major study of the industrial economy of North-West England concluded in 1969 that Merseyside was in fairly good economic health, especially in that "as a location for the motor industry, Merseyside now looks very good" (Smith, 1969, p. 165). At about the same time, in the Preface to the report of the Merseyside Social and Economic Survey Robert Steel, Wilfred Smith's successor as John Rankin Professor of Geography in the University of Liverpool, felt able to say of the 1960s that "the depression seemed a distant memory and confidence, as well as prosperity, in the region seemed high; was not Liverpool, in a special way, a symbol of the swinging 'sixties"? (Steel, 1970, p.vi).

The County of Merseyside was established in 1974 in the wake of that wave of great optimism, creating for the first time a potentially cohesive administrative and planning framework for the conurbation. However, during the 1970s and into the 1980s the problems of Merseyside, never fully solved, have intensified as national economic recession has cast deepening shadows over many of Britain's peripheral areas, and optimism has turned to disappointment, if not outright pessimism. The promise of the 1960s now appears to have been a false dawn. The port has continued to decline, while many of the new factories have closed or had to cut back in their output. The commercial centre has also suffered, and the industrial and residential areas of inner Merseyside have seen greater economic and physical devastation than even the bombing of the Second World War could achieve. Economic and social effects have gone hand in hand, and came to a head in the Toxteth riots of July, 1981, part of a wave of such riots in Britain's major cities. The immediate response of Westminster, to give special responsibility for the Inner Cities generally, and for Merseyside specifically, to the Secretary of State for the Environment, Michael Heseltine, has brought the problems into sharp focus, and initiated what may become a fundamental re-appraisal of the condition of Britain's major cities.

The 1982 Meeting of the British Association offers an opportunity to contribute to that re-appraisal. *The Resources of Merseyside* seeks to make its contribution by examining how and why aspects of economy and society in Merseyside have changed in recent years, and how these changes have been affected by the resources of the region. "Resources" are often equated with physical entities, such as oil, minerals, land or water, but they are more than that, more even than economically exploitable reserves. In this broadest sense resources include man's culture, skills and technology as well as the natural environment in which he lives. They include economic and social resources and the political will to activate them at any given time. The resource base is not only wide-ranging, but also dynamic. The resources of Merseyside in 1982 are not the same as thirty years ago; they differ in kind and in the way in which they are used. It is important, therefore, to ask whether this area has an adequate economic and physical resource basis as well as the human and organizational potential for continuing development.

This book is built round discussion of three major resource types—economic resources, environmental resources and social resources. The evaluation of economic resources is introduced by a general account of changes in the economy of Merseyside since 1945, illustrated principally by changes in the structure and spatial patterning of employment, and how past and current initiatives of local and central government have attempted to manage the resource base (Chapter 2). Chapters 3–6 consider particular aspects of that management. Changes in technology and international trading patterns have generally brought decline in the Port of Liverpool, yet new investments and technologies have diversified the land-use of the docklands (Chapter 3). Financial resources have been allocated to various public agencies to stimulate economic activity, particularly in the inner areas of the conurbation and particularly since 1978, and the use and impact of these resources and agencies provides the theme of Chapter 4. The tertiary sector has always been strong on Merseyside, as Wilfred Smith recognized in 1953, yet there have been major shifts in retailing and office employment in recent years even within this sector. While there are further possibilities for strengthening the resource base of the tertiary sector, as suggested in Chapter 5, these may have been used too late, and are in any case insufficient to compensate for losses in other sectors. The transport infrastructure is a necessary resource for any area, and in Merseyside there have been many changes and new initiatives especially since the creation of the Merseyside Passenger Transport Authority and Executive (Chapter 6).

The resources of the natural and built environments are examined in Chapters 7–10. Chapter 7, "The land of Merseyside", is a synthesis of the important work in resource inventory and assessment undertaken by the Natural Resources Unit of the County Planning Department since its creation in 1974. The management and use of one of these natural resources, woodland, is examined in rather more detail in Chapter 8, and this is followed by an assessment of the mineral resources of the County and the physical and economic bases of their exploitation. In any large conurbation the built environment has a direct impact on the people who live and work in it, and policies for management and control of the built environment of parts of the County, a subject of much public concern and pride, provide the focus for Chapter 10.

The final three chapters consider aspects of the population of Merseyside. Human resources are in the long-term the most important for any society, especially the channelling of human productivity and creativity for the benefit of all. In Chapter 11 the changing pattern and structure of population on Merseyside are examined, and this is followed by two chapters which deal explicitly with the City of Liverpool, each exploring one aspect of population change in the inner city. The characteristics and causes of poverty and deprivation of the population of the inner city are discussed in Chapter 12, and these are seen to be closely related to economic decline in the County as a whole and in the United Kingdom generally, as discussed in Chapters 2–5. Chapter 13 illustrates how political factors have intervened to prevent the sharp decline in school-age population being accompanied by the expected school closures and resulting financial savings. Taken as a whole this concluding section illustrates how people are affected by the changing use and management of resources, and also how the numbers and the conditions of people themselves can affect the processes of urban change.

The public image of Merseyside undoubtedly affects the realizing of its resource potential. That image is a complex one; Toxteth at the height of the riots of 1981 or the Merseyside of the Beatles, the Liver Birds and the Kop; an urban wasteland inhabited by work-shy and abrasive inhabitants or one of the United Kingdom's greatest centres of trade and commerce; an area of strike-ridden industries or a new and now more diversified economy with potential for growth. The reality is inevitably far removed from the caricature. While for many, too many, that reality is the Merseyside of the dole queue, of redundancy or the threat of redundancy, and of vandalism and "positive" policing, it is also an area of warm and strong local communities and with much to offer to families and industries, a worthwhile place to live and work. It has some of the finest architecture, art galleries and museums in Britain. It is the home of a symphony orchestra of international standing and, arguably, the finest football team in Europe.

But it is also an area that is urgently seeking an identity and direction that will re-establish its economic vitality and prosperity. Only with a thorough appraisal of the resources of Merseyside and a more purposeful commitment to their use can the trend of recent years can be reversed and economic dynamism restored.

W. T. S. GOULD
February 1982

Chapter 1

FROM THE PORT OF LIVERPOOL TO THE CONURBATION OF MERSEYSIDE

RICHARD LAWTON

In 1207 King John granted a Charter to a hitherto insignificant fishing hamlet on the Mersey estuary: that new borough was Liverpool. It is now a City and Metropolitan District of over half a million people, the focus of the County of Merseyside with a population of over 1.5 million and the regional capital of an area extending over South-West Lancashire, North-West Cheshire and much of North Wales. Though it has an ancient foundation, Liverpool's commercial growth effectively dates from the late seventeenth century. Most of the docks and waterfront industry, together with much of its urban fabric, are essentially creations of the nineteenth century from which come not only its waterfront and the fine commercial and civic buildings, but also the decaying infrastructure and housing stock of its inner areas and an outdated economic structure and persistent social problems rooted in marked class differences and pervasive poverty.

While the morphology and landscape of Liverpool and the character and activities of its people are the result of a long and complex history, Merseyside as an economic and social region is a product of modern times. The region has experienced marked changes, begun in the inter-war years, with the decline of the port and associated industry in the post-war period, only partly offset by new industrial development. Commercial activity, still mainly focused on central Liverpool, has weakened with the decline of shipping and marine activities. Meanwhile, since the 1930s massive slum clearance in the inner residential areas, has decanted tens of thousands of families to new suburbs and overspill towns. In short, the resource base on which rested the port-centred region of the nineteenth century has declined. Through the re-evaluation of these and other resources and the injection of new developments a new and different Merseyside is slowly and painfully emerging.

Early Liverpool

Throughout medieval times Chester was the main town and route focus of North-West England. Although the medieval borough has left its mark on the town plan of central Liverpool (Smith, 1953C, pp. 190–1), little is known of its activities and buildings. The population of three to four hundred at the 1379 Poll Tax were mainly "husbandmen". Merchants increased to about one-sixth of those recorded in the 1581 assessment, with one-quarter in shipping and nearly one-half in crafts and retailing. Welsh, Irish and Manx names point clearly to its trade links, and the concentration of merchants' residences on Water Street suggests an early functional zoning within the town.

At the Restoration (1660) the population of Liverpool was still only 900 to 1000, but the town was poised on the brink of great expansion. In 1660 the port became independent of Chester, and in 1699 the new Parish of Liverpool was separated from Walton Parish. Significant new trades were opened up with the Caribbean and North America for sugar, tobacco, indigo and, later, cotton. Exports of Lancashire textiles and Cheshire salt to these colonies, to West Africa and to the Baltic widened trade horizons, which generated such refining and processing industries as sugar, tobacco and salt, and also gave an impetus to shipbuilding and outfitting. Since river anchorages and wharfage along the Pool could no longer handle the traffic, the Old Dock was built in 1715 in the mouth of the Pool. By that time a population of some 5–6000 was expanding from the crowded medieval core across the Pool into the "New Town", acclaimed by Daniel Defoe in 1725 as "one of the wonders of Britain and unrivalled outside London for the fineness of the streets, and the beauty of the buildings".

Georgian Liverpool

Accelerating commercial growth and a major transformation of trade and industry produced rapid growth in the population and built-up area of eighteenth-century Liverpool. In its booming shipping and commodity trades slavery played a significant, though not dominant, role. Liverpool led Europe in the West African slave trade, providing 74% of slaving vessels by the turn of the century and carrying over 50 000 slaves per year at the height of the trade (Lawton, 1964). The West African trade was only one part of an increasing dominance in the Atlantic. An early lead established in the West Indies in the sugar trade was subsequently extended to North America and, after 1800, to Central and South America. Consequently the tonnage using the port increased from 36 762 in 1716 to 65 406 in 1751 and 708 314 by 1805. These links provided raw material imports which dominated trade and nurtured a growing range of processing industries, including tobacco, sugar, oil-seeds, grain, hides, cotton and timber, in Liverpool and its hinterland, while access to Lancashire coal, Cheshire salt and Cornish china clay was the basis of chemicals, soap, glass and pottery industries.

The first dock system was created between 1715 and 1825 to accommodate this rapidly expanding traffic, adding six docks from Coburg to Princes Dock (Chapter 3). The hinterland grew as more effective communication with Liverpool was provided by navigation on the Mersey and Irwell (1720) and the Weaver (1721–32); by turnpiking the routes to Prescot (1726) and Warrington (1753) and to Preston (1770); by pioneering the narrow-boat canals to St. Helens (via the Mersey and the Sankey Canal of 1757), to Wigan (1774) and then Leeds (1816); and to Runcorn via the extended Bridgewater canal (1776) which gave access to the West Midlands via the Trent and Mersey system (1777).

The widening hinterland of the port in the industrial North and Midlands and the extension of its trading foreland throughout the Atlantic and much of Southern and Northern Europe (Hyde, 1971) were responsible for its rapidly growing and increasingly cosmopolitan population. Its growing merchant élite was drawn not only from notable local families, such as the Gladstones, Rathbones, Roscoes, Claytons and Williamsons, but also from those attracted by prospect of economic and social advancement. But these were far exceeded by the labouring poor who, from the late eighteenth century, flooded into the city. This, one of the most explosive phases of growth in any modern British city, has left its mark on the physical and social environment and on its population, estimated to be 34 407 in 1773 and 53 853 in 1790. This had increased by some 22 000 (40%) in the 1790s, perhaps two-thirds of which was due to migration, not only from the North-West but also from distant British cities and areas of overseas trade (Laxton, 1981).

By the early nineteenth century the boundaries of the old Borough could no longer contain the rapidly expanding built-up area. Crowded courts and alleys within the town centre housed a largely unskilled and sea-faring population in increasingly congested and insanitary dwellings. Particularly in the dockside areas and the "North End" where, on ground often polluted by noxious industries, low-cost housing was thrown up at great speed, housing densities were high: of Liverpool's stock of 9976 dwellings in 1790, 16.2% were cramped and insanitary back-to-back houses and 17.3% were cellars; by 1801 these proportions were 14.3% and 14.7% respectively, and they housed more people despite the rapid growth of the housing stock. Claims for the "generally healthy state of the town" and its inhabitants doubtless applied to such spaciously planned middle-class areas as the Mount Pleasant–Rodney Street area, described by Wilfred Smith (1953C) as "Liverpool's Bloomsbury". Here and in other suburbs outside the Borough the merchant classes were increasingly concentrated by the early nineteenth century. Everton was perceived in 1817 to be "a place of genteel residence"; Waterloo and Woolton were fashionable residential suburbs; with the establishment of a growing number of cross-river steam ferries, settlements developed on the Wirral shore at Rock Ferry, Tranmere and Seacombe. Thus, even in advance of the growth of docks and industry at Birkenhead, an incipient Merseyside was emerging.

Victorian Merseyside

As residential areas expanded, parts of the town centre were increasingly given over to commerce and industry. By the 1840s merchants were concentrated in the Castle Street–Exchange Street–Water Street and Strand area, and the earlier focus of retailing in Castle Street and High Street had been replaced by a new "shopping area" along Lord Street, Church Street and Whitechapel and the fashionable Bold Street, spoken of in the 1830s as "the Bond Street of the North". Moreover, the increasing range and quality of the shops pointed to the emergence of Liverpool as a higher-order regional centre. The older industries, notably shipbuilding, pottery and chemicals, were progressively displaced from the waterfront and inner areas. In their place a wider range of processing industries, including oil-seed and grain milling and soap-boiling was added to sugar, tobacco and brewing. These industries flanked the docks and the Leeds–Liverpool canal, with extensive warehousing, storage and associated transport and handling facilities for timber, coal and a wide range of imports. Here and around the town centre a multiplicity of small industries for servicing shipping and trade developed: boatbuilders and coopers, sailmakers and chandlers, foundries and instrument-makers.

Between 1830 and 1860 the tonnage using the port trebled, and it had trebled again by 1913 (Hyde, 1971). The dawn of the age of the great shipowners and merchant princes of Merseyside—Brocklebanks, Booths, Bibbys, Holts, McIvers, Harrisons, Rankins and Wilsons—led to a zenith of shipping and commercial enterprise, and diversification of trade, shipping, handling and storage facilities required massive growth of docks and warehousing. Between 1825 and 1860 Jesse Hartley, the great dock engineer, built 21 docks and some 10 miles (16 km) of new quayage, more than half Liverpool's dockland, and some of the most innovative warehouses ever built in Britain, notably the Albert Dock complex.

The monopoly of the Dock Trustees, controlled by Liverpool Corporation, was challenged in the late 1820s when schemes were mooted for the development of docks on Wallasey Pool where already the small dormitory suburb at Birkenhead had been joined by William Laird's ironworks (1824) and shipyard (1828). Egerton and Morpeth Docks were completed in 1847, but a new phase in the history of the Port of Liverpool was inaugurated with the merger of the two systems in the Mersey Docks and Harbour Board in 1858 (Mountfield, 1965). After 1860 seven new docks, culminating in the massive Gladstone dock system (1913–27), were added to the Liverpool system. The entrance to Wallasey Pool was sealed, and Alfred (1866) and Wallasey (1877) Docks built. The Board was also involved in promoting better rail links with its industrial hinterland, adding to the early lines to Manchester (1830) and the West Midlands via the Grand Junction Railway (1837) and from Birkenhead via Chester (1840).

The registered tonnage of the port increased from 4.4 million in 1858 to 19.0 million in 1914. As its hinterland widened Liverpool's exports, mainly cotton piece goods, other textiles and engineering products, were £55 million in 1857 (45% of U.K. exports), and had increased to £170 million by 1913 (36% of U.K.). Although the import trade was proportionately less (one-third and one-quarter of U.K. respectively), with Liverpool second in importance to London, it profoundly affected activities in the port. While sugar and tobacco imports remained valuable, three bulk commodity trades assumed overwhelming importance. Cotton imports nearly doubled between 1850 and 1910 to a peak of 690 000 tons, 1910–13, despite the diversion of some of this trade after the opening of the Manchester Ship Canal in 1894. Wheat imports grew spectacularly from 120 000 tons in the early 1850s to 1 180 000 tons in 1913. Oil seeds, increasingly important from the late eighteenth century, gave Liverpool a near-monopoly in the West African palm oil trade by the mid nineteenth century, together with control of much of the U.K. imports of tropical oil seeds and other vegetable and animal fats. The organization of these trades and associated shipping, insurance and brokerage companies was backed by numerous specialist and professional services, providing some 10 000 commercial jobs by 1851 (6% of total male employment) and 32 076 by 1911 (7.8% of male employment).

In the late nineteenth century the manufacturing base of Merseyside moved further towards port processing industries. Refining of vegetable and animal fats, oil seed crushing and grain milling provided over 5000 jobs in Liverpool in 1851 (2.8% of the total) and 12 247 (2.6%) in 1911 when the scale of plant, for example in Lever's Port Sunlight works, had vastly increased. These and older processing industries such as sugar were the basis for brewing and a wide range of food industries employing 12 550 workers in 1851 (6.9% of the total) and 29 486 (6.2%) in 1911. Manufacturing was limited in range and significance, and declined in relative importance in the later nineteenth century. Shipbuilding and repairing, metals and engineering employed 13 846 in 1851 (11.3% of Liverpool's male workforce), but this had risen to only 25 377 (8.2%) in 1911, though shipbuilding employed over one-quarter of the male workforce of Birkenhead, largely at the Cammell Laird yards. Merseyside benefited from the growth of engineering at that time, but the industrial base remained perilously narrow.

Employment in Victorian Merseyside was progressively dominated by the port and by semi-skilled, unskilled and largely casual labour. Of Liverpool's total male workforce of 121 652 in 1851, 10.3% were labourers, another fifth employed in shipping and on the docks and 3.6% in transport; by 1911 these proportions were 2.6%, 15.7% and 8.2% respectively, out of a total male workforce of 313 089. To this may be added another 17 359 (5.5%) in the building industry.

Job opportunities for women were extremely limited, and their participation in the workforce relatively low. Apart from the clothing industries, which employed 17 048 (28.1%) and 19 046 (11.5%) working women in Liverpool in 1851 and 1911 respectively, only the processing and food industries (7.1% and 9.0%) and commercial jobs (4.3% and 4.5%) offered anything outside domestic service, which employed over 24 000 (40.1%) in mid century and 32 646 (19.9%) in 1911. Thus, while Merseyside attracted labour from all over the British Isles, much of the workforce was poorly paid. Moreover, the mass labour market was regulated by the trade of the port, and was vulnerable to cyclical fluctuations. Unskilled workers were hired or laid-off according to demand, and were employed by the half-day on the docks. This was a recipe for poverty and social and industrial instability which divided the mass of people from a rich élite in Merseyside's sharply differentiated society.

The growth in trade and employment brought a dramatic growth of population. Between 1801 and 1851 the population of the Borough of Liverpool grew five-fold from 78 000 to 376 000, and doubled to 746 421 by 1911. During that period there were four extensions to the Borough boundary (Fig. 1.1), as the built-up area advanced behind the docks, northward through Bootle to Waterloo and Crosby and southward towards Garston. By the late nineteenth century a ring of outer suburbs from Crosby through Walton, West Derby and Wavertree to Mossley Hill and Aigburth were already past their peak rate of population growth (Fig. 1.2). Growth in Wirral was no less spectacular.

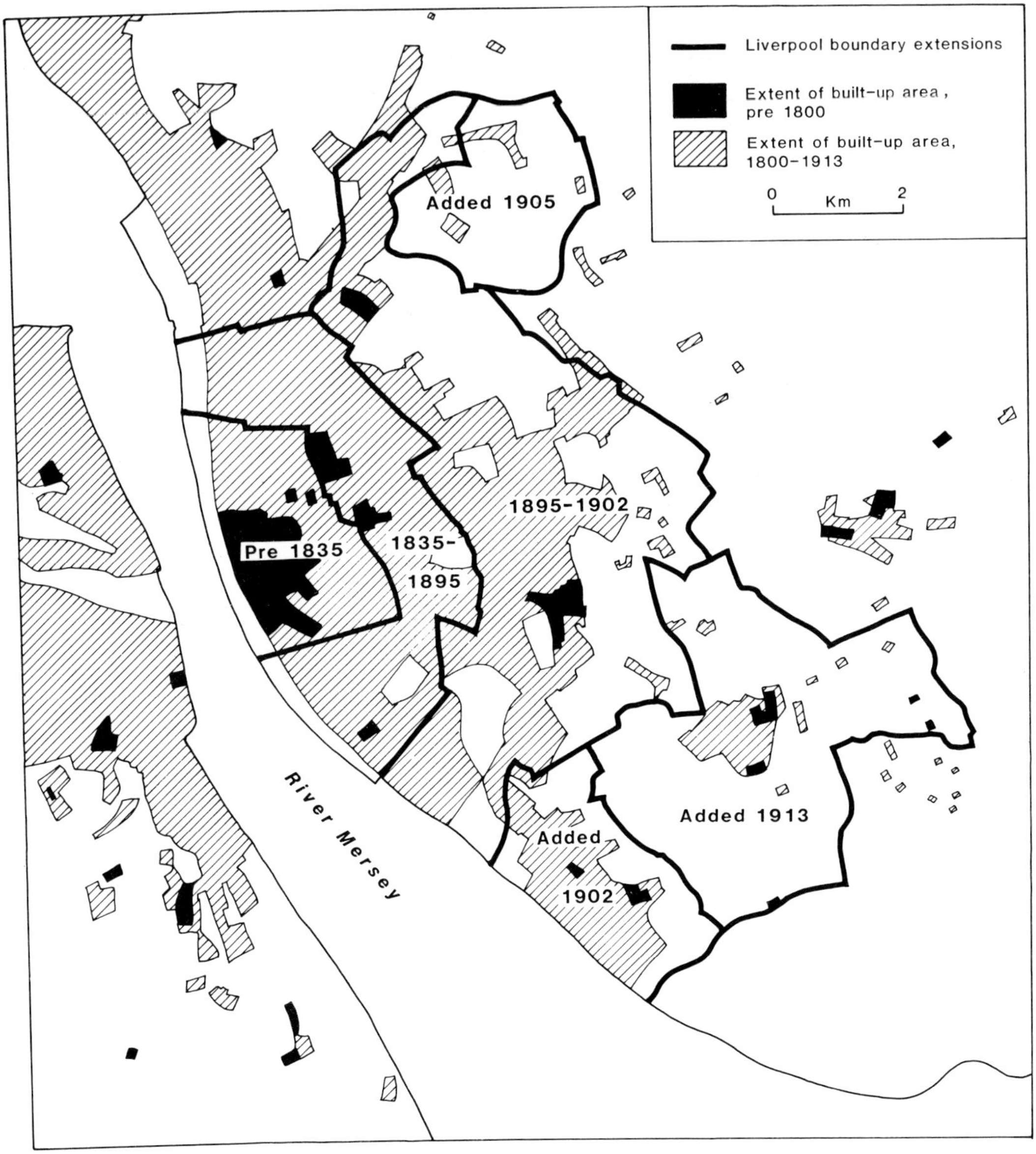

Fig. 1.1 Growth of Liverpool, 1835–1913. The dates of boundary extensions to the Borough and the extent of the built-up area in 1800 and 1913 are shown

Birkenhead, a hamlet of 110 people in 1801, was laid out by Price as a planned residential town in 1826, but was overtaken by industrial development associated with Laird's works and with the building of the docks. Its population rose from 24 233 in 1851 to 130 794 by 1911. Tranmere and Wallasey shared this rapid growth, and industrial developments at Bromborough Pool and Port Sunlight (from 1886) brought Bebington into the industrial and population expansion of Merseyside. After the opening of the Mersey railway tunnel

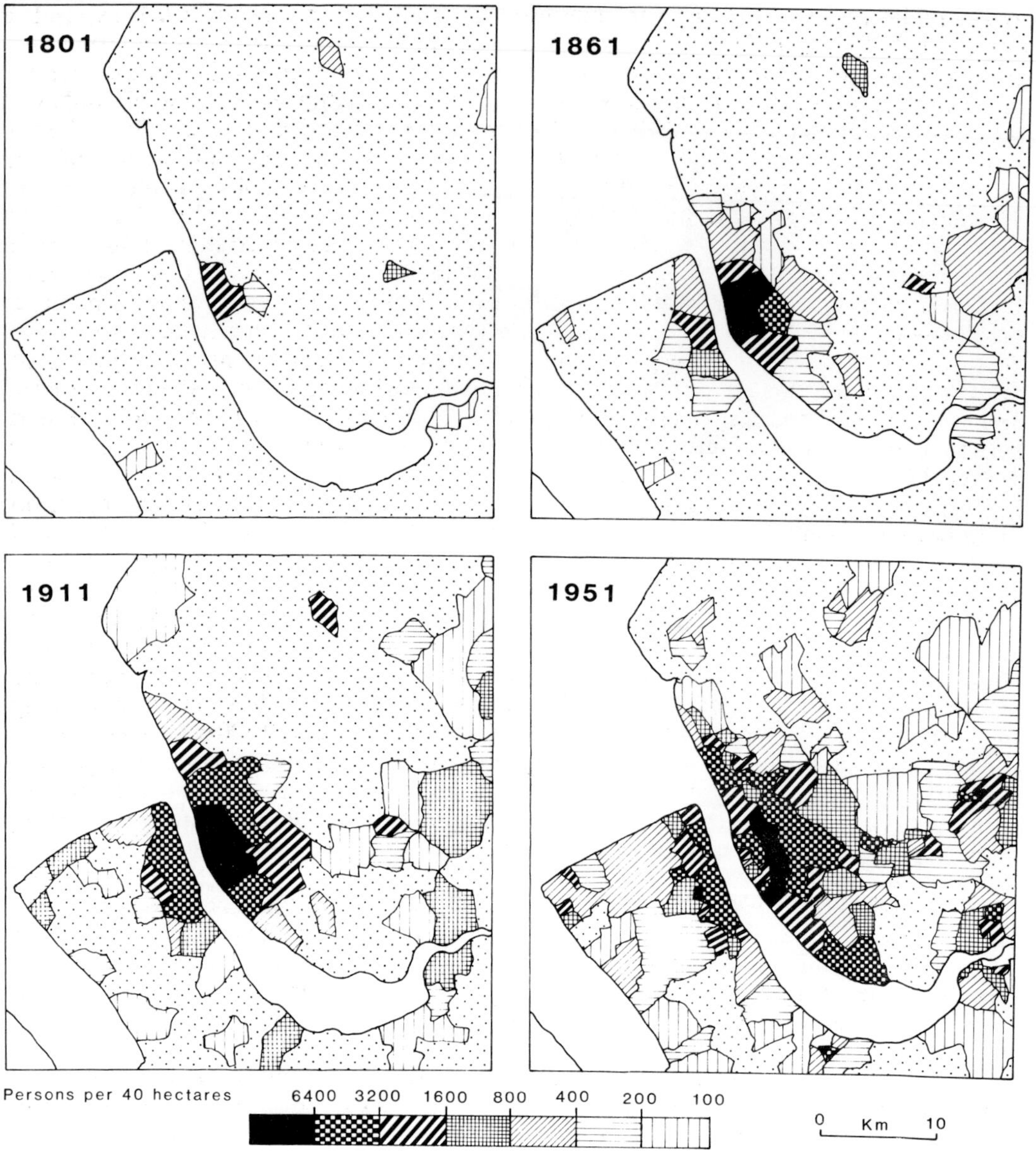

Fig. 1.2 Population distribution on Merseyside, 1801–1951. The density of population is shown by Ward and Civil Parish as designated at the specific dates

to Liverpool in 1886, commuter suburbs progressively reached out into all parts of Wirral, especially along its north shore to Hoylake and West Kirby. By 1911 the continuously built-up area stretched for several miles on either side of the Mersey estuary, and most of Wirral and much of South-West Lancashire, including Southport, looked increasingly to central Merseyside for services and employment.

Much of the phenomenal population growth on Merseyside from under 100 000 in 1801 to 1.5 million in 1911 was due to migration from all parts of the British Isles, and it influenced both population structure and social character. Many came from adjacent areas of Lancashire and Cheshire; others reflected Liverpool's old-established coastal trade, such as with Cumbria and the South West, and growing industrial and commercial linkages with London and the West Midlands. But the strongest and most distinctive migrant elements were from Ireland, Wales and Scotland. At mid century barely half of Liverpool's population was Lancashire-born; 22.3% were Irish, 5.4% Welsh and 3.7% Scottish born. The potato famine brought some 580 000 Irish in 1846 and 1847, 236 000 of whom subsequently emigrated. A steady flow of new Irish migrants continued throughout the later nineteenth century, ranging from 25 000 between 1851 and 1860 to 9300 between 1891 and 1900. The Irish were mainly unskilled—labourers, dockers, washerwomen and the like—and were highly concentrated in the areas of poorest housing, especially in the dockside zones of North Liverpool. The Liverpool Scots included many distinguished professional and commercial families in the high-status Mount Pleasant–Abercromby area and skilled workers, especially in shipbuilding and engineering, in Kirkdale and Birkenhead. The Welsh were prominent in building, maritime activities and in domestic service. More dispersed residentially than the Irish (though there were Welsh communities in Everton, Toxteth and Birkenhead–Wallasey), they retained a strong cultural cohesion united by chapel and language. Liverpool, dubbed "the capital of North Wales", hosted the National Eisteddfod in 1840, 1884, 1900 and 1929, and Birkenhead was the venue in 1917.

Rapid population growth brought overcrowding, disease and high mortality. In central Liverpool cheap slum accommodation for a rapidly growing and poorly paid workforce competed for land with commerce and industry, forcing up the cost of housing. There was a close-packed pattern of courts, one-third of the housing stock in 1850, and an exceptionally high proportion of inhabited cellars which perhaps accommodated 100 000 (one-third) of the Borough's population in the 1840s. Mortality rates were generally among the highest in England, consistently one-third above the national level between 1850 and 1910, and characterized by diseases associated with poverty and bad housing and sanitation: typhus, cholera, typhoid and tuberculosis.

Liverpool, however, was also a pioneer in municipal housing. It built the first municipal flats in Britain (St. Martin's Buildings, 1869), and demolished 10 000 houses and provided 2824 new dwellings between 1864 and 1914. Moreover, from mid-Victorian times bye-laws regulated the building of a mass of two-storey, four-room private dwellings which blanketed the older residential areas of Merseyside under successive layers of terrace housing. Despite widespread clearance, such terraces now form much of the sub-standard housing of the region.

By the end of the nineteenth century, migration from the first working-class "suburbs" was taking families into new Edwardian suburbs. Successive boundary extensions of the Borough of Liverpool in 1835, 1895, 1901, 1905 and 1913 (Fig. 1.1) followed the rapid spread of the built-up area (Fig. 1.3) which absorbed Bootle, Litherland and Crosby into a continuous conurbation. In Wirral the influence of the Mersey railway, electrified to Birkenhead in 1903, brought rapid growth in Birkenhead, Wallasey–New Brighton and Bebington, and created new commuter suburbs at Hoylake and West Kirby. From mid century the Southport and Ormskirk railways had brought these towns, together with settlements along the route to Liverpool's Exchange Station, progressively into the commuter hinterland of central Liverpool.

The middle classes had begun to desert the centre of the city from the early nineteenth century. One notable line of advance was along a sector from the merchant quarter of central Liverpool through the Mount Pleasant–Abercromby area towards Princes Park,

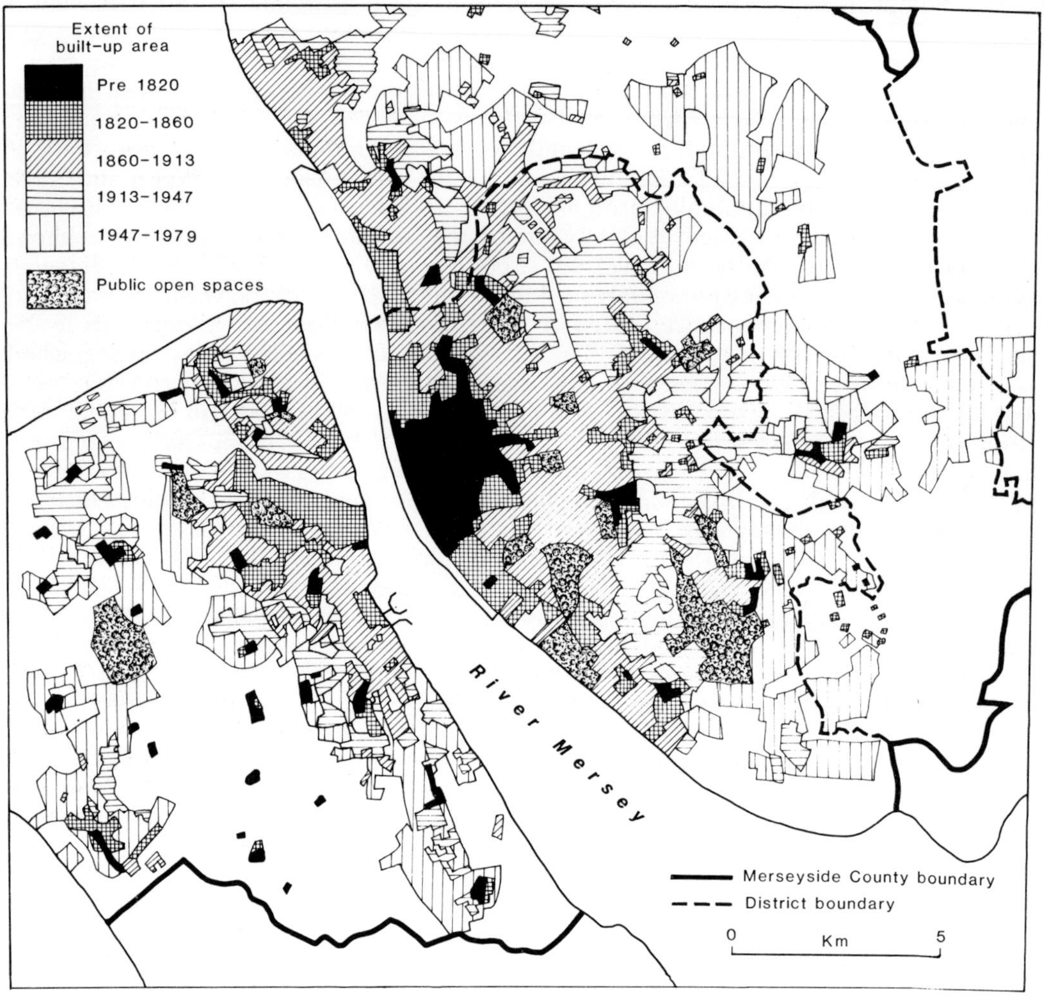

Fig. 1.3 Growth of the built-up area of Merseyside to 1981

one of the first of a great belt of parks which ring mid-Victorian Liverpool. Land for villa development was set aside around Sefton Park, Newsham Park and Stanley Park and in Bootle, while Birkenhead Park, laid out by Joseph Paxton of Crystal Palace fame and opened in 1847, provided 101 out of its 226 acres for high-class residential development, and drew "the quality" westwards from the early planned town which was already being overtaken by poorer quality housing. "Carriage folk" had already moved further afield, and travelled to business from up to 16 km from central Liverpool. Their mansions, sheltered behind sandstone walls in estates at Allerton, Childwall, Crosby, Mossley Hill or Oxton or behind the lodge gates of private residential parks, became a feature of upper middle-class Merseyside.

Both in their residential patterns and in their occupational and social status groups, Liverpool and other parts of nineteenth-century Merseyside were sharply segregated by mid-Victorian times. In that sense it was a "modern" conurbation rather earlier than those industrial cities in which a numerous artisan class was more upwardly mobile in social and residential characteristics.

Change and decline, 1919–1945

The inter-war years were difficult for Merseyside. Between 1915 and 1920 imports increased to one-third of the U.K. total compared with one-quarter pre-war, but between 1919 and 1939 changes in the national and international economy associated with the severe depression brought a substantial fall in the value of Liverpool's trade to 75% of the 1914 level and of imports to 74% and re-exports to 43%. A corresponding fall in exports to 82% of the 1914 level, especially in textiles, brought a loss of trade, mainly to London and the southern ports, averaging one per cent per annum between the Wars. The inter-war depression hit hardest such old staple industries as shipbuilding, cotton textiles, coal and heavy engineering, and meant a loss of jobs in Liverpool's hinterland. Shipping and associated industry and commerce declined, and unemployment in Liverpool rose sharply to a peak of 28% in 1932, as against 22% in Great Britain, and in the 1930s was never below 18%, one and a half times or more above the national level. Within particular areas and industries the loss of jobs was catastrophic, and reflected structural as well as cyclical problems. In Birkenhead 40% of men were out of work in 1932, and employment in shipbuilding in the town fell from 11 807 in 1921 to only 2868 in 1931.

That Merseyside was a depressed area, with an unbalanced economy over-dependent on declining industries, was widely recognized. With a shortage of skilled labour, a surplus of older unskilled workers and high juvenile unemployment, the auguries for the future were poor. New growth industries, including those offering employment to women, were needed. A campaign by the Liverpool Organization from 1926 (later joined by Birkenhead and Wallasey) brought the S.N.I.A. Viscosa artificial silk factory to Aintree which by 1929 provided 4000 jobs, mostly for women. Such efforts were later widened through the Lancashire Industrial Development Council and its successors L.I.D.A. and L.A.M.I.D.A. More importantly, under the Liverpool Corporation Act of 1936 new industrial estates were established at Fazakerley (Aintree) and Speke. The former had already benefited from the transfer of food processing industries from dock zone sites. Similarly Dunlops, who occupied a cramped site at Walton (Spellow Lane), and who were thinking of moving their entire U.K. operation to Birmingham, were attracted to the Speke estate in 1936. Other growth industries, including light engineering, chemicals and pharmaceuticals, helped to diversify the industrial structure and to disperse factories to the periphery close to new housing estates.

Port industries also experienced some movement towards the periphery of the region. Lever Brothers' widening range of products, especially margarine and cooking fats, gave South Merseyside a growth industry. At Ellesmere Port the growth of petroleum imports and the Bowater paper mill helped to offset the decline in the traditional sheet-metal industry and to provide the basis for a post-war boom based on oil-refining and petro-chemicals (Aspinall and Hudson, 1982). St. Helens, though highly dependent on coal and the glass industry, suffered less than the textile towns further east since glass-making was buoyant and helped a great deal by the building boom of the 1930s.

Thus, despite some diversification Merseyside between the Wars remained over-dependent on a narrow range of processing industries while the once-powerful commercial sector was weakening. The Second World War revived industrial employment, but it did less to change the traditional structure. One major development, however, was the Royal Ordnance Factory at Kirkby, later the core of the Kirkby Industrial Estate, which with other engineering plants, such as English Electric, along the East Lancs Road was to help post-war diversification. However, the port played the most vital role in the war effort, leaving 35% of Merseyside's population in shipping, services, transport and distribution in 1947, when, apart from the post-war boom in ship-building, the rapid run-down of activity brought a sharp increase in unemployment to 6.5%, two and a half times the national average.

Liverpool's population, 746 421 in 1911, reached a peak of 867 000 in 1937, and fell to 790 838 in 1951, a trend typical of inner Merseyside, where population fell by 80 000 between 1931 and 1951 despite a high natural growth rate. Residential migration removed some 80 000 of the total migration losses of 219 540 from inner Merseyside between 1931 and 1951, at a time when the outer areas of the conurbation gained 126 000 to add to their net gain of 32 093 between 1921 and 1931. Most of these were families removed by slum clearance into massive local authority housing estates around the periphery. Between 1920 and 1938 the four inner boroughs built nearly 42 000 new dwellings, 33 755 in Liverpool alone. Corporation estates, such as Norris Green with its 40 000 people by the late 1930s, were the first really major assault on the slum problem, though Liverpool's estimate of 13 000 "uninhabitable" houses in 1933 showed that they did not provide a complete solution. A more integrated approach to housing *and* planning was needed. Liverpool acted on this well in advance of the 1944 Town and Country Planning Act when in 1936 it initiated the development of Speke as a residential and industrial satellite for 22 000.

Nevertheless, massive investment in housing and construction benefited Merseyside's stagnant inter-war economy. Not only did those industries provide a substantial number of jobs, they also attracted some £40 million of investment between 1920 and 1939. As suburbs extended farther from the centre, communications required improvement. The electrification of the railways to New Brighton and West Kirby in 1938, together with further utilization of the electrified Southport (1904) and Ormskirk (1906–11) lines, contributed substantially to private house-building and rapid suburbanization in North Wirral and West Lancashire. Major improvements in road transport were even more vital. The significance of the road link between North and South Merseyside provided by the building of the Queensway Tunnel (1925–34) may be judged from the 3.25 million vehicles using it in 1935–6. The first steps towards Liverpool's ring road were taken before the First World War with the layout of Queens Drive (1903–27) through open country beyond the built-up areas. Likewise the East Lancs Road, built to give better access between Manchester and Liverpool (particularly the North Docks), attracted much pre- and post-1939 industry, and brought the adjacent areas of Lancashire, especially St. Helens, into closer contact with central Merseyside.

Physically the Merseyside which developed between the Wars was much more extensive, yet there were many common problems throughout the region, not least those relating to its future planning and government. The rapid peripheral spread of both housing and industry extended the continuously built-up area to some 10–16 km from Pierhead by 1940. The growing separation of home and workplace was reflected in increased commuting from periphery to centre and increasing daily movements within the suburban fringe (Chapter 11).

Structural change and the creation of the Metropolitan County, 1945–1974

In 1953 Wilfred Smith stated, "Merseyside is built and founded on commerce. Without the port there would be no Merseyside". At that time one-tenth of the labour force was directly employed by the port and one-sixth in port industries and commerce. The immediate post-war revival proved illusory. Despite rapid changes in the region's economy since the early 1950s, longer-term structural weaknesses and the need to

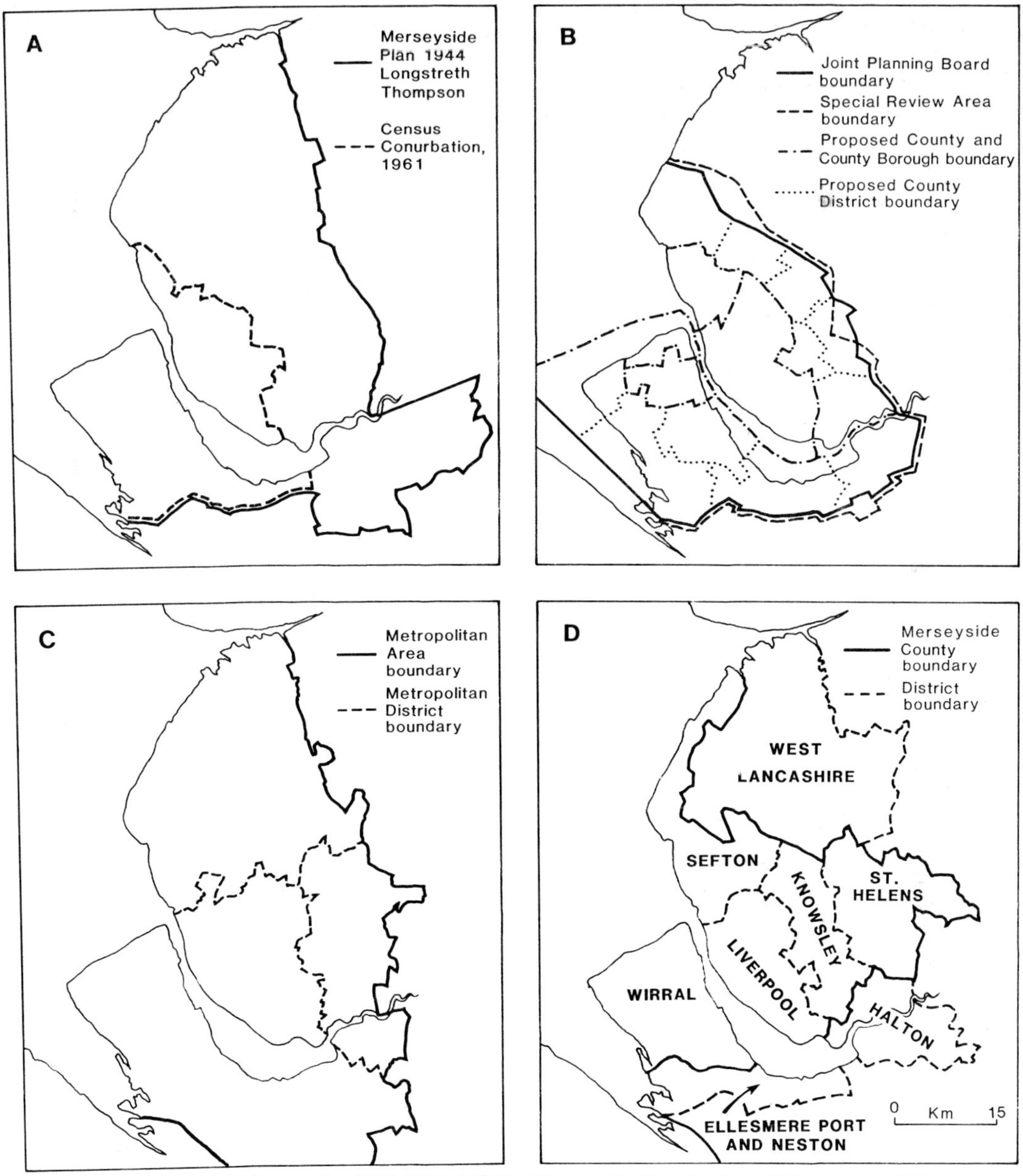

Fig. 1.4 Definitions of Merseyside, 1944–1974: (A) the Merseyside Plan Region of Thompson, 1945, and the Census Conurbation of 1961; (B) the Merseyside Special Review Area, 1965, and the proposed Joint Planning Region, with County and District boundaries; (C) the Merseyside Metropolitan Area and Districts proposed by the Royal Commission on Local Government, 1969; (D) the Metropolitan County of Merseyside and its constituent Districts, 1974, with adjacent Districts in Cheshire and Lancashire

generate new jobs for an expanding labour force have proved insurmountable. The considerable injection of new industries, massive housing and construction programmes, and the remodelling of the city centre have not solved Merseyside's unemployment problems.

The use of the port and its labour force declined sharply in the 1970s. From 28.0 million tonnes in 1967 total trade fell to 15.8 million tonnes in 1979, and the registered labour force fell sharply from 23 000 in 1963 to 9541 by 1972 (Chapter 3). Yet employment connected with the port is still considerable with 73 000 jobs in port-*related* industry (Kinsey, 1980).

That the industrial sector still employs about 40% of the workforce on Merseyside is due largely to new industries on the peripheral industrial estates and in the outer zone. But major problems of industrial balance and unemployment remain: job losses in old-established activities, the vulnerability of new firms to recession, are reflected in many early "exits" from the area (Chapter 2). Even in the good years of the 1950s and 1960s Merseyside's unemployment rates were 2.3–2.7 times those in Great Britain. Some 80 000 jobs were lost in the inner boroughs from the mid 1960s to the mid 1970s, and employment in the conurbation centre as defined by the Census declined by 46 720 between 1966 and 1971. In the peripheral industrial areas there have also been major losses, including both old-established firms such as Dunlops (2300 jobs) and new ones such as British Leyland Motors, both at Speke. The New Towns have not been immune, and disastrous closures at Skelmersdale have brought unemployment and social problems indistinguishable from those of parts of inner Merseyside. Runcorn with its older-established industrial base and diverse new industries has been more fortunate. Nor have the towns of outer Merseyside fared much better. St. Helens, long dependent on glass and coal, has seen mining decline to 2300 jobs, but has been worst hit by the weakening of the glass industry involving the closure of Rockware, substantial redundancies at United Glass Bottles, and 1200 jobs shed by the mighty Pilkington works, which with 10 000 jobs still dominates the town.

Even with a massive inter- and post-war housing programme it was doubtful if Liverpool could meet more than one-quarter of its housing needs within its boundaries. Hence the urgency for overspill and New Town development. Under the Town Development Act, 1952, the city sought overspill arrangements for 41 000 people with Ellesmere Port, Widnes, Winsford and Central Lancashire New Town. The New Towns for Liverpool were essentially another form of overspill, though rapid industrial development in the 1960s promised more. Despite the recession, Skelmersdale had a population of 39 144 at the 1981 Census, a four-fold growth since its inception in 1961. Runcorn, established in 1964, is well on the way to its target of 12 000 dwellings by 1980, and had nearly 100 advance factories, a major new shopping centre and a population of 63 813 in 1981.

From the 1920s it was obvious that closer liaison between local authorities was needed to tackle the growing economic and social problems of Merseyside on a regional scale and to integrate the planning and administration of a distinctive, interdependent and spreading region which was divided between four County Boroughs and the County Councils of Lancashire and Cheshire. The Merseyside Advisory Joint Committee's plan for the future development of the region (Thompson, 1945; Fig. 1.4A), however, covered a much wider area than the Local Government Boundary Commission of 1945 which was appointed to examine areas around major cities as a possible basis for defining new metropolitan areas. While the Commission suggested the desirability of an administration focused on Liverpool, it was left to the 1958 Local Government Special Review to define such an area. Its proposals fell short of the continuous county which Liverpool sought, but it did suggest a Joint Planning Board while leaving the constituent local authorities essentially unchanged (Fig. 1.4B). The Royal Commission on Local Government, reporting in 1969, recommended that Merseyside should be one of three metropolitan counties. The area proposed embraced the Mersey estuary, and extended deeply into West Lancashire and North-West Cheshire (Fig. 1.4C). Although the government of the day accepted the Report, its White Paper of February, 1970, noted that precise boundaries for the new local authorities would require further discussion.

However, under the Local Government Act, 1972, introduced by a new government, the mid-Mersey towns of Runcorn (Halton District) and Widnes were excluded from Merseyside, and transferred to Cheshire. Moreover, South Wirral, which had throughout resisted inclusion in Merseyside despite its close industrial and commuting links, became in 1974 the Cheshire District and Borough of Ellesmere Port, which in 1976 incorporated Neston. In North Merseyside the inclusion of St. Helens and Southport in the Metropolitan County gave an extensive area within which strategic planning, development control, transportation, certain environmental matters and police and fire services could be integrated. It brought to an end, if not to a fully satisfactory conclusion, a century over which the case for a more unified structure of local government for the region had become increasingly apparent. It recognized the transition from the port of Liverpool to the conurbation of Merseyside. Yet the County still faces massive economic and social problems far beyond the power of local and regional governments to resolve, as recent interventions by central government on behalf of Merseyside and the other British conurbations indicate.

Chapter 2

THE ECONOMY OF MERSEYSIDE, 1945–1982: QUICKENING DECLINE OR POST-INDUSTRIAL CHANGE?

TREVOR CORNFOOT

For Merseyside and all other British conurbations the period since 1945 has been one of aggregate decline, reflected in growing problems of employment, income, housing and infrastructure. Until relatively recently this urban decline went unrecognized as a national problem, and received little attention from policy makers. Throughout most of the period the application of policies of regional assistance to Merseyside and other "depressed" or development areas was viewed as a means of contributing to national efficiency by improving the distribution or promoting the efficiency of factors of production. In Merseyside this took two forms: firstly, the utilization of the labour surplus caused by the contraction of the port and the rapidly growing labour force through the attraction of new industries from more prosperous regions; and, secondly, the use of the new instruments of physical planning to restructure and develop the conurbation by the creation of expanded and New Towns on its periphery.

The operation of regional policies has had distinctive impacts on the Merseyside economy which are discussed later in this chapter. In the orthodoxy of Keynesian macroeconomic management, however, the policy was not attuned to local circumstances. Thus a major Government study of the area, "The Problems of Merseyside", by the Department of Economic Affairs in 1965 confirmed the need to maintain a manufacturing-based regional policy, but neglected to note the significance of, or investigate the reasons for, the slowing of growth in services, Merseyside's traditional employment base. This was all the more serious when local policies for economic development in Merseyside were relatively undeveloped, greater attention being devoted to the area's overspill housing and city centre redevelopment schemes.

By the early 1970s employment in Merseyside and other conurbations was declining sharply, although it was not until the availability of appropriate employment statistics that the extent of the problem was realized. The international recession after 1973, by exposing economic problems in hitherto "prosperous" regions, challenged conventional views of regional prosperity and problems. It led to a growing questioning of the relevance of regional assistance and to the identification of conurbations, and particularly their inner areas, as the principal locations of economic malaise. This shift in interest from regional to specifically urban problems came at a time when the new local authorities, created in 1974, were providing a new source of political demands to design appropriate policies and to provide more resources to tackle their fundamental economic problems. Thus on Merseyside, the preparation and approval of the County Council's Structure Plan (Merseyside County Council, 1980) involved a conscious effort to seek Government support for relevant and locally co-ordinated economic policies for the area (Struthers and Williamson, 1979). Faced with continuing economic problems and a serious loss of jobs in the current recession, the need for such a sensitive application of policy is pressing, and Merseyside's employment crisis now appears to demand radical measures.

In this chapter discussion of Merseyside's changing economic fortunes over the last thirty-five years is based upon employment statistics. With the growing capital intensity of industry, it is acknowledged that in themselves employment statistics increasingly provide only a partial view of economic change. The greater availability and use of information on output, productivity and added-value at the Merseyside level will, in the future, permit a broader view of relative economic health than is possible here.

Development Area policies to 1959

The Merseyside economy of the late 1940s can be characterized as being over-dependent upon the port and port services. Despite pre-war industrial diversification and expansion on peripheral industrial estates, one-third of all jobs in Merseyside in 1949 were in shipping, shipbuilding, transport and distribution. This over-specialization was a source of national concern, and, together with manifest inability to absorb the high growth of the local labour market, led to Merseyside being designated a Development Area in 1949. This sought to use the new instruments of regional policy to promote manufacturing employment, largely by influencing the movement of industry from other regions. Merseyside received some two-thirds of the moves of manufacturing industry into the North-West between 1949 and 1959, and 40 000 jobs were created (Table 2.1). Greatest success was achieved before and shortly after designation as a Development Area, and vacant munitions factories provided a ready home for new industrial concerns. From 1952 the number of industrial movements fell nationally as credit squeezes and enhanced industrial competition reduced the willingness of firms to move. The national economic environment was unfavourable to growth, yet over 28 000 new manual jobs were created in new factories in Merseyside, 1949–1959. This apparent success, however, was tempered by an increasing rate of factory closure and a continuing decline in port-related employment. The insured employment of the Development Area increased by only 20 000 (3.6%) between 1950 and 1958, enabling it to keep pace with a growing labour force only after a net out-migration of 50 000 people. The industrial structure of Merseyside was changed only slightly, expansion being greatest in electrical engineering and vehicles. This decade in Merseyside's industrial history has been summarized thus: ". . . there was some sign of an emergence of a new element in the economic base but no sign at all of a growth process by which newer industries could progressively dominate the economy in a cumulative growth of expanding industry" (Lloyd, 1969, p. 386).

The Development Area phase intensified the pre-war trend towards industrial

TABLE 2.1 *Manufacturing industry moves into Merseyside, 1945–75*

	Moves from outside N.W. to Merseyside			Employment created by moves from elsewhere in North-West	Total Employment created
Period of Opening	Moves	% of total moves to North-West	Employment created		
1945–51	23	67	24 000	3 000	27 000
1952–59	18	63	17 000	3 000	20 000
1960–65	32	71	32 000	2 000	34 000
1966–75	97	57	10 600	4 100	14 700
1945–75	170	66	83 600	12 100	95 700

Source: Department of Industry.

Notes: Statistics for 1945–65 refer to the Merseyside subdivision of the North-West. Those for 1966–75 refer to the Merseyside Development (later Special Development) Area.

Employment refers to that still surviving at the end of 1967 for the period 1945–65 and at mid 1975 for the period 1966–75.

decentralization. The inner areas of Liverpool and Birkenhead and the docklands experienced a high turnover of labour which was associated with post-war reconstruction and industrial reorganization, especially in Merseyside's food and engineering industries. It was, however, in the outer urban fringe on pre- and post-war industrial estates that most employment growth occurred. Important new job opportunities in industries hitherto not well represented in the area were created on estates at Aintree, Kirkby, Huyton, Speke, Bromborough, Ellesmere Port and Capenhurst. New industries predisposed to output and employment growth at the urban fringe contrasted sharply with the traditional industries of inner Merseyside.

The impact of the motor industry, 1960–66

Merseyside was the major beneficiary of a stronger policy for the redistribution of industry following the 1960 Local Employment Act. Planned expansion of the British motor industry in Merseyside—Ford and Standard Triumph at Speke, Vauxhall at Ellesmere Port and motor components firms, notably at Kirkby—brought over £65m in new investment and the expectation of 30 000 new jobs. So successful was the initial impact of new industries judged to be that Merseyside was descheduled from its Assisted Area status in 1960, only to be rescheduled in 1963 as local unemployment rose to 40 000 in a period of national recession. The coming of the motor industry should not have been expected to "solve" Merseyside's employment problem. The attraction of new well-paid jobs and the recruitment policies of the companies involved led to a threefold increase in labour turnover within industry, 1960–66, compared to the 1950s, rather than a reduction in the number of unemployed. The gain of 32 000 manufacturing jobs (Table 2.1) was considerably offset by the closure of factories whose demise may have been hastened by the high labour turnover, loss of skilled labour, and wage competition engendered by the rapid establishment of new, mobile industry and by only a slow growth in employment in established firms (Salt, 1967).

The net gain in manufacturing employment was a modest 10 500, but a major success was that during the mid 1960s, at a time when other conurbations were beginning to experience the ebbing tide of economic growth, Merseyside was the only conurbation growing in employment (Danson, Lever and Malcolm, 1980, p. 195). The main impact of the motor industry was to stimulate a rapid restructuring of the Merseyside economy and to accelerate the processes of dispersal evident in the previous decade. For the only time in Merseyside's history manufacturing became the driving force in employment growth, and the dependence upon the port economy was fundamentally weakened. Thus, while employment in vehicle manufacture increased by 47% and in electrical engineering by 15%, 1961–66, the port industries of shipbuilding and transport and communications declined by 12% and 30% respectively. Employment change within manufacturing followed the spatial patterns established in the 1950s, with high closure rates in inner and dockland areas and peripheral expansion, notably at the new growth points of Speke–Halewood and Bromborough. In addition there was continued growth at Ellesmere Port, and the beginnings of significant overspill expansion to the New Towns of Runcorn and Skelmersdale.

In the general optimism of the 1960s the conclusion among many commentators was that Merseyside's employment problems were nearing a solution, and that despite "neither a spectacular increase in the availability of jobs nor a substantial reduction in unemployment, forces were set in motion which in the long run should forge a new, more successful economic base for the region" (Lloyd, 1969, p. 408). Others were wary of Merseyside's continued dependence upon the attraction of inward investment. Concern was expressed that the application of regional policy over the previous twenty years had

TABLE 2.2 *Employment in Merseyside, North-West England and Great Britain, 1966–81*

	1966	1971		1976	1981	% Change 66–71	71–76	76–81
Manufacturing	285 820	243 356		208 707	154 400	−14.9	−14.2	−26.0
Blue collar services	263 720	225 164		212 827	196 200	−14.6	−5.5	−7.8
White collar services	128 915	157 631		172 434	170 950	+22.3	+9.4	−0.1
Primary & construction	58 195	44 075		36 498	32 450	−24.3	−17.2	−11.1
MERSEYSIDE COUNTY	736 650	670 226		630 466	554 000	−9.0	−5.9	−12.1
		NI Card	Census			NI Card		
NORTH WEST REGION (000)	2 999	2 779	2 657	2 637	2 425	−7.3	−0.7	−8.0
GREAT BRITAIN (000)	23 301	22 027	21 648	22 047	20 729	−5.5	+1.8	−6.0

Notes: Merseyside County defined by "nearest fit" of employment office areas.
Manufacturing: Standard Industrial Classification orders 3–19; blue collar services: SICs 21–23 & 26; white collar services: SICs 24, 25, 27; Primary & construction: SICs 1, 2, 20.
Data 1966: National Insurance Card Count.
1971: NI Card Count & Census of Employment.
1976: Census of Employment.
1981: Merseyside County Council & Department of Employment (all figures at June '81).

concentrated upon the creation of manufacturing employment almost to the exclusion of the faster-growing service sector, with the risk that "the employment pattern being created is designed to take advantage of the growth which has already occurred rather than what is to come" (Lawton, 1970, p. 489).

Employment decline to the mid 1970s

The benefits brought by the motor industry proved to be short-lived, and from the mid 1960s to the mid 1970s the area failed to gain an appropriate proportion of nationally growing office service employment. In total, employment declined by over 106 000 (−14.4%) in the decade to 1976, with decline at its most rapid in the late 1960s (Table 2.2). Merseyside's rate of employment decline was greater and apparently more sustained than that of either the North-West or Great Britain, and the area experienced the fastest employment decline of any conurbation outside London.

A number of inter-related factors appear to account for the inability to build upon the earlier "success". National economic stagnation slowed employment growth, and greatly reduced the flow of mobile industry at a time when Government was unwilling to direct new industrial investment to the Assisted Areas in the manner of the early 1960s. The operation of the Redundancy Payments Act, 1965, and the Prices and Incomes Board (from 1966) also contributed to a shakeout of labour from manufacturing, which may have been slowed in Development Areas only by the Regional Employment Premium. In such an unsympathetic economic environment manufacturing firms moving into Merseyside, though annually a larger number than in the early sixties, brought with them considerably fewer workers: only 100 jobs per move compared with about 1000 jobs per move in the earlier period (Table 2.1). In addition Merseyside's attractions as a Development Area were progressively weakened, first by the creation of Special Development Areas (S.D.A.) in the Northern Region, in Scotland and South Wales in 1967, and by the designation of most of the rest of the North West as an Intermediate Area in 1972 (Pounce 1981, p. 70). Moreover, from the mid 1960s a rising tide of plant closure and out-movement from Merseyside began to produce a net decline in employment. Between 1966 and 1977 over 350 plants closed or transferred production, affecting over 40 000 employees, half the closures and removals being between 1969 and 1974. The overall effect of these changes in manufacturing was that, despite the creation of over 28 000 new manual jobs, there was a slight net decline in employment.

The inability to maintain the momentum of employment growth in manufacturing was all the more serious when, as Lawton had feared, Merseyside failed to gain significant benefits from the rapid growth of the service sector. This appears to be due to both structural features, notably a high proportion of employment in nationally declining services, and to local performance. In "blue collar" services, port employment declined sharply as a result of the changing pattern and technology of Britain's overseas trade and decasualization of dock labour. The effect on employment was dramatic with a 21 000 (25%) decline in Transport and Communication employment, 1966–76 (Figure 2.1 and Chapter 3). Declining population and employment in the Merseyside sub-region depressed demand for locally-orientated blue collar services such as Passenger Transport, Retailing and Miscellaneous Services, all of which experienced rates of growth less than those of the country as a whole.

Equally significant was that Liverpool, unlike other major cities, failed to experience a speculative office boom (Chapter 5). While "white collar" service employment increased by 43 000 (33.7%), 1966–76, in line with national growth rates, most of this increase was attributable to growth in Education and Health Services, in which Merseyside continued to serve as a regional centre. Between 1966 and 1971 Merseyside benefitted substantially

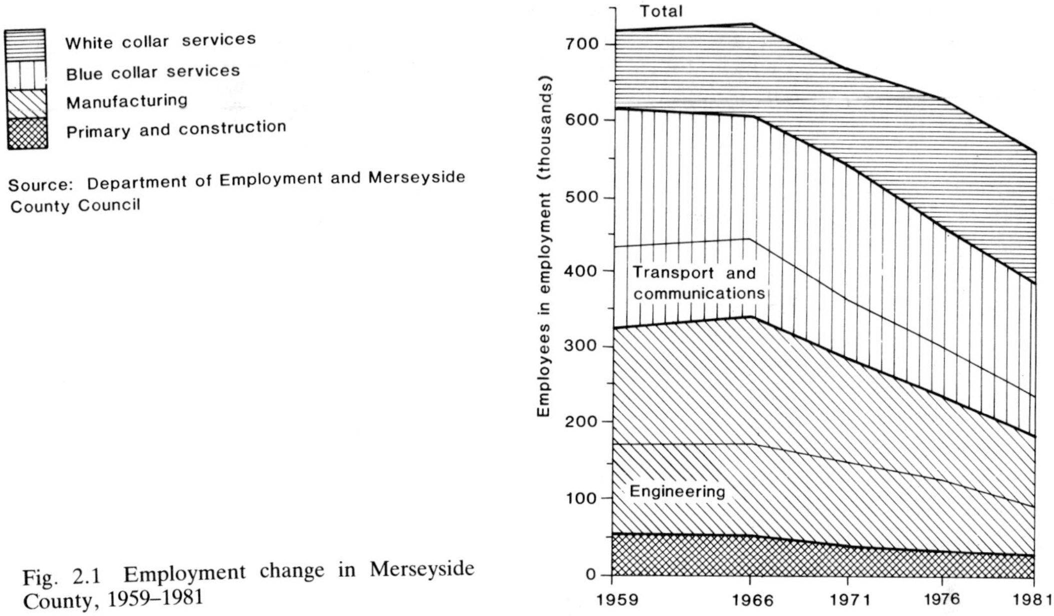

Fig. 2.1 Employment change in Merseyside County, 1959–1981

from the decentralization of government offices, most spectacularly at Bootle, with an increase of office floorspace in excess of 150%, and education and health services were expanded substantially by new capital schemes. In the following five years to 1976, the virtual cessation of government office decentralization, the ineffectiveness of the Location of Offices Bureau in promoting moves to Merseyside (only 1200 jobs were so created) and the failure to experience a private office boom led to a growth of only 3800 jobs in detached offices. Over two-thirds of the increase of 14 800 white collar employees, 1971–76, was attributable to the continued expansion of education and health services.

The widening disparity between the economic fortunes of the Inner and Outer areas of Merseyside was of particular significance during this period of quickening employment decline. In Inner Merseyside, 1966–75, there was a net loss of 18 291 (25%) manufacturing jobs. The 7970 jobs created were offset by an *in situ* decline of 9167 jobs and by a loss of 17 094 jobs through closure or outward movement (Lloyd, 1979, p. 45). All industrial sectors suffered considerably over the period, but about a dozen large plants, each employing over one thousand workers and together providing 47% of the 1966 employment in Inner Merseyside, accounted for half the total manufacturing job loss. Furthermore, it was of course in Inner Merseyside where the decline of the dock labour force and population-related services was taking place, leading to a loss of 47 500 jobs (10%), 1971–77, from the Liverpool travel-to-work area. By contrast employment growth continued in Outer Merseyside and beyond. In manufacturing there was a net gain of 19 500 jobs, due both to the growth to maturity of the firms that had moved into Outer Merseyside, 1945–66, and to the continued success—at least up to the early 1970s—of the peripheral industrial areas established in the 1950s and 1960s in attracting further mobile investment. Employment in services continued to grow in the Outer County with over 6000 new service jobs, 1971–76.

The employment decentralization of the earlier post-war periods continued. In the decade from 1966 Merseyside County lost 106 000 employees, while the rest of the Special Development Area gained 20 000. By the mid 1970s the focus of employment growth had shifted totally from the S.D.A. to locations such as Wigan and Warrington which were better served by the regional motorway network and which attracted not only jobs moving to the region but also employers transferring out of the North-West's two conurbations.

The economy in the late 1970s

Modest economic success in the 1950s, followed by spectacular job creation in the early 1960s and the haemorrhaging of employment that has occurred since then, were reflected in the Merseyside economy of the late 1970s. Certainly the local economy was still characterized by a large number of port-related activities, with about 12% of the county's employees in port or port-related jobs in 1976, and the growth of white collar service employment had biased the Merseyside economy even more towards services. As a result of the operation of regional policies a new manufacturing base had grown. Merseyside had become a highly capitalized area with local manufacturing producing a net output of over £2000 millions in 1979.

But the twofold legacy of port-related industries, many involved in mergers and takeovers with the growth of corporate capitalism, and the investments of the 1960s and 1970s had led to a manufacturing economy dominated by large plants. In 1976 half of Merseyside's employment was to be found in establishments with over 200 employees, and 28% of the workforce were employed in establishments with over 1000 employees, compared with a national figure of 18%. Moreover, the success of regional policy measures had made manufacturing employment dependent upon branch plants of U.K.-based trans-national or foreign-owned multi-national companies. Less than 20% of the employment in Merseyside's 29 largest establishments (employing 150 000 people) could be said to be truly controlled from within the County (Merseyside County Council, 1979, p. 67). Regional capital subsidies had encouraged the establishment of branch plants of manufacturing firms which already employed large labour forces. Faced with declining markets, increased overseas competition and/or rapidly escalating labour costs, the industrialists' response was to cease production in the most labour-intensive plants or to seek productivity improvements by a combination of reduced manning levels and further capital investment in new technology. In such circumstances, the Merseyside economy was extremely vulnerable to further employment contraction.

However, Merseyside's declining fortunes cannot be solely, or even substantially,

TABLE 2.3 *Inner and outer city employment change, 1952–76: Merseyside and British conurbations*

Area	% Change per annum				Total change 1952–76
	1952–63	1963–68	1968–73	1973–76	
Inner Merseyside	+0.60	−0.58	−2.67	−2.32	−50 000
Inner Conurbations	+0.97	−0.92	−2.60	−3.15	−1 160 000
Outer Merseyside	+1.13	+3.16	−1.11	−1.18	+29 000
Outer Conurbations	+1.88	+0.76	+1.66	−0.04	+557 000

Source: Adapted from Danson, Lever & Malcolm, 1980, p. 193.

Notes: "Inner" areas defined on basis of Employment Exchange Areas with a job ratio over 100, i.e. net importers of labour.

"Conurbations" are West Midlands, South-East Lancashire, Merseyside, Tyneside Clydeside and London, and are generally defined in terms of journey-to-work figures from the 1971 Census.

attributed to the unforeseen effects of regional capital subsidies. All Britain's major industrial centres were in employment decline, 1966–71, with the small net national growth of employment occurring in previously non-industrialized regions (Keeble, 1980, p. 945). At a smaller scale Danson, Lever & Malcolm (1980, p. 193) have illustrated the decline in employment in the older conurbations, with inner city decline followed by suburban decline as the net shift of employment favoured non-urban places. A comparison of Merseyside with the average for six conurbations (Table 2.3) further identifies the general trends in employment decentralization. Although employment growth on Merseyside between 1952 and 1963 was less than the average for the six conurbations, the tendency to employment decentralization was equally apparent. However, in the mid 1960s the success of the introduction of the motor industry to Outer Merseyside is clearly seen, with a job growth over four times the conurbation average. By the late 1960s and early 1970s job growth had turned to decline and Merseyside was the only conurbation to lose jobs from both its outer and inner areas. This pattern of job loss continued into the later period when Merseyside experienced the largest rate of job loss of any outer conurbation. Thus, far from being solely the consequence of the varying fortunes of regional policy, employment decline in Inner and then Outer areas was part of a general decline of conurbation employment. For Merseyside, however, this was made the more extreme by the sudden expansion, and subsequent longer decline, of employment induced by regional incentives to the Outer area of the conurbation.

Recent changes in employment

The continued loss of employment at a sharply increased rate in the recession from 1979 confirmed the vulnerability of the Merseyside economy already evident in the mid 1970s. Between 1976 and 1981 Merseyside County lost 76 500 jobs (12.1%) (Table 2.2, Fig. 2.1). The major decline was from manufacturing with the loss of 54 000 jobs, 26% of the sector's employment. The service sector, for so long the growing element in Merseyside's employment structure, had begun to stagnate, with characteristic losses from "blue collar" services and the slight decline in "white collar" services.

The decline of Merseyside's traditional manufacturing sectors has continued at faster rates, with, for example, the food industry shedding over 18% of its workforce in five years. Of equal concern is the dramatic decline of employment in many manufacturing industries established in Merseyside in the era of an active regional policy. The recession has hastened corporate rationalization and reorganization, resulting in cutbacks or closures in branch plants on Merseyside. Eight of the seventeen industrial "orders" in manufacturing have lost 25% or more of their workforce, nearly all associated with the contraction or closure of a small number of large firms in each industry—for example Cammell Laird and Western Ship Repairers in Shipbuilding, Courtaulds in Textiles, Dunlop and Meccano from Other Manufacturing, Pilkington in Glass, Lucas and Plessey in Electrical Engineering, and Ford and British Leyland in Vehicles.

The number of notified redundancies indicates the rising impact of recession in an already vulnerable economy. Redundancies (involving 10 or more persons) in the Merseyside Special Development Area increased from 12 600 in 1977 to 23 580 in 1981, an increase of 87%. The greatest job losses have been in Liverpool, the employment focus of the County, but other areas that in the past enjoyed growth or stability of employment, are now experiencing sharp decline. Of the net loss of 54 000 employees from manufacturing, 24 000 were from Liverpool, over 9000 from St. Helens, nearly 8000 from both Wirral and Knowsley. Decline in construction and service employment was heavily focused on Liverpool, accounting for a further loss of over 9000 employees.

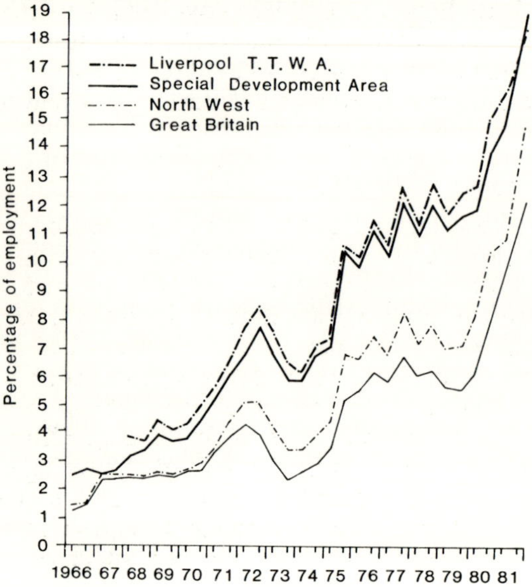

Source: Department of Employment, Monthly Statements

Fig. 2.2 Unemployment rates: Liverpool, Merseyside, North-West England and Great Britain, 1966–1981

Economic problems and prospects

Such a dramatic decline in employment over such a short period has led to a rapid rise in unemployment (Fig. 2.2). The rate of unemployment in September 1981 was 18.9%, higher than that of any other Special Development Area in Britain with 130 000 people unemployed in Merseyside County. The majority are men of whom about half are unskilled, a legacy of the past requirements of the area's traditional industries. Since there has been a low rate of job creation, the area has a high proportion of long-term unemployed (over 30% of the total unemployed have been out of work for more than one year) and the largest concentration of youth unemployment outside London. The labour force is characterized by a low level of skills, which has not been conducive to new investment, and the preponderance of larger manufacturing firms means that there is an insubstantial base of small and medium-sized firms from which future employment growth is expected.

The economic weaknesses of the area are reflected in a number of associated problems. Firstly, Merseyside has a declining population, net outward migration being in the order of 12–15 000 persons per year. Many of the migrants have been young, skilled and mobile; the less skilled, the poor and the unemployed have been left behind (Chapter 11). Secondly, the poor industrial relations image of the Merseyside workforce is known to have deterred investment. The problem is related to the legacy of decline and to the indirect effects of past policies; it may be more a feature of the local industrial structure than a reflection of the area's labour force. Thirdly, there are large numbers of vacant and obsolete buildings and extensive areas of dereliction. The generally poor physical environment is a disincentive to managers, incoming skilled workers and outside investors alike.

The problems of chronic unemployment, lack of skills, loss of jobs and poor environment are concentrated in particular locations in Merseyside. The spatial concentration of such problems is not confined to inner Liverpool, but includes many post-war peripheral developments. In older areas the massive decline in jobs for the unskilled and semi-skilled has been responsible for high rates of unemployment (estimated to exceed 40% in some areas and among Merseyside's black community). The presence of equally high rates in parts of peripheral housing estates is more related to the nature of nearby employment, characterized by rapid labour turnover and increasingly prone to contraction and closure.

Employment prospects to 1986

Prospects for future employment in Merseyside are frighteningly bleak. The number in employment could decline by a further 60 000 between 1981 and 1986 (Merseyside County Council, 1981). Low national growth of output, continuing capital intensification, few significant industrial relocations and dependence upon investment decisions made elsewhere in Britain or overseas all suggest that most manufacturing sectors can be expected to experience continuing employment decline. Some large sectors, such as Electrical Engineering and Vehicles, could experience contraction of over 25% of their workforce. Poor prospects in service sectors are a consequence of public expenditure restraints upon local public services, the future of the Port of Liverpool and the raising of output by increased productivity as a result of new office and distribution technologies rather than by additional labour. Most service sectors can be expected to decline slightly, although transport and distribution are both expected to be more severely affected.

This continuing loss of employment in Merseyside needs to be put in national perspective. For British conurbations in general "all the evidence points to ... employment trends less favourable than those for the rest of the nation" (Cameron, 1980, p. 69). Certainly the expected reduction of employment of 10% in Merseyside to the mid 1980s is notably worse than the decline expected for the North-West (−6%) and for United Kingdom (−5%) over a similar period (Manpower Research Group, 1981, p. 40). Out-migration is less likely than in the 1970s to suppress rising unemployment as low rates of job creation and high unemployment throughout Britain are likely to reduce inter-regional migration flows. Unless there is an increase in special employment measures, reduced economic activity rates and significantly increased levels of unemployment will occur.

Initiatives of Central Government

Regional development policy has operated with varying degrees of commitment, but is an enduring feature of government assistance to Merseyside. However, as a mechanism for promoting new employment in areas of high unemployment, regional assistance is increasingly unsuccessful, acting instead as a capital subsidy to already large, well-informed and capital-intensive industries. Experience of the operation of regional policies in the Merseyside Special Development Area indicates that for some industries, such as basic chemicals, nuclear power and vehicles, the receipt of assistance should be recognized as part of a national, rather than a regional, policy. Further, to avoid excessive subsidy to capital-intensive industry there is a case for an employment criterion such as a cost-per-job limit.

The greater potential of services compared to manufacturing for creating or maintaining employment has been almost ignored, yet, with its traditional bias towards the tertiary sector, Merseyside could benefit considerably from service sector assistance. It is also apparent that regional policy is not adequately co-ordinated with, or related to, other policy fields, in particular national industrial, inner city, economic planning and manpower policies. Greater subtlety and awareness of the local consequences of these programmes could be achieved through a devolution of decision making and policy development to Merseyside, rather than policy being formulated and assessed at a distance from the area.

Central Government policies to stimulate employment have led to a range of programmes and initiatives at the Merseyside level. Central Government financial assistance to new and small firms is provided under the Business Opportunity Programme, which provides tax incentives and loan guarantees. As both schemes are operated nationally, no priority is accorded to Assisted or Inner Areas, nor are they integrated with regional or inner city policies. Advance factory construction is undertaken by English Industrial Estates (E.I.E.) as successors to the Department of Trade which has been active in Merseyside for many years. Since 1980, E.I.E. has been developing a more commercial approach to industrial development which appears to have resulted in a lack of interest in more difficult sites, of which Merseyside has many, and much more interest in the more commercially attractive opportunities (Chapter 4). The Merseyside Development Corporation (M.D.C.), established early in 1981, is one of two bodies responsible for the regeneration of disused docklands. The M.D.C. is seeking to encourage developers to parts of the Mersey docks, to promote the development of small businesses, and to reclaim land for amenity uses. Although the top priority of M.D.C. is stated to be employment generation, the nature of the problems in its "designated area" requires that, initially at least, the largest proportion of its considerable resources must be devoted to derelict land reclamation and environmental enhancement. The Speke Enterprise Zone in south Liverpool is one of eleven such zones resulting from an initiative by the Chancellor of the Exchequer in his 1980 budget. Relaxation of rates, taxation and planning regulations in the zones will, the Government hope, encourage new businesses and help rejuvenate the local area. In the case of both the Enterprise Zone and M.D.C. concern has been expressed that new jobs created will not be attracted from outside Merseyside, but will merely cause the redistribution of existing employers.

Despite the above doubts and criticisms, these Government initiatives ought to be seen as worthwhile, particularly where they involve the introduction of new skills or processes, inter-firm linkages, serve new markets, or, in the case of the M.D.C., promote major environmental improvements. For Merseyside and particularly its inner area the introduction of new enterprises is a crucial element in the diversification of its large-scale, externally controlled employment structure. However, in view of the growing capital intensity of industry and the possibility of losing up to a further 40 000 jobs from manufacturing by 1986, it would be totally unrealistic to expect these initiatives to directly redress the substantial prospective employment loss.

Given the expected decline in employment, especially of semi-skilled and unskilled workers from process and mass-production industries, and given national demands for an increasingly skilled and adaptable industrial and office workforce, there can be only a growing mismatch between available and required skills. Taken with the continuing restriction of job opportunities for school leavers, this mismatch is likely to lead to increased pressures on education and training facilities. The scale and scope of training provided by local authorities and the Manpower Services Commission will need to be substantially increased above current intentions. There will undoubtedly be a continuing need for Special Programmes, with better marketing directed to disadvantaged groups such as ethnic minorities. However, the severity of Merseyside's job crisis and the loss of self-respect caused by enforced youth idleness is now so starkly obvious that there is a strong case for making "permanent" the "temporary" Special Programmes in the area, thereby creating "real" jobs.

Further recognition by Central Government of the severity of Merseyside's economic problems was indicated in the announcement in October 1981 that the Secretary of State for the Environment was to head a taskforce comprising civil servants from the Departments of Environment, Industry and Transport and the Manpower Services

Commission. Although falling short of the range of proposals that had been expected following the Secretary of State's extended visit to Merseyside in July/August 1981, the announcement holds substantial promise. The objectives of the task force are to promote the best use of the Central Government resources which are committed to Merseyside; to make proposals to modify policies or switch resources between existing programmes; to generate new initiatives; to examine how additional resources could most usefully be used; and to develop longer-term proposals (Department of the Environment, 1981). Given criticisms of co-ordination, the misdirection of regional development policies, the relative ineffectiveness of current job creating initiatives and the need for expanded and new Manpower Services Commission programmes, the objectives of the task force are encouraging. While local authorities are rightly cautious of any suggestion of increased central control over local affairs, the announcement appears to offer Local Authorities on Merseyside a major opportunity of influencing the development of more sensitive and appropriate Central Government policies in the area.

Local policy initiatives

Local Authorities in Merseyside have long been aware of their responsibilities for economic development and employment promotion. Liverpool City Council in 1936 was the first local authority in Britain to use parliamentary powers for the establishment of industrial estates, at Speke and Aintree. The 1970s saw the widening of activity from traditional industrial land provision to the development of full-scale economic policies and political initiatives. Those of Merseyside County Council include the establishment of an Economic Development Committee drawn from councillors from the County and District Councils; a Merseyside Enterprise Forum drawn from the commercial, industrial, educational and church life of the County, and the establishment of a County Economic Development Office (Struthers and Williamson, 1979). Both the County and the five District Authorities have various programmes of industrial land servicing, industrial and environmental improvement areas, as well as schemes of financial assistance and the provision of advice and information to businesses, often in conjunction with private sector trusts, as in St. Helens. These activities foster local enterprise by improving co-operation with the private sector and liaison with public agencies, Central Government and the E.E.C. as part of the County Council's Structure Plan strategy of urban regeneration (Merseyside County Council, 1980).

In the absence of wide ranging industrial or economic powers such as those possessed by the Scottish and Welsh Development Agencies and in the face of increasing Central Government pressure to reduce public expenditure, local authorities on Merseyside are responding to their severe economic problems with increasing innovation. Examples include the creation by Merseyside County Council, in conjunction with the University of Liverpool and Liverpool Polytechnic, of a Merseyside Innovation Centre to help develop the ideas of local companies. The County Council has established a private company, Merseyside Economic Developments Limited, to make full use of available resources in the provision of a considerably enhanced contribution to Manpower Services Commission Special Programmes and youth training. It now intends to set up a Merseyside Co-operative Development Agency to promote local co-operative enterprise.

These local economic initiatives are vital to Merseyside's future. The area cannot turn its back on new industry and commerce since they are crucial to the restructuring of the local economy, to retraining the workforce, to rebuilding the area's social capital and to the encouragement of private investment. But the future requirements of industry and increasingly of commerce are likely to involve fewer workers. The current job-creating initiatives of central and local government and the private sector can have only a limited effect. Indeed, the greatest contribution to closing the disparity between the labour force and available jobs in recent years has been M.S.C. Special Programmes which in late 1981 provided places for about 25 000 persons in Merseyside.

The need for radical change

The features of a post-industrial society identified by Trist (1974) have been evident in Merseyside throughout the 1970s—the dominance of the service sector in employment and output, control by multi-national companies, significant social costs generated by society, the rise of permanent unemployment and the interlinking of urban communities. But, as Trist argues of the post-industrial society, what has not occurred is any change in our values, organizations or ecological strategies. In Merseyside the already critically high levels and local concentrations of unemployment, poor local and national economic prospects and fears for the impact of new technology appear to herald an era of permanently high unemployment and increasing social tension that will demand a radical change of attitudes to work and leisure. The need for alternatives to conventionally defined unemployment was suggested both in the County Structure Plan (Merseyside County Council, 1980, p. 18) and by a panel of the Merseyside Enterprise Forum which recommended the development of socially useful work and "the negative approach of paid employment being replaced by the positive concept of transitional employment coupled with training or retraining" (Merseyside Enterprise Forum, 1980).

The Special Programmes of the Manpower Services Commission have begun in part to redefine unemployment. However, much more can be done to extend and redirect these programmes into longer-term (and ultimately self-sustaining) social and environmental activities supplying Merseyside's needs for more welfare services, housing and environmental improvement and for the provision of leisure. Perhaps, too, it is time to reappraise the purpose of unemployment and retirement benefits and to seek their redirection toward non-compulsory social activity payments. In this regard, local budgets for the provision of community activities by the voluntary sector, the creation of community co-operatives and tax changes which would encourage increased self-employment are further ways to break from convention. Above all, however, it is the urgent need created for investment in comprehensive, co-ordinated programmes of education and training which would provide the workforce with the necessary new skills required for modern technologies and for the promotion of a more flexible use of time in and out of employment.

There are those who argue that such fundamental changes are a matter for national attention, and imply that a consensus at that level is necessary before action can be taken. A Merseyside view would be that the changes in the economy over the last 35 years have left the area with some of the worst features of post-industrial society, and that Merseyside's problems and needs are so pressing that action on these issues locally, if only experimentally, is urgent.

Chapter 3

DOCKLAND ACTIVITIES: TECHNOLOGY AND CHANGE

SIDNEY GILMAN and SHARON BURN

The Port of Liverpool was a giant of the age of conventional general cargo shipping which lasted until the middle of the 1960s. It had a large estate of impounded docks covering several miles of waterfront both in Liverpool and Birkenhead, employed many thousands in cargo handling and associated commercial activities, and was the home of some major shipping lines. There was little change in the technology of dock working from the middle of the nineteenth century to the middle of the twentieth, so for many years increases in trade had to be accommodated by increases in scale in the ports, and those like Liverpool which served large trading hinterlands grew to giant size. When change did come, first in the form of bulk handling technologies for products like grain, coal and ores, and later in container and other unit load systems for general cargo, it was revolutionary, reversing the process of growth and setting in motion a major reduction in the physical scale of ports and in the employment of dock labour. In almost all the major conventional ports of the developed world, as in Liverpool, large numbers of old docks lie unused and derelict, and work only the occasional ship. Port authorities have had very difficult problems to face in managing this transition, and nowhere were they greater than in Liverpool, where there was a financial collapse in the early 1970s. This chapter examines some of the main changes in traffic, employment and land use in the Port of Liverpool since the 1960s to provide a perspective on its adaptation to the forces of revolution in maritime transport.

Transport technology

Liverpool and London were the two major general cargo ports of the United Kingdom from the beginning of the Age of Steam up to the late 1960s. They were sustained by close relationships to large hinterlands, appeared to be well placed to benefit from new developments and certainly embraced them with enthusiasm. However, the very size of these ports was a major disadvantage, given the re-adjustments they had to make in physical facilities and in the labour force in response to new transport technologies. In addition, their strong position in the market was weakened by the changing transport geography of container systems which broke many of the links between ports and their established hinterlands.

The initial effect of new technologies for handling both bulk and general cargoes was to allow a considerable increase in the speed of cargo handling and throughput per berth. The throughput of the typical general cargo berth of the conventional era was about 50 000 tonnes per annum, but container berths can handle between about 400 000 and 1 500 000 tonnes per annum over a single linkspan. Thus, even if there had been continued growth in traffic, container and roll-on/roll-off systems would have led to an enormous reduction in the size of any dock estate, affecting Rotterdam and New York as much as Liverpool and London. The change did not come all at once. From the early and mid-1960s to the middle of the 1970s the short-sea trades and the major deep-sea routes between developed countries underwent transition, whilst many of the routes to developing countries continued to be served by conventional ships and conventional handling systems. Indeed many of them believed that the capital-intensive container technology was basically unsuited to their needs. However, since modern transport technologies reduce the amount of capital required in ships and ports in the long run, modern systems began to spread to Third World countries, and most of their routes are now in a process of rapid transition which will be complete within a few years.

As well as reducing the total demand for facilities, the new transport technologies also changed the style of facility required. The most severe demands on existing facilities occur when there is a large increase in size of ship and in the size of cargo exchange, so that new dock-entrances and large areas of land are required. Although high speed handling systems allow ship size to be increased without the ship having to spend an excessive length of time in port, it is only on long deep-sea routes and on those with large flows of traffic that it is economic to use very large ships. The short-sea trades have tended to use converted conventional facilities, and investments have been relatively modest, whilst on the deep-sea trades there has been a combination of conversion and new development, the scale of which has varied tremendously depending upon site conditions and the strategy adopted. Southampton, for example, has natural deep water combined with a moderate tidal range and large areas of land on which container berths could be built; London retains an impounded dock system, although the latest addition to the container system (a terminal for third generation ships requiring up to 12.8 m of water) has been built on the riverside, located behind one of the existing berths to form a joint complex; at Felixstowe, which manages without an impounded dock system, a first berth was built with only 9.75 m of water, which has recently been supplemented by two new berths in 12.8 m of water enabling the port to handle a substantial throughput. Liverpool has an impounded dock system, and in the mid 1960s was considering a new development at Seaforth to cater for the growth in traffic. This large conventional scheme was converted to a more modern complex containing a grain terminal, deep-sea container berths, timber berths and a meat berth, and provision was made for a substantial expansion of the facility should need arise. Thus Liverpool's approach to the requirements of the new era in maritime transport was on a relatively large and ambitious scale.

Liverpool also has facilities suitable for the short- and medium-sea trades. However, in this market sector only relatively shallow water is required, and there are a number of alternative sites on the North-West coast and on the Manchester Ship Canal. There are

TABLE 3.1 *Trends in N.W. share of U.K. foreign trade in traffic other than fuels*

	Eire	Continental Europe	Scandinavia & Baltic	Iberia & Mediterranean	Deep-Sea	Total
1966						
U.K. Total	1620	11613	21562	8235	41284	84314
N.W. Ports	793	882	2908	1397	12614	18596
N.W. Share	49%	8%	13%	17%	30%	22%
Liverpool	497	469	704	968	10130	12769
Liverpool Share	30%	4%	2%	8%	24%	15%
1979						
U.K. Total	2729	27906	19440	13845	49461	113381
N.W. Ports	1283	1374	1363	1612	7849	13481
N.W. Share %	47%	5%	7%	12%	16%	12%
Liverpool	410	340	431	337	6839	8357
Liverpool Share	15%	1%	2%	2%	14%	7%

Source: National Ports Council Annual Digest of Port Statistics.

particular advantages to operators who can employ a small, self-contained labour force with practices closely tailored to the particular needs of the terminal. The facilities themselves could also be made available at modest cost, and, though the alternative terminals have often been constrained by the deficiencies of their site, the old dock systems of Liverpool have also caused problems, particularly because of the large areas of back-up space that are required today. The alternatives have often been preferred.

A further major effect of the introduction of new transport technologies has been the enormous reduction in labour requirements. A typical conventional berth operating with three gangs (a total of about 60 men) would handle about 250 tonnes a shift; the same number employed in two container gangs would move about 220 boxes containing about 2500 tonnes of cargo through the terminal. It was only in 1972 that the Port Authority became responsible for the dock labour force, at just about the time that the effects of new handling systems began to bite. Since then Liverpool, in common with other major U.K. ports, has had to bear the burden of the reduction in dock labour, with the cost of very substantial redundancy payments and the problem of developing efficient working practice with a labour force that was frequently too large for its needs (see below).

Trading patterns

Liverpool is mainly a deep-sea port, and the orientation of U.K. general cargo trades has been increasingly with Europe, the deep-sea sector as a whole being fairly static. Within this sector Liverpool has lost its market share, partly as a result of geographical factors and partly as a result of its performance. It has also been hit by a sequence of isolated events in bulk and semi-bulk trades, like the development of the Amlwch Terminal off Anglesey to serve the Stanlow oil refinery and the recent closure of the Tate & Lyle sugar refinery. In total there has been a substantial loss of traffic, although this still leaves Liverpool as a major port with an important hinterland and traffic potential (Table 3.1). Containerization has led to an increase of up to six times in the size of deep-sea general cargo ships. In order to fill these large ships and to operate with the same frequency of service it became necessary to serve even larger catchment areas, and this led to increased integration between U.K. and Continental European routes. Ships serving Continental Europe tend to have one French, one Dutch, one German and one U.K. port in their basic itinerary, and for the U.K. port it is clearly convenient to choose either London, Southampton or Felixstowe, which are all close to their main route alignment. However, this trend is not universal. Ships, for example, which have a large proportion of North-West cargo on board, can justify a call at Liverpool; on some routes, particularly those to the Americas, a call at a west coast port does not represent a particularly large ship diversion. However, Liverpool lost its important Far East and South African trades and part of the Australian trade. In routes to Europe there have also been some losses of traffic as certain trades which traditionally used west coast ports have re-located on the east coast, and use the improved road network for distribution. Conversely the North-West has gained from a concentration of Irish traffic, but, as suggested above, there is a tendency for such traffic to use small ports outside the jurisdiction of the Mersey Docks and Harbour Company.

The map showing world trade through Liverpool indicates the proportion of trade to and from Europe and deep-sea areas (Fig. 3.1). There has been an overall decrease in trade on all routes except that to North America, which consists largely of grain to Royal Seaforth Grain Terminal. The map gives a false impression of stability in the Far Eastern trade in terms of the total proportion of imports and exports to and from this area, for the exports of manufactured goods from Liverpool have fallen tremendously from 342 000 tonnes in 1966 to 121 000 tonnes in 1979. The total trade has been offset by increased imports of basic materials.

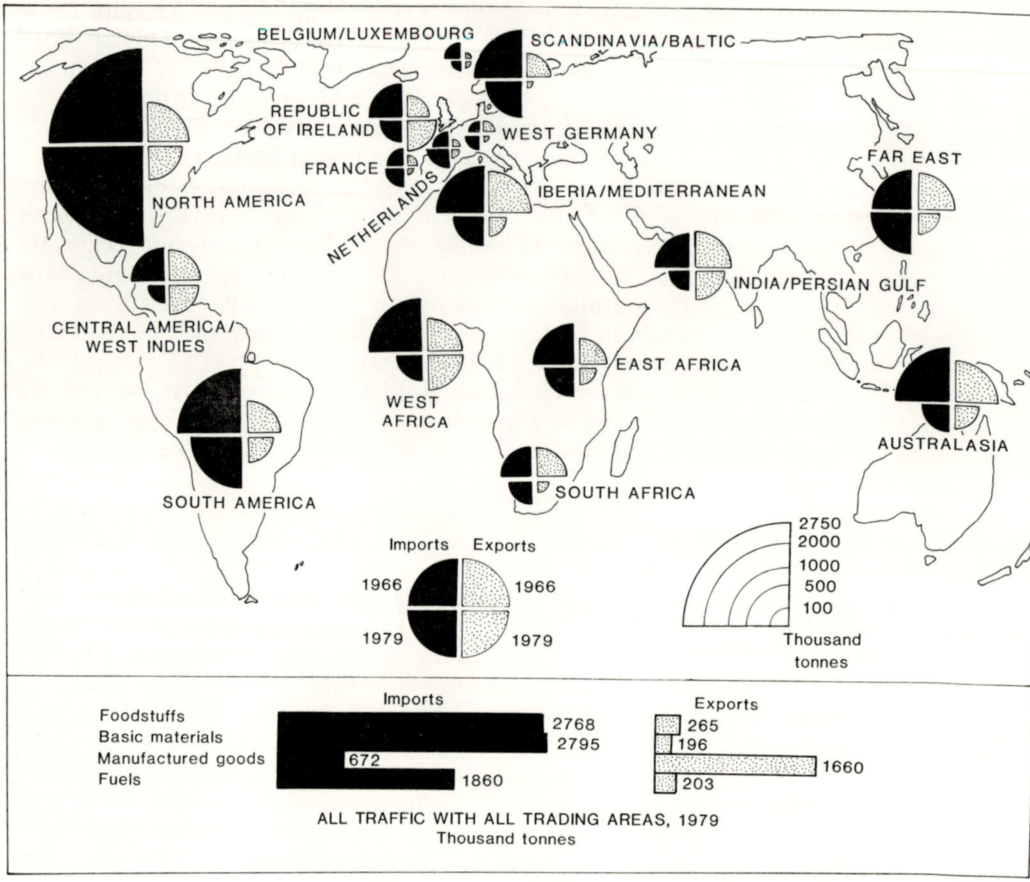

Fig. 3.1 World trade through the Port of Liverpool, 1966 and 1979 (source: National Ports Council, Annual Digest of Statistics)

Port facilities and activities

The Port of Liverpool responded to changes in transport technology and trading patterns with a combination of policies of investment and rationalization. The major investment was in the Royal Seaforth complex, begun in the mid 1960s (with a late conversion of the design from conventional to modern), and the main rationalization was the closure of the whole of the South Docks in 1972. In the rest of the North Docks and in Birkenhead there has been a mixture of some smaller scale and planned investments with some areas of low intensity use and pending closure (Fig. 3.2).

The current patterns of activities in the port, described in Figures 3.3. and 3.4, are now concentrated on five main areas of the northern part of the Liverpool system and on Birkenhead. The Pier Head complex is used principally by short- and near-sea services. This includes the Belfast Ferry and the Dublin Ferry terminals in Princes Dock and Trafalgar Dock respectively, whilst at the Waterloo Container Terminal Hispania Maritima operates a container service to Portugal, Morocco and Spain. To the north on the Liverpool side is an area of general cargo and small bulk terminals. Among these are the operations of the independent stevedores, Liverpool Maritime Terminals, which have a

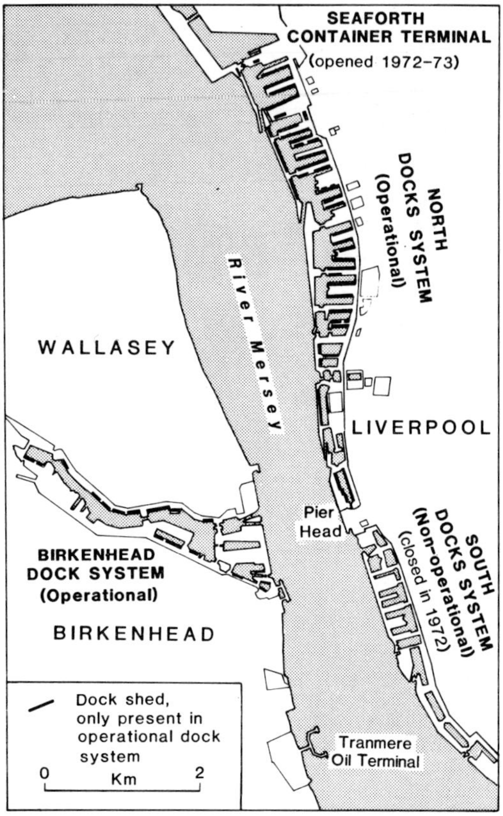

Fig. 3.2 Docks owned by the Mersey Docks and Harbour Company

semi-container service to West Africa as well as a service to the West Indies. There is a new bulk wine and spirit terminal at the Nelson Dock, where bulk spirits are piped directly into Stanley warehouse, and facilities are available for in-bond blending, colouring and reducing. Between the Liverpool Maritime Terminals base at Huskisson and the Gladstone end of the North Docks system is an area of low intensity use. Some partial redevelopment has taken place in this area as the Langton Graving Dock and Branch 1 of the Alexandra Dock have been filled in. This was part of the redevelopment plans for the North Docks where the intention was to develop an efficient new, combi-terminal for mixed container break-bulk operations. However, traffic is not buoyant, finance is short, and progress has been fairly slow. The Northern end of the dock system (Plate 3.1), Hornby Dock, Gladstone Dock and the Royal Seaforth complex, is the busiest part of the port.

Royal Seaforth Dock was the last to be built by the Mersey Docks and Harbour Company (M.D.H.C.). Officially opened in 1973 at a final cost of some £50 m, it is a modern, well equipped complex of specialist berths (Plates 3.2 and 3.3). The grain terminal is the most successful of Liverpool's operations, with extensive storage facilities and direct conveyor links from the terminal to three mills. The container terminal is a substantial one with 1100 m of quay, five Panamax gantries and 48 hectares of land. Groupage facilities for part container loads are also available on the site. The timber terminal is a modern, well equipped berth, capable of handling large amounts of cargo quickly and efficiently, but has been hit by the recession in the construction industry.

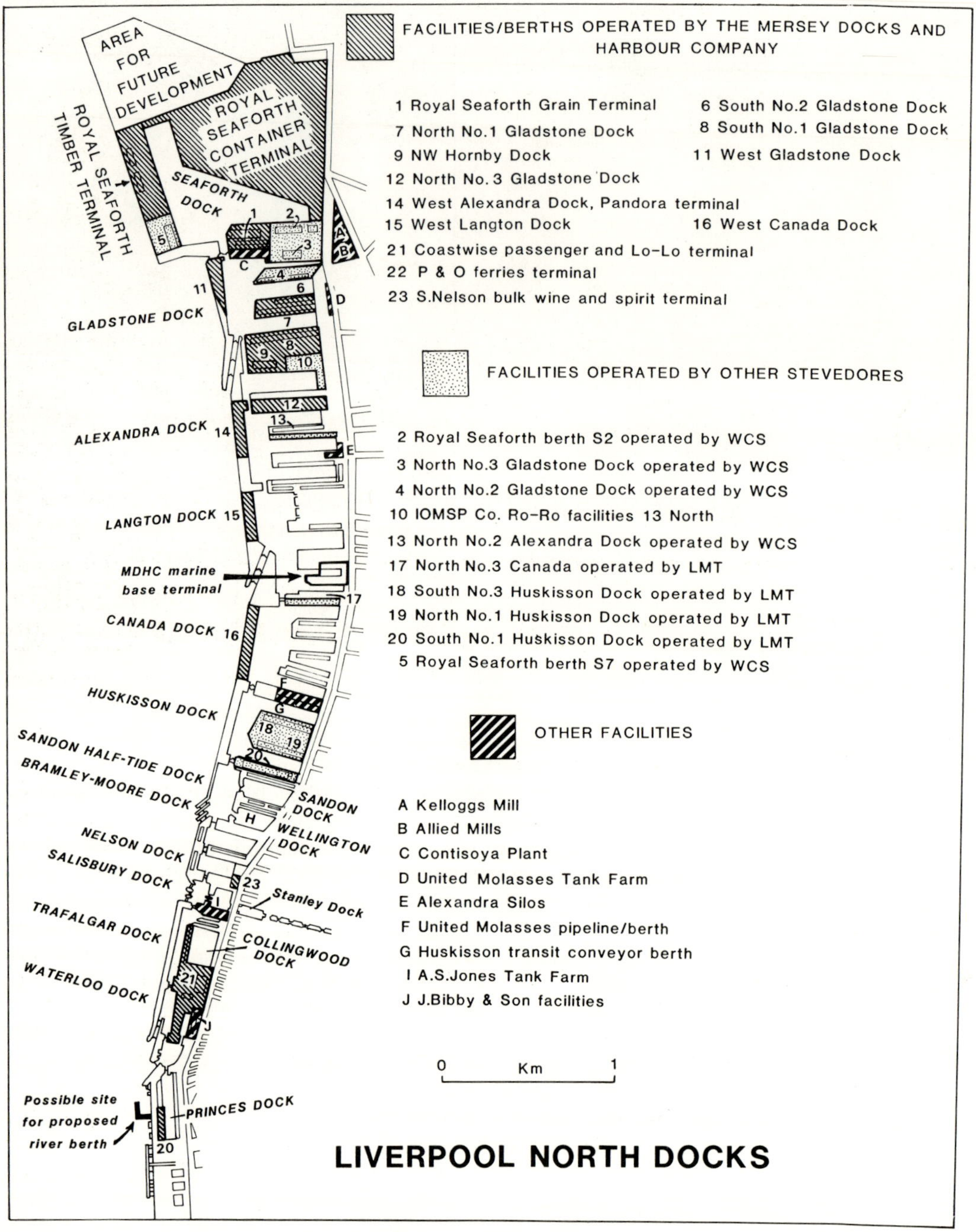

Fig. 3.3 Facilities of the North Docks System (source: M.D.H.C.)

Plate 3.1 North Docks System, showing the configuration of conventional docks with finger piers, transit sheds, self-sustaining general cargo ships and conventional quay cranes, before the Royal Seaforth Container Terminal was fully operational (photograph: Photo Graphic, Birkenhead)

The main activities on the Birkenhead side of the river are concerned with grain transhipped from the terminal at Royal Seaforth to one of several mills which are situated within the dock complex, and operated by companies leasing land from M.D.H.C. (Fig. 3.4). There are modern general cargo facilities at Vittoria Dock used by the Harrison Line to East African ports and by the Pacific Steam Navigation Company serving the west coast of South America, together with a bulk discharging facility for handling coal and bauxite. Operating problems at Birkenhead are primarily a consequence of the 8.68 m draught limitation to the whole complex, including Vittoria Dock. Bidston Dock is largely disused, and the older part of Birkenhead Docks (Egerton Dock and Morpeth Dock) is now closed. The Tranmere Oil Terminal, once an active receiver of tankers, has suffered a loss in trade since the opening of the Amlwch Mooring where tankers can moor offshore and have their cargoes pumped to the mainland. Tranmere is mostly used for coastal imports of oil at the present time.

Figure 3.5 summarizes the different operational areas in the port estate, including the pockets of activity remaining between closed docks. It shows the extent of cargo-handling operations in the port, illustrating this by measuring intensity of usage of various berths.

Changing patterns of employment

There have been three main components of the changing employment pattern. The first of these relates to the perennial problem of fluctuations in the demand for labour and the

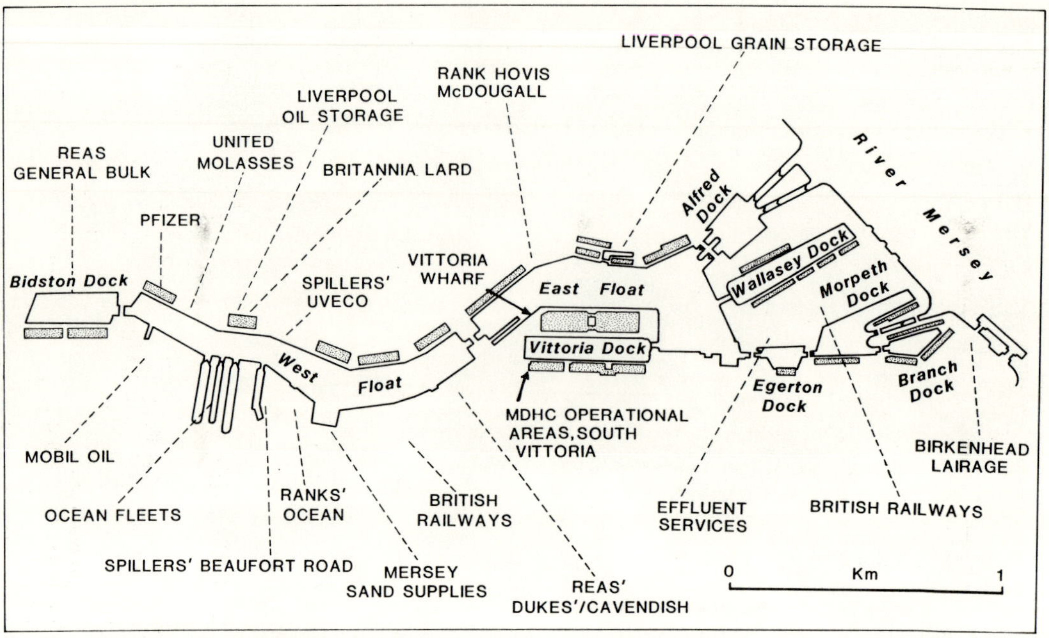

Fig. 3.4 Facilities of the Birkenhead Docks System (source: M.D.H.C.)

need for casual employment which were the familiar features of cargo handling in the conventional era. The second has been the transition from a labour-intensive industry into one which employs large resources of capital and a substantially smaller work force undertaking work of a very different character. The third has been the decline of the traditional stevedoring companies. All three components came together in the 1960s and 1970s to place an enormous financial burden upon the port and to create great difficulties for operating practice.

The first attempt in the U.K. to find a solution to the abuses of the casual labour system was in the form of a Dock Workers' Employment Scheme administered by the National Dock Labour Board (N.D.L.B.) which came into being in 1947. Its twin aims were to ensure that dock work was undertaken only by workers registered by local Boards and to improve the regularity of dock work. Whilst employment did become somewhat more regular under this scheme, it provided only a partial solution to the problem. The report of the Devlin Committee of Inquiry of 1965 into port employment recommended that all registered dock workers should be employed on a permanent basis, but also suggested that the number of dock workers should be substantially reduced. In 1967 a revised Dock Workers' Employment Scheme implemented the recommendations: a licensing system was introduced for the employers, who were then allocated registered dock workers on a permanent basis. Dockers who could no longer be offered permanent employment were held on the Temporarily Unattached Register (T.U.R.) while awaiting a fresh permanent location. Decasualization was thought by port employers to be the answer to the problem, but the dockers remained suspicious. A bitter six-week strike preceded decasualization, a spate of strikes followed, and in Liverpool alone there were 159 stoppages costing 130 554 man-days in 1969. There was a lack of leadership on the Trade Union side, with shop stewards exercising industrial muscle yet not accepting responsibility, whilst on the

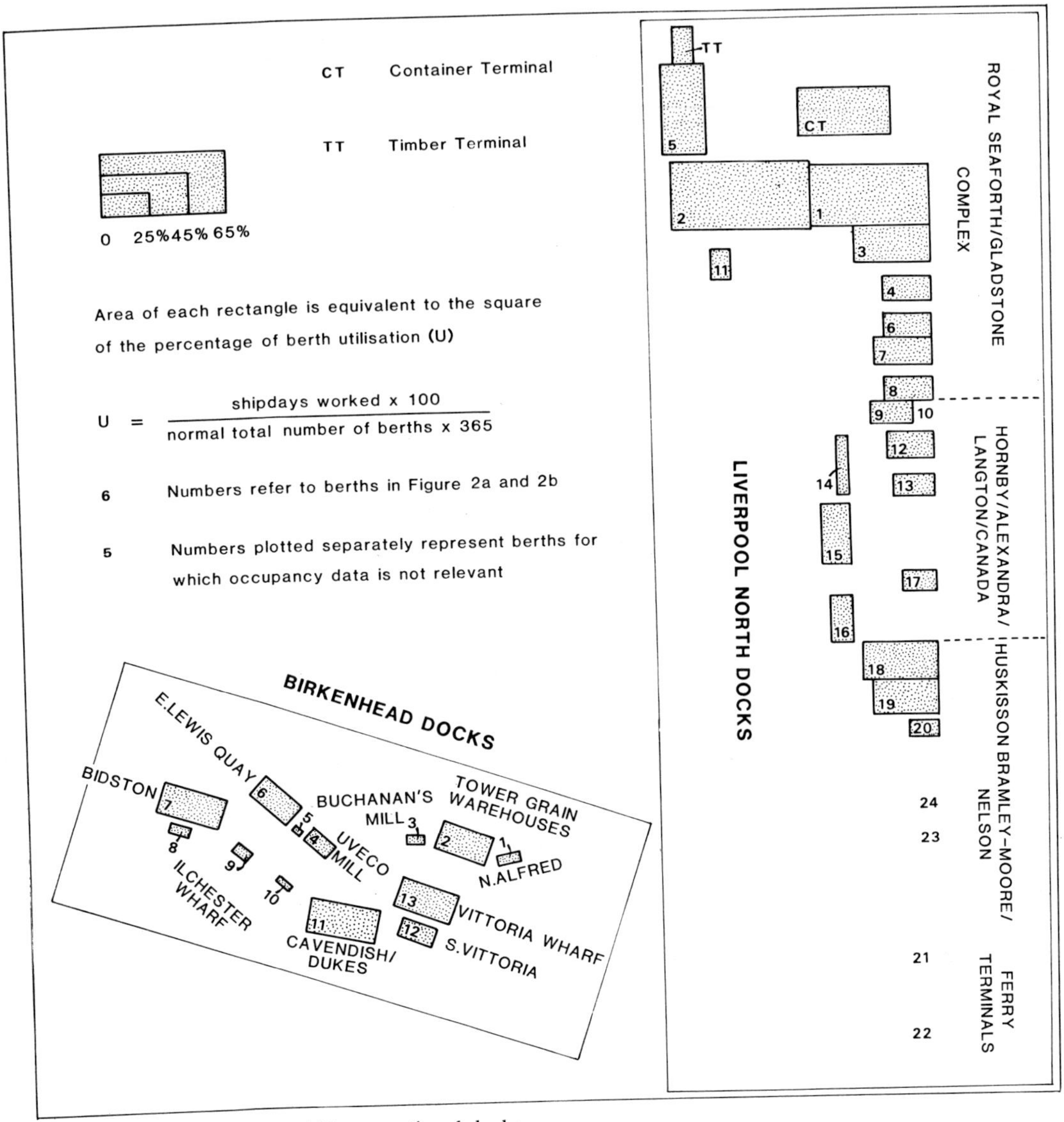

Fig. 3.5 Berth utilization within operational docks

management side firms often acceded to unreasonable demands rather than risk further confrontation and inevitable delays to sailings. Shortly after this three of Liverpool's major stevedoring companies ceased trading. The Mersey Docks & Harbour Company had no choice but to take over their services and personnel, and its registered dock labour force was increased from 1700 to 5100 in the short space of time between January 1972 and February 1973.

Since the implementation of the Devlin Report there have been a number of important developments in the form of the severance schemes devised to deal with the chronic surplus of labour which followed the introduction of new handling technology. The

TABLE 3.2 *Employment by the Mersey Docks and Harbour Company*

	Registered dock workers	Others	Total
January 1967	None	6297	6297
January 1968	716	6528	7244
January 1969	1989	5886	7875
January 1970	1896	5396	7292
January 1971	1783	4563	6346
January 1972	1734	4068	5802
January 1973	3336	4388	7724
January 1974	4830	4804	9634
January 1975	4766	4788	9564
January 1976	4661	4235	8896
January 1977	4182	4115	8297
January 1978	4066	4250	8316
January 1979	3771	4077	7848
January 1980	3253	3535	6788
January 1981	2989	3336	6325
October 1981	2300		

Source: M.D.H.C.

Plate 3.2 Royal Seaforth Container Terminal, showing the layout of a modern cargo handling terminal with a large back-up area, groupage sheds for part container loads and modern container gantry cranes (photograph: Stewart Bale, Liverpool)

Plate 3.3 Royal Seaforth Grain Terminal, discharging a bulk grain carrier. This is one of the most successful terminals within the port (photograph: Mersey Docks and Harbour Company)

Aldington-Jones severance scheme (1972–73), originally conceived to reduce the chronic labour surplus in London, was applied nationally, and as a result Liverpool lost some 2800 dockers. This was rather too many, and Liverpool suffered a serious labour shortage which was to prove even more damaging to the port than the industrial relations problems mentioned above. Ships diverted from the Mersey at the rate of fifty a month. Shipping conferences applied surcharges, and ships lay idle because of the shortage. Eventually the National Dock Labour Board was forced to concede a temporary register of 500 men with safeguards, but much damage had been done. Rationalization of the new enlarged company labour force became a long and difficult process against the background of continuous decline in general cargo. With the approval of the N.D.L.B., a series of voluntary severance schemes was introduced in an effort to reduce the over-manning problem as well as to minimize the cost of fallback payments to registered dock workers for whom there was no work available.

As a result of these agreements the number of registered dock workers employed by the company increased with take-over from private companies (Table 3.2). The large number of "others" is accounted for by a combination of activities including administration, pilotage services, dredging, hydrographic surveying and continuing radar surveillance, together with lockgate men, warehousemen and security men and a large workforce involved in the running and maintenance of engineering works and buildings on the dock estate. Table 3.2 also demonstrates the reduction of the workforce of M.D.H.C. between

1974 and 1981 by around 34%. However, this was still larger than the port's activities could sustain, and the M.D.H.C. suffered a cumulative loss of some £24 m from 1972 to 1981. At this stage the Company presented a profitability plan to the Government indicating the urgent need to shed 1000 dock workers and 500 general staff, as well as to improve efficiency and reduce overheads. In response to this, the Government introduced the Ports (Financial Assistance) Bill, 1981, which permitted the Secretary of State for Transport to give financial assistance to M.D.H.C. and the Port of London Authority to reduce the numbers employed. A special voluntary severance scheme was introduced for two months only, ending on 30th April, 1981, under which registered dock workers could apply for redundancy payments of up to a maximum of £16 000 if they had seen twenty years service in the ports. The scheme proved to be successful, with the first men leaving the docks as early as the beginning of April. By the end of the period the target had been achieved and the number of registered dock workers was reduced to 2300 which is the port's estimate of requirements for labour with improved working practice. The number of registered dock workers employed by outside stevedores had also dropped by 200 to 1200, with a total of 3500 in the port as a whole. Voluntary severance payments made by the Company between 1971 and 1979 amounted to some £20 m, and fallback pay to registered dock workers had cost over £13 m by the end of 1980. This was an enormous financial burden, particularly as many of the workers joined the Company only in the early 1970s.

Redevelopment of the dock estate

The closure of the South Dock system in 1972 made available for redevelopment a complex of docks, quays and buildings, extending for two miles from Albert Dock south to Herculaneum Dock and covering an area of some 95 hectares. This is the largest area of vacant land and buildings in the southern area of the inner city, and represents a major resource and development opportunity, but is endowed with a highly individual and difficult set of problems. The physical nature of the site, docks with narrow quays and large water areas, is foremost of these. Dock basins have silted up, and in some cases their in-filling would only be satisfactory if they were dredged to a firm base. The amount of fill required would also be quite large, and, if it has to be brought any distance, fill is expensive. The buildings are dilapidated. The Albert Dock for example, is in a state of almost total disrepair, and the cost of rehabilitation and conversion to modern standards will be substantial, perhaps greater than the cost of a new building. The scale of potential development is also very large. Even to develop one old dock complex can cost tens of millions of pounds, as was the case with the St. Katherine Dock in London, and the potential long-term cost of redevelopment of the South Docks could dwarf the cost of re-investment in the port itself.

The history of the area has been one of ambitious and comprehensive long-term planning which has so far borne only modest fruit. Currently the South Docks contain a great deal of interim small-scale use, some of it in very poor surroundings. The area has approximately 115 small firms which were all on short leases from the M.D.H.C. pending more substantial redevelopment. The area is best described as one of mixed industrial use, some of which is loosely port related, although most is totally unconnected with the port (see also Chapter 4). Activities on the Estate range from warehousing and storage of bulk feeds to road haulage, printing, and even a sculptor's studio. The buildings are in varying states of repair and the services available to many are at best basic—in some cases there is no running water and only a makeshift electricity supply. To the north of the Albert Dock the County Council has developed a Maritime Museum and there are plans for its further extension.

The agencies concerned with planning have included the M.D.H.C. as landlord,

Liverpool City Council, Merseyside County Council and Central Government (Chapter 2). Liverpool City Council set out its proposals in a report 'South Docks: Principles of Re-Development', in November 1972, which envisaged the comprehensive redevelopment of the area with a mixture of industrial and residential uses and open space. The M.D.H.C. then sought to dispose of the Dock Estate in the context of these proposals, but met with little success in the economic climate of the mid and late 1970s. Merseyside County Council's policy, set out in a 1976 report, 'A Strategic Policy for the South Docks', focused on the possibility of filling in unwanted areas of water with domestic refuse, thereby increasing the land area available for development. However, even this did not produce much more actual development, and after many years of very strict regulation, planning permission for short-term use has been eased, with some leases of up to seven years, and there has been a tendency to use the buildings on a short-term basis for a variety of industrial and storage purposes.

Most of the earlier initiatives have now been superseded by the formation of the Merseyside Development Corporation, created by Central Government and officially inaugurated on April 1st, 1981, and invested with planning authority for most of the area. The objective of the Corporation is to secure the regeneration of the under-used and derelict docklands on both sides of the Mersey, mainly by attracting private sector investment, since funds available from Central Government will be sufficient only for limited physical restructuring and redevelopment. Negotiations have taken place for the purchase of M.D.H.C. land including most of the South Docks complex, together with pockets of land in Bootle and Birkenhead. In this way the Development Corporation will relieve the M.D.H.C. of the responsibility for redevelopment.

Conclusion

Much of the physical transformation of the port is now complete. The activities of the M.D.H.C. will be concentrated at the Gladstone, Seaforth complex, with some short-sea traffic in the Pier Head area and perhaps a general cargo terminal at Birkenhead. Private stevedores will continue to operate, chiefly in the Huskisson complex. At the same time the labour force of the port has been substantially reduced, and is now at a level commensurate with the current needs, but with some scope for improvement in working practice and cuts in operating costs. However, 1981 has also seen the loss of some important traffic and the development of further financial crises so that the future of the M.D.H.C., currently dependent on government grants, is yet again under review.

The effect of the revolution in transport has been to take Liverpool out of the front rank of U.K. container ports. It is not the change in transport technology *per se* which has done this, but the secondary changes in transport organization and trading patterns and in particular the integration of U.K. traffic with that of continental Europe. However, bulk and semi-bulk cargoes and other non-containerizable cargoes still tend to use ports close to origins and destinations, sustaining the old hinterland relationships, and this spills over to services where containers are carried in association with these cargoes. In addition, where container lines specialize to some extent and can accumulate a fairly large container exchange at Liverpool, it will still pay to bring in a deep-sea ship. There are some prospects for gaining traffic, particularly in the newly containerized routes to countries of the Third World and with new national shipping lines. What is clear is that the port cannot survive, even in the reduced form described above, in a weak trading environment and with much weakened links with its hinterland if it is also less competitive in price and quality of service. In this respect the port has some way to go in re-establishing its somewhat tarnished reputation.

Chapter 4

ECONOMIC PROMOTION AND THE INNER CITY

P. H. LISTER

Physical and economic planning strategies before 1970 transformed the economic and spatial structures of the Merseyside conurbation by diversifying the regional economy and by decentralizing population and economic activity irrespective of consequences for inner urban localities (Chapters 1 and 2). The planning priorities of both national and local governments then changed. The inexorable growth of unemployment stimulated concern for Merseyside generally, but this was tempered by awareness of increasing welfare disparities within the County, particularly the problems of inner city communities in Liverpool, Wirral, St. Helens and south Sefton (Chapter 12). The "Strategic Plan for the North West" recommended the concentration of public resources in the older urban areas (North West Joint Planning Team, 1974), and the "Merseyside Structure Plan" in 1979 adopted inner urban regeneration as its strategic planning priority. National government also recognized these problems, and accepted that existing spatial planning policies were inappropriate to the scale and character of inner city needs. Regional policies assisted broadly-defined "areas for expansion", but were inadequately discriminatory at sub-regional level. New approaches were clearly required, and this chapter examines the nature of policies adopted since 1970 by the several tiers of government for economic promotion within inner urban areas.

National government and inner city policies

National responses to the social and economic deprivation of inner urban areas emerged piecemeal from the late 1960s (Cameron, 1980; Lawless, 1981). Innovative but unco-ordinated and vestigial programmes of area-based, positive discrimination were developed, particularly under the Home Office "Urban Programme" from 1968. This supported local authority expenditures on approved social and environmental projects in areas of "special social need" by 75% grant aid under the Local Government (Social Needs) Act, 1969, and by additional loan sanction allocations for their residual expenditure. Research studies of the Department of the Environment (1977A) highlighted a "collective deprivation" in areas such as inner Liverpool, providing "... an important argument for discriminating in favour of the inner areas in the working out of public policies and programmes" (p. 4). This brought major changes in the aims and character of existing area-development policies and in the spatial allocation of financial resources, with new measures specifically related to the needs of inner cities. The White Paper *Policy for the Inner Cities* (H.M.S.O., 1977) promised these areas "... an explicit priority in social and economic policy, even at a time of particular stringency in public resources" and "... a long-term commitment to tackle their problems" (p. 1). The main policies and programmes of central government departments were amended where these affected inner areas development. In April, 1977, the New Towns programme was curtailed to reduce decentralization of population and employment from the inner conurbation areas. This involved rejection of extensions to Skelmersdale and Runcorn and reductions in the proposed population intake to the Central Lancashire and Warrington New Towns. Regional policies were also amended (p. 46), and an inner city emphasis given within manpower programmes.

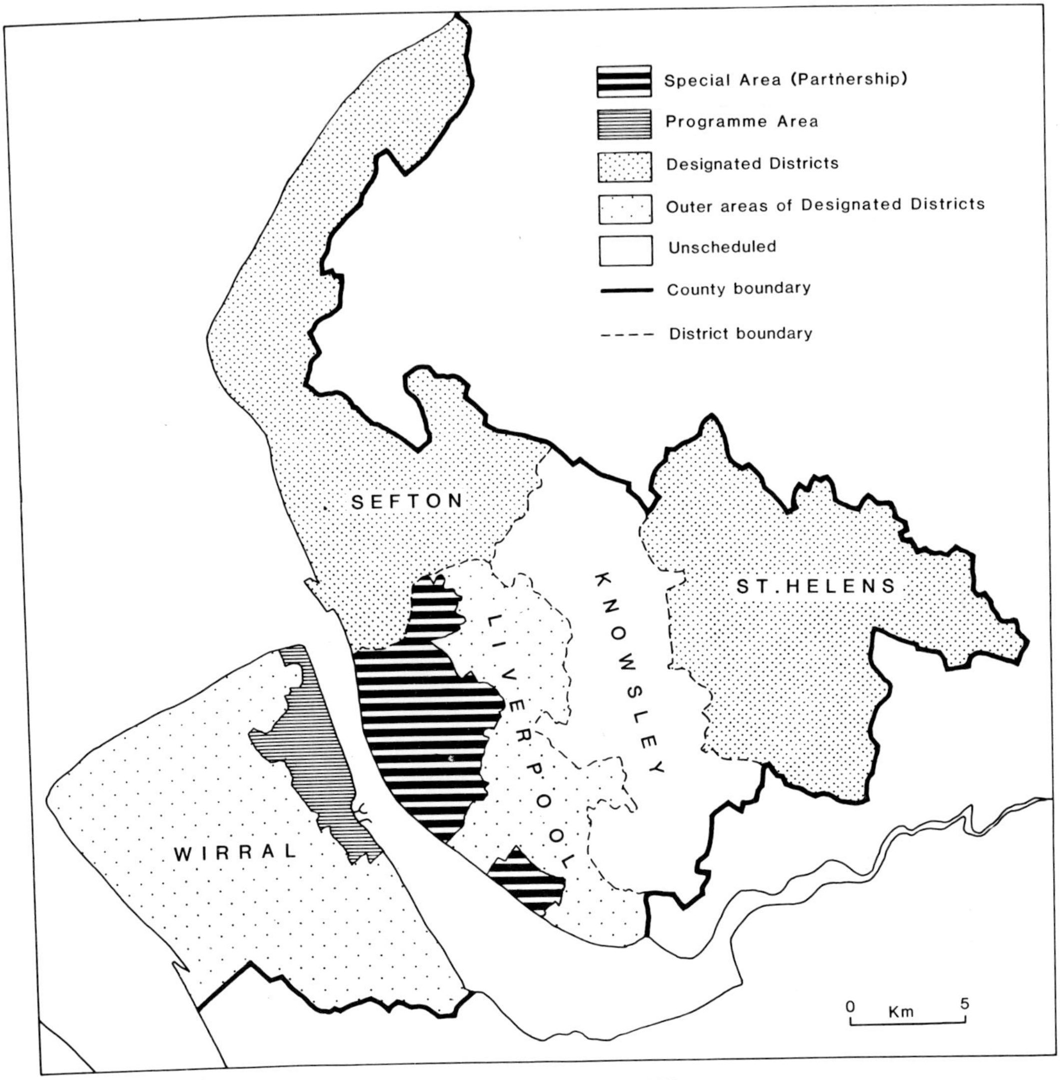

Fig. 4.1 Areas designated under the Inner Urban Areas Act, 1978

The Urban Programme was also recast to support industrial and commercial projects in addition to social schemes. Its resources were quadrupled from 1979/80 to £125 m for expenditures within England and Wales (1977/78 prices), and administrative responsibility was given to the Department of the Environment. Priority in the geographical allocation of these resources was narrowed in favour of local authorities with deemed inner area problems scheduled as Designated Districts under the Inner Urban Areas Act, 1978. These included Liverpool, Sefton, St. Helens and Wirral, but not Knowsley. The latter competes for residual Urban Programme resources with other "outer areas" with special social needs. Three tiers of priority exist within the Designated Districts (Fig. 4.1). First priority is given to the Liverpool Special Area ("Partnership Area"), where partnership machinery established between national and local governments was to draw up and implement regenerative measures using Urban Programme resource allocations of £12.1 m in 1979/80, £18.1 m in 1980/81 and £17.5 m for 1981/82 (Liverpool Inner City Partnership Committee, 1978, 1980). As second priority the Department of the Environment (D.O.E.) declared Wirral to be a Programme Authority Area, and invited the Council to submit an inner area programme focused on the older urban areas of the Mersey waterfront and the docklands of Wallasey and Birkenhead. Resources were more circumscribed than to the Special Area, being £1.875 m in 1979/80, £2.690 m in 1980/81 and £2.794 m for 1981/82. No formal partnership machinery was established. Third priority were the St. Helens and Sefton Designated Districts, whose local authorities submitted no formal programmes but bid for resources for industrial and commercial projects in their inner areas against a limited North-West regional pool of £1.4 m and £2.0 m in 1979/80 and 1980/81 respectively. Each District received an annual provisional allocation, St. Helens receiving £0.26 m in 1979/80, £0.54 m in 1980/81 and £0.3 m in 1981/82. Sefton has received similar provisional allocations, but has committed only one project, its unexpended balances being redistributed between other authorities.

The revised Urban Programme from 1979/80 clearly introduced a new dimension to the geography of state aids for area development within Merseyside by providing varying levels of support for initiatives by its constituent local authorities. These emphasized schemes for economic and environmental regeneration and experimental and "pump-priming" expenditures likely to stimulate private-sector investments. Variations between authorities largely reflect their varying resource endowments. Furthermore, and more immediately to initiate measures of assistance for inner areas and to stimulate the construction industry, a national "Construction Package" of additional public capital projects totalling £100 m was announced in March 1977 for completion by March 1979. £11 m was allocated for projects within the Liverpool Partnership Area with £0.47 m, £0.42 m and £0.44 m to Sefton, St. Helens and Wirral respectively. Knowsley was omitted. Priority was suggested for schemes of economic significance within their inner areas, and important programmes of economic promotion resulted. The period 1977–79 was thus a transitional phase of enhanced resources for inner area projects, foreshadowing more radical measures from 1979/80.

The Inner Urban Areas Act, 1978, also increased the statutory powers of County and District Councils to provide financial assistance to the private sector of industry and commerce within Designated Districts. Within the Districts generally loans could be provided for land and building costs incurred by private developments. Moreover, within the Liverpool Special Area the partnership authorities could provide loans with interest rebates for costs of site preparation and servicing, an important provision given the deterrent costs of site predevelopment in areas of urban renewal. They could also provide grants towards rents on leased industrial or commercial buildings or towards interest charges on loans for land acquisition or building works by small firms. Statutory "Improvement Areas" could also be scheduled by the local authorities in which even more financial aids could be given. They comprised old and decaying industrial or commercial localities, within which loans or grants were authorized for converting, extending, improving or modifying buildings. The sensitive definition of Improvement Areas promised a more discriminatory tailoring of financial assistance to local circumstances, and this is now central to policies for inner area economic regeneration by the County Council and the Liverpool and Wirral Councils (Fig. 4.2). Neither St. Helens nor Sefton have scheduled Improvement Areas, and Knowsley is ineligible. Clearly the inner city policies of national government, largely effected through local authority intermediaries, had created by the late 1970s a hierarchy of sub-regions within the County with marked

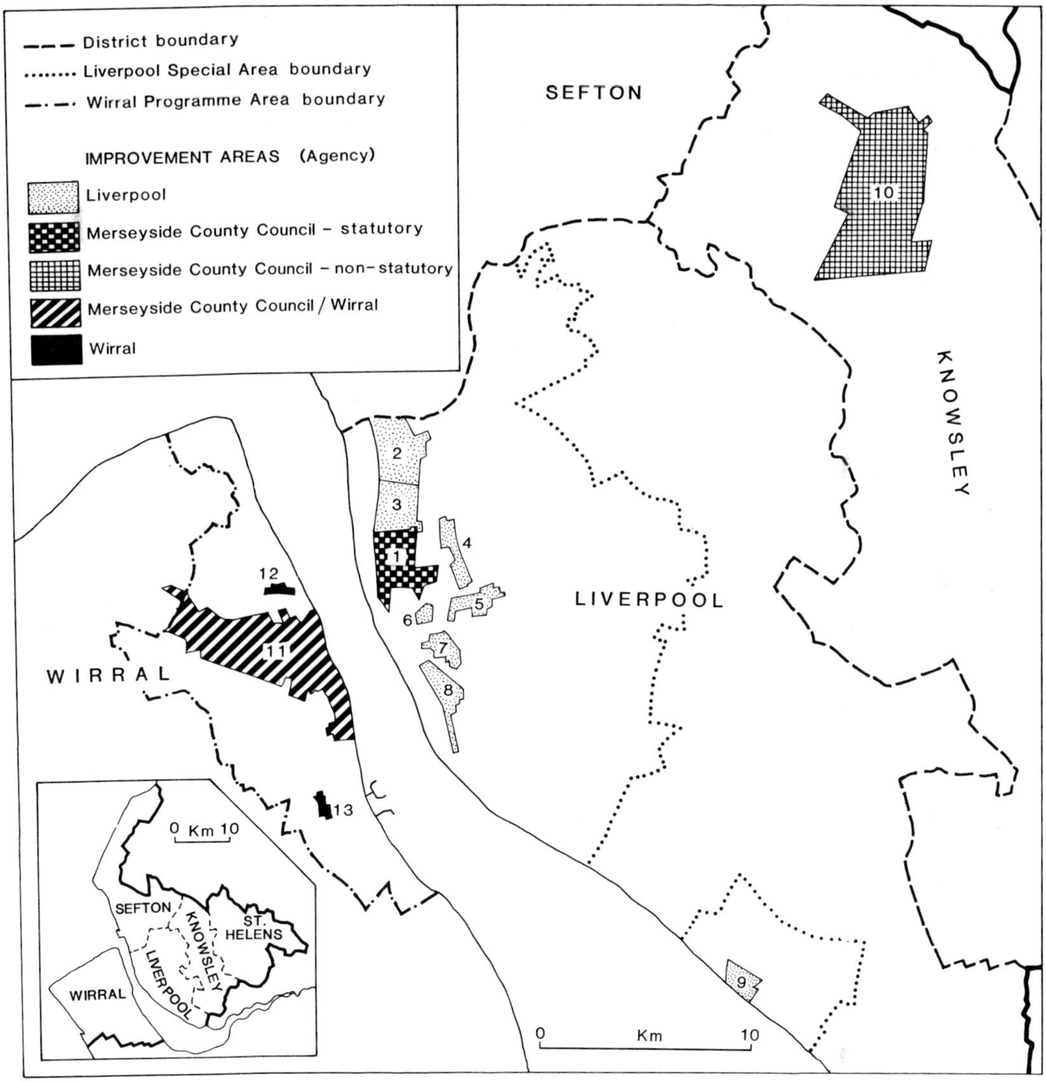

Fig. 4.2 Improvement areas designated by Merseyside local authorities, 1977–1981 (1 Great Howard Street; 2 Bankhall; 3 Boundary Street; 4 St. Anne Street; 5 London Road; 6 Temple/Victoria Street; 7 Duke Street; 8 Parliament Street; 9 Garston; 10 Kirkby Industrial Estate; 11 Wirral Docklands; 12 Borough Road; 13 Old Chester Road)

variations in the access of local authorities to incremental financial resources and to statutory powers related to economic development and promotion.

This complexity was increased in 1981 by further measures by national government to stimulate economic and environmental regeneration within Merseyside through the creation of the Merseyside Development Corporation (M.D.C.) and the designation of two Enterprise Zones. The M.D.C. was formed in March 1981 to facilitate the redevelopment of 865 acres (350 ha) of derelict docklands in Liverpool, south Sefton and Wirral embraced by newly-scheduled Urban Development Areas (Fig. 4.3). The

Fig. 4.3 Urban Development Areas and Enterprise Zones, 1981

Corporation became the local planning authority, and was given both wide powers in these Areas and also considerable financial resources to promote industrial, commercial and residential developments and environmental improvements. These resources, broadly equivalent to the Urban Programme allocation to the Liverpool Partnership authorities, are an important additional commitment to the inner areas of the region from central government. The M.D.C. published its "Initial Development Strategy" in August 1981, but most budgetary decisions and the nature and phasing of development proposals currently await detailed economic, financial and engineering evaluations.

The Enterprise Zones were created to encourage economic development in areas of high unemployment, not necessarily inner urban areas, by relaxing or abolishing certain planning, fiscal and administrative impositions of local and national governments on business enterprises. Two Zones were designated in August, 1981, at Speke, an outer district in south Liverpool seriously affected by the closure of manufacturing plants (Fig. 4.3). They include some of the few large tracts of undeveloped industrial land in the City, though they are in part constrained by continuing airport uses pending the relocation of terminal and control-tower facilities. There are also vacated industrial premises awaiting redevelopment with a floor space of over 2.5 m sq ft (232 258 sq m), equivalent to the total floorspace of factory buildings financed by Central Government within the County under regional policies since 1967 (p. 46). Controversially experimental, the effects of Enterprise Zones on economic growth both within and beyond the designated areas remain conjectural, but they add a further element to the mosaic of area-specific initiatives for economic promotion in Merseyside.

National government and regional policies

The region remains eligible for regional aids currently provided by Central Government under the Industry and Local Employment Acts of 1972 and associated legislative and administrative provisions. Areas so assisted in the review period comprise the Development Area, scheduled in 1966, and the Intermediate Areas of 1972, the former uprated to Special Development Area status in 1974 (Fig. 4.4). However, regional policies proved markedly less effective through the 1970s than in the 1960s as demands placed upon them increased with rising unemployment. The decline of manufacturing industry nationally undermined policies based on the induced mobility of manufacturing plants and

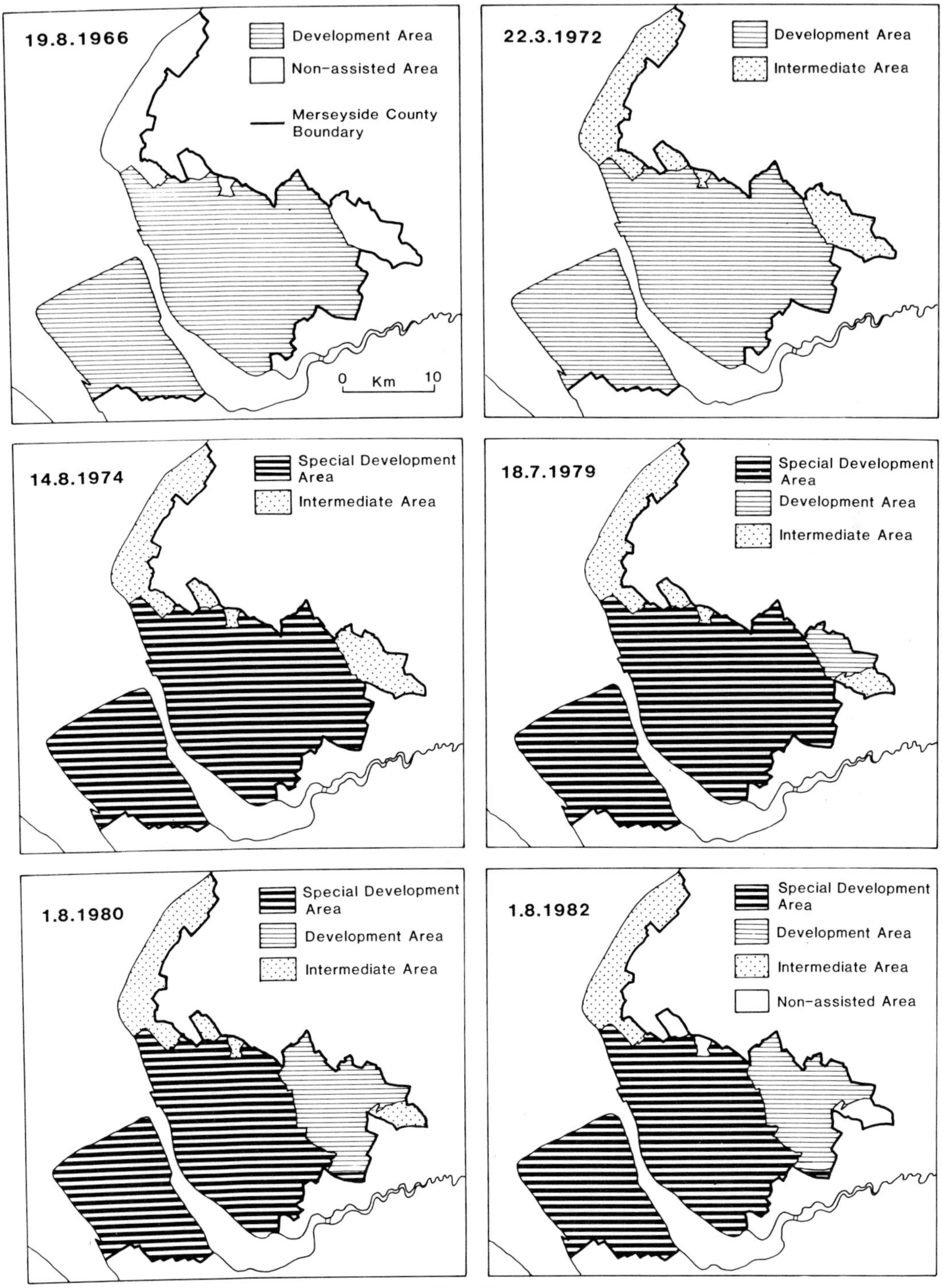

Fig. 4.4 The Assisted Areas of Merseyside, 1966–1982

on the premise of manufacturing growth. Location control policies were also progressively relaxed, and suspended indefinitely in December 1981, reducing pressures on investing enterprises to relocate. Expenditure cuts eroded financial incentives, particularly Regional Development Grants which were reduced and concentrated within more limited priority areas. Within Merseyside the Special Development Area contracted in August, 1980, when St. Helens was downgraded to Development Area status, and other localities revert from Intermediate Area to non-assisted area status in August 1982 (Fig. 4.4). Grants paid on manufacturing investments were reduced in August 1980 in the Development Area from 20% to 15%, widening the differential with that of 22% in the Special Development Area, while the 20% grant formerly paid on new buildings in Intermediate Areas was abolished (Department of Industry, 1980). The hierarchical structure of assisted areas within Merseyside is now more clearly pronounced, with enhanced priority given to the Special Development Area and sharp spatial discontinuities in the provision of financial aids.

The weakened efficacy of traditional regional policies at the same time as growing regional and intra-urban problems encouraged an increasing emphasis on support for indigenous industrial and commercial enterprises, rather than inducing the migration of large firms into Merseyside. This required revision of the Treasury-financed factory building programme within the region, historically one of the principal instruments of regional promotion (Lister, in press), representing a further response of national government to the changing scale and character of the region's economic problems.

Within Merseyside the provision of factory buildings by Central Government agencies, currently by English Industrial Estates (E.I.E.), dates from the 1940s. Until 1967 these overwhelmingly comprised large factories built for sale or lease specifically for known firms ("bespoke" buildings), the companies largely originating outside the region. Of the 2.39 m sq ft (222 038 sq m) of floorspace provided within the County, 1947–1966, 80.5% consisted of new, bespoke premises and 13.5% of extensions. Only 6% comprised "advance factory units" (A.F.U.s) built speculatively to enhance the available building stock and to provide immediate accommodation for incoming industry (Fig. 4.5). Most of this public investment was located at the periphery, with industrial estates built at St. Helens (Parr), Huyton and Birkenhead, and large, individual factories at Speke, Fazakerley, Kirkby, Bromborough and Birkenhead (Fig. 4.6). However, the nature and spatial pattern of building then changed markedly. A new programme of A.F.U.s began in 1967, and these have since predominated. Between 1967 and 1981 premises totalling 2.53 m sq ft (235 045 sq m) were either built or under construction, of which 74.8% comprised A.F.U.s (Fig. 4.5). Bespoke building almost ceased after 1970. The A.F.U.s built until 1975 consisted of small numbers of large factories between 10–25 000 sq ft (929–2415 sq m), and were reserved for manufacturing firms originating outside the region. However, in 1975 and 1976 terraces of small "nursery" units were started at Knowsley, Rock Ferry and Sandon Dock (Fig. 4.6), and E.I.E. activity within Merseyside since then has emphasized the provision of large numbers of small factories. Between 1975 and 1981 406 units were built or started, of which 301 were under 5000 sq ft (465 sq m), including "Beehive Workshops" of under 1000 sq ft (93 sq m) introduced in 1979 at Wallasey and in 1981 at Birkenhead, Bromborough, Netherton and Speke. Since these are largely inappropriate to the needs of inter-regionally-mobile firms, this recasting of the E.I.E. programme reflects the accepted improbability of regional policies generating industrial movement into Merseyside on a scale commensurate with that achieved in the 1960s. It also emphasizes the need to encourage the indigenous small-business sector and local entrepreneurship by providing modern premises (Lister, 1982).

The geographical pattern of E.I.E. factory building also changed in the 1970s to place

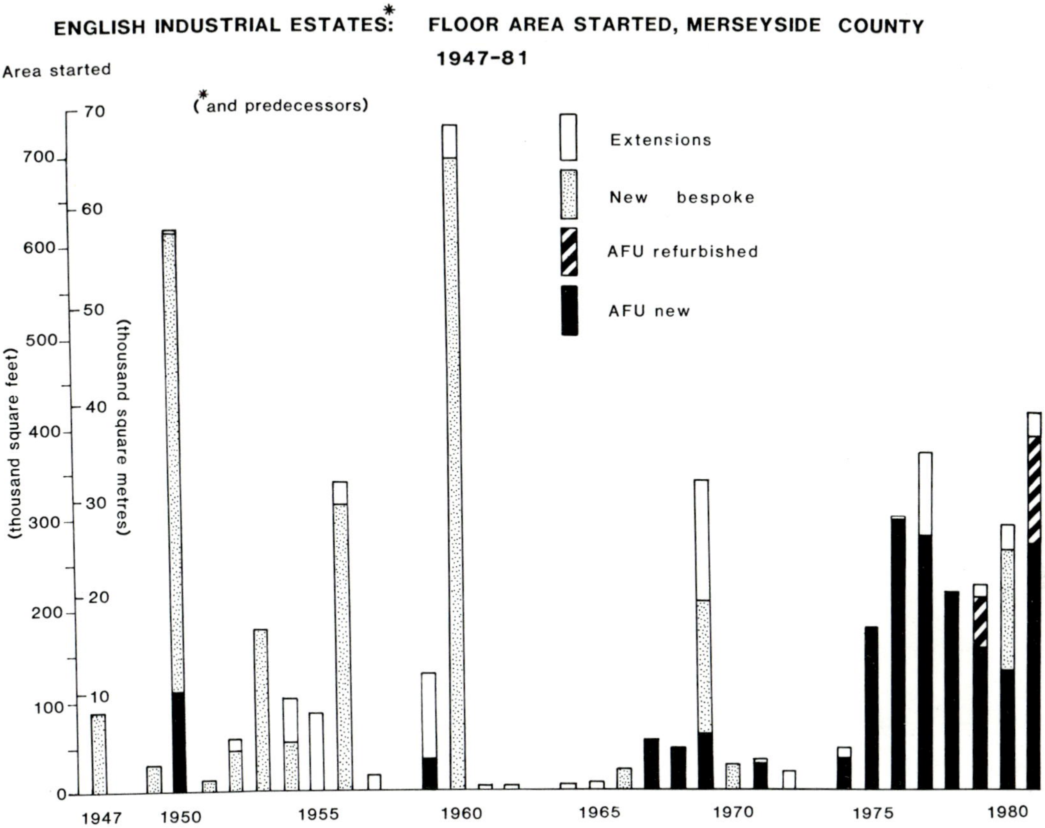

Fig. 4.5 Factory building by Central Government in Merseyside: annual floor area started, 1947–1981 (includes E.I.E./private sector partnership schemes, 1981)

regional policy more in accord with inner urban area policies. The E.I.E. programme was originally focused on peripheral, greenfield sites, a pattern reinforced by the rapid development of the Knowsley estate from 1967 and, potentially, by the location of its remaining land holdings. However, it was increasingly diverted to the inner areas following pressure from the County Council in 1975. Initial developments of small advance units at Rock Ferry in Wirral and Sandon Dock in Liverpool were followed by extensive A.F.U. construction within inner areas generally. Changes in the size, structure and spatial pattern of E.I.E. building are clearly consistent with the amended promotional objectives and "target population" of regional policies and with inner city priority. Unfortunately the achievement in these areas, particularly in relation to small business needs, is countered by the concurrent loss of employment arising from the high closure rate of large factories occupied over previous decades (Chapter 2).

Local government and economic promotion

These national responses to the mounting problems of Merseyside were accompanied by, and often stimulated, symbiotic responses from local authorities. Their role in economic promotion and development increased dramatically, if unevenly, across the County in the 1970s. This role had been previously limited by both statutory and financial restrictions,

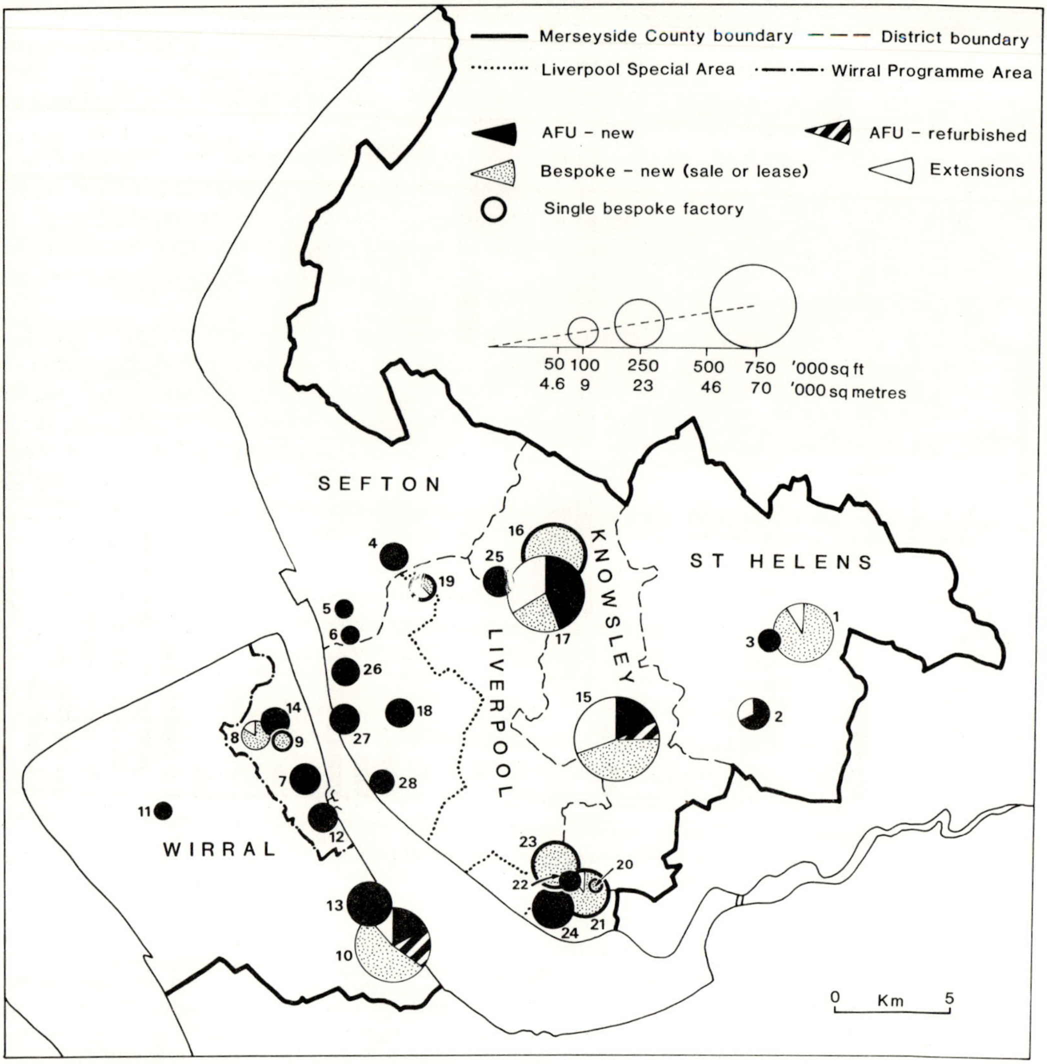

Fig. 4.6 Central Government industrial estates and sites: total floor area completed or under construction 1947–1981, including factories sold (1 Parr; 2 Lea Green; 3 Sherdley Road; 4 Netherton; 5 Strand Road; 6 Brasenose Road; 7 Argyle Street; 8 Beaufort Road; 9 Cleveland Street; 10 Tebay Road; 11 Upton; 12 Rock Ferry; 13 Croft; 14 Wallasey; 15 Huyton; 16 Kirkby; 17 Knowsley; 18 Erskine Street; 19 Fazakerley; 20/21/22/23 Speke (individual sites); 24 Speke Hall Avenue; 25 Gillmoss; 26 Sandon Way; 27 King Edward Street; 28 Grain Street)

but these were eased by the Inner Urban Areas Act and by Construction Package and Urban Programme resources. However, authorities varied markedly in the priority given to economic policies and programmes, as these are generally discretionary functions rather than statutory obligations. They are therefore properly influenced by political philosophies and competition for resources. In addition authorities had differential access to powers and finance under inner city policies.

Local government's promotional role may be summarized as the adoption of measures appropriate to the successive stages of the land development process likely to create at each stage a more positive climate for private-sector investment in preferred locations. These include an explicit recognition of responsibilities in economic promotion and development. New policies were introduced to provide a framework for public and private-sector initiatives and to provide a rationale for new resource commitments. Decisions by Liverpool City Council in 1970 to encourage industrial growth within the city limits and in 1974 to give priority to inner area development were particularly significant. Wirral Council agreed new inner urban policies in 1977 and an associated economic policy and programme from 1980. Knowsley and St. Helens introduced "industrial strategies" in 1978 and 1979 respectively. The County Council also approved economic development and employment policies in 1978, Sefton alone having no comparably explicit policies for economic promotion.

Authorities also adopted new administrative mechanisms to promote private investment through marketing strategies, the provision of advice and consultancy services to potential developers and the coordination of public-agency activities in specific developments. Significant here was the creation by Liverpool in 1970 of an Industrial Development Unit, succeeded in 1979 by the Liverpool Development Agency. In 1981 Wirral and Knowsley agreed the formation of an Economic Development Unit and an Industrial Development Office respectively, the County Council having formed in 1974 the Merseyside Industrial Development Office, now the Merseyside County Economic Development Office. In 1980 the County also incorporated a private development company with major promotional responsibilities, Merseyside Economic Development Company Limited. This direct involvement in economic promotion, Sefton apart, reflects the deepening employment crisis and defensive reactions to the existing activities of adjacent Councils and the New Towns.

A third function of local government has been to improve the supply and quality of land zoned for industrial and commercial development. The availability of serviced sites is a major determinant of the pace and spatial pattern of economic development, and inner urban regeneration strategies are seriously constrained by poor land resources. In 1978 the County Council concluded that "... there remains a serious lack of sites in a serviced condition which are immediately available" (Merseyside County Council, 1978) and Liverpool Council that "... the industrial land situation particularly in the inner city is critical ... If economic regeneration is to occur ... then the available land resource in its current state will be patently inadequate to cope with the demands placed upon it" (Liverpool City Council, 1978, p. 7). Local authority responses have included the acquisition of land and assembly of sites, clearance of dereliction, predevelopment and servicing operations and cosmetic improvements (Chapter 7). Although derelict land reclamation was encouraged by the availability of 100% grants under the Local Employment Act from 1975, the general record of Merseyside authorities has been poor. Furthermore, new capital expenditure controls began to bite in 1981. Most progress has been made where specialist land reclamation units were created, as by the County Council in 1977 and by St. Helens in 1976, generating a necessary level of professionalism, commitment and programme continuity. The County programme by March, 1982, will have cleared 344.5 acres (139 ha) on thirty-eight sites, 121 acres (49 ha) for industrial after-use predominantly in St. Helens and inner Liverpool. The Liverpool and Sefton authorities have less-formalized programmes, and Wirral and Knowsley have been uninvolved.

Given the obsolescence of existing fixed capital in inner areas and the deterrent costs of renewal to the private sector, the servicing of development sites and provision of related physical infrastructure present important areas for "pump-priming" expenditure by local government. Programmes have been supported by varying combinations and degree of

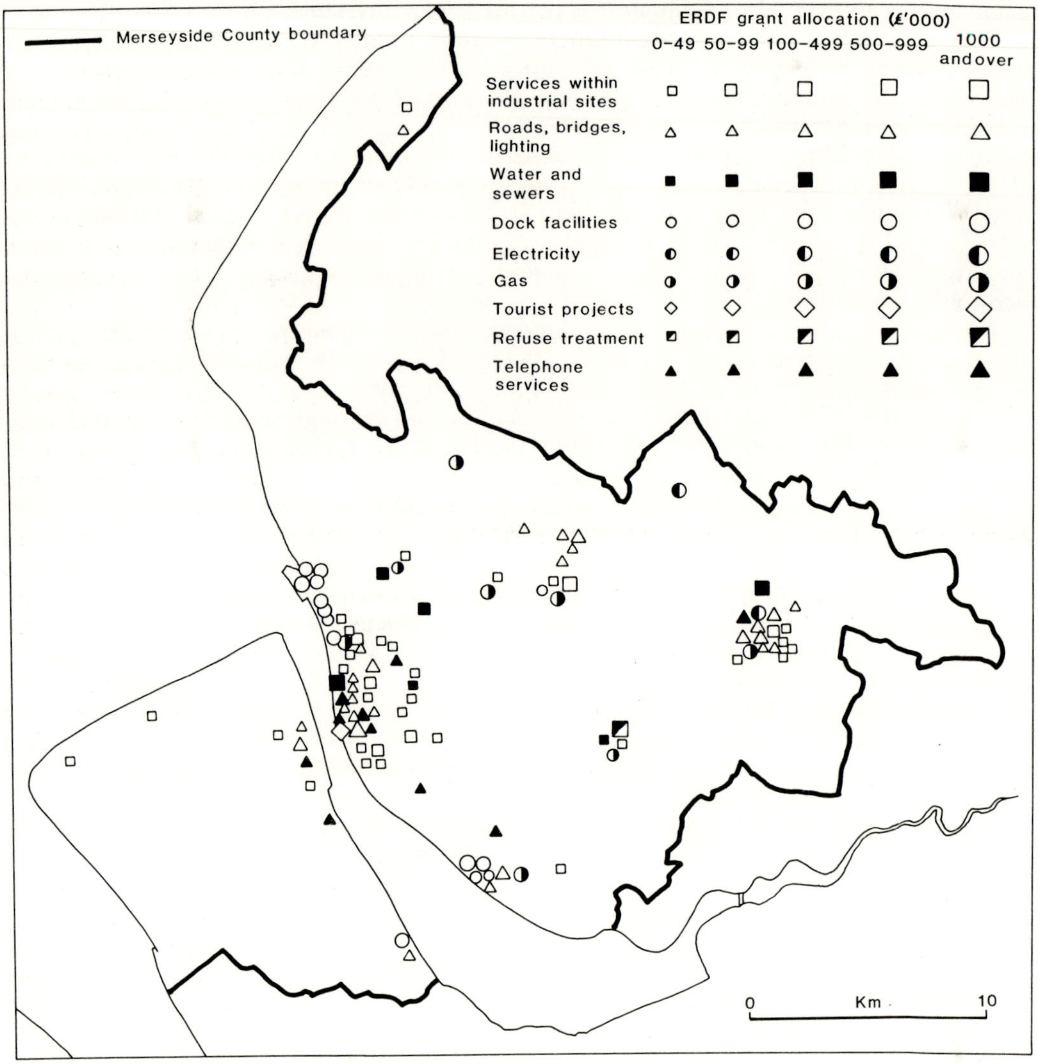

Fig. 4.7 European Regional Development Fund: grant allocations approved, 1975 to October 1981, for infrastructure projects in Merseyside (allocations not always fully paid if projects amended; allocations for "grouped" projects equally divided between individual sites; five projects not shown as not specifically located)

grant aids relative to the status of areas and authorities under regional and inner city policies. From 1975 grants from the European Regional Development Fund (E.R.D.F.) supplemented those from national government under the Local Employment Act, with Construction Package and Urban Programme resources added from 1977. Depending on the mix of grants available, residual costs to local authorities range between 70% and 17½% of expenditures. Priority in the allocation of E.R.D.F. grants, 30% of infrastructure costs, is given to projects in the County's Special Development and Development Areas, eighty-six schemes being aided between 1975 and October, 1981, with total grant allocations of £13.6 m. Most use of E.R.D.F. resources has been made by the County Council and Liverpool City Council. Projects of economic significance by other public bodies have also been assisted, the general focus of E.R.D.F. aid being the inner areas (Fig. 4.7). Construction Package and Urban Programme resources stimulated site-servicing programmes by the County, Liverpool, Wirral and St. Helens Councils particularly, given 75% grant aid on expenditures. Local Employment Act grants of 30% provide some assistance to projects not so supported. Industrial site-servicing has been undertaken by the County Council since 1975, primarily in St. Helens and the inner docklands of Liverpool, south Sefton and Wirral, and in association with land-owning public bodies and local authorities. Liverpool's activities were initially focused on its peripheral industrial estates at Knowsley and Netherley from 1969 and 1971 respectively, but subsequently have emphasized inner area sites. Despite Partnership resources from 1979/80, the programme has been subject to considerable slippage and underspending, suggesting that constraints on industrial land schemes are now legal, technical and administrative rather than financial. Wirral Council has serviced industrial sites in and beyond the Programme Area, and also sites for commercial and office development in Borough Road (Seacombe) and at the former Birkenhead market. St. Helens has acted on industrial sites both independently and in partnership with the County Council, including major road and bridge improvements to facilitate industrial development on land with access problems. Sefton has also serviced industrial sites in Bootle, Southport and Litherland.

These programmes are clearly a prerequisite for the successful implementation of strategies for regional economic development and inner area regeneration, yet serious imbalances persist between demand for and supply of serviced land. Its availability has markedly influenced the pattern of investment by both private and public sectors, for private developments are drawn to sites serviced by local authorities, and the locational pattern of advance factory construction by the E.I.E. and by the local authorities is itself similarly influenced. Conversely, land shortages deflect or deter investment and undermine spatial planning strategies. In 1980, for example, greenfield peripheral sites in St. Helens were rezoned for industrial use pending the treatment and servicing of inner area sites.

Local authorities have also promoted economic development by the speculative building of premises for lease to private firms. These are primarily advance factories, but also include some warehouse and office accommodation. By 1981 all Merseyside authorities except Sefton had such programmes, introduced by Liverpool City Council in the late 1960s, by St. Helens from 1976 and the County and Wirral Councils in the 1980s. Knowsley approved a project at Huyton in 1980, as yet in abeyance. This activity reflects deemed deficiencies in the scale, location, size range and tenancy terms of developments by the private sector and E.I.E. Until 1977 expenditures for speculative building fell upon local finances, thus precluding major initiatives unless given priority within capital budgets, as in Liverpool and St. Helens. Construction Package and Urban Programme resources then facilitated substantial new developments by recipient authorities. In the 1980s priority is being placed upon A.F.U. provision by the private sector in forms of financial partnership with local Councils, and upon the refurbishment and subdivision for A.F.U.s of large, vacated industrial premises (Lister, 1982).

The Liverpool programme was initially to rehouse firms displaced by central area redevelopment and by land acquisition and construction works associated with the second Mersey tunnel and the proposed inner ring road. The E.I.E. programme was limited, peripherally-located and its unit sizes too large for most of the affected concerns. It was subject to tenancy policies excluding non-manufacturing firms and those originating within the region. Liverpool's activities were conceived as complementary, comprising the refurbishment and subdivision of redundant warehouse buildings in the South Docks by

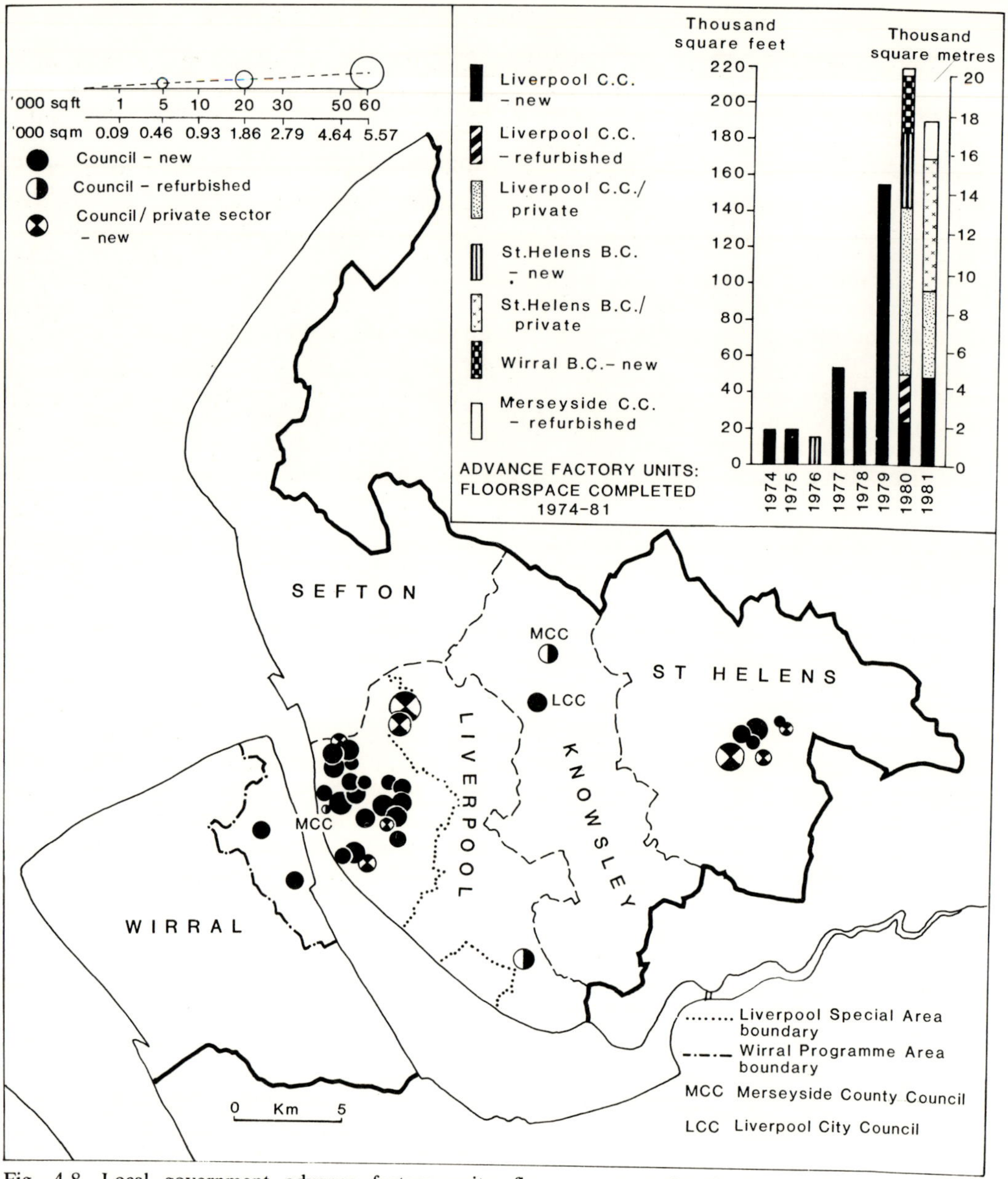

Fig. 4.8 Local government advance factory units: floor area completed, 1947–1981 (includes local government/private sector partnership schemes from 1980)

1969 and a new multi-storey block completed at Canning Square in 1970. From the mid 1970s, however, Liverpool saw A.F.U.s as instruments of economic regeneration in inner areas, and emphasized the needs of new business and existing small firms moving within Merseyside as well as the attraction of mobile industry from elsewhere. A new programme commenced in 1974, and by December 1981 the Council had completed, either itself or in partnership arrangements, some 529 000 sq ft (49 146 sq m) of premises comprising 164 factory and warehouse units, overwhelmingly in the inner urban areas (Fig. 4.8). This total was only slightly less than the 590 000 sq ft (54 000 sq m) concurrently built within Liverpool by E.I.E. The City had also encouraged the speculative provision of office accommodation in the central area, using Partnership resources to provide rent guarantees on private-sector developments.

Other Merseyside authorities undertook A.F.U. schemes from the mid 1970s. These were responses to perceived local needs, the adoption of new economic development strategies and the availability of additional resources, as well as to fears of "cross-border" migration by local firms to premises in Liverpool and the New Towns. St. Helens constructed thirty-nine units totalling 130 500 sq ft (12 123 sq m) between 1976 and 1981, latterly in private-sector partnerships, and Wirral completed twenty-seven units totalling 31 000 sq ft (2879 sq m) in Birkenhead in 1980. From 1980 the County Council also sought to encourage private A.F.U. schemes by partnership financing, including rent guarantee and leaseback arrangements, and agreed in 1981 that the Merseyside Economic Development Company Limited should so sponsor up to 200 000 sq ft (18 580 sq m) annually. If achieved this will almost equal the annual average level of A.F.U.s started within Merseyside by E.I.E. in the period 1975–81. Both County and District Councils have also provided A.F.U.s by refurbishing existing buildings, the potential for which increased greatly in the mid 1970s as a result of factory closures. Private capital is not easily mobilized for such schemes. From 1980 projects were completed by Liverpool at Speke and by the County Council in the Liverpool North Docks and at Kirkby, while substantial commitments of Partnership and Programme Funds have been made by Liverpool and Wirral Councils for further schemes from 1982.

These local authority A.F.U. programmes effected the completion of 245 units totalling 713 800 sq ft (66 312 sq m), 1974–1981 (Fig. 4.8). These are undoubtedly valuable in stimulating private demand for modern premises and the formation, growth and efficient operation of tenant firms. Environmental amenities were improved with capital investment in areas of dereliction and obsolescence, and private investment was encouraged by tangible evidence of a public commitment to their regeneration. Their direct impact on employment is, however, marginal in relation to employment needs, for even if all completed units were occupied and at a reasonable job density of four per thousand sq ft (41 per 1000 sq m), and all jobs were additional to the region rather than relocated within it, then total employment within local authority A.F.U.s would be only 2860. The programme must also be judged against a long-term objective of stimulating economic development by the seeding and growth of indigenous enterprise and the small-firms sector. Future programmes need review in relation to market requirements and the need to co-ordinate the activities of the many public agencies involved, both to prevent market saturation and to avoid negative impact upon private-sector proposals.

Finally, local government has promoted economic development by financial incentives for private investments. Before the acquisition of new powers and resources in the later 1970s, the provision of incentives by local councils was limited. Such aids were then primarily granted by national government within assisted areas scheduled under regional policies. Regional Development Grants mainly supported major capital-intensive investments by manufacturing firms, and the peripheral location of large plants within the conurbation suggested these aids largely by-passed inner city areas characterized by small enterprises and non-manufacturing concerns. Local authority schemes of financial aid were thus designed to complement national aid, both sectorally and spatially, by assisting otherwise ineligible projects and by supplementing national aid in priority locations, particularly in the Improvement Areas (Fig. 4.2). The County Council initiated such policies from August, 1977, in a pilot scheme in the north Liverpool docklands where the Great Howard Industrial Improvement Area (G.H.I.I.A.) was scheduled to test the

Council's economic regeneration strategy. An experimental programme aimed at "... the restoration of local business confidence, the improvement of the area's image, the retention and creation of employment and improvements to working conditions and the operational environment" (Struthers and Williamson, 1979 p. 177). Included in the package of measures was a County scheme of grants and loans for small-scale construction works to be completed by both manufacturing and service firms by March, 1979, and financed from Construction Package resources. The provision of incentives continued from September, 1978, under the County's C.H.A.S.E. scheme ("County Help for Active Small Enterprise"). This was financed initially from local rate precepts, and applies throughout the County. However, greater incentives apply within "Special Areas" selected by the authority, namely the G.H.I.I.A. and the Kirkby Industrial Estate, the latter designated an Industrial Improvement Area in June, 1978. The C.H.A.S.E. scheme is periodically endowed from County revenues, supplemented from 1979/80 by Urban Programme allocations for projects within the Designated Districts and, at higher rates of aid, statutory Improvement Areas designated under the Inner Urban Areas Act. The G.H.I.I.A. was statutorily scheduled from April, 1979, and in September the County and Wirral Councils jointly scheduled the Wirral Docklands. C.H.A.S.E. expenditures in this case are supported by Wirral's Programme finance. The Kirkby Industrial Improvement Area remains non-statutory since it is located within Knowsley. The County Council also used European Social Fund grants to finance C.H.A.S.E. from 1981/82, and the scale and characteristics of the scheme have changed with the resources and funding available. By October, 1981, some £2.66 m had been committed for grants under the C.H.A.S.E. scheme since its inception, involving 402 projects and total project costs of £21.79 m.

Both Liverpool and Wirral Councils have independently provided financial aid to the private sector from Partnership and Programme resources. The limited Urban Programme allocations to St. Helens and Sefton preclude such measures, and only the County C.H.A.S.E. scheme applies. Priority is given by Liverpool to eight Improvement Areas created from March, 1979 (Fig. 4.2), five being industrial areas in the city docklands and three commercial areas in and adjacent to the city centre (Liverpool City Council, 1979). Financial aid is provided for private schemes of environmental improvement or for productive investments. By March, 1981, the City had approved ninety-four "amenity" schemes with total grant aid of £0.51 m, and 202 "production" projects with grants and loans totalling £3.8 m. In 1979 and 1980 Wirral Council scheduled two "Shopping Improvement Areas" at Borough Road (Seacombe) and Old Chester Road (Rock Ferry), grants and loans being provided for improvements to obsolescent retail premises, a novel use of the new statutory powers.

Conclusion

If public policies and programmes in themselves resolved problems, the economic and employment stresses of the Merseyside region and its inner urban areas could be expected to respond to the cumulative impact of measures adopted since 1970 by national and local governments. Despite these measures it was still being asked at the end of the decade "... whether in that troubled area some special bold type of scheme is necessary to bring about the aim of redevelopment from its heart" (H.M.S.O., 1979, p. 24). It is clearly easier to suggest the need for such a scheme than to define its nature and to provide the political, financial and administrative frameworks necessary for its implementation.

Considerable expenditure and effort have been deployed in pursuit of regional and urban regeneration, but economic and employment growth remain chimerical. This does not necessarily invalidate the promotional policies of the period, which could only partially offset the effects of continuing plant closures and redundancies. The benefits of such activities as the enhancement of land resources, of environmental quality and of building stocks will be felt only when private projects in the manufacturing and service sectors are stimulated, based as they are on the encouragement of private capital formation and production. Similarly, the provision of financial incentives or the offer of partnership arrangements generate results only in the presence of reciprocal demand from private developers. To this extent public programmes are demand-sensitive. Their success depends largely upon circumstances beyond local influence, especially the resumption and character of economic growth both nationally and internationally. Private investment, however, remains at a low level or in abeyance, and there is risk of over-provision of publicly-financed infrastructures, serviced sites and speculatively-built premises. Such expenditure, however, may accelerate or inwardly-deflect private projects, or push economically-marginal schemes into commercial viability.

Perhaps questionable is the relationship between the incidence of area assistance within the County and the geography of its welfare disparities. The concentration of financial resources within the Liverpool Partnership Area is remarkable, and clear difficulty has been experienced in conceiving and implementing projects within the Partnership's economy programme commensurate with the financial resources allocated. Conversely, St. Helens has encountered resource constraints, and the ineligibility of Knowsley is certainly anomalous. Political attitudes also condition the relative roles of local authorities in economic development. Liverpool and Sefton Councils are at opposing ends of the spectrum of involvement.

The political and administrative structures of Merseyside are clearly less than ideal as bases for programmes of economic promotion. The proliferation of public agencies involved in development lends itself to unco-ordinated or competitive action, particularly when compounded by the weak joint-consultative machinery and political conflicts endemic in the region. Whether these problems will be ameliorated by the delegation of greater roles to quasi-official and nominally apolitical bodies such as the Merseyside Development Corporation and E.I.E. is arguable. In this area, at least, the problems of Merseyside are capable of self-improvement and the creation of the "Merseyside Task Force" in 1981 may engender greater co-ordination and co-operation between agencies.

Current policies and resource commitments are unlikely in themselves to be of more than marginal significance in the restoration of economic vitality and full employment to, and within, the region. The current emphasis upon encouraging the indigenous small-firms sector, although welcome and positive, developed *faute de mieux* given the failure of conventional regional policies. It will bear fruit only in the longer term. Meanwhile it is difficult to avoid the conclusion that ". . . on Merseyside we appear to be running to go backwards" (H.M.S.O., 1979, p. 24).

Chapter 5

SERVICES: THE GROWTH SECTOR FOR THE 1980s?

P. W. DANIELS

The structure and distribution of service industry

Service industries are important for sustaining employment opportunities on Merseyside, as elsewhere, during a period of significant national structural change which involves a shift from manufacturing. Currently, the service sector* accounts for some 60% of national employment, but an estimated 64% of all employment on Merseyside in 1980 (Merseyside County Council, 1981). While service industries have been expanding nationally, this has not been the case on Merseyside where service employment declined between 1973 and 1980, although at a slower rate than for other industry sectors or the overall average of 11.8% (Fig. 5.1). It is important to distinguish between the performance of "white" and "blue" collar service industries, the former including activities in Insurance, Banking and Finance, which have only marginally declined by comparison with Transport and Communications or the Gas, Electricity and Water industries, the "blue" collar services. Forecasts for the period to 1986 suggest that white collar services will be the only source of employment expansion on Merseyside, but that they will not return to the level prevailing in 1973.

The difference between employment trends in white and blue collar services reflects the steady restructuring of the service sector throughout the 1970s (Fig. 5.2). In 1971 blue collar services comprised 59% of total service employment; by 1980 this had fallen to 55%. The shift is largely a product of labour shedding in the Transport and Communications sector, which includes the Post Office, British Rail, Merseyside Passenger Transport Executive, some large shipping companies, such as Ocean Transport, and the Mersey Docks and Harbour Company. Almost 3500 jobs were lost through contractions and a further 476 through closures between mid 1978 and the end of 1980 alone (Merseyside County Council, 1981). There were no openings or expansions during the same period. In total 20 000 jobs have been lost in the Transport and Communications services since 1971, and the only expanding blue collar sector has been the Miscellaneous group (2.5% per annum), a performance attributable to particular activities such as sport and recreation and tourism-related functions such as hotels. Merseyside also benefits from the presence of some very stable employers in Miscellaneous Services, including Vernons Pools and Littlewoods Pools, whose labour needs appear not to fluctuate widely in response to economic cycles.

While it is clear from figure 5.2 that the white collar services have increased their share of all employment on Merseyside since 1971, the extent of the shift is less than expected in relation to national trends. Insurance, Banking and Finance services experienced a declining absolute and proportional share of total service employment on Merseyside during a period when they have been a major national growth sector. The failure of

*Service industries comprise Orders XXI–XXVI of the Standard Industrial Classification—Public Utilities (Gas, Electricity and Water), Transport and Communications, Distributive Trades, Insurance, Banking and Finance, Professional and Scientific Services, Miscellaneous Services and Public Administration and Defence.

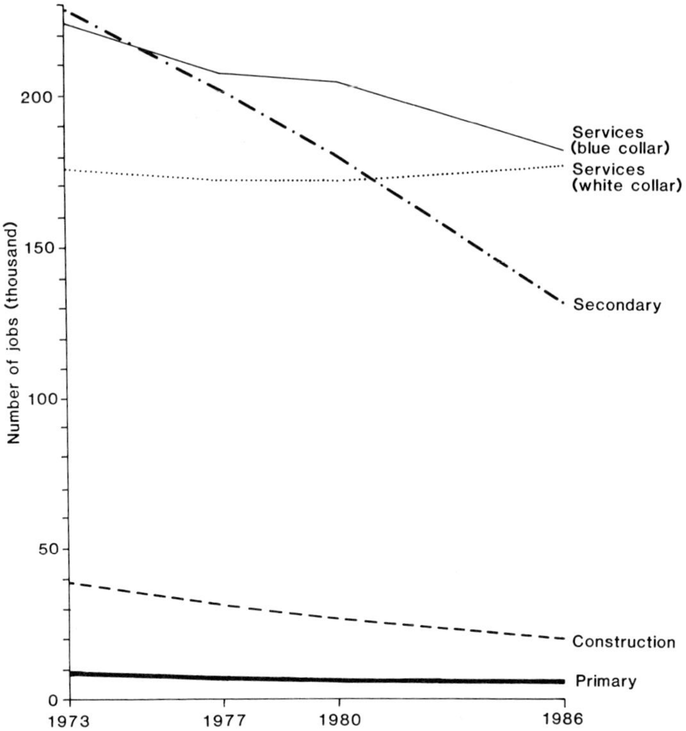

Fig. 5.1 Employment trends and prospects by industry sector, 1973–1986

Merseyside to share in this growth may not be attributable to any single factor, but the steady emergence of Manchester as the regional capital of the North-West seems to have ensured its attraction for a disproportionate share of office-based services, mainly at the expense of Merseyside. Royal Insurance, the Royal Liver Friendly Society and the National Giro are among the big local employers in this group, and their future growth plans could be crucial. Professional and Scientific Services have, however, expanded in much the same way on Merseyside as nationally, but the division between private- and public-sector activities in this group could hold back any prospect of further expansion during the 1980s. Educational services increased their share of Merseyside employment from 6.8% in 1971 to almost 8.2% in 1977, but reductions in education expenditure, such as the 17% cut in finance for the University of Liverpool for 1981–84, will inevitably lead to labour-shedding or, at best, a static labour force. Employment in medical and dental services has also increased steadily during the 1970s, but the possible abolition of the Merseyside Area Health Authority alone will suggest a 10% reduction in administrative staff. Accountancy, legal or research and development services represent the private sector component, and, since many of these are producer services, i.e. they mainly serve the needs of other firms and industries, they are very dependent on the performance of, for example, the manufacturing sector. Since this has been consistently contracting on Merseyside, it is likely that this source of demand for professional services will continue to fall.

The prospects are little better for Public Administration and Defence which is divided into National and Local Government service. Together, these comprised just over 7% of employment in Merseyside in 1977, but their significance could begin to diminish in the face, firstly, of requests to local authority employers to stay strictly within their approved

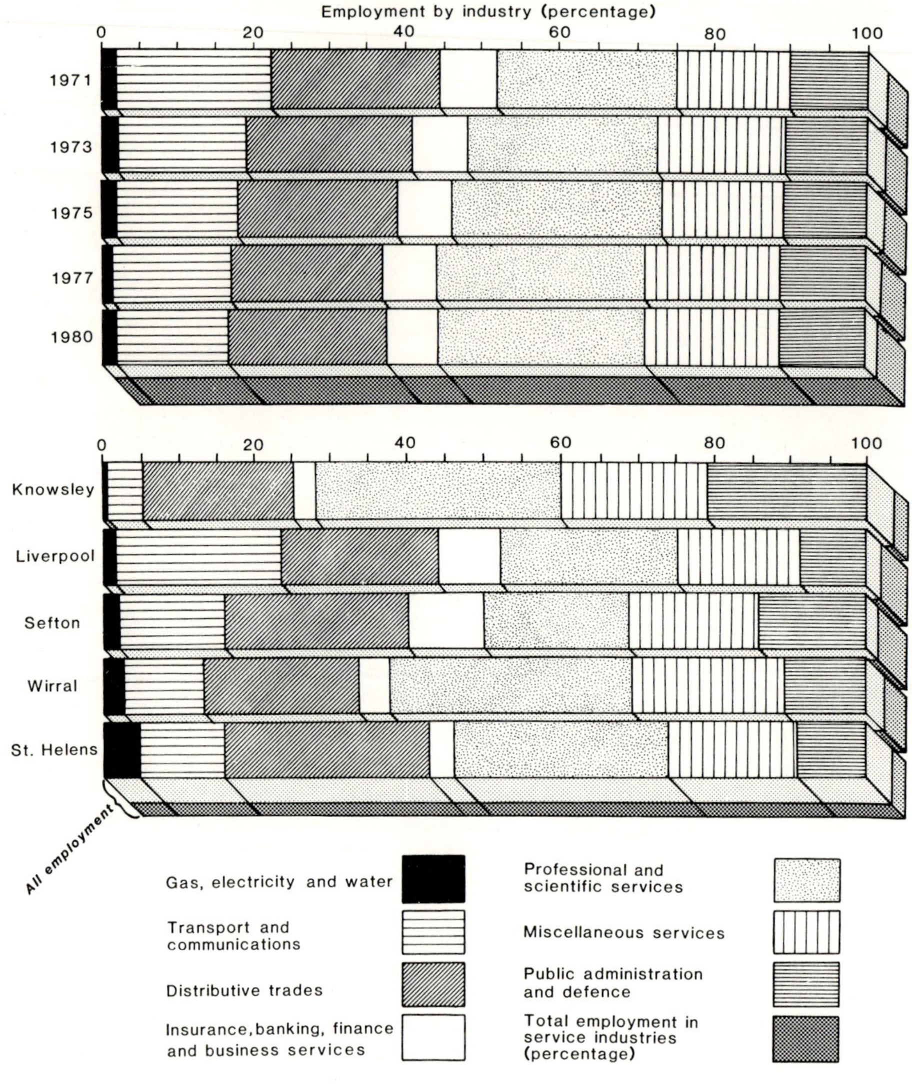

Fig. 5.2 The changing structure of service employment, 1971–1980, Merseyside and individual Metropolitan Districts

budgets through undertaking staff and other cuts, and, secondly, as a result of the marked slow-down in the decentralization of civil servants from London and the South East. The principal example of the latter is the decision not to undertake a planned dispersal of 3000 civil service posts in the Ministry of Agriculture.

Yet, just as in the 1930s, Merseyside remains dependent for its continuing economic viability on the performance of its service industries. The only difference now is that Transport and Communication Services which were the original "anchor" activities, but very vulnerable to the vagaries of world trade and business cycles, have been replaced to a large degree by those services financed from public funds. These are mainly incorporated within Professional and Scientific Services (e.g. education, medical, dental) and Public Administration. But these are vulnerable to fluctuations in government policies and expenditure priorities. Those private services which are relatively independent of such constraints and which are performing well nationally are, unfortunately, tending to under-perform on Merseyside. This dismal prospect is likely to be enhanced by the increased automation of many tasks performed in the service sector using a combination of micro-processor technology and greatly improved telecommunications networks. Displacement of many routine clerical jobs, as well as some lower and middle management jobs, seems inevitable. Merseyside County Council (1981) has forecast that employment in all services could decline by as much as 40 000 between 1980 and 1986. Such projections are hardly the basis for contemplating a restructured Merseyside economy better geared to the needs of the 1980s.

These services are not evenly distributed within Merseyside. A distinction may be made between producer services, sometimes described as intermediate services, which meet demand largely from other industries, and consumer or final services which meet demand directly from members of the public. This means that some services must seek more widely accessible locations than others, and this should be reflected in variations in their distribution within Merseyside (Fig. 5.2). Hence, it is notable that Professional and Scientific Services are prominent in St. Helens, Knowsley and Wirral, but many of these belong to the slowly growing public sector rather than the private sector activities performing a producer role, which are more likely to be located in central Liverpool. Employment in the Distributive Trades comprises a consistent proportion of total service jobs in each District, apart from St. Helens, which is probably far enough removed from the major concentration of retail services in central Liverpool to be able to attract regional or sub-regional retail activities as well as those servicing the local population. As might be expected, Liverpool and Sefton have the largest proportions of Transport and Communications employment, with 72% in Liverpool compared with its overall share of 57% of service employment on Merseyside. Insurance, Banking and Finance also reveal an above average concentration of employment in Liverpool (66%). All the other sectors are slightly under-represented in Liverpool, with Public Administration and Defence (46%) showing the largest negative difference.

In the remaining sections of this paper a selective approach has been taken to focus on three significant sub-elements of service industries: retail services, office services and tourism. Each of these represents different facets of Merseyside service infrastructure. Retail services underpin the socio-economic organization of the region since they meet particular consumer needs ranging from daily shopping for non-durable and perishable goods through to less frequent durable goods speciality shopping. Office-based services are widely distributed throughout the service sector, but well represented in Insurance, Banking, Finance and Business services and the Professional services. Up to 90% of the labour force in these services may be accommodated in office premises of one kind or another. The particular significance of these office-based activities is that they have been a consistent source of employment growth since 1945 during a period when most other types of employment have been contracting. Tourism has been selected as the third element because of its relatively untapped potential for generating employment expansion.

Retail services: the mis-match between supply and demand

In 1977 the Distributive Trades, which include wholesale distribution and dealing, provided 76 000 (12%) of Merseyside's jobs with almost 20 000 engaged in retail distribution. Retail turnover on Merseyside was £460 m in 1971, and Liverpool, one of the

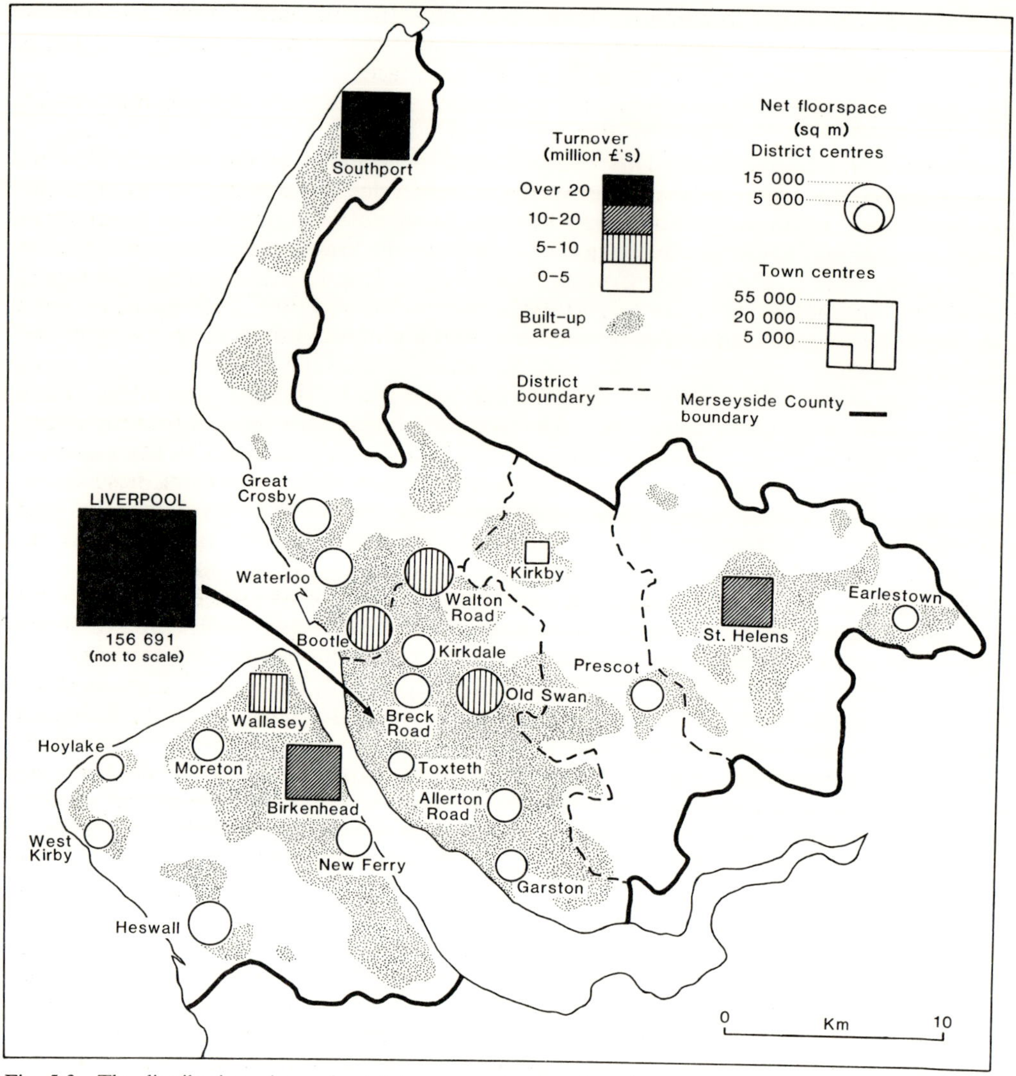

Fig. 5.3 The distribution, size and retail turnover of major shopping centres, 1971

two major regional shopping centres in the North-West, had the second largest turnover for centres outside London (£77 m) (Merseyside County Council, 1975A, 1979B). The hierarchy of shopping centres is dominated by two town centres with turnover exceeding £20 m (Liverpool and Southport) and four secondary town centres at Kirkby, St. Helens, Birkenhead and Wallasey (Fig. 5.3). Much of the retail floorspace in the town centres is devoted to the sale of durable goods and the operations of service trades such as building societies, which are increasingly located within major retail nucleations. District centres are both smaller and have a lower turnover than the town centres, and, as at Kirkdale, Allerton and New Ferry, often comprise ribbon-like development along major arterial roads. Consumer and durable goods are more evenly balanced in these centres, which have more compact consumer catchment areas, but they are still larger than the diverse collection of local centres which are almost exclusively devoted to consumer goods retailing and have less than 5000 sq m of retail floorspace.

Local and district shopping centres tend to be in high density areas of the County which were built-up before the First World War. With the possible exception of the Wirral, outer suburban areas are less well served by district centres. There is an over-supply of retail units and services, whether measured in terms of floorspace or number of retail units, in areas of population decline, and there is under-provision in the growth areas. A survey of selected shopping centres, in district centres such as Kirkby, Garston and Huyton as well as in local centres such as New Brighton, Rock Ferry, Edge Hill, London Road and Smithdown Road (Merseyside County Council, 1976B), showed that 1 in 5 of all shop units were unoccupied. Most of these are inner urban shopping centres in those parts of the County which have experienced the largest population losses, so that in many instances floorspace provision far exceeds the requirements of the catchment population. High vacancy rates amongst older local shopping areas in the inner city are not therefore very surprising. The dispersal of population to other districts within the County has not, unfortunately, been matched by a proportional increase in retail services in these areas. Such is the seriousness of the deficiency in the outer estates, such as Netherley and Croxteth, that mobile shops, normally associated with rural shopping provision, are an important element in their retail system.

Although many parts of the area have levels of car ownership well below the national average, the use of cars for shopping purposes has increased, especially for convenience goods. This has taken trade from less accessible stores, which are often located on busy traffic routes in inner district centres and suffer from congestion and tight parking restrictions, e.g. Edge Hill, Rock Ferry, Waterloo or Breck Road, to car-oriented accessible sites in the suburbs. For shoppers dependent on public transport, the alignment of routes and frequency of service to shopping centres may also affect the level of trading activity in those centres. Rising overheads but stable or declining turnover in areas with diminished catchment populations also discourage retailers from remaining in business; conversely, high rents for newer retail premises in the outer suburbs have discouraged new start-ups by smaller independent retailers. In addition, retail services are themselves undergoing extensive structural and operational changes as they strive to reduce overheads and to offer competitive prices through bulk purchasing or centralized warehousing. Supermarkets began the transformation during the 1960s, and have been followed by the larger superstores, hypermarkets and discount stores operating on a cash-and-carry basis. These represent severe competition for the small non-specialized retailer, who may eventually cease operations and thus add to the catalogue of vacant, often obsolescent, retail premises. Durable goods stores tend to replace convenience goods shops, reducing the important role of local shops as neighbourhood "community" centres.

There is certainly little scope for adding to the existing stock of retail floorspace in Merseyside, and the only prospect seems to be for replacement or renewal of retail units, preferably in locations where the benefits can be shared by both the consumers and the retailers. The dilemma confronting planners dealing with these problems is the degree to which they can balance the need to counter the worst effects of obsolescence with the need to accommodate the demand for edge-of-town retailing. The Merseyside Structure Plan (1980) promulgates a strategy for urban regeneration which means that the policy for retail services involves reinforcement of viable existing shopping centres rather than the development of strategically located peripheral or outer suburban locations. An extremely good case will therefore have to be made for an edge-of-town hypermarket or superstore, and firms making such proposals encouraged to look towards district and town centre locations. The Asda superstores in Birkenhead town centre, at Kirkby and Huyton are recent examples.

Some of the priorities involved in a centre-oriented strategy for retailing can be illustrated with reference to Liverpool (City of Liverpool, 1980A, 1980B). In view of its role as the principal centre within the District as well as its importance as a regional shopping centre, considerable efforts have been made to sustain the dominance of the City Centre in the retail system. The City Centre has approximately 40% of the District's retail floorspace (200 000 sq m), and according to a survey of shoppers undertaken in 1978 some 42% come from outside the City boundary, attracted by the wide range of opportunities for durable goods purchases; almost 46% of the shoppers from outside Merseyside considered Liverpool to be their main centre (Liverpool Polytechnic, 1978). But the survey also revealed that 40% of all shoppers thought that they shopped less frequently than a year before in the City Centre. The growth of competing centres elsewhere on Merseyside, such as Southport and St. Helens, as well as the injection of major new centres into the regional shopping hierarchy, such as Shopping City (Runcorn) or Golden Square (Warrington) have also contributed to the reduced attraction of the centre of Liverpool. Service employment in the City Centre declined from 84 500 to 78 000 between 1971 and 1975 (Department of Employment, 1976), and served further to reduce the demand for retail services. The decline of London Road and the changing character of Bold Street, a former "quality" shopping area, as a result of colonization by non-retail services may be one symptom of the changing status of the City Centre.

It has therefore been important for the City Centre to try to maintain its attractiveness in order to protect investment and redevelopment. Since the late 1960s there have been a number of new developments, including St. John's Precinct (48 600 sq m), and redevelopment or extension of existing retail facilities such as Marks and Spencer (10 620 sq m) and C. & A. Modes (9754 sq m). This private sector investment has been supported by publicly financed pedestrianization of the shopping "core" in Church Street, where rents in excess of £40 000 per annum are amongst the highest outside London (City of Liverpool, 1980B), as well as partial schemes in adjacent areas such as Bold Street (Chapter 6). A number of multi-storey car parks have been strategically located within easy reach of the retail area, but, since the 1978 survey found that only 26% of shoppers arrived by car (Liverpool Polytechnic, 1978), it has been important to ensure that public transport passengers can alight or board buses and trains as near to the principal shopping streets as possible.

During recent years, however, the momentum of retail development in the City Centre has slowed, and the development of the Central Station site (8000 sq m) is the only current activity. Planning permission has also been granted for some time for the Pavilion (18 600 sq m) and Trade Centre (14 000 sq m) developments in the South Docks area. However, the benefits of these for the City Centre are unclear, and any which they might confer will most likely accrue to residents in an area which has experienced the largest decline in the number of shops during the 1970s and has some of the highest levels of obsolescence (Fig. 5.4). There are other possibilities for development in the Bluecoat Chambers area and in London Road.

Consolidation of retail services in the other town and major district centres in the County has also occurred during the 1970s. The most important example has been the major reconstruction of central Birkenhead in the form of the Grange Road Precinct (45 000 sq m), Grange Market (8000 sq m), which replaced the former Birkenhead Market gutted by fire in 1976, and an Asda Superstore (4530 sq m). The latter incorporates parking facilities, and, along with other municipal car parks located on housing clearance areas

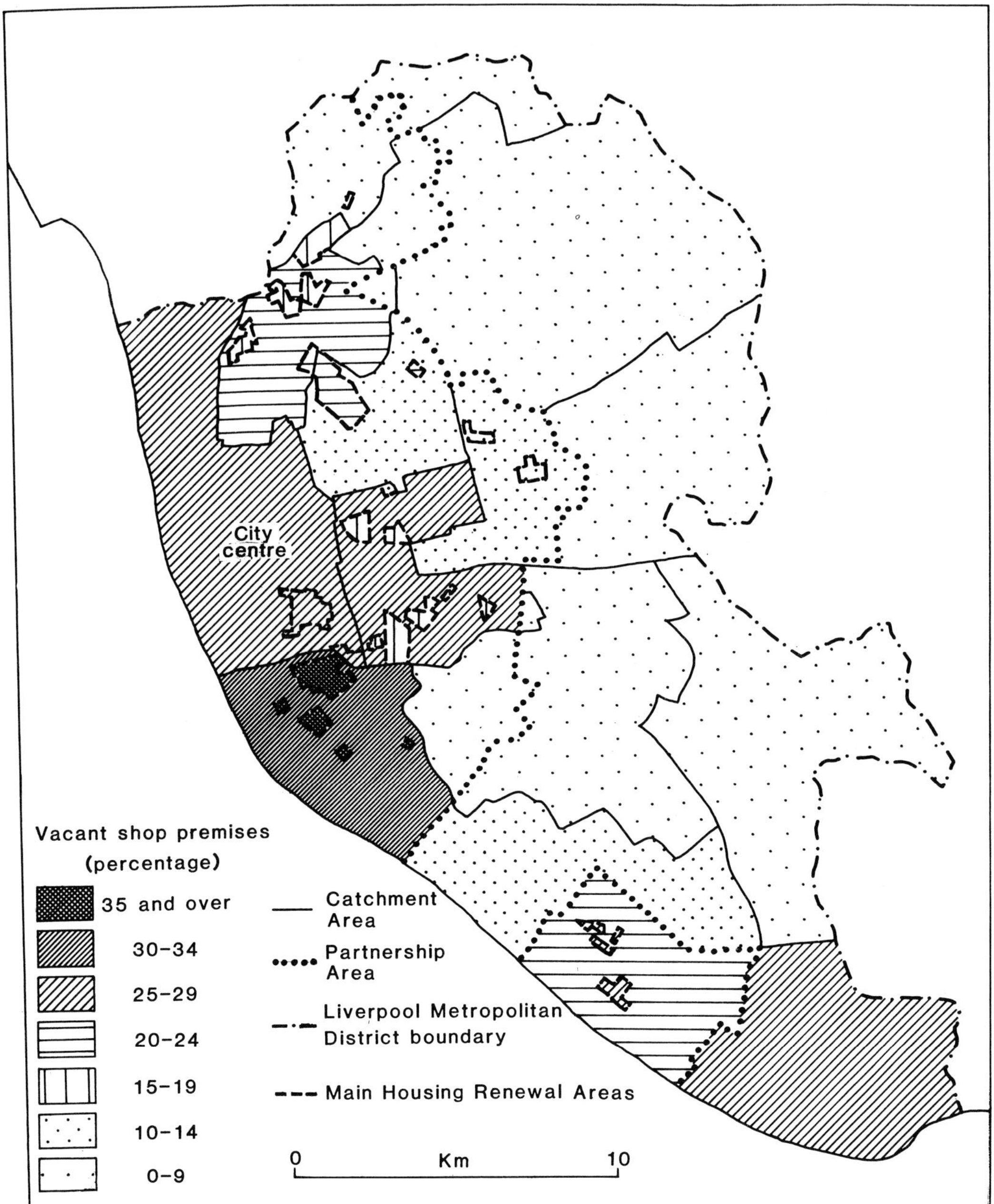

Fig. 5.4 The distribution of vacant shop premises, Liverpool District, 1978

adjacent to the shopping centre, has proved a powerful magnet for car-borne shoppers who might otherwise use Liverpool city centre (see Fig. 10.2). Although near to a number of competing centres outside the County, St. Helens commands a substantial catchment area, and the St. Mary's Precinct and Tontine Market (40 500 sq m) completed during the early 1970s have attracted several new retail functions and greatly enhanced the attraction of the town centre. Southport dominates retail provision in the north of the County with a range of specialist and multiple retailers, attracted by its role as a holiday and convention centre. There have been no major developments since 1970, although the low levels of obsolescence and vacancy rates point to a successful shopping centre.

Despite the emphasis on regeneration of retail services in established centres, it is inevitable that retailers have been pressing for permission to develop superstores and hypermarkets on edge-of-town sites near motorway or major highway interchanges, to be dependent primarily on car-borne shoppers. While recognizing that a case can be made for such development in the outer parts of the County, official policy is largely negative. There are therefore no hypermarkets on Merseyside, although applications have been received for strategic sites at motorway junctions on the M53 in Wirral and the M57 in Knowsley at its interchange with the A57 at Prescot. Woolco have also made application for a site in Huyton. The only example of a superstore (5400 sq m) on an edge-of-town site is the Leo (formerly Co-operative) store at Woodchurch, Birkenhead, adjacent to a major junction on the M53.

Office-based services: a role unfulfilled

Liverpool has not been able to capitalize on its early advantages in the office sector. Shipping-related office activities have contracted as the port has lost almost all its passenger traffic and much of its import and export trade (Chapter 3). As a result many of the overseas banks have either closed their Liverpool branches, or have been taken over or merged with larger banks with headquarters offices in London. The role of the Stock and Commodity Exchanges in Liverpool has also declined, and it has become increasingly clear during the 1970s that Merseyside is highly dependent on the public sector as a source of office employment. In the centre of Liverpool, the principal office concentration in the County, the office-dominated Professional and Scientific Services and Public Administration and Defence orders were the only categories to have experienced employment growth, 1971–75 (City of Liverpool, 1980C). Employment in the other major office-dominated order, Insurance, Banking and Finance, fell by 7% over the same period. Since such a large proportion of private sector office employment is concentrated in central Liverpool, the dependence on public sector office employment becomes especially significant for the other metropolitan districts such as Sefton, which had almost 29% of Merseyside's Central Government employment in 1973 (Table 5.1).

TABLE 5.1 *Distribution of public office employment, 1973*

District	Central Government Employment (%)*			Local Government Employment (%)		
	Males	Females	Total	Males	Females	Total
Knowsley	2.7	2.4	2.5	10.3	2.8	14.9
Liverpool	61.4	49.3	55.1	49.3	31.2	44.5
St. Helens	3.2	4.8	4.0	7.5	8.8	7.8
Sefton	22.9	34.4	28.8	13.8	12.9	13.6
Wirral	9.8	9.1	9.6	19.1	19.4	19.2
Total	6585	7510	13735	19958	7838	27296

Source: Merseyside County Council (1975).
Note: *Column totals sum to 100.

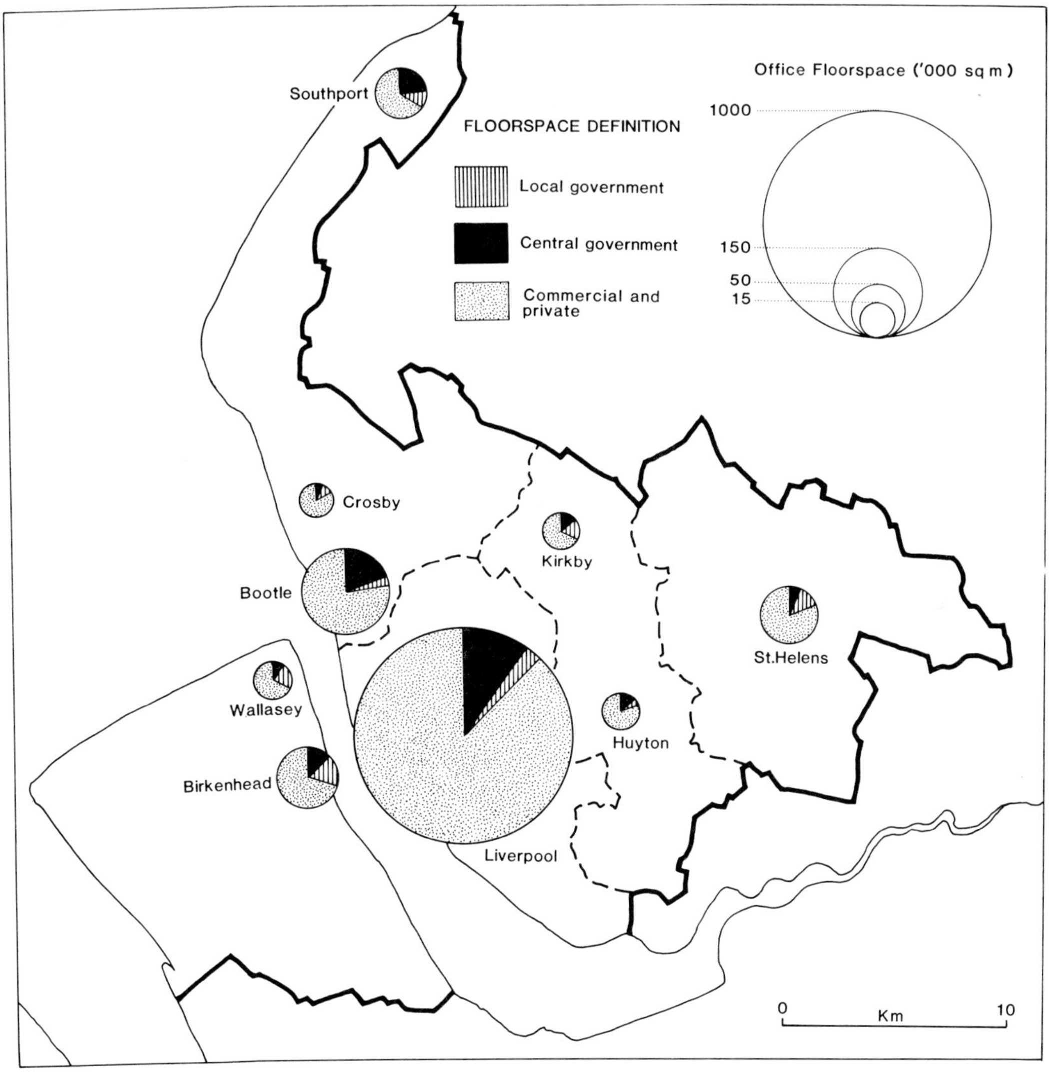

Fig. 5.5 The size and functional composition of office centres, 1973

There are five principal concentrations of office space on Merseyside (Fig. 5.5). Almost two-thirds of the 1.5 m sq m of commercial, central and local government floorspace in 1973 was located in Liverpool, mainly in the city centre, with secondary centres at Bootle (10%), St. Helens (6%), Birkenhead (5%) and Southport (3%). There has since been a 50% increase in the office floorspace located in Bootle. The policy of the former County Borough of Bootle prior to local government reorganization proved particularly successful in attracting the National Giro to set up its headquarters in the area, and this encouraged a number of office schemes, mainly in the public sector, in the centre of Bootle which were in direct competition with the principal office centre in Liverpool. Both areas were hoping to benefit from the increased mobility of office firms from London. In the event Merseyside suffered more than most parts of provincial Britain from the reluctance of most office-based services to move much beyond suburban London, let alone to a Special Development Area with a wide range of economic and social problems (both real and perceived) which would be difficult to "sell" to both employers and any employees they would wish to bring with them. Hence between 1963 and 1976 nine firms moved 1020 jobs from London to Liverpool, with 90% accounted for by just two companies, Blue Star Ship Management and United Biscuits (City of Liverpool, 1980 D and E). The image of Merseyside has created a paradox which is most clearly manifest in central Liverpool: office vacancy rates are low, rents amongst the highest for provincial city office markets, but, contrary to the "normal" development industry response to such conditions, the supply of new office space has been negligible.

The growth of secondary office centres on Merseyside has been very limited (Fig. 5.5). Since current attention is being given to methods of retaining existing office-based services in the County, to encourage them to expand if at all possible and to provide sufficient new office space to represent an attractive prospect for enterprises considering moving their office into the area, the provision of accessible and attractive suburban sites outside existing office centres has not been a significant feature on Merseyside. Preference has been given to increasing the supply of new and vacant office space in the central area. There is a potential for 230 000 sq m of new office space in central Liverpool, of which 35% already has full or outline planning permission (City of Liverpool, 1980D). Together with 54 000 sq m originally granted for a Central Government development at Exchange Station (now being marketed for private sector development), this comprises a more than adequate supply for potential demand during the 1980s, and the City of Liverpool has adopted initiatives designed actively to stimulate new office development (City of Liverpool, 1980E). Rates will not be levied on new office space until it is occupied, and, in certain instances, a similar arrangement applies to refurbished space which has not been re-let. Financial support will be given to suitable schemes to encourage advance office building in the city centre, and developers will be invited to bid for council-owned sites. The partnership approach to office development does appear to have increased the interest of the private sector institutions and investors and some 25 000 sq m has already been underwritten using Urban Programme finance (Chapter 4).

Local initiatives have to some extent been "forced" by the failure of Central Government policies directed at the service sector as a whole. Merseyside received only £3.2 m in Regional Development Grant or Selective Financial Assistance for service industries between 1976 and 1980, an average of £8.3 per head compared with £928 per head for manufacturing (Merseyside County Council, 1981B). Given Merseyside's above-average dependence on service industries and the non-local or export function of activities such as business and some professional services, this is a major deficiency. Grants need to be made available for services, other than those which meet "local" needs, which stimulate office-based services as well as the final element of the service sector to be considered in this paper, the tourist industry.

The potential for tourism

Employment in hotels and other residential establishments increased by more than 30% on Merseyside between 1972 and 1977 (Merseyside County Council, 1979C). This growth exceeds that of most other sources of service employment in the County, even though until recently the area has not been actively promoted as a tourist resource. Liverpool's image is clearly not helpful; but Southport or most of the Wirral are not tarnished by the same image. The County's strong overseas connections, particularly with the United States, New Zealand and Canada, developed during its heyday as a great port and commercial centre, could provide a useful source of overseas visitors, many with family connections. In

1976 Merseyside attracted some 12% of the domestic tourism to the North-West (Merseyside County Council, 1979C). During the same year the International Passenger Survey found that overseas visitors expended approximately £12 m on Merseyside. This level of expenditure was achieved before recent initiatives to develop some of the world class attractions in the County were introduced. These attractions include the Maritime Museum and Park (commenced but not yet complete), the Pilkington Glass Museum in St. Helens, Port Sunlight Village and the Lady Lever Art Gallery, Ellesmere Port Boat Museum, the Beatles, the Grand National at Aintree and Liverpool City Centre (which incorporates the Ferries, the County Museum and Walker Art Gallery, the Waterfront at Pierhead, Bluecoat Chambers, and the two Cathedrals).

Tourism will help to generate badly needed employment, for its multiplier effects are considerable. A study in 1977 by the English Tourist Board suggested that 400 jobs are directly generated and a further 300–400 jobs indirectly by each £1 million of tourist expenditure. Thus, the £34 m expended in 1976 is likely to have directly supported 13–14 000 jobs. Marketing is clearly important, and preliminary indications are that active promotion by the English Tourist Board and the County Council has been successful. Enquiries at Liverpool City Centre Tourist Information Office (one of six such offices on Merseyside) increased by 30% between mid 1977 and mid 1978 (Merseyside County Council, 1979C), and approximately 11 000 enquiries from overseas, six times the level during the previous year, were made directly to Merseyside County Council public relations office in 1978. Development Areas such as Merseyside also qualify for financial assistance from, for example, the English Tourist Board for projects which will attract tourists, and help to revitalize local economies. Unlike other Development Areas such as Northumbria or parts of Yorkshire, Merseyside has not taken full advantage of these opportunities.

Conclusion: the uncertain prospect for service industries

This selective view of the service sector on Merseyside may be considered excessively negative. But the fact is that the County has not been able to increase its share of employment generating services in a way which reflects national trends. The problem has been compounded by the failure of the local service sector to shift from dependence on port-related services which are no longer dynamic to business and professional services which offer the most potential for the future. Urban economies cannot depend on the strength of the past; they must be able to adapt to the needs of the present.

Unfortunately, because of the influence of factors beyond the control of local agencies, there may not be time to rectify some of the deficiencies in the service economy. A major current issue is the possible impact of micro-electronic technology on office-based services, where the advances in information processing systems, telecommunications and personal computers are changing the relationship between output and employment growth. The most vulnerable to reduced employment demand, or indeed contraction, are precisely those sectors recently forecast to be expanding—Miscellaneous Services, Insurance, Banking and Finance, and, to a lesser extent, Professional and Scientific Services. The strength of Manchester as the regional capital continues to divert functions, such as regional headquarters, which might otherwise come to Merseyside. Public sector offices have followed a similar trend to generate in Manchester an office complex which is more diverse and better able to attract other enterprises. The prospects for retail services are not enhanced by the continuing population decline within Liverpool and, at best, stability within the County as a whole. Other consumer-oriented services, such as the public utilities or some of the professional services, will be similarly affected. The prospect of continuing decline in the Port of Liverpool also directly affects the future for employment in Wholesale Distribution, Transport and Communications, Insurance and some aspects of Banking, and, due to public expenditure cuts, the growth of public sector employment will also slow down during the foreseeable future.

To a degree, the debate about the most appropriate planning strategy for Merseyside is superfluous. There is much to commend the strategy of urban regeneration in so far as it encourages the reinforcement of the existing City Centre and district centres where office-based and retail services can benefit from maximum accessibility for employees and clients. In practice, Merseyside will probably be glad to accommodate the expansion of existing services anywhere within reason, including the suburban "campus" sites designated in the Merseyside Structure Plan. However, there are major obstacles to the rejuvenation of the service industries on Merseyside, even though initiatives directed at untapped opportunities such as tourism or the encouragement of export services, combined with the creation of the Merseyside Development Corporation and the Enterprise Zone at Speke, may provide some relief. But the scale of this relief is unlikely to compensate for the forecast decrease of some 28 800 in service industry jobs between 1980 and 1986 (Merseyside County Council, 1981), let alone the overall decrease of 78 000 jobs.

Chapter 6

TRANSPORT ISSUES AND POLICIES

D. A. HALSALL

Merseyside has a continuing tradition of urban transport innovation, including Britain's first street tram (Birkenhead, 1860), the first underground railway outside London (Mersey Railway, 1886), also the first in Britain to be electrified (1903), Britain's only electric overhead railway (1893–1957), and the first road tunnel under a major waterway outside London (1934). Merseyside was also the first Passenger Transport Executive to complete new urban railways and introduce a Zone Ticket system.

Innovation is, however, only one part of urban transport development. Changes in transport policy and infrastructure create new patterns and levels of accessibility, and should therefore be seen within a wider social and economic context. This chapter examines trends, issues, policies and actions in transport within the county area of Merseyside since the 1968 Transport Act provided for the designation of Merseyside Passenger Transport Authority and Executive. As in other conurbations, the decentralization of population and employment and increasing use of private transport place considerable stress upon the transport infrastructure. Public transport services face the difficulties of widening gaps between costs and revenue and between the areas and population they are required to serve. "Numbers of passengers fall, but simultaneously the areas needing public transport widen" (Merseyside County Council, 1980, p. 5). Despite low car ownership rates in Merseyside, increased use of private vehicles strains the road system, aggravates environmental problems and widens inequalities in personal mobility.

Merseyside and the national transport networks

Liverpool's position as a port ensured the development of a radiating pattern of inter-urban routes, strengthened by recent investment in trunk routes. However, Merseyside's relatively isolated west-coast location is reflected in its late and weak connection to the motorway network. Liverpool ranks twenty-eighth (equal to Cambridge and Darlington) and Birkenhead twenty-third in relative accessibility rankings of thirty-nine British major towns connected by the motorway network of the mid 1980s (Williams, 1977). The same calculations show Birmingham in first place, Sheffield eighth, Manchester tenth and Leeds thirteenth. Merseyside waited ten years for direct motorway access (M62) to the M6, and the important Tarbock-Queen's Drive extension allowing access via the A5080 to Liverpool city centre opened only in 1976. Merseyside now has three motorway links with the M6—the M58 and two major east-west routes (M62 and M53/M531/M56) to Manchester and beyond (Fig. 6.1). The M62 forms part of an international sea/land route linking north-east U.S.A. and Europe. These motorways also perform several local functions. The M62 between Queen's Drive and Rainhill is an important route through eastern Merseyside, linked via the M57 to Prescot, Kirkby and Aintree, thence along the widened A567 to Seaforth container terminal. The M58 provides direct access to Skelmersdale, Wigan and the M6, allowing north-south traffic to avoid congested areas of the A59. The M53 Mid-Wirral motorway diverts traffic from the residential/industrial west bank of the Mersey. Its connection with the second Mersey road tunnel, opened in 1971, allows through traffic from the North and Liverpool docks for North Wales, Cheshire and Ellesmere Port to avoid Liverpool city centre. Its continuation via the M531 provides the Wirral with a fast link along the M56 to Runcorn, Warrington and Manchester.

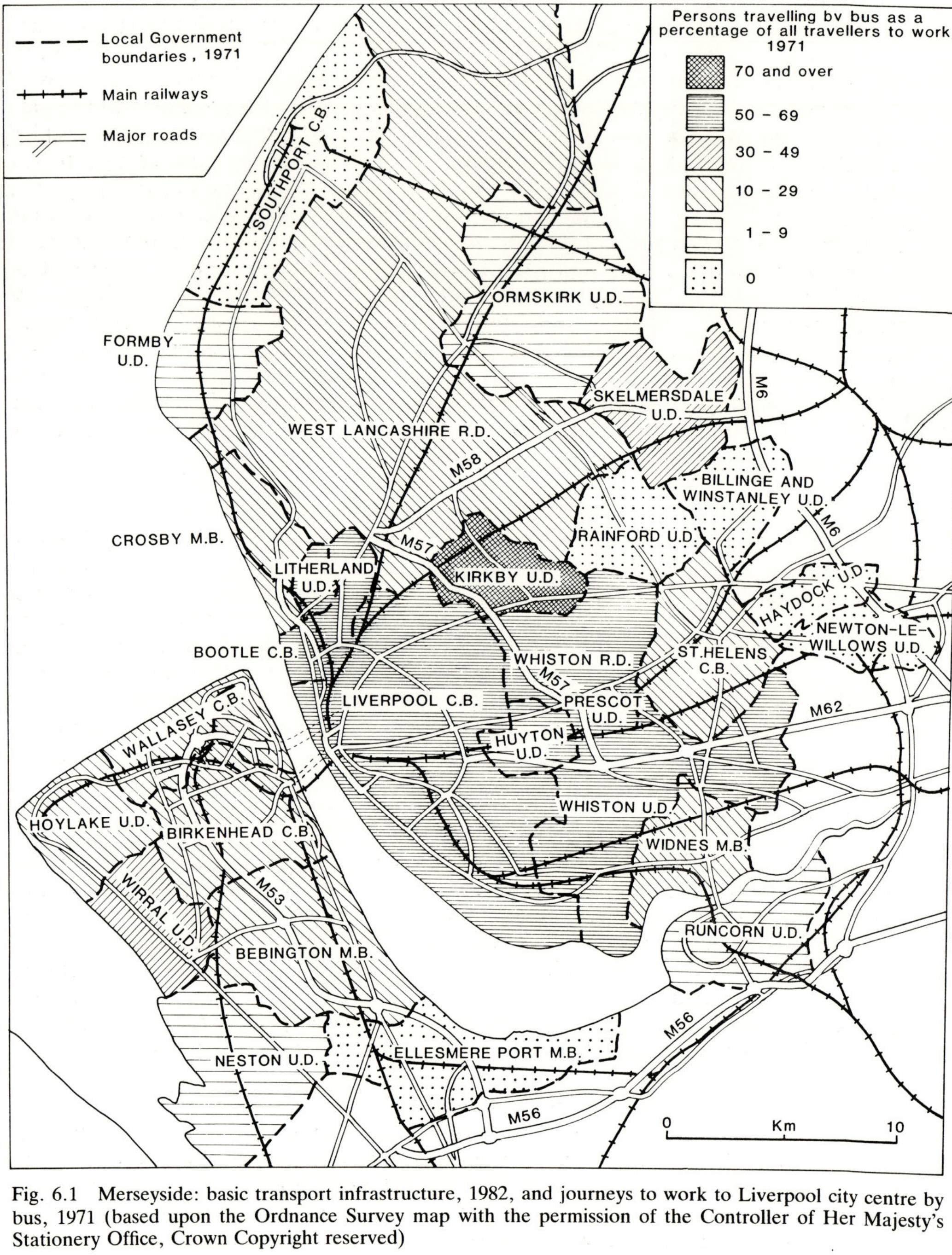

Fig. 6.1 Merseyside: basic transport infrastructure, 1982, and journeys to work to Liverpool city centre by bus, 1971 (based upon the Ordnance Survey map with the permission of the Controller of Her Majesty's Stationery Office, Crown Copyright reserved)

Investment in main line railway electrification linked Liverpool to Birmingham and London in 1967, seven years before electrification of the West Coast main line to Preston and Glasgow. The establishment of a fast regular interval service, with fastest journey times of 2 hr 36 minutes between Liverpool Lime Street and London Euston (311.4 km) and 1 hr 46 minutes between Lime Street and Birmingham (142.0 km), considerably reduced contemporary air and road competition for passenger traffic between the three cities. Electrification to Glasgow was completed in 1974, but trains are still diesel hauled between Liverpool and Preston. The remaining link (Edge Hill-Earlestown) is scheduled for electrification by 1985. Otherwise, there has been relatively little change in the Inter-City rail network serving Merseyside during the last decade, although the frequency of certain services and journey times have improved. Liverpool's position within the main line rail network is much higher than in the motorway system. In terms of total rail travel time, Liverpool is sixth, after Birmingham, London, Manchester, Sheffield, and Leeds in an accessibility hierarchy of twenty major towns (Williams, 1977). The most striking recent feature for passengers is the introduction of special cheap "Saver" fares between Liverpool and selected cities to compete with reduced coach fares on National Bus Company services, following the increased competition permitted by the Transport Act, 1980. The reduced fare to London, for example, is approximately 25% of the Ordinary return fare. This is still higher than the cheap coach fare, but the shorter journey times of trains appear adequate compensation for many passengers.

Freight traffic

External freight flows utilize the trunk road and rail routes, and the County Council supports applications by industry for government grants for rail freight handling facilities (Merseyside County Council, 1980, p. 109). Data on the movement of goods within Merseyside are sparse, but internal urban goods traffic is carried exclusively by road. Goods movements in Merseyside in 1966, surveyed for the Merseyside Area Land Use and Transportation Study (M.A.L.T.S.), were mainly to industrial, commercial and residential areas and deliveries to retailers (80% of trips), and of perishable foods and manufactured goods. Most commercial vehicle journeys are in short stages with a number of stops. Predictably both the average sizes of loads and of vehicles increase as journey distances increase. In contrast to passenger movements, there is little variation in goods vehicle movement throughout the working day. The complex spatial pattern of goods vehicle trips may be divided into three main types of origin/destination categories embracing about 250 000 daily trips: internal movements in which both origin and destination are within the M.A.L.T.S. study area predominate (approximately 86%); external movements in which either the origin or the destination are within the study area; and through movements, a minute proportion (under 500 trips, less than 0.25%), where both origin and destination lie outside the study area (Fig. 6.2). The M.A.L.T.S. survey reveals an intense localization of trips, with about three-quarters terminating in the same study zone as they originate, and a concentration of movement in and around the city centre. Residential destinations dominate (Daniels and Warnes, 1980, pp. 83–108).

Roads and road improvement

Three aims have characterized road improvement in Merseyside: to by-pass areas of congestion, although this is no longer a serious problem; to provide good access to industry; and to relieve environmental problems in older areas with inadequate road systems. Major road construction in the 1970s was dominated by motorways and their connections to local roads and by-pass schemes, but the local impact of smaller scale developments has also proved worthwhile, especially where these are an integral part of

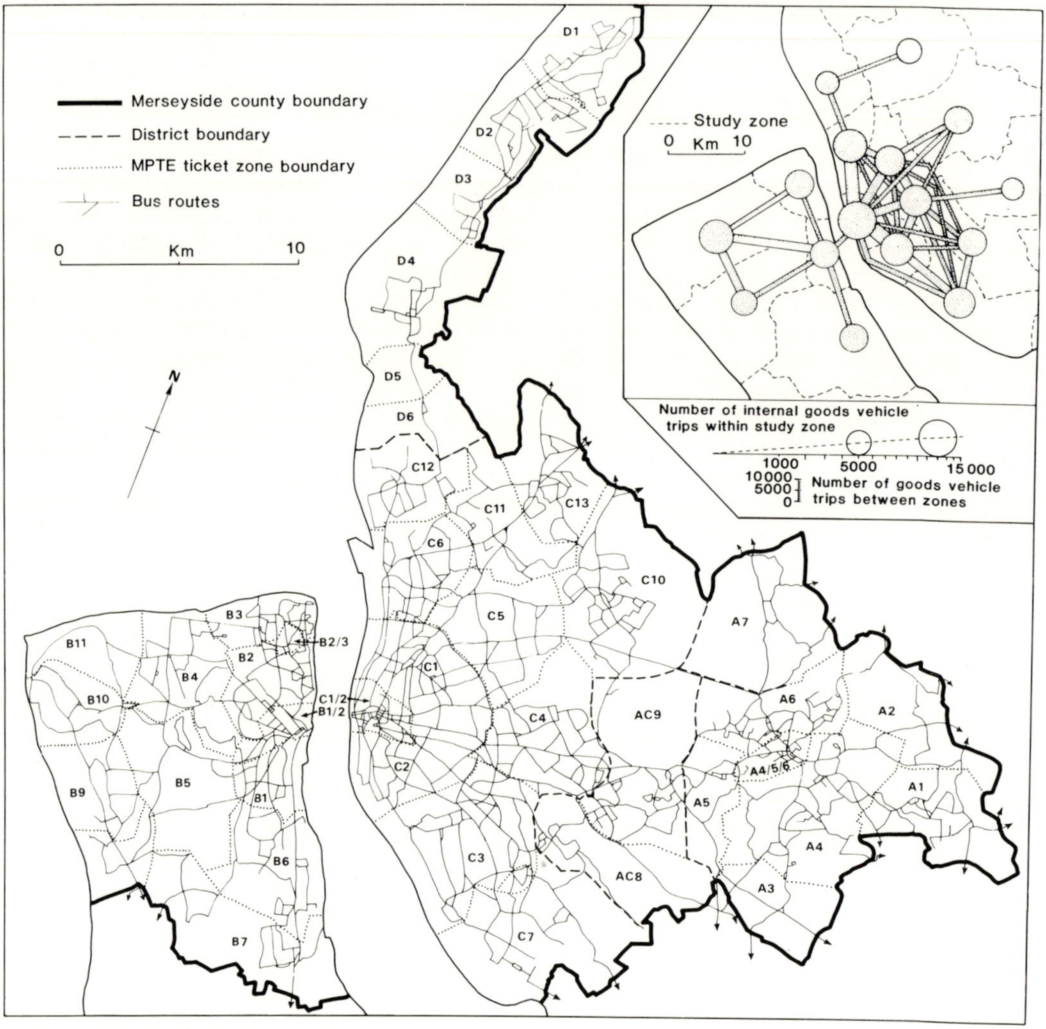

Fig. 6.2 Merseyside Passenger Transport Executive bus routes and ticket zones. Inset: number of internal goods vehicle trips within and between study zones in Liverpool, 1966 (only inter-zonal flows of over 1000 trips are shown) (source: Traffic Research Corporation, 1969)

wider local improvements. Road plans inherited in 1974 by the County Council were optimistic in their expectations of increasing population, employment and available capital. Many proposals have been abandoned, and current policy aims to make best use of existing resources with limited expenditure: to "help commerce and industry, reduce accidents, improve the environment, help the operation of buses" and "reduce excessive traffic delay" (Merseyside County Council, 1980, p. 110). Blight remains a major problem especially in inner areas, and the County Council is currently seeking to rescind all improvement lines except where new roads still appear necessary. Four phases of the Liverpool Inner Ring Road, supported by central government and E.E.C. funds are under

Plate 6.1 Widened access roads to the Mersey tunnels, August 1973. Byron Street and Scotland Road—view north showing part of Churchill Way flyover to segregate local and Liverpool-Birkenhead traffic, and in the centre, flyover and access roads to the Liverpool-Wallasey tunnel, opened in 1971

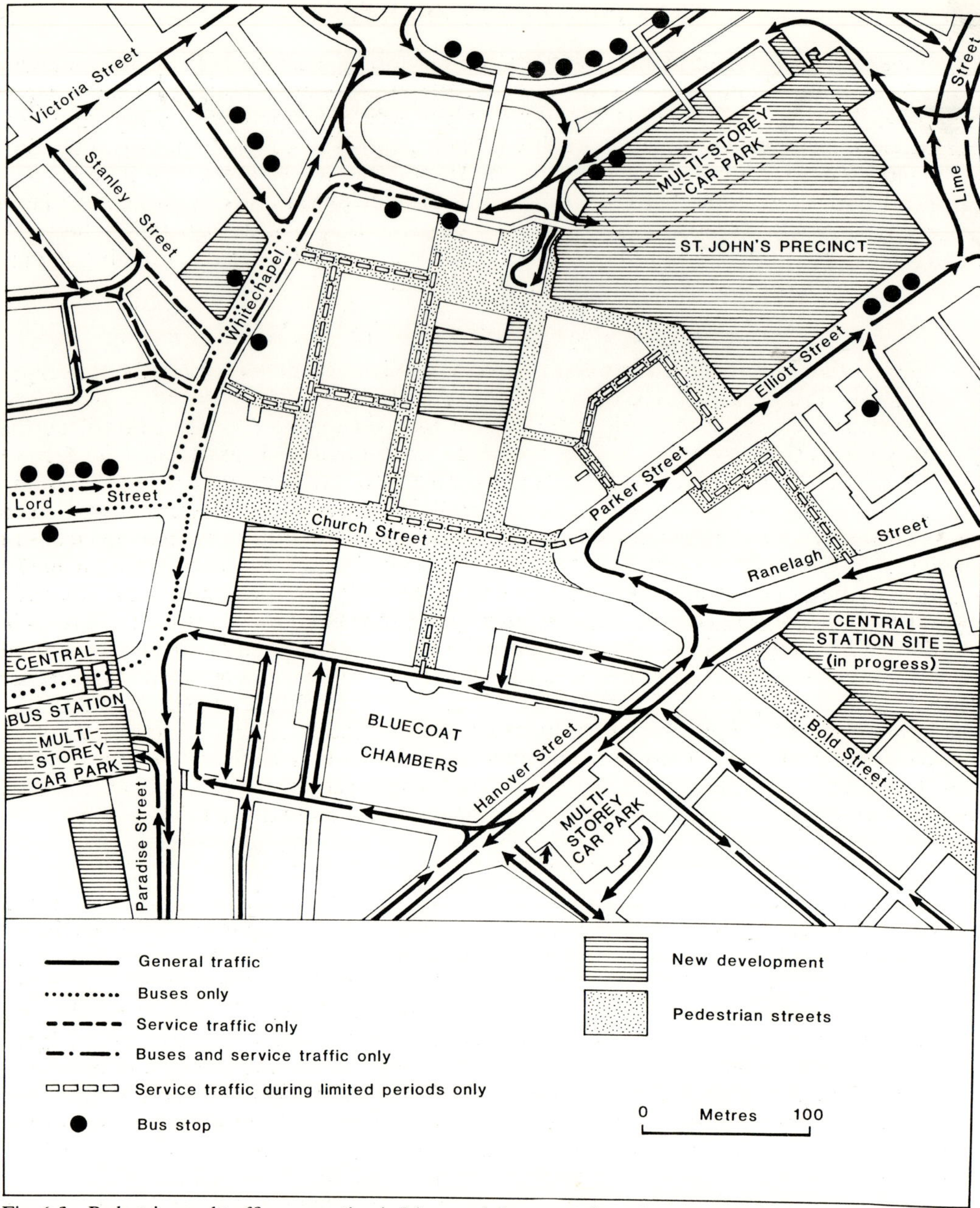

Fig. 6.3 Pedestrian and traffic segregation in Liverpool city centre (based upon the Ordnance Survey map with the permission of the Controller of Her Majesty's Stationery Office, Crown Copyright reserved)

construction, but the remainder is now abandoned. The need for the road is questionable especially within a constrained budget, and selective improvement of existing roads along the route should greatly reduce disruption to local communities (Merseyside County Council, 1976, p. 55; 1980C, pp. 110–15; 1981C, p. 21).

Current policy favours the utilization of public transport by increasing its efficiency and attractiveness rather than by markedly restraining private transport. However, one-way systems and pedestrian-traffic segregation in Liverpool city centre (Fig. 6.3) and in small centres such as St. Helens speed traffic flow, reduce accidents, segregate through and local traffic and improve environmental quality (Daniels and Warnes, 1980, p. 325). Together with restricted and controlled parking in central areas, they help redress some imbalance in flexibility and convenience between public transport and private cars. A partly completed walkway system in Liverpool C.B.D. provides limited vertical segregation between pedestrians and traffic. The Council has not as yet adopted cycle routes, a valuable asset in a period of increasing energy costs, as a major policy.

Public passenger transport: the M.P.T.E.

The present organization of public transport services by the Merseyside Passenger Transport Authority and its Executive (M.P.T.E.) results from the Transport Act, 1968, and the Local Government Act, 1972, which established the County Council as the Passenger Transport Authority. The M.P.T.E. co-ordinates all local bus (the former Liverpool, Birkenhead, Wallasey, St. Helens and Southport Municipal undertakings and National Bus Company services within the M.P.T.E.), rail and ferry services to provide "a properly integrated and efficient system of public passenger transport to meet the needs of that area" (Transport Act, 1968, Section 9(1)). Rail and N.B.C. bus services are run under operating agreements with the two nationalized bodies. The N.B.C. agreement, presently pending re-negotiation, guarantees bus mileages within the area—11.16% for Crosville (N.B.C.), 12.8% for Ribble (N.B.C.) and 75.95% for M.P.T.E. A further agreement gives control over services operated by Lancashire United, now part of Greater Manchester Transport, within the M.P.T.E. area (Swallow, 1981). M.A.L.T.S. recommendations and priorities were incorporated into the first M.P.T.E. transport plan, stressing major improvements to the suburban rail network, investigation of bus-rail and "park and ride" integration and "optimization of bus services to meet changing patterns of travel" (Merseyside Passenger Transport Authority and Executive, 1972, p. 30).

The Merseyrail network (Figure 6.4)

Rationalized local rail passenger services in 1969 radiated from Liverpool serving three areas. The electrified Wirral line linked West Kirby, New Brighton and Rock Ferry (Birkenhead) to Liverpool Central via the Mersey rail tunnel. Diesel services provided connections to Neston, Chester and Helsby. Northern line services from Liverpool Exchange were electrified to Ormskirk and Southport and diesel hauled to Kirkby and Wigan, whilst City line services from Lime Street served St. Helens, Wigan, Newton-le-Willows and Warrington (for Manchester) and, using 25kV. a.c. overhead electrification, Runcorn and Crewe (Halsall, 1978). These services contrast with the problems of blight and re-use of land left by the selective rationalization of the rail network (Paul, 1980). The idea of suburban railway electrification was approved in 1962 by Liverpool Corporation to save expensive major road construction. M.A.L.T.S. recommendations of a Liverpool terminal loop to connect the three termini, a burrowing junction at Birkenhead to increase capacity, a link line between Exchange and Central termini and extended electrification were the basis of the Loop and Link schemes opened in mid 1977. The Link extended electrification to Kirkby (1972) and Garston (January, 1978), the latter service reopening the Garston line to passenger traffic after six years closure. Extension of 650 V.d.c. electrification from Garston to Hunts Cross is scheduled for completion in May, 1983, and a similar scheme from Rock Ferry to Bromborough or Hooton awaits M.P.T.E. authorization. Loop and Link services are operated on an interval basis with weekday frequencies of twenty minutes (Ormskirk and Kirkby) and

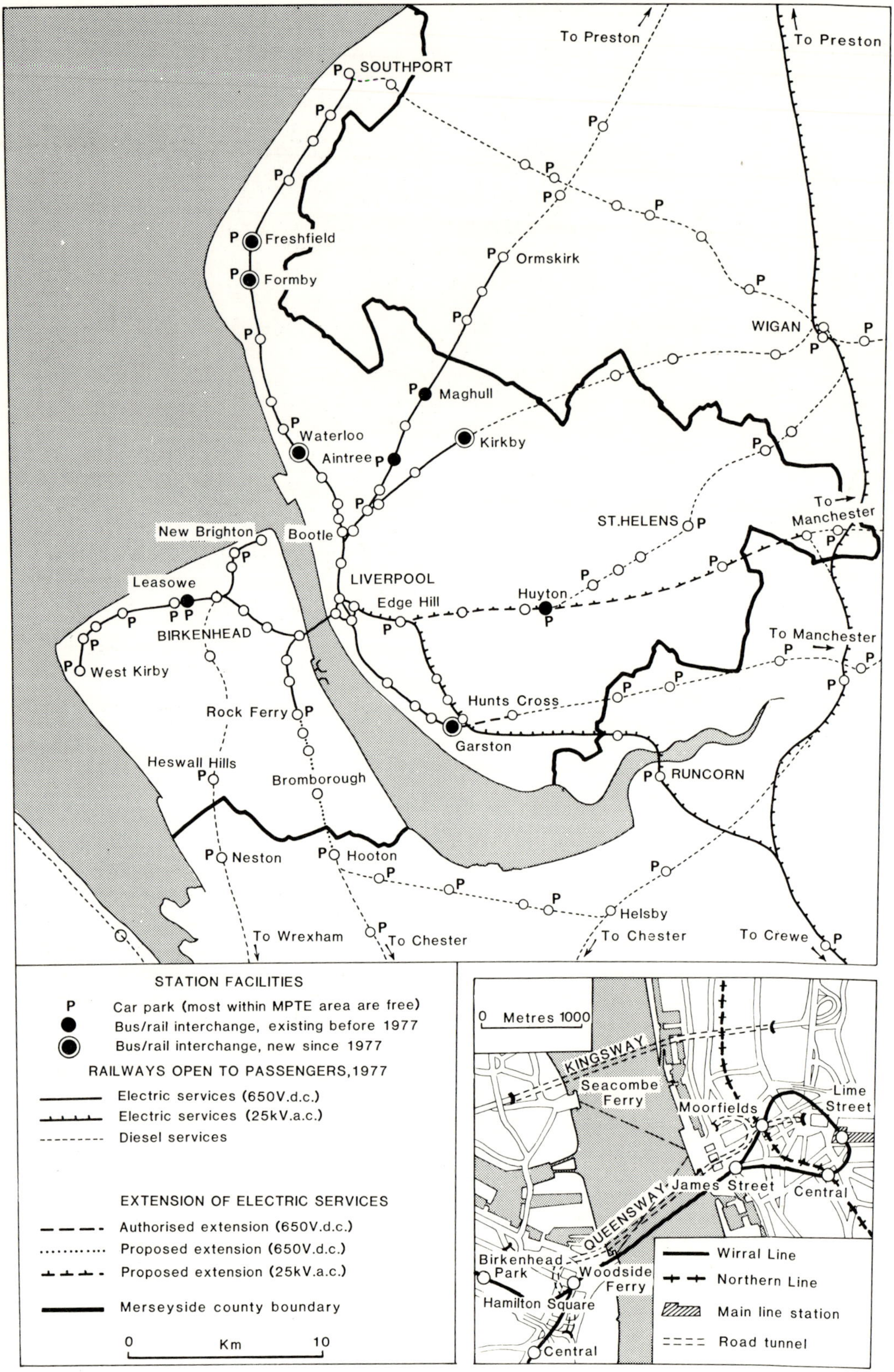

To Preston
To Preston
SOUTHPORT
Freshfield
Formby
Ormskirk
WIGAN
Maghull
Waterloo
Kirkby
Aintree
Bootle
New Brighton
ST.HELENS
To Manchester
Leasowe
LIVERPOOL
Edge Hill
Huyton
BIRKENHEAD
West Kirby
To Manchester
Rock Ferry
Hunts Cross
Garston
Heswall Hills
Bromborough
RUNCORN
Neston
Hooton
Helsby
To Wrexham
To Chester
To Chester
To Crewe
P
STATION FACILITIES
Car park (most within MPTE area are free)
Bus/rail interchange, existing before 1977
Bus/rail interchange, new since 1977
RAILWAYS OPEN TO PASSENGERS, 1977
Electric services (650V.d.c.)
Electric services (25kV.a.c.)
Diesel services
EXTENSION OF ELECTRIC SERVICES
Authorised extension (650V.d.c.)
Proposed extension (650V.d.c.)
Proposed extension (25kV.a.c.)
Merseyside county boundary
0 Km 10
0 Metres 1000
KINGSWAY
Seacombe Ferry
Moorfields
Lime Street
James Street
Central
QUEENSWAY
Birkenhead Park
Woodside Ferry
Hamilton Square
Central
Wirral Line
Northern Line
Main line station
Road tunnel

Plate 6.2 New and old lines from Liverpool to Southport, Ormskirk and Kirkby, April 1977, showing (on left) new link line avoiding Exchange station and (on right) original lines with Exchange station (closed 1977). Since that time derelict railway land at Great Howard Street (on right) and Waterloo Dock (on left) has been subject to Derelict Land Clearance Schemes and Industrial Site Servicing by the County Council. Tate and Lyle (left, middle-distance), closed in 1981, is to be redeveloped by English Industrial Estates (see Chapter 4)

fifteen minutes (Southport, New Brighton, Rock Ferry and West Kirby) with strengthening in peak hours. Equivalent frequencies in 1971/72 were fifteen minutes (Southport), twenty minutes (New Brighton and West Kirby) and thirty minutes (Ormskirk).

Passenger transport integration (Figure 6.4)

Experiments in passenger transport integration in the 1970s included bus-rail services at Aintree, Hillside, Huyton, Leasowe, Maghull, Neston and Waterloo, and car-rail schemes at Ainsdale, Aintree, Formby, Hooton, Leasowe, Ormskirk, Rock Ferry and Wallasey. There was also a bus demonstration project at Formby with a feeder bus service to Formby railway station to assess affects on modal split and particularly private car usage. Although this made an operating loss, it attracted passengers and brought an overall financial gain to the Merseyside transport system (Department of the Environment, 1974). The frequent Kirkby train service allowed withdrawal of limited-stop bus services from Liverpool.

In practice, the new rail system is regarded as "a backbone to public transport services . . . which enables measures to integrate bus and rail transport" (M.P.T.E., 1981, p. 7). Thus, revised bus services focus on rail interchanges introduced at Waterloo (1977), Formby and Freshfield (1978), and Kirkby and Garston (1980). In addition, the through Ribble Liverpool-Southport bus service was replaced by separate Southport- and Liverpool-Formby/Freshfield services integrated with local Waterloo, Formby and Southport services (1978), and a bus/rail feeder service was introduced from Speke to Garston (1979) (Swallow, 1981).

Fig. 6.4 (opposite) Merseyside railways and passenger stations, 1982. Inset: the Loop and Link underground system

TABLE 6.1 *M.P.T.E. bus operating characteristics, 1960–78*

	Passengers carried		Bus miles operated	
	Actual no. (m)	Base 1960	Actual mileage (m)	Base 1960
1960	516	100	58.5	100
61	511	99	58.6	100
62	491	95	58.8	101
63	479	93	57.2	98
64	464	90	56.1	96
65	440	85	54.2	93
66	415	80	52.7	90
67*	365*	71*	47.6*	81*
68*	299*	58*	39.0*	67*
69	333	65	45.5	78
70	309	60	43.4	74
71	284	55	44.2	76
72	281	54	44.1	75
73	288	56	43.2	74
74/75	297	58	41.7	71
75/76	274	53	43.7	75
76/77	265	51	40.4	69
77/78	246	48	36.8	63
78/79	236.4	46	36.2	62
79/80	229.7	45	35.9	61
80/81	228.1	44	37.1	63

Source: M.P.T.E. Note: *1967/68 figures affected by industrial dispute.

Changing bus services

The bus network is more dense and comprehensive than the rail network. Older urban areas, such as Southport, St. Helens and Newton-le-Willows, and the main centres of Birkenhead and Liverpool, support dense clusters of routes, whilst settlements based on the railway (e.g. Hightown) or with large middle-class housing areas (e.g. West Kirby and Heswall) have sparse route provision (Fig. 6.2).

Since its formation, the M.P.T.E. has contended with rising financial pressures from salaries and operating costs and diminishing returns from passenger numbers and local authority budgets. The number of passengers fell by 55% between 1960 and 1980, but variable change precludes an identical reform of operations (Table 6.1). The amalgamation of local authority services and co-operation with the N.B.C. and British Rail provided a valuable opportunity for the M.P.T.E. to rationalize its bus services. General rationalization of M.P.T.E. services in Liverpool and Sefton (1978), St. Helens and Wirral (1979), and co-ordination of services with the N.B.C. have eliminated much wasteful duplication and restrictions, and have reduced bus and staff numbers. Areas served by the M.P.T.E. and N.B.C. in Huyton (1973), Bootle and Crosby (1975) and Wirral (1979) have been considerably revised. New services include express buses ("Rapidride") between Liverpool and Halewood (1970) and via Kingsway tunnel to New Brighton, Liscard and Heswall. A new N.B.C. (Ribble) "Timesaver" service (1980) from Liverpool to Skelmersdale via the M58 received M.P.T.E. support. Two inner area midibuses, the "Vauxhall Round-a-bout" and "Toxteth Link-up", were introduced by the M.P.T.E. in 1980 despite an unsuccessful appeal for government finance. In contrast to long-distance services, there has been no attempt by private competition to operate local services under the terms of the Transport Act, 1980.

Mersey ferries

The opening of the Kingsway tunnel in 1971 and new rail and bus services have reduced the divisive effects of the Mersey, leaving the long established ferries (Patmore, 1970, p. 53) as a nostalgic but very costly anachronism, rather than an essential element of the passenger transport system. Passengers declined from twenty-eight million in 1955 to three million in 1980, and public support for the remaining Woodside- and Seacombe-Liverpool services cost £1 million (i.e. 33p per journey compared with average public transport subsidy of 7p per journey) in 1978/79 (Merseyside County Council, 1980, p. 119). Withdrawal of ferry services would cause little hardship and reduce the financial burden upon the M.P.T.E. Their value remains as a leisure and educational cruise facility rather than as a transport link.

Fares structures and policies

A fully integrated fares structure aids efficiency and convenience in any transport undertaking. Fares structures inherited from M.P.T.E. constituents demonstrated a basic correlation between fare levels and distance, tapered in favour of longer distances. N.B.C. fares were generally higher, and British Rail operated a market pricing system with off-peak discounts. Local bus fares varied according to former operator, and the problem was compounded with the absorption of the St. Helens and Southport undertakings in 1974. Standardization of bus fares throughout Merseyside, based on a relatively coarse scale with increments every three miles (4.8 km) was achieved in November, 1975, after an evolving system of adjustments. Rail fares and bus/rail integration of fares were separate problems. The 1970s experiments demonstrated the crucial importance of equalizing bus/rail fares and providing through bus/rail tickets to achieve successful integration. Market pricing was dropped on rail lines within the M.P.T.E. when the Loop and Link were opened in 1977, and a coarse mileage base using single tickets only was adopted for journeys up to nine miles (14 km) parallel to bus routes. On longer journeys, higher rail fares reflect higher rail speeds. Rail season tickets were standardized and off-peak discounts adjusted to give a larger discount at the upper end of the fare scale. Ferry fares remain lower than rail for the Mersey crossing to attempt to increase their attraction.

By 1977 the M.P.T.E. had thus achieved a degree of fare standardization, but no real integration between modes. The Traveller Ticket, introduced as "a flat fare, all modes season ticket" in 1974 was too highly priced to achieve good market penetration, and was never set a clear role. The unique thirty-seven zone fares system, introduced in October 1978 after an extensive policy review, replaced fare stages and B.R. and Traveller Ticket season tickets (Fig. 6.2). It aimed to simplify the fares system, to maximize off-bus ticket sales, to develop a through ticketing system and to provide season tickets for bus as well as rail passengers. It has marketing and administrative advantages in the grouping of zones, saves the passenger money by pre-purchase, and allows unlimited travel on all public modes. It provides through facilities for season ticket holders, includes concessionary fares and can be used for single tickets. When complete, the system should ease inter-modal transfer, allowing full benefits of integration (Coleman, 1979).

Progress and success?: monitoring decisions and services

In general, there is a lack of information about the elements aiding the success of urban transport projects, for many urban transport planning projects have not been monitored closely. A monitoring project by the Department of Transport and M.P.T.E. suggests

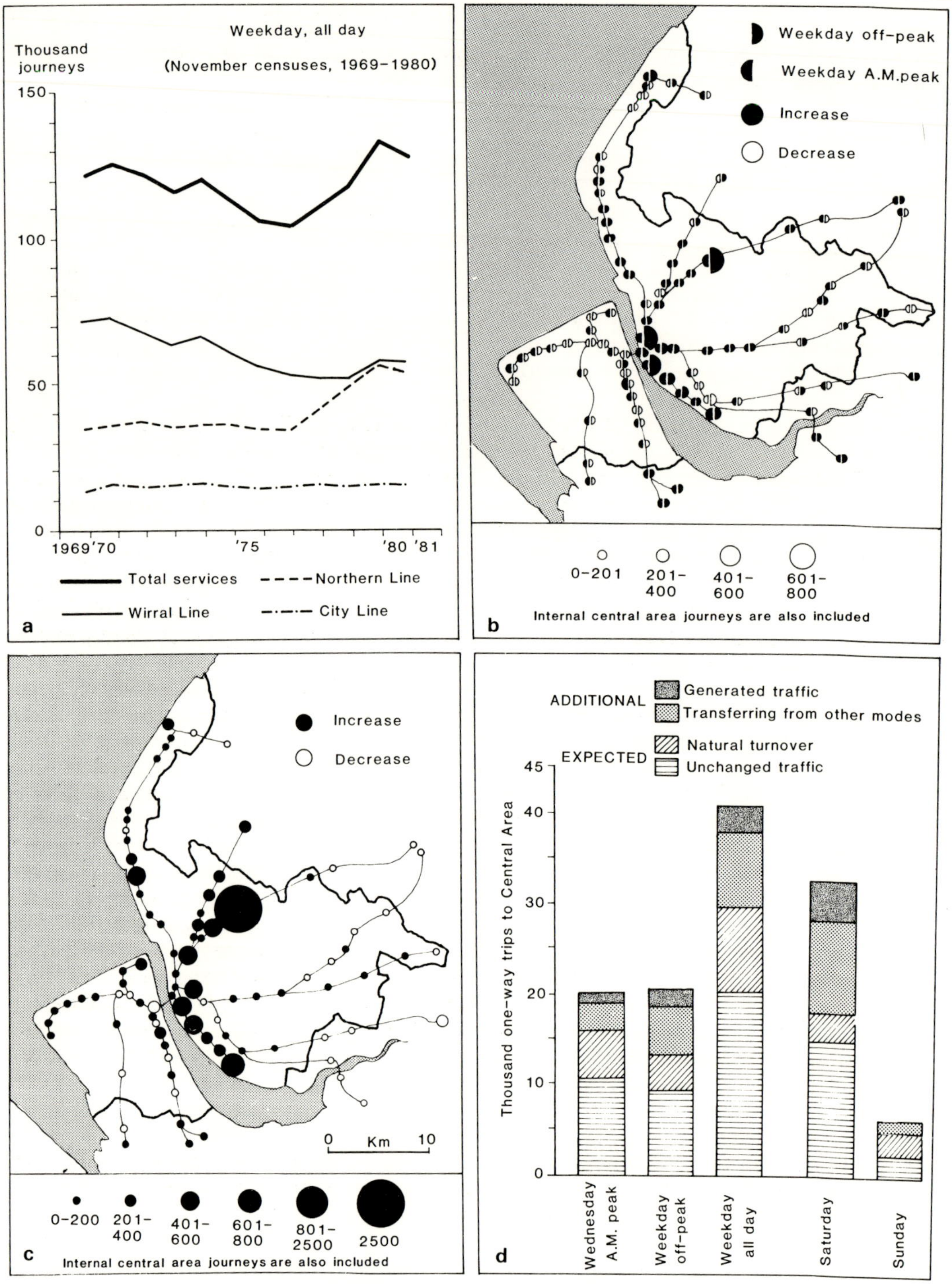

Fig. 6.5 Merseyside rail services: a. total journeys on local rail services, 1969–1980 (weekdays); b. changes in passenger journeys from each origin station to city centre, 1977–1979 (weekdays); c. changes in passenger journeys from each origin station to city centre, 1977–1979 (Saturdays); d. additional rail traffic entering Liverpool central area in March, 1979 as a result of Merseyrail projects (source: MPTE, 1981)

TABLE 6.2 *Trips to city centre on Merseyrail, March 1979*

Traffic source	Generated traffic		Transferred traffic	
	Weekday	Saturday	Weekday	Saturday
Overall	3000	4100	8300	10300
Former car-users			1900	2800
Former bus-users			4400	6100
Former ferry-users			1100	1000
Others			900	400

Source: M.P.T.E. (1981).

considerable success of the new Merseyrail system (M.P.T.E., 1981). In contrast to the steady decline of passengers using Merseyside's suburban railways, 1969–76, the period 1976–79 shows increases of 27% in total weekday patronage (76% for off-peak weekday traffic on Wirral and Northern Lines electric services). The decline in 1980, especially on the Northern Line, is probably due to the economic recession (Fig. 6.5). The new rail system has stimulated greater use of the purpose designed bus-rail interchanges. There was a 71% increase (680 journeys) during the weekday peak 1976–79. Park-and-ride facilities show a much more modest rise of 8% over the same period. By March, 1979, 39% of passengers used zone tickets, mainly for journeys to work, although there is evidence of increasing use for shopping and leisure trips. Journeys to work (93% of peak journeys) are always a significant proportion of total trips even on Sundays, whilst 39% of Saturday trips are for shopping. Overall, the new system has successfully generated entirely new trips to the central area, and has encouraged existing passengers to change their travel patterns to use the new system (Table 6.2). In particular, the Kirkby-Garston electrification has increased the line's optional traffic by 61% in week-day off-peak and by 273% on Saturdays. Saturday optional traffic on the Wirral line has increased by 41%.

The M.P.T.E. is particularly encouraged by the survey, taken before the extension of concessionary travel, the introduction of the Kirkby bus revision and the Speke-Garston feeder bus service. In financial terms, the system is also promising annual savings of £0.6 m from bus-rail integration, and rail revenue is substantially higher, by £2.0 m in 1980, than would have been expected without the scheme. The Merseyrail and bus-rail integration measures thus more than cover their operating costs, but not the total additional costs of provision (including capital charges). "However, while the value of the additional income gained by the Merseyrail projects will be retained in real terms, that of the corresponding capital repayments will decrease. This will result in a continuing improvement to the financial position of the Merseyrail system over future years" (M.P.T.E., 1981, p. 20).

Conclusions

Policies through the 1970s have succeeded in alleviating conflicts between intra- and inter-urban traffic, private and public passenger transport, passenger and freight handling and pedestrian and road traffic in Merseyside. Overall policy objectives are now broader, and recognize that "transport facilities help achieve wider social and economic aims rather than being an end in themselves", especially in a period characterized by declines in population and employment. Thus, the improvement of existing facilities by "finding an acceptable balance between the level of passenger transport services, fares charged and subsidy required, minimizing the conflict between traffic and environment" and "preventing the environmental and physical deterioration of some areas" (Merseyside County Council, 1980, p. 100) is now emphasized.

Transport patterns within conurbations depend on the distribution of people and of their activities and their available means of transportation. Developments in Merseyside in the 1970s have been closely linked with transport provision, both in infrastructure and vehicles. A more equable and convenient fares structure with simplified, integrated regular services aids individual mobility. The problem is whether these developments reflect wider economic and social change within the conurbation, and the location of real demand for transport services. Daniels and Warnes (1980, p. 337) suggest that "while the logic of the new (Merseyrail) network is clear enough, it may well prove to be a good example of the difficulties of providing a new transport system on the basis of apparently reasonable passenger forecasts", before "the very steep decline in city centre employment upon which the new system would depend for a substantial part of its payload." The capacity of the Merseyrail network does exceed its present traffic, especially as Liverpool central area employment has fallen by about 50% since 1961. However, the network has successfully attracted optional traffic, but it remains to be seen whether these trends will continue after the 1980/81 setbacks. Whilst doubts may be expressed over the effectiveness of public transport services between suburbs to cope with inter-suburban travel, not just to get to work but also for shopping and social trips, extension of railway electrification, greater ease of interchange and frequency of cross suburban bus services and a fully integrated fares system combine to ease the situation. However, much inter-suburban traffic is by private means, and the public transport system may too heavily emphasize access to Liverpool's central area. Many realities of personal mobility and mobility deprivation remain unassessed in transport planning.

Many transportation issues are overwhelmed by the importance of financial and political decisions. Financial support from central government, which has tended to favour capital expenditure, has been dramatically cut. Additional finance is urgently required for both highway and public transport maintenance. The election of a Labour-controlled County Council in May, 1981, revolutionized transport policies, resulting in the cancellation of substantial fare increases and capital intensive projects (such as the Liverpool Inner Ring Road), the retention of services planned for abandonment, and the introduction of a subsidized cheap fare policy which was specifically related to the 1981 supplementary rate demand, rather than transport policy reasons (Merseyside County Council, 1981D), although the M.P.T.E. has exploited the situation with the adventurous "Save Away" all zones/all modes day ticket. The long-term effects of these initiatives are awaited, particularly in a period of reduced central government support and of declining individual financial ability and need to travel. Unless cheap fares dramatically boost passenger usage to increase income from ticket sales substantially, rising subsidies could threaten necessary capital and current expenditure to the detriment of transport provision in the County.

Acknowledgements

I am most grateful for information and ideas provided during discussions with officials of various bodies concerned with the operation and planning of transport in Merseyside. In particular, I should like to thank Mr. R. Owen of British Rail, Liverpool Division; Messrs. A. H. Coleman, D. Jackson and K. W. Swallow of Merseyside Passenger Transport Executive; Messrs. B. Knowles and G. M. Lamb of Merseyside County Council Joint Transportation Unit; and Mr. Corking of the Department of Transport, North-West Road Construction Unit.

Chapter 7

THE LAND OF MERSEYSIDE

JOHN HANDLEY

The urbanization of Merseyside has proceeded rapidly since the emergence of Liverpool as a port of national importance two or more centuries ago (Chapter 1). The radial expansion of the built-up area enabled a fast growing population to be housed at progressively lower densities. During the 1970s, with fertility and mortality more or less in balance, an underlying trend of out-migration became increasingly evident (Chapter 11). These changed circumstances coincided with a renewed concern for environmental quality, both within the older urban areas most affected by slum clearance and in the surrounding open land which had been eroded by peripheral development. This is reflected in the Stage 1 Strategy of the Merseyside Structure Plan: "the proposed strategy would concentrate investment and development within the urban County and particularly in those areas with the most acute problems, enhancing the environment and housing and economic expansion on derelict and disused sites. It would restrict development on the edge of the built-up areas to a minimum"; and "there would be a reciprocal effort to enhance and conserve the natural features of the County's open land and its agriculture while ensuring that its capacity to meet the County's needs for leisure, recreation and informal education is exploited" (Merseyside County Council, 1975A).

This approach, which became known as the Urban Regeneration Strategy, lies at the heart of contemporary land-use planning on Merseyside (Merseyside County Council, 1980). This chapter elaborates this planning strategy, drawing heavily on a series of Reports of Survey prepared by the staff of Merseyside County Council and submitted to the Secretary of State for the Environment in 1979 as supporting documents to the Merseyside Structure Plan (Merseyside County Council, 1979D, E, F, G).

Throughout the nineteenth century Liverpool grew rapidly, and maintained its position as the second-largest city in Britain. By the time of the First World War, Liverpool and Birkenhead together had a population of over 850 000, yet the built-up area was still largely confined to within a three-mile radius of the Pier Head. But even before the end of the nineteenth century a process of rapid suburban expansion was gaining momentum. Local railways served developing commuter settlements on the Wirral and Lancashire coasts, and tramways linked the new areas of bye-law housing around the edge of Liverpool with places of work. Between the Wars, with the expansion of motor transport suburban growth occurred on a much more extensive scale. Semi-detached houses with gardens became the norm, and Liverpool Corporation contributed by building estates such as Norris Green on the outskirts of the city.

Since the Second World War urban development has continued, but, influenced by planning policies, it has taken a somewhat different form (Fig. 7.1). Several large housing estates were built around the outer fringes of Liverpool and Birkenhead, to be supplemented by "overspill" settlements such as Kirkby in the 1950s and the New Towns of Runcorn and Skelmersdale in the 1960s. At the same time physical constraints, Green Belt policies and increasing personal mobility caused private developers to concentrate their activities further away from the city than they had previously done, in places such as Formby, Maghull, Bebington and in the St. Helens area. Nevertheless, by far the largest post-war allocation for private house-building, made by Liverpool Corporation in the early 1970s, lies within the city limits at Croxteth Park, the former estate of the Earls of

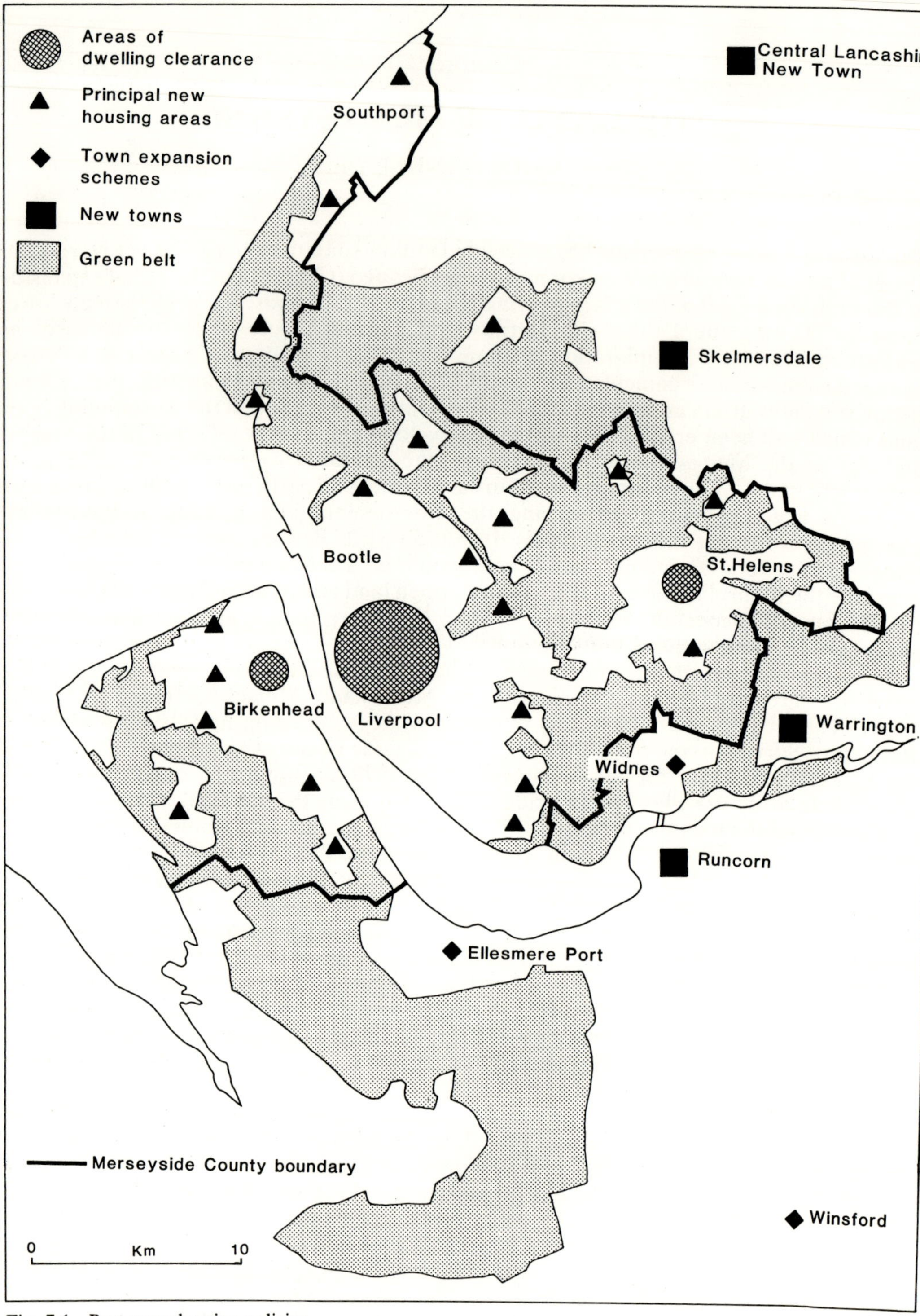

Fig. 7.1 Post-war planning policies

Sefton. Meanwhile, slum clearance proceeded apace in the older urban areas, and during the 1960s outstripped the process of redevelopment by a considerable margin.

The recent pattern of land-use change

It is by no means straightforward to translate this qualitative description of the physical growth of Merseyside into quantitative data on land-use change. Despite the panoply of planning legislation affecting land-use decisions, there is no systematic record of land-use change. Best and Campion (1970), using data on the rate of conversion of farmland to urban uses, have shown that Merseyside, in common with much of North-West England, experienced a conversion rate substantially higher than that recorded in most other parts of England and Wales. The North-West Economic Planning Council (1978) pointed out that, although the proportion of land in urban use in the North-West is three times the average for England and Wales, the agricultural output is 25% above average. In view of the productivity of the region's farm economy, the prospect of continued development of green-field sites for urban use was viewed with concern. The standard of provision of urban open space improved substantially between 1950/51 and 1970 (from 26 to 31 ha/1000), but the North-West remained one of the most densely populated regions with some of the worst housing conditions in the country, so that a greater rate of increase than in other regions in its open space requirements was to be expected.

The pattern of land-use change can best be revealed by analysis of land-use survey maps. Fortunately, successive surveys of Merseyside have taken place during the 1960s and 1970s using a standard classification (Coleman and Maggs, 1968). The 1960s survey extended over the period from 1960 to 1968, with most of the maps (31 out of 41) completed during 1967–68 (Coleman, 1978). The 1976 survey was commissioned by Merseyside County Council, and completed within the year. Both surveys have been analysed by Coleman using a point-sampling technique (8 points per sq km) to produce data on land-use change. Because the 1960s maps were completed over a period of years the data cannot be used to determine rates of land-use change. However, the pattern of land-use change between decades emerges clearly in Table 7.1. The distribution of land uses and net changes between surveys are summarized in Table 7.2.

The area of developed land increased by some 53 sq km (17%) between surveys, principally due to residential development and associated greenspace. Most of this new urban land was derived from farmland, but the land take was not evenly drawn from the three categories of farmland, and there was also a significant contribution from rough grassland. The total area of arable land was maintained between surveys by conversion of land in horticultural use (7.6 sq km) and improved grassland (8.6 sq km). A significant area of improved farmland (11.6 sq km) reverted to rough grassland and scrub, whilst only 2.4 sq km was improved. The net increase in rough grassland suggests that farmland is being taken out of productive use in anticipation of development taking place. Meanwhile, within the built-up area some 600 ha of land became 'derelict' principally by slum clearance, and 600 ha fell into a neglected condition as rough grassland. It should be noted that the definition of derelict land in the Land Utilization Survey is wider than the official definition used by the Department of the Environment. Whilst the total extent of damaged and neglected land is proportionally small, its visual impact is considerable, and this secondary land resource may help to meet future development needs. Development also took place at the expense of the natural environment, notably sand dunes and woodlands. On the Wirral peninsula a whole fifty-one woodlands have been lost since 1954, whilst only seventeen have been added by replanting (Roberts, 1975). The progressive loss of sand-dune habitat in what is now the Borough of Sefton has also been documented (Jackson, 1979). In drawing attention to the absolute losses of farmland and natural

TABLE 7.1 *The pattern of land-use change, 1960s–1976*

1976 \ 1960s	Settlement							Farmland			Vegetation					Total Losses (square kilometres)
	Mixed Urban	Industry	Extractive	Waste Disposal	Derelict	Transport	Open Space	Arable	Horticulture	Improved Grass	Coastal	Heath, Moss and Marsh	Rough Grass and Scrub	Woodland	Water	
Settlement																
Mixed Urban	137.5	1.5	—	—	2.1	1.1	1.7	0.1	0.3	0.1	—	—	0.5	—	—	7.4
Industry	3.5	13.6	—	—	0.9	0.1	0.1	—	—	—	—	—	0.1	—	—	4.7
Extractive	—	0.1	0.3	0.3	0.4	—	—	—	—	—	—	—	0.1	—	—	0.9
Waste Disposal	—	0.4	—	0.9	0.6	0.4	0.1	—	—	—	—	—	2.3	—	—	3.8
Derelict	0.6	0.5	0.1	—	0.4	0.1	0.6	—	—	0.5	—	—	0.9	—	—	3.3
Transport	2.0	0.6	—	0.1	1.4	75.8	0.4	—	0.3	—	—	—	1.5	0.3	—	6.6
Open Space	3.4	0.4	—	—	—	0.8	51.6	0.1	0.1	0.4	—	—	1.0	0.1	—	6.3
Farmland																
Arable	4.8	1.0	—	0.1	—	2.6	4.4	46.7	12.5	19.6	—	—	4.4	—	—	17.3
Horticulture	4.6	0.8	—	0.3	0.1	1.4	1.9	20.3	10.6	6.2	—	—	1.6	—	—	10.7
Improved Grass	10.4	0.1	—	0.5	—	3.8	7.8	28.0	6.4	47.3	—	0.1	5.6	0.8	—	29.1
Vegetation																
Coastal	0.4	—	—	0.1	—	0.4	0.5	—	—	1.0	18.5	0.1	1.6	0.5	0.4	5.0
Heath, Moss and Marsh	—	—	0.4	—	—	0.1	0.1	0.1	—	—	—	3.0	0.1	0.6	—	1.4
Rough Grass and Scrub	3.5	1.5	0.3	0.8	0.4	1.0	4.3	0.9	0.1	1.4	—	0.5	8.5	0.3	—	15.0
Woodland	1.3	—	—	—	—	0.5	0.8	0.4	0.3	0.5	0.1	0.5	0.4	22.4	—	4.8
Water	—	—	—	—	—	0.1	0.3	0.1	—	0.1	—	—	0.4	—	5.4	1.0
Total Gains	34.5	6.9	0.8	2.2	5.9	12.4	23.0	1.7	1.1	4.0	0.1	1.2	20.5	2.6	0.4	117.3

TABLE 7.2 *Summary of land-use change in Merseyside, 1960s–1976*

Category of use	1960s (sq km)	1976 (sq km)	Net change (sq km)
Residential/Commercial	144.9	172.0	+27.1
Industry	18.3	20.5	+2.2
Mineral extraction	1.2	1.1	−0.1
Waste disposal	4.7	3.1	−1.6
Derelict land	3.7	6.3	+2.6
Transport	82.4	88.2	+5.8
Open space	57.9	74.6	+16.7
TOTAL SETTLEMENT	313.1	365.8	+52.7
Arable	96.1	96.7	+0.6
Horticulture	47.8	30.6	−17.2
Improved grass	110.8	77.1	−33.7
TOTAL IMPROVED FARMLAND	254.7	204.4	−50.3
Coastal	23.5	18.6	−4.9
Heath, Moss and Marsh	4.4	4.2	−0.2
Rough Grass and Scrub	23.5	29.0	+5.5
Woodland	27.2	25.0	−2.2
Water	6.4	5.8	−0.6
SEMI-NATURAL HABITAT	85.0	82.6	−2.4

environment we may in fact be underestimating the full impact on nature conservation and the farm economy, for fragmentation of habitat and disruption of farm structures are significant factors in the urban fringe.

The farmland

Within Merseyside, an area with an equable climate and unspectacular topography, the principal determinant of land capability for agriculture is soil type (Agricultural Development and Advisory Service, 1969; Taylor, 1952) (Fig. 7.2). In association with this, the Ministry of Agriculture, Fisheries and Food has devised an agricultural land classification system with five grades (Ministry of Agriculture, Fisheries and Food, 1966; Table 7.3). Grade 1 land has very minor or no physical limitations to agricultural use. Yields are consistently high on these soils, and cropping is highly flexible since most crops, including the more exacting horticultural crops can be grown. At the other extreme Grade 5 land has very severe physical limitations. Land in this grade is generally under grass or rough grazing, except for occasional pioneer forage crops.

The resulting Agricultural Land Classification Map is reproduced diagrammatically in Figure 7.3. It is immediately apparent that a substantial area consists of farmland of the highest quality. The distribution of land quality by agricultural grade in Merseyside is compared with England and Wales as a whole in Table 7.4. The best quality land is associated with soils developed on alluvium, peat and Shirdley Hill sand in a broad tract of land north of the Mersey between Hightown and Billinge. Large-scale reclamation of these mossland areas began in the eighteenth century. The introduction of steam pumps in the next century increased the rate of reclamation, and at the present day extensive tracts of

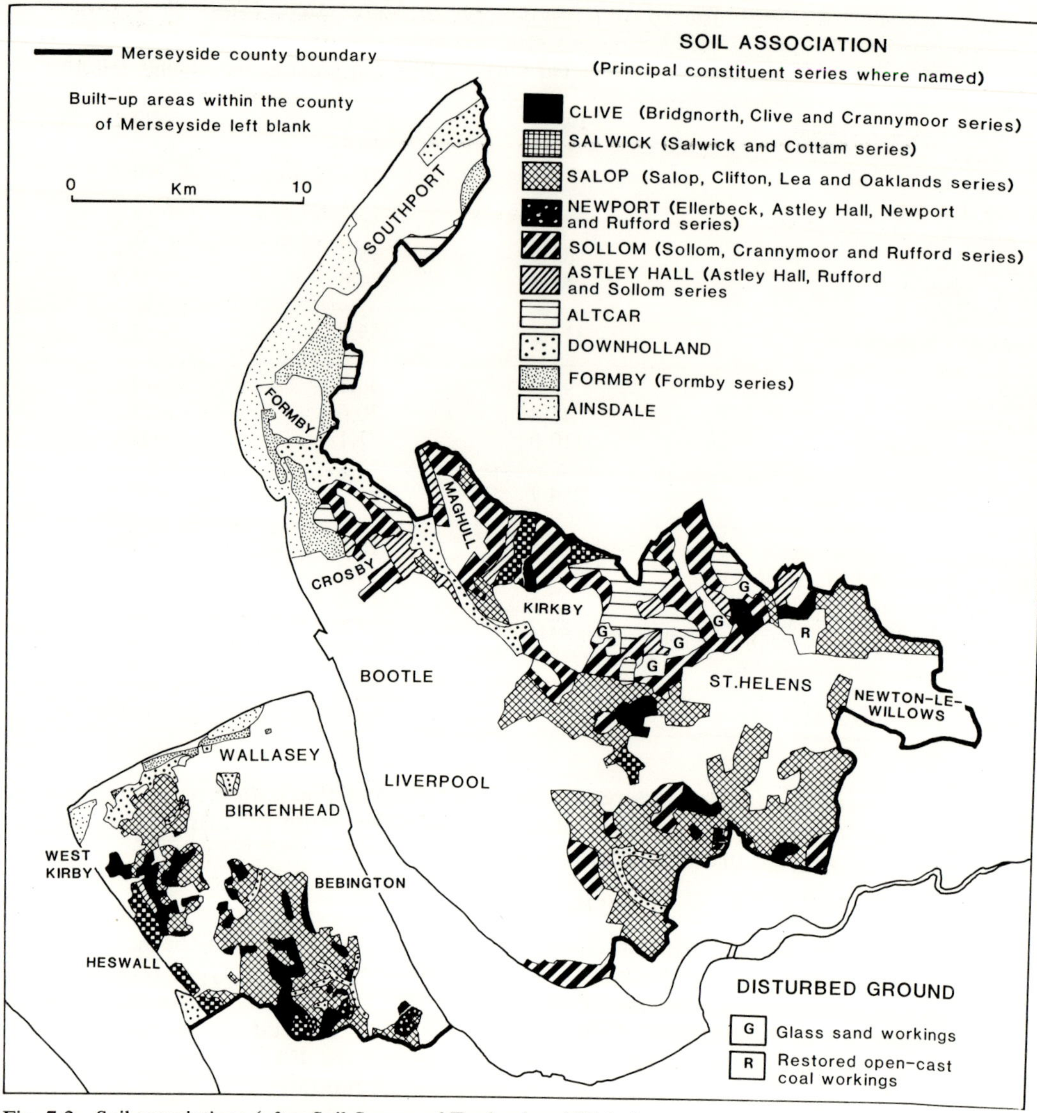

Fig. 7.2 Soil associations (after Soil Survey of England and Wales)

low-lying land are dependent on pump drainage for their security (Mersey and Weaver River Authority, 1972; Prus-Chacinski and Harris, 1963). Some of the peat deposits have a dome-shaped profile, e.g. Simonswood Moss, and special techniques are required to bring these areas into agricultural production. However, following drainage and fertilizer application these "raised mosses" may be transformed from Grade 5 to Grade 1 farmland within a few years (Hall and Folland, 1970).

Where soils have developed on glacial till they are more usually classified in Grade 3, but the area between Halewood and Bold Heath is mostly Grade 2, despite the predominance of the Salop soil association. The overall cropping pattern in Liverpool, Knowsley, Sefton and St. Helens is remarkably constant with a large cereal acreage and a substantial area of

TABLE 7.3 *The principal soil associations of Merseyside*

Parent material	Soil Association	Grade	Typical farming system and present land use
Calcareous blown sand	Ainsdale	V	Asparagus, amenity, afforestation
Non-calcareous blown sand	Formby	III & IV	Dairying and livestock rearing, mixed arable
Fen peat and raised moss peat	Altcar	I to V	Intensive arable (some mosses unreclaimed)
Active and recent alluvium	Downholland	I to V	Mixed arable, dairying and livestock rearing, rough grazing on unreclaimed salt marsh
Shirdley Hill sand	Astley Hall, Sollom	I & II	Intensive arable
Medium to fine textured glacial till	Salop, Salwick	II & III	Dairying and livestock rearing, mixed arable
Triassic sandstone	Clive	III to V	Mixed arable, heathland and amenity woodland

Sources: "Soils of Lancashire" by B. R. Hall and C. J. Folland, *Soil Survey of Great Britain*, Bulletin No. 5; "Soils of the West Midlands" by D. Mackney and C. P. Burnham, *Soil Survey of Great Britain*, Bulletin No. 2.

TABLE 7.4 *Quality of agricultural land in Merseyside and England and Wales*

Grade of agricultural land	MERSEYSIDE		ENGLAND & WALES
	Farmland area (ha)	% of total farmland	% of total farmland
I	5755	20.8	2.8
II	8937	32.3	14.6
III	10 127	36.6	48.9
IV	968	3.5	19.7
V	1882	6.8	14.0
Total	27 670	100	100

Source: Ministry of Agriculture and Fisheries, 1974.

potatoes, sugar beet and vegetables. This land forms part of the principal area for arable cropping in western Britain, and the horticultural output is of national significance (Ministry of Agriculture, Fisheries and Food, 1967). In Wirral, medium to heavy clay soils predominate and the farming pattern contrasts sharply with the rest of the County. There is a large area of permanent grass, with dairy farming the principal enterprise. Whilst cropping flexibility is somewhat limited on these soils, their inherent fertility is high, and, given the comparatively long growing season, they support highly productive grasslands.

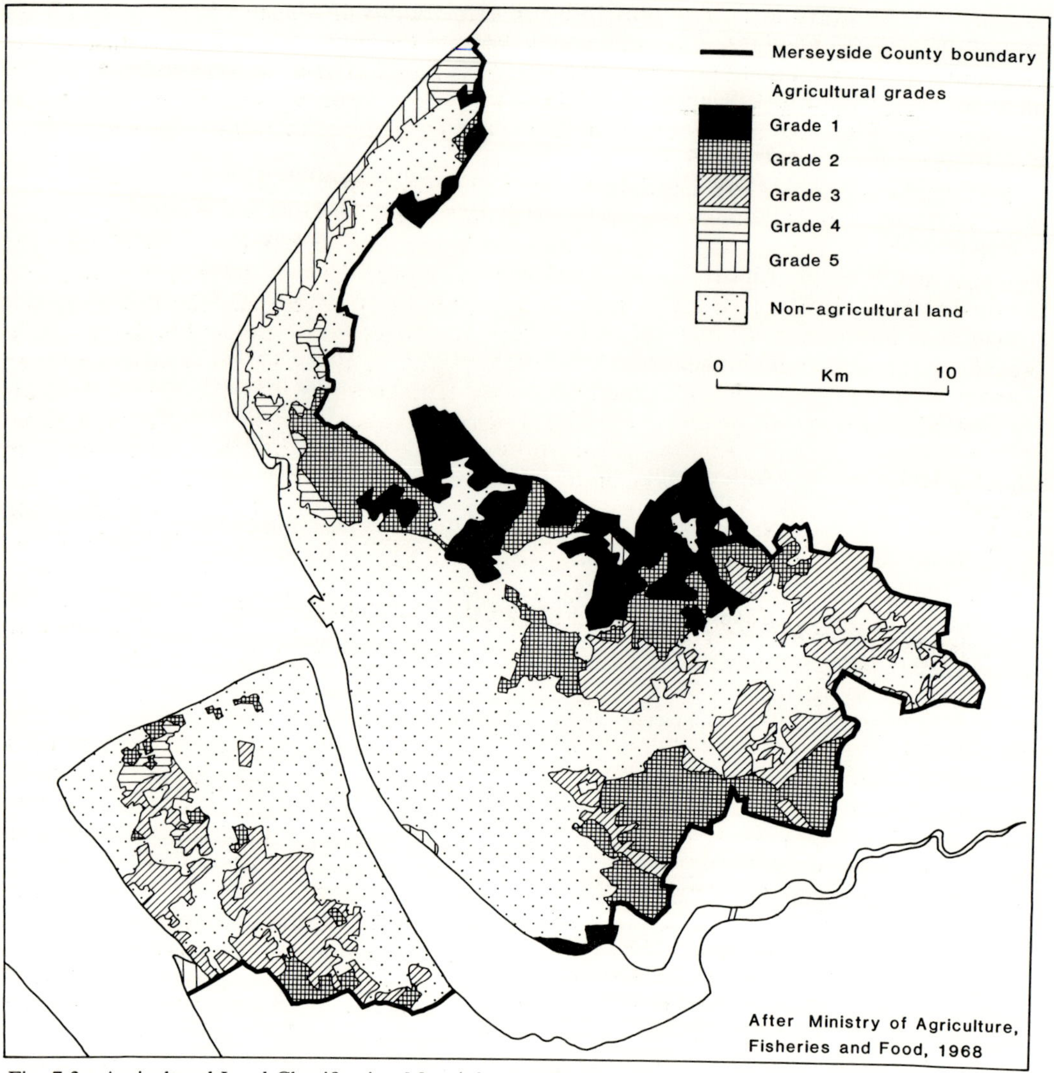

Fig. 7.3 Agricultural Land Classification Map (after Ministry of Agriculture, Fisheries and Food)

The distinctive market gardening area of north Wirral on blown sand (Grade 2) has supplied spring vegetables and salad crops to the conurbation since the eighteenth century (Smith, 1953D).

Grade 4 agricultural land occurs on thin sandy soils around Formby and on heavy, poorly drained alluvial and clay soils behind Hoylake. An arterial drainage scheme could increase the agricultural potential of north Wirral, but cost-benefit analysis by the Agricultural Development Advisory Service indicates that this would be uneconomic. The soils around Formby are productive when expertly farmed, but much of the area is under permanent grass. The species diversity of these permanent grasslands is high, and they are of considerable ecological interest. Where grazing is excluded, as on Woodvale aerodrome, heathland has developed. The Grade 5 land includes sand dunes, salt marshes and unimproved mossland. The raw sandy soils of the dune belt are quite unsuited to conventional agriculture, but asparagus is well adapted to these conditions. In the recent past Formby was well known as a northern outpost of asparagus growing (Ministry of Agriculture, Fisheries and Food, 1969), but the industry has contracted steadily since 1945, and less than 10 ha remain.

Because of their apparent unsuitability for agriculture the coastal areas remain in a near natural state, and are the parts of the County of greatest importance for nature conservation. Nevertheless, reclamation of salt marshes in the Dee and Ribble has produced soils of the highest agricultural quality. Approximately 1500 ha of salt marsh were reclaimed from the Ribble estuary during the last century, and the resulting soils (Grade 1) support a wide range of arable crops and vegetables (Hall and Folland, 1967). Land reclamation in the Dee estuary began early in the eighteenth century, and continued until 1916 by which time 5000 ha had been reclaimed. These alluvial soils are used in part for mixed arable cropping and good yields of cereals are obtained (Furness and King, 1973). Further land reclamation within these estuaries holds out the one prospect of making good some of the losses of top quality farmland which the North-West has experienced. A recent survey by the Ministry of Agriculture (1981) confirmed the potential of the Ribble estuary, but demonstrated that extensive salt marshes in the Mersey were less suitable for agriculture due to sediment composition and serious contamination by heavy metals. The heavy metal pollution of the Mersey estuary was not unexpected, but the finding that the agricultural potential of the Dee estuary was also prejudiced, though to a lesser extent, by metal pollution was more remarkable.

The estuaries

The contrasting hydraulics of the Mersey, Dee and Ribble estuaries have exerted a profound influence on the pattern of economic development in the North-West region. The Dee estuary, once more important for shipping than the Mersey, has been silting up since the eleventh century. Land reclamation at the head of the estuary reduced tidal scour, which was naturally weak due to the steady widening of the Dee estuary seawards. The Chester Haven was abandoned in the fifteenth century, after which port facilities gradually migrated up the eastern shore of the estuary as far as Parkgate which was finally superseded by Liverpool early last century. The process of salt marsh development was further accelerated by the introduction of the vigorous hybrid grass, *Spartina anglica*, at Connah's Quay in 1922. Today, the Dee estuary, except at high spring tides, is at least two-thirds dry, with large areas of exposed sand banks and salt marsh.

The Mersey, by contrast, with its narrow neck and a large inner basin, develops a strong tidal scour. This is further assisted by the construction of training walls flanking the channel in Liverpool Bay for some 16 km, to direct and control the waters as they enter the sea. The training walls were required in the first instance to stabilize the Crosby channel following changes initiated by dredging to increase clearance on the outer bar. Maintenance dredging of the seaways continues, and further improvements in dredging efficiency may require relocation of the dumping ground or removal of material from the system in a major land reclamation project (McDowell, 1973).

The main channel of the Ribble is notoriously unstable, and training walls were constructed around the turn of the century to provide a permanent shipping lane to Preston. These developments increased tidal scour within the walls, but reduced it greatly outside them encouraging rapid development of mudflats and salt marshes. *Spartina anglica* was also introduced to the Ribble estuary, and following the construction of a new coastal road enclosing Marshside and Crossens Marsh, a herbicide spraying programme

TABLE 7.5 *Waders and wildfowl of international importance in the Dee, Mersey and Ribble estuaries, 1969–75 (percentages of the North-West European population)*

	Dee	Mersey	Ribble
Teal	1	4.3	—
Pintail	5.7	14.4	3.3
Shelduck	3.3	1.4	—
Pink-footed Goose	—	—	18.7
Bewick's Swan	—	—	(1)*
Oystercatcher	2.6	—	(2.7)†
Ringed Plover	1.3	—	—
Grey Plover	1.2	—	1.9
Curlew	1.0	—	—
Black-tailed Godwit	1.8	—	2.7
Bar-tailed Godwit	5.6	—	7.9
Redshank	2.9	1.4	1.7
Knot	6.2	—	14.1
Dunlin	2.3	3.1	3.6
Sanderling	3.1	—	12.0

Notes: *Over 1% have been recorded since 1975; †2.7% have been recorded since 1975.
Source: Birds of Estuaries Enquiry.

has been needed to prevent salt marsh development on the holiday beaches of Southport. The closure of the Port of Preston and cessation of dredging in 1981 will, in time, bring further changes to the Ribble estuary.

Despite the management of these estuaries as seaways and their alteration by land reclamation and effluent disposal, the inter-tidal sand banks, mud flats and salt marshes constitute one of the most extensive wilderness areas in lowland Britain. The biological productivity of the estuaries is considerable, and this, together with their relative inaccessibility, makes them ideal staging posts and wintering grounds for migratory wading birds and wildfowl. The importance of these estuaries for nature conservation is apparent from Table 7.5. Since the presence of 1% or more of a North-West European species population of wading birds and wildfowl is one of the accepted criteria for assessing the international importance of a wetland area, the Nature Conservancy Council has scheduled the great majority of the inter-tidal area as Sites of Special Scientific Interest (S.S.S.I.s). But whilst this designation confers a degree of protection, it does not guarantee that management will be in accordance with conservation objectives. It has been possible to accommodate a variety of land-uses including grazing, wildfowling, shell fishing and, more recently, sand winning, without prejudicing the ecology of the estuaries, but other pressures may be more damaging. There is some indication that, as the gross organic pollution of the Mersey estuary is progressively reduced, the influence of persistent pollutants, such as heavy metals, will be increasingly felt. In the late summer of 1979 and again in 1980 a substantial mortality of wading birds and wildfowl seems to have been associated with organic lead pollution, a problem which has since been alleviated.

But the pressure for large-scale land reclamation continues to be the major threat to the integrity of the estuaries. The agricultural potential of the Ribble is such that in 1979 a private developer proposed the enclosure and reclamation of 2000 ha of salt marsh at Banks Marsh. Opposition to this scheme on nature conservation grounds eventually led to purchase of the site as a National Nature Reserve by the Nature Conservancy Council, and

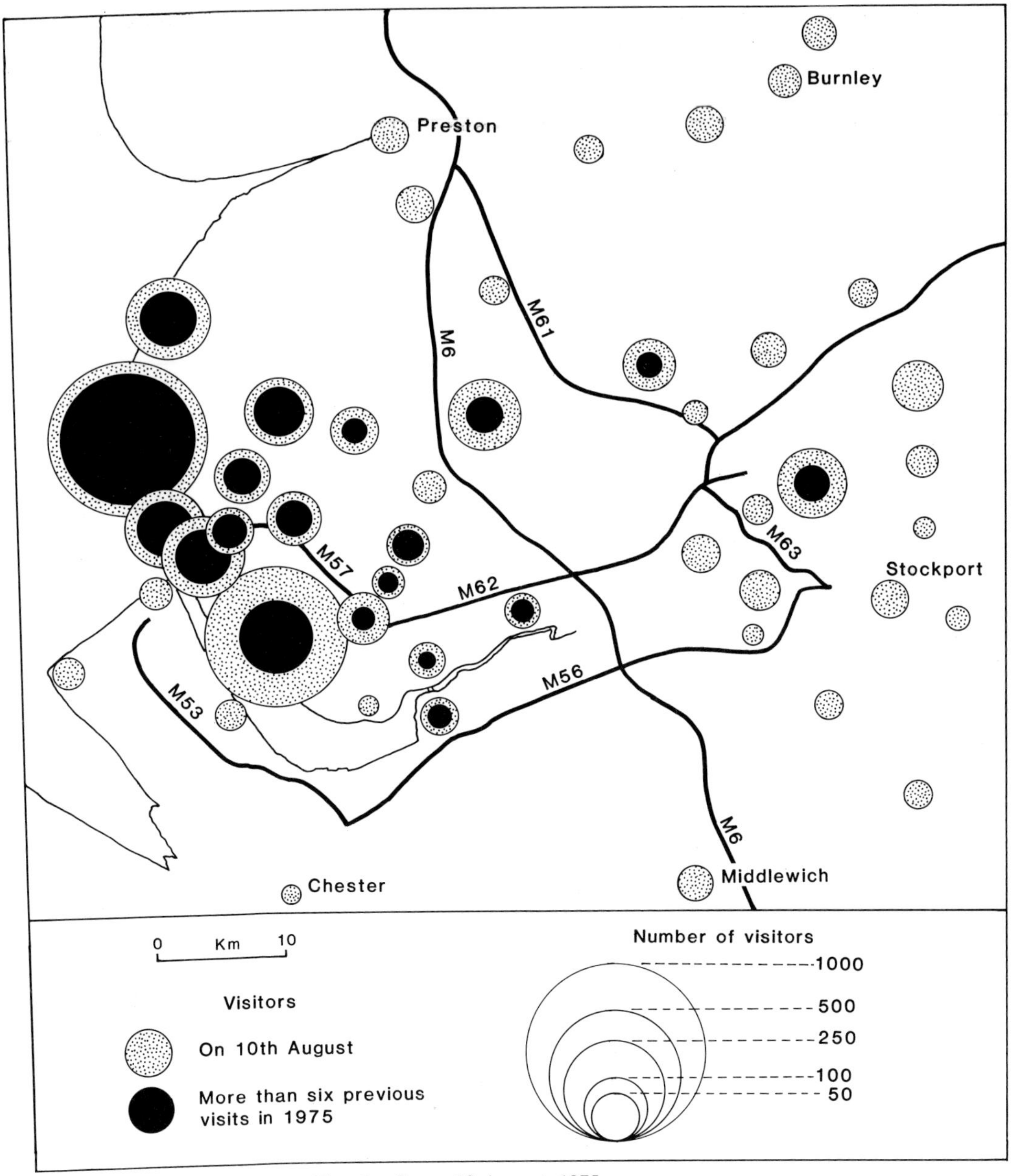

Fig. 7.4 Origins of visitors to Formby Coast, 10 August, 1975

reclamation was restricted to some 300 ha on Hesketh Out-Marsh further up the estuary. The main impetus for land reclamation in the Mersey estuary is to provide new land for industrial development and to an increasing extent for disposal of solid wastes from domestic and industrial sources. The proposal for a tidal barrage across the Mersey estuary for electricity generation (Mersey Barrage Panel, 1981) is likely to be more benign ecologically than a proposed road crossing of the Dee estuary with upstream lagoons for storage of fresh water. The prospects for nature conservation in the Dee estuary were greatly advanced by the establishment of the Gayton Sands Reserve (2040 ha) by the Royal Society for the Protection of Birds in 1979, which protects a strategically located area of salt marsh and tidal flats fronting the Cheshire shore.

The sand dunes

Effective management of large natural systems, such as estuaries, is made more difficult by the large number of agencies involved and the complexity of administrative boundaries. Fortunately a precedent does exist within Merseyside for a co-ordinated approach to coastal resource management. In 1979 a joint management scheme was adopted for the sandy foreshores, dunes and woodlands fronting the Sefton coast between Hightown and Southport. The management scheme is intended to reconcile the requirements of countryside recreation with the objectives of coast protection and conservation of nature and the landscape. The Merseyside County Council, Sefton Borough Council, major landowners and government agencies are represented on a Sefton Coast Steering Group. As shown by Fig. 7.4 the dune coastline is a regional recreational facility. Under this type of pressure, in the absence of management the protective plant cover is weakened, exposing bare sand to wind erosion. The amenity value of the sand dunes deteriorates, and the role of the dunes as a sea defence is weakened. Sand blown further inland damages woodlands and inundates wildlife habitats such as dune slacks. Analysis of sequential aerial photographs, spanning three decades, reveals persistent and spreading erosion features. These damaged areas recover very slowly, and are avoided by visitors who therefore contribute to further erosion elsewhere.

Dune management is labour-intensive, and there is considerable evidence for a positive approach prior to the Second World War (Gresswell, 1953), but the increasing cost of labour in the post-war period, coupled with increasing visitor pressure, contributed to the deterioration in the dune system. Ironically, the restoration of damaged areas at Formby Point has only been possible because of the availability of labour under the government's Special Temporary Employment Programme. The management scheme seeks to accommodate considerable numbers of people in the more accessible parts of the dune system by measures to increase carrying capacity, such as construction of board walks, careful design of car parks and creation of inland lakes on the site of worked-out asparagus beds and mineral workings. Continual maintenance is required at these pressure points, but the remainder of the dune system requires a much lower management input. A substantial area is managed for nature conservation by the Nature Conservancy Council (461 ha) and Sefton Borough Council (205 ha) with varying degrees of public access. There are also golf courses (300 ha) and land used for military training.

The parklands and fringe lands

A careful inventory of vegetation surfaces in Merseyside which are not intensively farmed or managed for recreation has been provided by analysis of panchromatic aerial photographs (Collins, 1975A). Those tracts of land of greatest interest for nature conservation are scheduled by the Nature Conservancy Council (N.C.C.) as Sites of Special Scientific Interest. The aerial survey (Table 7.6) shows that the extent of semi-natural habitats in 1974 greatly exceeds the area scheduled by N.C.C. In the most recent (1979) edition of the schedule there is a significant increase in the proportion of sand dune, dune heath, salt marsh and marshland with S.S.S.I. status. The mosslands are excluded because these areas are used for peat extraction and waste disposal. The

TABLE 7.6 *Natural environments with statutory protection compared with total resource*

Environment type	Area identified by aerial survey (ha) 1974	Area included in SSSI schedule July 1977 (ha)	Area included in SSSI schedule March 1979 (ha)
Coniferous woodland	421	154	173
Mixed woodland	81	20	32
Broadleaved woodland	2504	49	92
Sand dunes	1289	467	636
Salt Marsh	574	481	543
Freshwater marsh	31	10	10
Freshwater ponds and lakes	350	½	½
Dune heath	25	—	16
Sandstone heath	117	30	50
Unimproved mossland	156	—	—
Scrub	1319	12	30
Rough grassland	3039	4	17

Sources: Nature Conservancy Council, Schedules of Sites of Special Scientific Interest. Collins (1975b), Remote Sensing Unit, Aston University.

heathlands of the Wirral peninsula, in common with the sand dunes, are in need of urgent and careful restoration work in the face of intense visitor pressures.

The proportion of broad-leaved woodland with S.S.S.I. status is very low, but this reflects the fact that most of Merseyside's woodlands are of comparatively recent origin (Roberts and Burnett, 1977; Chapter 8) whilst high species diversity characteristic of natural woodland may take centuries to develop (Peterken, 1974). Most of the woodlands were in fact planted on the great estates during the 18th and 19th century to improve visual amenity and to provide cover for game. These estate woodlands have been eroded to a varying degree in recent decades (Table 7.7), but even in areas where the woodland is more or less intact there is an urgent need for positive management. The previous use, followed by years of neglect, has tended to produce overmature woodlands with much dead and dying timber, a plight accentuated by the ravages of an aggressive strain of Dutch Elm Disease. The scale of the problem is exemplified by the management issues confronting Merseyside County Council at Croxteth Park, the former home of the Earls of Sefton (Merseyside County Council, 1982). By contrast, the experience of the neighbouring Knowsley estate demonstrates that sound woodland management can provide a firm basis for landscape continuity in the 1980s.

The area of rough grassland (3039 ha) and scrub (1319 ha) in Table 7.6 is broadly comparable with the estimated combined area of rough grassland and scrub in the 1976 Land Utilization Survey (2900 ha). This is a substantial area of land and a characteristic feature of the urban fringe of most large conurbations (Coleman, 1976). The prevalence of this type of land, especially along major transportation routes, has a blighting effect on the landscape, and gives an air of neglect. In practice the condition is often temporary for the land may be in the process of structural change. There is, however, a need for management of this land, even as an interim measure, to realize its potential for agriculture, informal recreation, afforestation and nature conservation. This will be a key objective in a major urban fringe experiment "Operation Groundwork", which is being promoted in the Metropolitan Boroughs of St. Helens and Knowsley by the Countryside Commission. The principal aim of the experiment is to test whether, through a co-ordinated effort in the countryside around a city, the standards of land management, access, environmental

TABLE 7.7 *Woodland condition in selected historic landscapes*

Landscape	Historical Association	Woodland Area (ha)	Woodland lost since 1845	Condition
Bold Hall, St Helens	Present estate laid out in 1732	32	48%	Ownership fragmented, severed by M62, woodlands require urgent attention
Croxteth Park, Liverpool	Seat of Earls of Derby, 1473–1973, now a Country Park	100	None	Woodland intact but remedial work urgently needed. Extension housing development on adjoining land
Garwood Park, St. Helens	Present estate dates from 18th century	28	63%	Mature woodland used for game management in past. Fragmented by A580
Halsnead Park, Knowsley	Seat of de Halsneads from 1246–1422	22	54%	Intruded by Cronton Colliery, caravan site and M62. Mature woodlands require management
Haydock Lodge Park, St. Helens	Original home of Legh family	50	10%	Mature woodland intruded by A580 and housing development
Ince Blundell, Sefton	Seat of Blundell family from 13th to 18th century	45	9%	Active woodland management in past but parkland requires attention
Knowsley Park, Knowsley	Home of Earls of Derby, fine 18th century designed landscape	441	4%	Effective woodland management to provide timber and retain landscape integrity
Little Crosby, Sefton	Former home of Blundell family	41	5%	Active woodland management, including replacement of losses due to Dutch Elm Disease
Meols Hall, Sefton	Home of the Hesketh family	15	Planted since 1845	Active woodland management
Rainford Hall, St. Helens	Victorian home of Pilkington family	45	13% but extensive new planting since 1845	Effective woodland management
Speke Hall, Liyerpool	Reference to Speke Manor in Domesday Book, 1086	15	None	Derelict woodland requires urgent attention
Thornton Hough, Wirral	Model estate village with tree lined avenues on Leverhulme estate	4+	Avenues planted since 1845	Replacement planting under way following losses due to Dutch Elm Disease

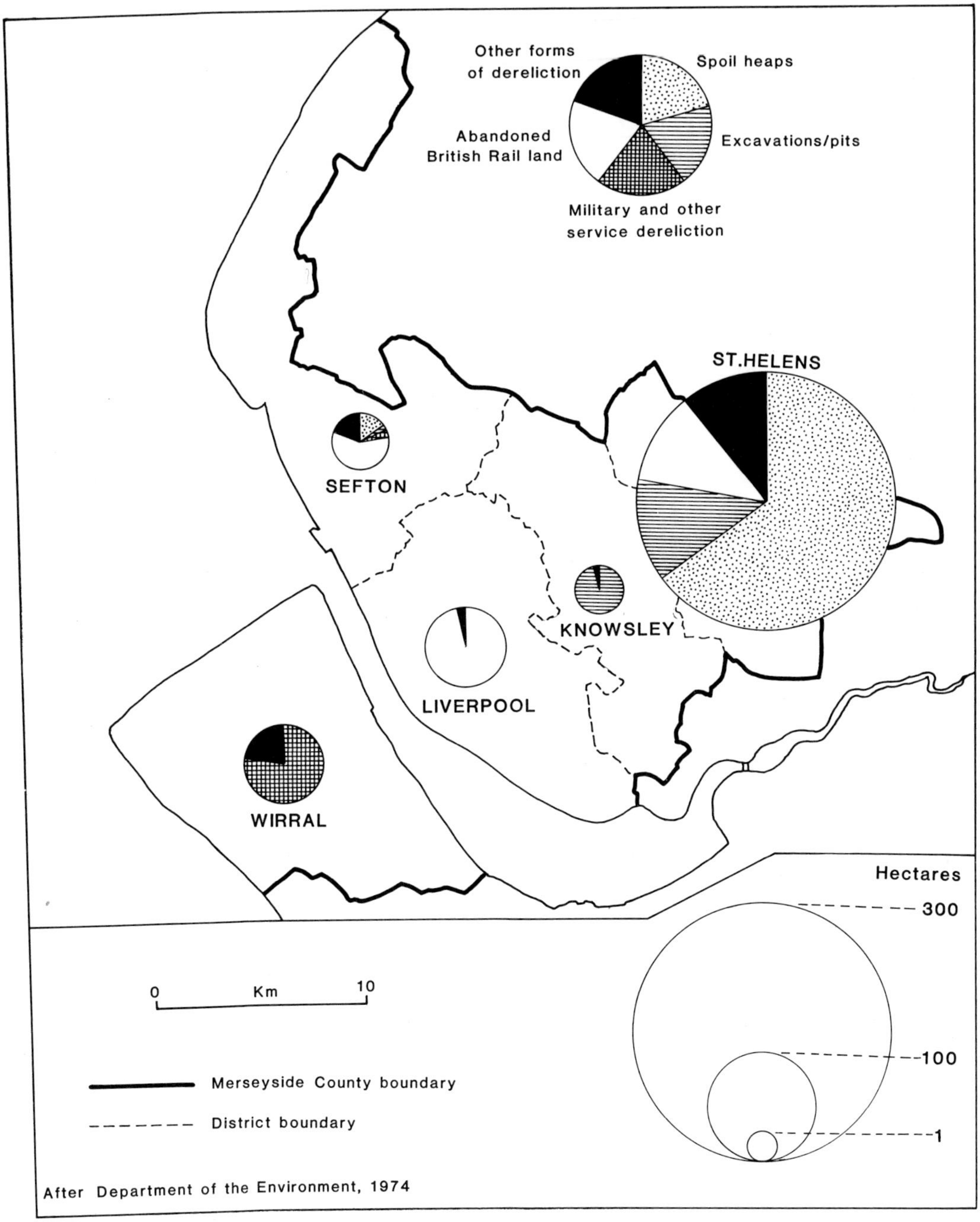

Fig. 7.5 Distribution of derelict land

quality and food and timber production can be improved for the benefit of the city and surrounding settlements and the economy generally. The pioneering work of Merseyside County Council and St. Helens Borough Council in creating a Country Park extending for 8 km along the Sankey Valley gives some indication of what this project is intended to achieve.

Derelict and despoiled land

The government defines derelict land as "(l)and so damaged by industrial or other development, that it is incapable of beneficial use without further treatment" (Department of Environment, 1975). The extent of derelict land in Merseyside was surveyed by the local authorities in 1974 when 529 ha were identified. The distribution of this land between Districts is shown in Fig. 7.5 which shows that the core of the problem (59%) is in St. Helens. This reflects the long history of mineral working in that area for coal, glass sand, brick clay, fire clay and sandstone aggregate, together with disposal of industrial waste materials notably alkali waste and burgy sand, formerly a by-product of glass manufacture.

The official definition of derelict land, stringently qualified by a number of conditions, is used by the Department of Environment to determine the eligibility of derelict land reclamation schemes for grant aid. Steady progress has been made with the reclamation of derelict land, and there are some notable achievements, particularly the restoration of 33 ha of severely damaged land at Sutton Heath, St. Helens, by Pilkington Brothers Ltd., in 1977 in preparation for a new float-glass plant. But much despoiled land fails to qualify for grant-aid, e.g., land to which after-treatment conditions apply, land in active use (e.g. for waste disposal), dereliction of natural origin and buildings vacated or sites cleared with a view to programmed urban redevelopment. The full extent of the problem was revealed by aerial survey (Collins, 1975B) which identified more than 3000 ha of derelict and despoiled land. The planning status of each land-parcel has been examined by the District Councils, and this information, together with an indication of development potential, has made an important contribution to the Land Resources System of the County and District Councils (Merseyside County Council, 1979G) which identifies some 3400 ha (5% of the area of the County) of unused land in Merseyside. The urban regeneration strategy aims to make use of this land for development or return it to agriculture, and, where this is not practicable, to improve its appearance. Local authorities own 40% of the unused land with private developers and other private owners owning 36%. The balance is owned by statutory undertakings, such as British Rail and the Mersey Docks and Harbour Company. The establishment of the Merseyside Development Corporation should accelerate progress in the most intractable area of dereliction, the abandoned docklands. The treatment programme for vacant urban land in Liverpool and Birkenhead has also benefited from their status as Urban Programme Authorities, which attract favourable rates of government grant for land treatment (Chapter 4).

The aerial survey of derelict and despoiled land revealed that much of the unused land is associated in one way or another with waste disposal. It is not unexpected that industrial and mining wastes should prove recalcitrant, but the fate of land formerly used for disposal of domestic waste is more disturbing. The summary table of land-use changes (Table 7.1) reveals that 76% of land used for tipping in the 1960s was in a derelict or neglected condition in 1976. There are some examples of good practice from the past, notably the creation of an attractive parkland at Otterspool in Liverpool, but it is to be hoped that the creation of a unified waste disposal authority in 1974 will ensure higher overall standards of restoration and after-management than was previously possible.

Whilst the consequences of solid-waste disposal are often all too obvious, the impact of air-borne pollutants on the land may be more insidious. The long history of sulphur pollution in Merseyside has produced amenity grasslands with an acidic reaction, about half their area having pH values between 5.0 and 7.0 whereas nearly half the farmland area has pH values over 7.0. In some parklands the acidity may greatly reduce the carrying capacity of the turf, and the nitrogen cycle is effectively blocked. Fortunately, this situation is fairly easily reversed by careful applications of ground limestone (Vick and Handley, 1977). Contamination by persistent pollutants such as heavy metals is potentially more damaging, and is less reversible. There is a general contamination by lead in the older parts of the conurbation and a marked concentration of copper and cadmium in the vicinity of Prescot, Knowsley (Merseyside County Council, 1979F). Some gardens within this zone are unable to support vegetation, except for special strains of grasses which have evolved tolerance to copper (Wu & Bradshaw, 1972).

Despite these findings it should be emphasized that atmospheric pollution is becoming much less of a constraint on land-use than hitherto. There has been a sustained improvement in ground-level concentrations of smoke and sulphur dioxide over the last three decades. The situation even in central Liverpool has ameliorated to the point where lichens, sensitive indicators of air quality, have begun to recolonize after an absence of a century or more. Furthermore, legislation and pollution control technology have advanced considerably so that we should no longer regard industrial development and maintenance of air quality as mutually exclusive goals. Indeed, modern technology, especially that based on the micro-chip, is itself demanding high air-quality standards.

Prospects

This discussion has traced the changing pattern of land-use on Merseyside through a period of rapid urban expansion to one of marked economic decline. The success of strategy for urban regeneration will depend on substantial funding from central government coupled with a vigorous response to the agreed planning framework by both private and public sectors on Merseyside. But the opportunity exists to move beyond the exploitive relationship between the city and surrounding countryside to a more benign position of dynamic equilibrium.

The first requirement is to define the limits of development for the foreseeable future within a Merseyside Green Belt. The Green Belt Subject Plan prepared by Merseyside County Council is now (February, 1982) on formal deposit prior to adoption as a statutory plan. Draft Green Belts for Merseyside were submitted by both Cheshire and Lancashire County Councils, but, although accepted as Green Belt for development control purposes, they were not formally approved by the Secretary of State. The new Merseyside Green Belt represents a substantial extension on the former position (Table 7.8). The rationalization of local government boundaries in 1974 has enabled the Green Belt to be

TABLE 7.8 *Green Belt extension proposed by Merseyside County Council, October, 1980*

	Open land in 1974 not included in the Green Belt* (ha)	Open land to be covered by extended Green Belt (ha)	Percentage increase	Residual open land (ha)
Wirral	1524	820	53.81	704
Liverpool	892	444	49.78	448
Knowsley	652	140	21.47	412
Sefton	1732	1240	71.59	492
St. Helens	3056	2324	76.05	732

extended across "white land" lying within the former County Boroughs. Consequently, the most marked extension of the Green Belt has occurred in St. Helens, Southport, Birkenhead and Wallasey. In addition, the outer boundary of the Green Belt has been extended to the north and east of St. Helens as far as the County boundary to cover open land which had not been included in the original submission. There has also been a re-appraisal of land needed for housing and industrial development and of the capacity of derelict or neglected land within the built-up area to satisfy new requirements. Finally, in the methodology used to delimit the Green Belt much greater attention has been paid to including or excluding land on the basis of its intrinsic value with respect to the various open land policies which have been adopted in the Structure Plan. Fifty-six per cent of the residual open land (2788 ha) was firmly committed to development of various types in 1974. It includes two substantial areas (Crossens Marsh, Southport, and the M53 corridor, Wirral) where the extent of any land release will be defined by Local Plans. In addition there remain areas of open land which, whilst separated from the Green Belt, are likely to remain undeveloped because of their current use and position (e.g. Royal Liverpool Golf Course and Liverpool Airport).

The Green Belt will help to reduce uncertainty amongst the farming community, and we may anticipate greater investment by farmers with holdings on the edge of the built-up area. But a variety of conflicts will remain in the countryside, and these can only be alleviated by joint working between those concerned. Elsewhere on Merseyside there is a need for a similar co-operative effort of the type offered by the Sefton Coast Management Scheme. The major urban-fringe experiment, Operation Groundwork, is an encouraging development in St. Helens and Knowsley. A management scheme has been set up to protect the fragile woodlands of Dibbinsdale on the Wirral, and some form of joint working is in prospect for the Dee estuary. Within the built-up area the urban regeneration strategy is properly focused on the older parts of the conurbation through the Merseyside Development Corporation and the Inner City Partnership. The land reclamation teams of the County and District Councils are increasingly getting to grips with the hard core problem of derelict land. The North-West Water Authority is bringing forward a major programme of investment in the interception and treatment of crude sewage flows to the Mersey estuary.

These investment programmes are being pursued in a volatile political climate. The temptation persists to achieve a short-term gain by returning to an expansionist strategy of peripheral growth. This would prejudice not only Merseyside's precious open land resources, but also the prospects for much needed physical regeneration in areas of acute social and economic deprivation.

Acknowledgements

The urban regeneration strategy was developed by the Planning Department of Merseyside County Council under the direction of Audrey M. Lees, formerly County Planning Officer and now Controller of Planning and Transportation, Greater London Council. The development of strategic policies for the environment was the particular responsibility of Dr. John Ritchie, now Director of Development, Merseyside Development Corporation. The author was privileged to work under their guidance from 1974–1980. Much of the source material was made available by the hard work of close colleagues in the Department, notably Michael Brummage, Richard Evans, Sally Kelly and Dr. Graham Parry. The brief description of the physical growth of Merseyside is freely adapted from an excellent account by Michael Chitty. Finally the author is grateful to Peter Wood, Director of Development and Planning, Merseyside County Council, for permission to reproduce material prepared within his Department.

Chapter 8

THE WOODLAND RESOURCE: MANAGEMENT AND USE

PAMELA M. BERRY and ROBERT A. PULLAN

Woodlands have always been regarded as a resource, but during the past twenty years there has been a significant change in the perception of smaller woodlands by both government agencies and private organizations. The Countryside Act, 1968, the Town and Country Planning Act, 1971, and the White Paper on Forest Policy, 1972, led to reappraisals of the future roles and importance of woodlands by such bodies as the Timber Growers Association, the Nature Conservancy, the Countryside Commission, the Country Landowners Association and the Forestry Commission. As a result there has been renewed interest in woods as a source of locally used timber, as shelter for grazing animals, for the rearing and shooting of game animals and for visual amenity, all of which are traditional uses. In addition, woods have become more important for ecosystems and species conservation, for recreational use and as components of landscapes. The last of these roles is especially important in Merseyside as elsewhere, for it requires that woodlands provide varied social benefits not only for their owners, as in the past, but also for many rural and urban residents.

However, the very varied nature of these woodland roles has resulted increasingly in conflicts of interests over existing and future land-uses. These conflicts are most complex in the peri-urban areas of the Metropolitan Counties, such as Merseyside, where both urban and rural needs must be considered. It is not uncommon for woods to be destroyed or fragmented during residential, civic or industrial developments and the associated expansion of the road, rail, motorway and power transmission line networks. Even where woods remain after urban developments, many seem destined to suffer total neglect and ultimate dereliction. In the peri-urban zone there is a great need, as well as scope, for formal and informal recreational facilities. At the same time the viability of agricultural enterprises must be maintained. Thus, in order to ensure that sound decisions about the existence and role of woodlands are taken, information is required about the characteristics and history of each wood. Merseyside is fortunate in having two recent major studies of its woods (Roberts, 1974; Berry, 1980), and it is from these that much of the information presented in this chapter is derived. There are 679 woods larger than 0.2 hectares in Merseyside today, 74% of which are less than two hectares. Few are located within the built up area, and the peri-urban woods are irregularly distributed (Fig. 8.1).

Woodland history

Documentary evidence suggests that for several centuries before 1800 there were very few woods in Merseyside. Land suitable for farming had been cleared and enclosed by the early eighteenth century (Elliott, 1973), and grazing, burning and wood collection maintained the sandy heaths and peaty mosslands in a treeless state. A few small woods were located near the long-established country houses (Burdett, 1777; Yates, 1786) and in the steep-sided valleys in Wirral (Greenwood, 1819). The increasing prosperity and growth of Liverpool, Birkenhead and St. Helens during the next fifty years was accompanied by the planting of many new woods, initially within the parklands of existing estates (Fig. 8.2), and then throughout the estate farmlands, newly-drained mosslands and heaths (Fig. 8.3); (see also Table 7.7). Between 1840 and 1875 new country estates with parklands and new

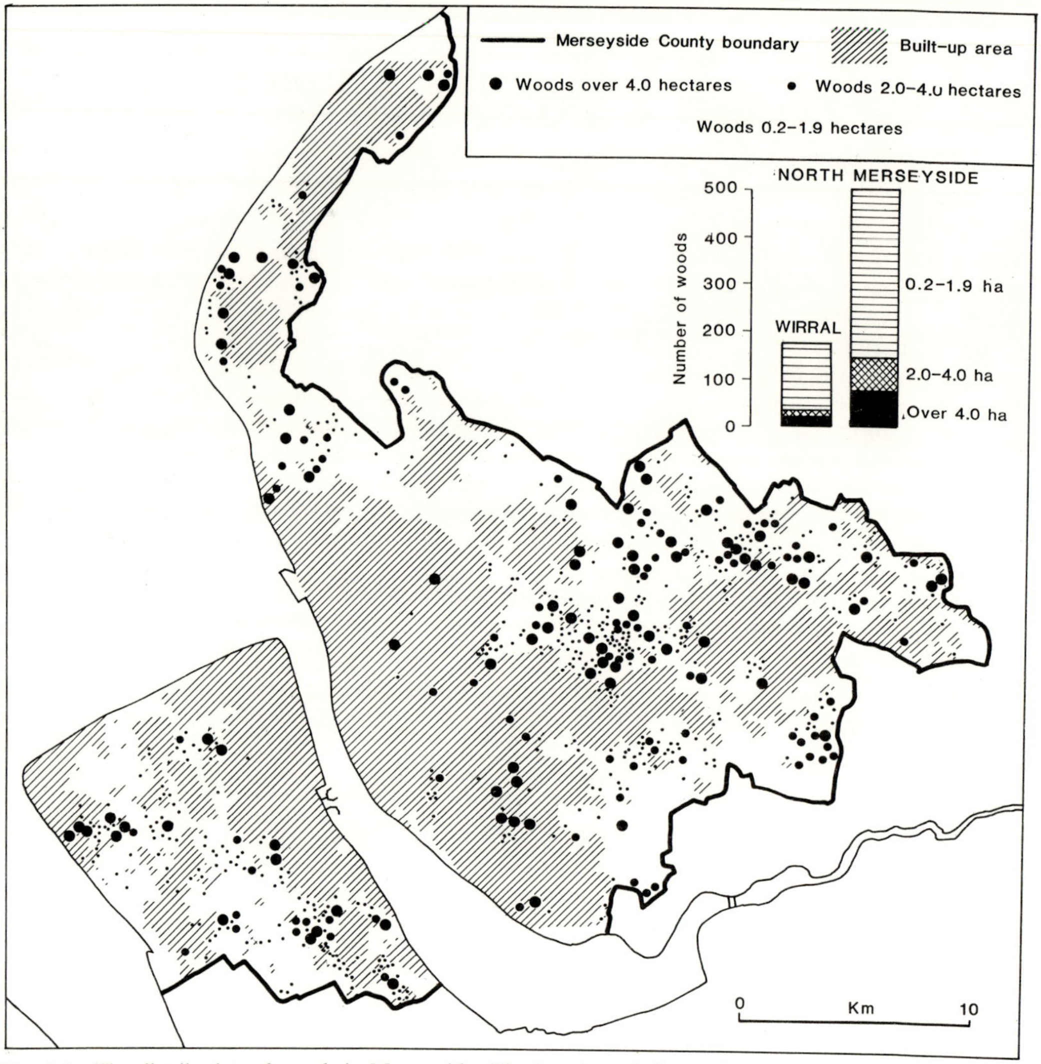

Fig. 8.1 The distribution of woods in Merseyside. The location of all woods over 0.2 hectares is shown in relation to the urban areas (see Fig. 8.6 for locations)

Fig. 8.2 (opposite) Woodlands on the Halsnead Estate. The parkland of Halsnead was transformed by the planting of woods, shelterbelts and single specimen trees between 1810 and 1840. Possibly only the Old Wood predates these plantings. There are many boundary woods, but the names of others indicate the close association with pheasant shooting and fox hunting. Estate planting accompanied the development of coal mining in the immediate vicinity, and reflected the growing interests in field sports in Victorian England. Woods were also planted in the surrounding farmlands. Today Halsnead Park has lost woodland to farming, to housing estates, to colliery buildings and to spoil tips. The colliery railway, power lines and, most recently, the motorway and its new feeder roads have fragmented the remaining woods (based upon the Ordnance Survey map with the permission of the Controller of Her Majesty's Stationery Office, Crown Copyright reserved)

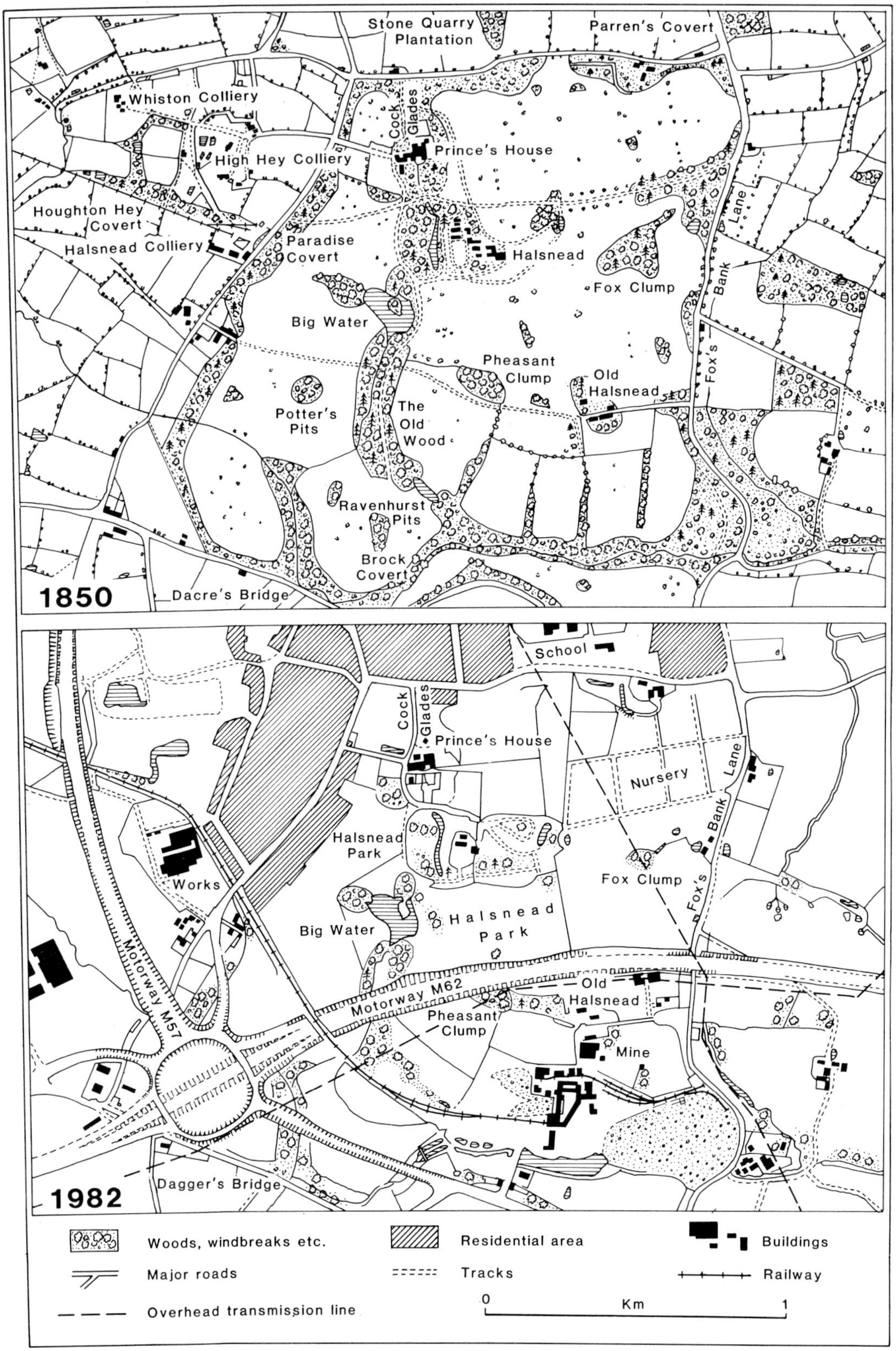
Stone Quarry Plantation
Parren's Covert
Whiston Colliery
Cock Glades
Prince's House
High Hey Colliery
Houghton Hey Covert
Halsnead Colliery
Paradise Covert
Halsnead
Fox Clump
Big Water
Pheasant Clump
Old Halsnead
Potter's Pits
The Old Wood
Fox's Bank Lane
Ravenhurst Pits
Brock Covert
1850
Dacre's Bridge
School
Cock Glades
Prince's House
Nursery
Fox's Bank Lane
Halsnead Park
Fox Clump
Works
Big Water
Halsnead Park
Motorway M57
Motorway M62
Old Halsnead
Pheasant Clump
Mine
Dagger's Bridge
1982
Woods, windbreaks etc.
Residential area
Buildings
Major roads
Tracks
Railway
Overhead transmission line
0
Km
1

woods were established throughout Merseyside (Fig. 8.4), whilst small woods were planted in civic parks. This process of woodland growth is well documented on successive editions of the Ordnance Survey maps. They record the establishment of 246 new woods between 1840 and 1910, forty of which were in Wirral. However, 156 woods were also destroyed on urban, industrial and farmland sites during the same period. For example, forty woods and shelterbelts were planted on the Garston Hall estate between 1800 and 1840, but most were destroyed completely or fragmented by 1900 through the development of the railway marshalling yards associated with Garston Docks. The remaining woods were destroyed in the next thirty years by residential developments. The net result was an increase in the number of woods in Merseyside from 455 to 505 during the period from 1840 to 1910, and the area of woodland rose from 1371 to 1651 hectares. The inter-war years brought little overall change for woodlands, but there was fragmentation of some larger woods. This resulted in a reduction of their area, but was more than matched by large plantations on the coastal dunes.

The fate of woodlands during the post-war period has varied. The private estate woods of Knowsley Park, Crosby Park, Ince Blundell and Thornton Manor remain virtually unchanged. A large number of the woods of Croxteth Park have passed into public ownership. Other estates have been sold for development however. Upton Manor estate is now completely urbanized, but modern planning control has preserved most of the woods (Fig. 8.4). Halsnead estate woods have, however, suffered loss and fragmentation from colliery, rail, motorway, power lines and residential developments (Fig. 8.2). Overall, eighty-five woods have been destroyed in Merseyside in the post-war period, 59 to housing, 14 to industrial plants, seven to the Liverpool airport extension and five to motorways. Fifty-three woods have been affected by fragmentation, and others have suffered partial losses through various developments. Twenty-five woods have been surrounded by urbanization, but still exist (Fig. 8.5).

Woodland characteristics

Woodlands cover less than five per cent of Merseyside. Since the national average is 8%, it is clear that woodland is poorly represented in the county, and this enhances the value of those woods which remain. The total area of woodland is about 3000 ha, and there are 679 woodlands with an area greater than 0.2 ha. Seventy-four per cent of these are less than two hectares, and there are only sixteen woods larger than twenty hectares. The distribution of woods (Fig. 8.1) has an irregular pattern which is related to the location of the urban area and country estates (Fig. 8.6). The larger woods are usually associated with sandstone ridges, dune sands and mosslands, and are located on boulder clay only on the largest country estates.

As far as can be ascertained all the woods have been planted or replanted during the past 150 years. Very many contain old trees from the original plantings which are now damaged or diseased, but many large fine trees remain. Less than twenty estate woods have been clear-felled and replanted in the past thirty years, and many smaller woods appear to have escaped the selective felling that was common in British woods during the two World Wars.

Twenty-three native broad-leaved tree species have been recorded in the woods, and these are commonly found in mixed stands. The oak (*Quercus robur*), the beech (*Fagus sylvatica*), the ash (*Fraxinus excelsior*), the elms (*Ulmus glabra*; *Ulmus procera*) and the birches (*Betula pendula*; *Betula pubescens*) occur individually in more than half the total woods. Most of the broad-leaved exotic species have a low frequency, and were planted as single specimens in amenity woods near large houses, as for example the evergreen oak (*Quercus ilex*), but the sweet chestnut (*Castanea sativa*), the horse chestnut (*Aesculus

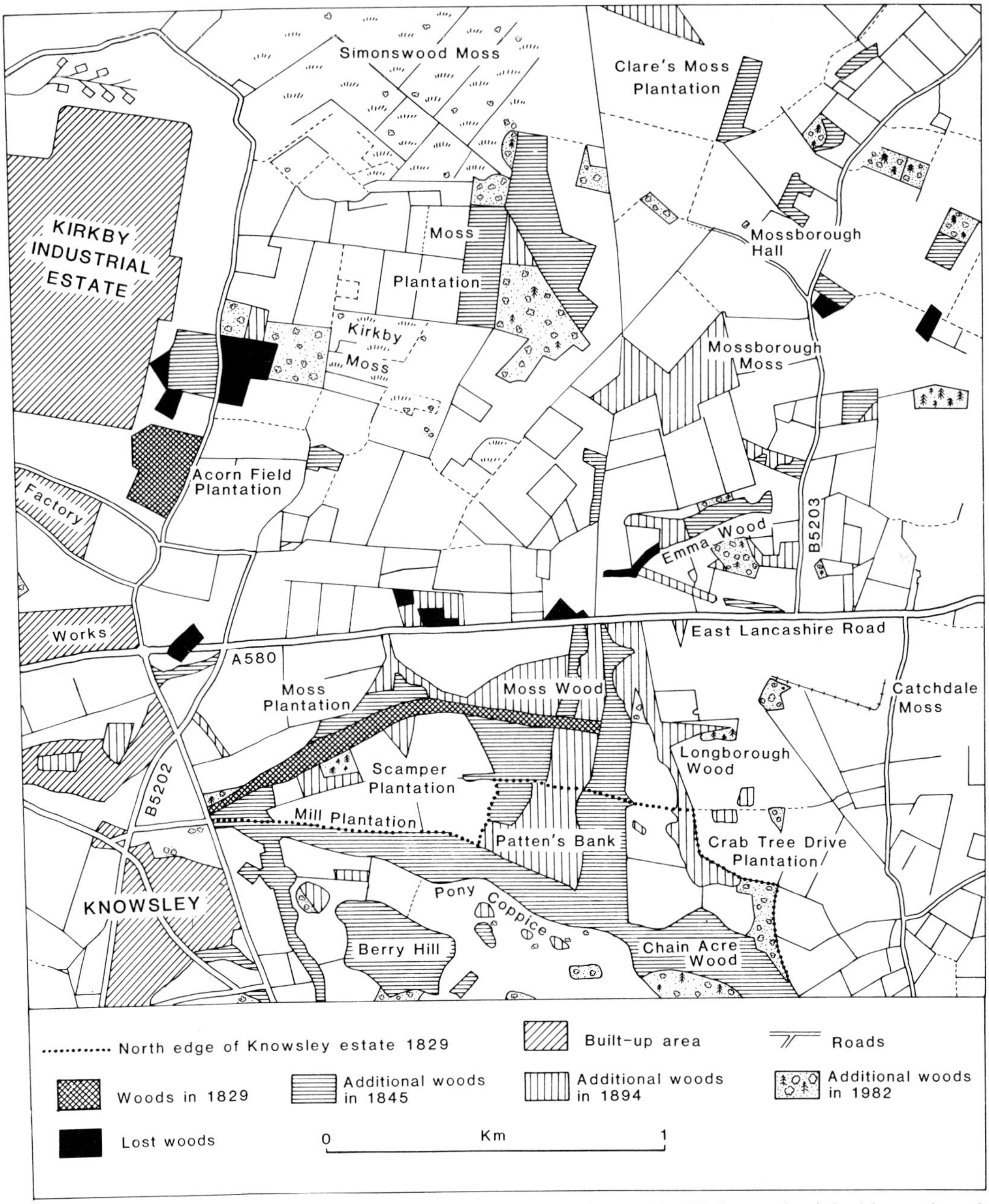

Fig. 8.3 Woodlands on the Knowsley Estate. The parkland of Knowsley Hall was planted with woods and landscaped by Lancelot Brown in 1775, but only two woods were recorded in the surrounding area in 1829. By 1845, however, boundary woods, plantations and coppice woods had been established on a north extension of the estate, and the first woods on drained mosslands near Simonswood had been planted. Subsequent woods were not confined to peat areas though these contain the largest woods. The present pattern of woods had become established by 1900, and subsequently only a few woods have been lost, mainly during the building of the East Lancashire Road

hippocastanum) and the Turkey oak (*Quercus cerris*) occur in at least twenty-five per cent of the woods, and may be locally common. Today by far the most common tree in many woods is the sycamore (*Acer pseudoplatanus*). This exotic was planted sparsely in many woods originally, but has regenerated freely and spread widely throughout the woods. It occurs in ninety per cent of all woods in Merseyside.

Many of the larger woods are coniferous, and pines were planted as single species stands. The native Scots pine (*Pinus sylvestris*) is found largely on sandstone ridges and on the Shirdley Hill sands, while the exotic Corsican pine (*Pinus nigra var. maritima*) occurs on the dunes. Scots pines were also planted in some estate woods amongst the broadleaved trees, as were European larches (*Larix decidua*). Self-seeded birches are commonly found in many woods today. Native understorey shrubs and small trees are not a common feature of the woods. The most widely distributed, hawthorn (*Crataegus monogyna*) and elder (*Sambucus nigra*), are found in over 60%, but holly (*Ilex aquifolium*) and hazel (*Corylus avellana*) in less than 20% of the woods. The exotic *Rhododendron ponticum* occurs in 60% of all woods, and frequently forms a dense cover. Twenty-four other exotic shrub species occur, all with a low frequency. Blackberry (*Rubus fruticosus agg.*) is found in 80% of the woods, and is abundant in many.

Over 200 species of flowering plants have been recorded in the field layers of Merseyside woods, but very few woods contain more than fifty of these. Indeed, 70% of the woods surveyed in North Merseyside contained less than twenty-one species. The woods on the sandstone ridges, the dune sands and the mosslands are floristically poor. Typical woodland species, such as the wood anemone (*Anemone nemorosa*), wood sorrel (*Oxalis acetosella*), wood millet (*Milium effusum*), dog's mercury (*Mercurialis perennis*) and ramsons (*Allium ursinum*), all have a frequency of less than 7% in North Merseyside, though the bluebell (*Endymion non-scriptus*), which has greater ability to persist after woodland is cleared, is found in 30% of the woods. Species which might be indicators of primary woodland sites* are very rare. Weed species, derived from non-woodland sites and often introduced into the woods by man or animals, are widely distributed, and frequently common. These characteristics confirm the documentary evidence for the secondary nature of most of the woods.

Woodland ownership

Before the early nineteenth century the woods were owned by country gentry and farmers (see Table 7.7). This pattern of private ownership continued until the mid nineteenth century, though many small estates were bought or created by wealthy citizens from the

*Primary woodland derives directly from fragments of the prehistoric forest which were brought into some degree of management by man without ever having been cleared of trees. Secondary woodland consists of woods established by man on areas which in the historical period were arable or pasture lands, heaths, moors, bogs or dunes.

Fig. 8.4 (opposite) Woodlands in North Wirral. The woodlands of Arrowe Park were established on boulder clay farmlands over a period of fifty years after the estate lands had been acquired by a wealthy Liverpool warehouse owner in 1835. The park was bought by Birkenhead Council for public use in 1927 and there have been very few changes to the woodlands in subsequent years. The woodlands of Upton Manor were largely planted after 1857, when the estate was established by a shipping magnate. Residential and motorway developments have engulfed the estate but most of the woodlands remain, though some have been reduced in size. The woodlands of the Vyner Estate on Bidston Hill were established on heathland before 1876. They were purchased as a 'lung' for Birkenhead after 1893. Three woods have been lost south of Arrowe Park to residential developments, but the one remaining, Harrock Wood, was given to the National Trust in 1927. This is probably a primary woodland site in an incised Valley, but is now suffering from vandalism, horse riding and overuse. Prenton Wood, another valley wood, is now derelict

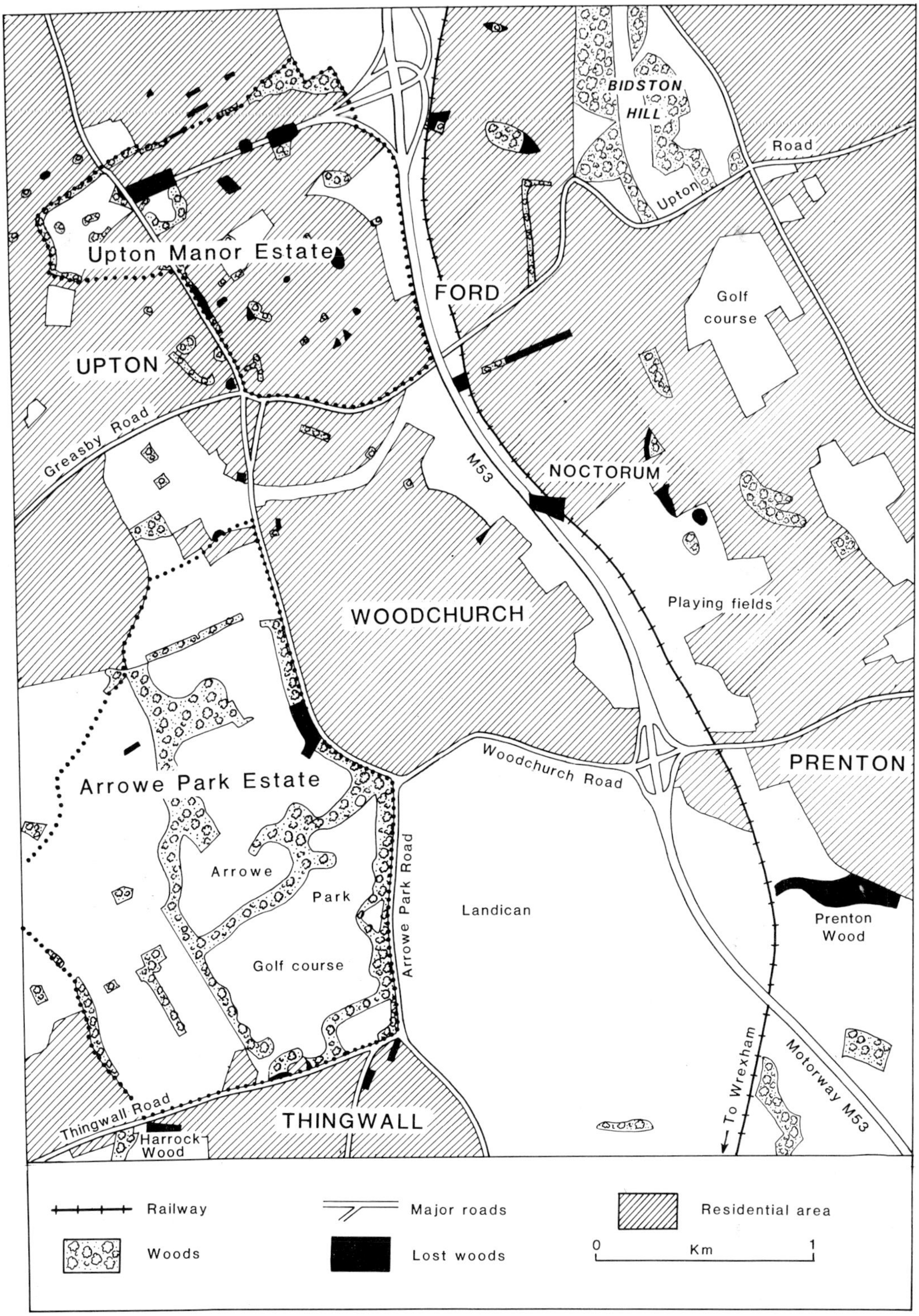

BIDSTON HILL
Upton Road
Upton Manor Estate
FORD
UPTON
Golf course
Greasby Road
M53
NOCTORUM
Playing fields
WOODCHURCH
Woodchurch Road
PRENTON
Arrowe Park Estate
Arrowe Park Golf course
Arrowe Park Road
Landican
Prenton Wood
To Wrexham
Motorway M53
Thingwall Road
THINGWALL
Harrock Wood
Railway
Major roads
Residential area
Woods
Lost woods
0 Km 1

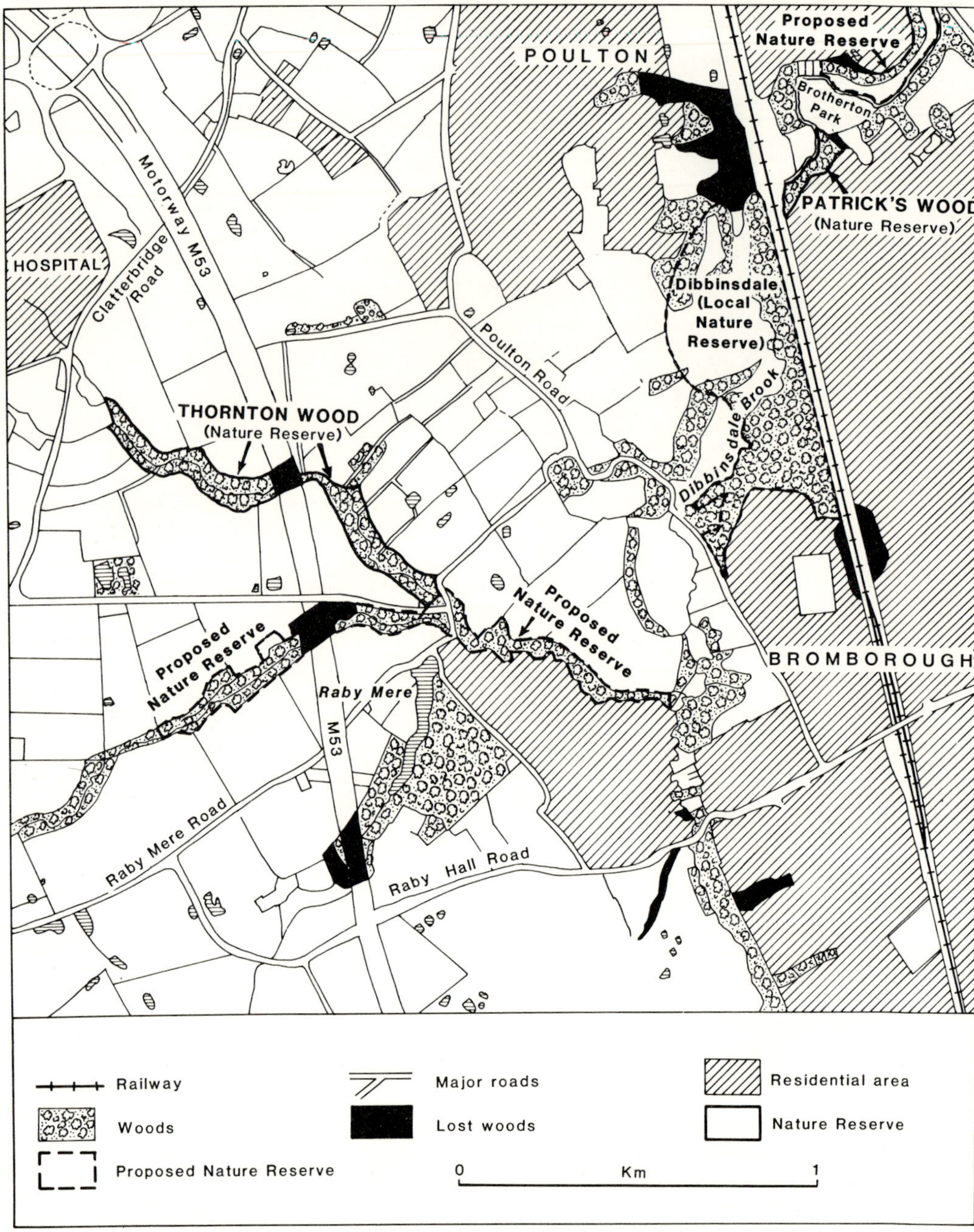

Fig. 8.5 Woodlands in Dibbinsdale, South Wirral. The woodlands escaped clearance owing to their location on steep valley sides, but recent encroachment by residential developments has increased the threat to these primary woods. Fragmentation has occurred initially as a result of some farm clearance, and then by the railway (1840), roads and by the motorway (1972). One wood was destroyed by the creation of a refuse tip near Poulton, the site of which has now been rehabilitated for playing fields. These woods are probably the most important in Merseyside from the point of view of their diverse flora and fauna, and existing and proposed conservation designations are shown. The area is subject, however, to trespass and some vandalism. Implementation of the proposed management plan with some measure of wardening is badly needed.

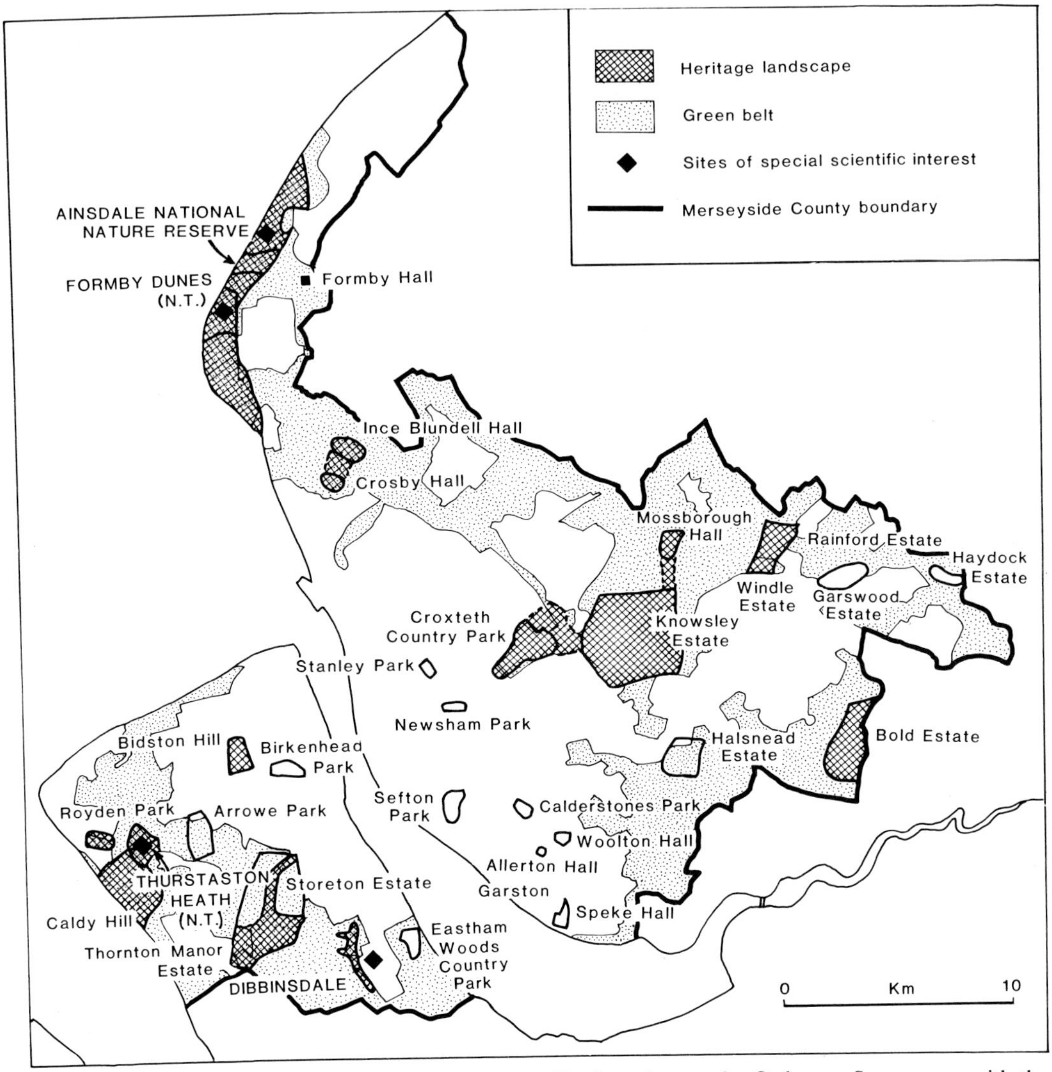

Fig. 8.6 Protected areas containing woods in Merseyside (based upon the Ordnance Survey map with the permission of the Controller of Her Majesty's Stationery Office, Crown Copyright reserved)

expanding towns. Public ownership of woods began with those planted for amenity in the newly laid out park in Birkenhead, opened in 1847. Subsequently new parks were established, as for example Sefton Park (1872), and small estates with woods were acquired by the civic authorities. By the end of the century demand for informal recreation in public open space led to the purchase of Bidston Woods from the Vyner estate (from 1893) and this process of acquisition has continued through the twentieth century as Arrowe Park (1927), Royden Park (1961) and Croxteth Park (1974) came into public ownership. Woods have also been acquired by institutions, and are found in the grounds of public buildings such as schools and hospitals. In recent years the purchase of land for council housing and industrial estates has brought more woods into public ownership.

Increasing urbanization during the past thirty years has resulted in woods being

TABLE 8.1 *Ownership of woods in Merseyside, 1976*

Public		Private	
Local Authorities	105	Estates	169
National Trust	7	Farmers and Individuals	167
Nature Conservancy	3	Industry	7
		Estate Agents	10
Totals	115		353

Information has not been collected for 202 woods (smaller than two hectares) on North Merseyside, but it is believed that the majority of these are owned by farmers, private individuals or large private estates. At the time of writing, in August 1981, two woods in Wirral had been purchased by the Cheshire Nature Conservation Trust from private owners.

Source: Roberts, 1974; Berry, 1980.

purchased by estate agents and property developers and by industry through the purchase of "green field" sites for factories. Conservation organizations are also increasing the number of woods they own (Table 8.1). Private owners, however, still govern the destinies of over 500 woods in Merseyside.

Woodland uses

With few exceptions, Merseyside woods were planted originally on estates for visual amenity, social prestige, the supply of estate timber, as a capital investment, or in association with the development of game shooting and, more rarely, fox hunting (Fig. 8.2). Today many of the woods have different uses resulting from new social and economic pressures, changes in ownership and modifications in the characteristics of the woods. In particular, the growing need for additional recreational opportunities for urban dwellers on Merseyside has led to the establishment of the peri-urban Country Parks of Croxteth (1981) and Eastham Woods (1970). In contrast, the parklands of the Bold and Haydock estates are now highly productive farmlands, and, though the farmers may regard the woodland as unnecessary and would wish to increase their arable acreage, Merseyside County Council (1976) regards these areas of woods and arable fields as having considerable importance because "of the excellence of the landscape" as seen from the motorways (the M6 and the M62), and because the woods made other more intrusive elements, such as cooling towers, chimneys and mines, "not unattractive" in this framework. The Bold estate has now been declared a Heritage Landscape.

Information on the use of woods for 1974–6 (Table 8.2) indicates that one of the most common traditional uses is for visual amenity. Woods in urban parks and most woods in estate parklands were planted for visual amenity, and have kept this use today (Plate 8.1). Many are also used for recreation. In recent years the changing geography of Merseyside has given certain woods an enhanced amenity value. This is particularly true of woods now surrounded by private and public housing developments. Examples are found in Upton (Fig. 8.4, Plate 8.2) and near Bromborough (Fig. 8.5).

Woods used for shooting are particularly well represented in North Merseyside, and there has been continuity of their original use on the larger estates (Plate 8.3). Most (73%) of these woods are larger than two hectares, and they contain mixed tree species. The original plantings of exotic shrubs, especially rhododendron, for game protection persist in many such woods. Game coverts on the large private estates such as Thornton Manor (Lord Leverhulme) and Knowsley Park (Lord Derby) are well managed, but smaller woods on farmlands which are also used for shooting are usually neglected. Most of the

Plate 8.1 Part of the mixed deciduous woodland planted along the southern boundary of the Knowsley estate. These woods have been fragmented by the M57, but the woods to the right of the motorway are important as they separate it from a housing estate. Part of the wood (foreground right) has become derelict as a result of motorway construction (G.R. 435 932 to E)

Plate 8.2 Mixed deciduous-coniferous woodlands in the Fender Valley, Moreton, Wirral. These woods formed part of the northern boundary of Upton Manor Estate (Fig. 8.4), and were planted about 1860. They now lie between a large council housing estate, the M53 and the Upton spur and form part of a public open space including the adjacent grassland. Walking, cycling and horse riding are a feature of the uses of these woods, but they are being increasingly subject to vandalism. In the far distance (right) are the public woodlands on the sandstone of Bidston Hill (G.R. 265 892 to ENE)

TABLE 8.2 *The use of woodlands in Merseyside, 1974–1976*

Use	Number of Woods		
	Wirral	North Merseyside	Total
Major uses			
Environmental protection	0	22	22
Nature conservation	10	5	15
Game management	19	67	86
Grazing	28	21	49
Timber production	0	17	17
Recreation	67	72	139
Visual amenity	26	70	96
No use	25	54	79
Ancillary uses			
Vandalism to trees	11	29	40
Refuse disposal	73	52	125

Note that many woods have two or three uses in either part or the whole of the wood.

Access to twelve woods in Wirral was not granted and so their use was not ascertained. Information for 202 woods of less than two hectares was not collected for North Merseyside.

Source: Roberts and Burnett (1976).

woods associated with game shooting are located far from roads and footpaths, and so have a long history of protection from disturbance. Though nearly all are secondary woodlands, their considerable age has resulted in a great diversity of plant and animal species to the extent that many may be considered important Merseyside biotic reserves. Such woods may also be used for timber production as this is compatible with game management. Woods are no longer used for fox hunting. The use of woodlands by farm animals for grazing and shelter is incompatible with other uses apart from environmental protection. Some small woods on dune sand, peat and boulder clay are used for these purposes. The designation of woods for environmental protection applies to the establishment of pine woods on dune sands at Formby and Ainsdale. These were established after 1915 to prevent sand blowing on to first-class arable land. Though some linear woods may have been planted as shelterbelts on estates, most of them appear to be visual indicators of estate boundaries.

Merseyside woods contain a considerable volume of mainly hardwood timber in the form of large mature trees, but timber production is not an important use of woodlands. The small size of most of the woods, the wide range of species present, and the diversity of ownership prevents commercial exploitation. Equally important, however, are other considerations which reduce the motivation of owners to utilize their woodland resources for timber. All seventeen woods established for timber production are on the Knowsley estate. Though broad-leaved species were commonly planted in these woods before 1901, conifers have been more extensively used during the last thirty years.

Nature Conservation is very poorly represented as a use, especially in North Merseyside. Since nearly all the woods have been recently established, they do not contain woodland species of plants and animals which are rare in either a regional or national context. However the pine woods planted on sand dunes are now important in conserving the dune habitats and their flora and fauna. Two of Britain's rarest animals, the sand lizard (*Lacerta agilis*) and the natterjack toad (*Bufo calamita*), live in these dunes which are

Plate 8.3 Mixed deciduous woodlands on reclaimed mossland, Rainford. These woods form part of the Mossborough Hall Estate (Fig. 8.3), and are managed today for pheasant cover. They were planted in the early years of this century on what is today regarded as Class 1 farmland. The younger woods in the far distance (right) are conifers planted on the edge of Reed's Moss (G.R. 470 992 to E)

Plate 8.4 Mixed deciduous woodland on the steep west-facing slope of the Dibbinsdale Valley, Bromborough. This mature woodland occupies what is believed to be a primary site, though many of the trees may have been planted. The floodplain contains well-grown willows. This part of the valley is designated as a local nature reserve (Fig. 8.5). Some young standard trees have been planted (middle right) (G.R. 338 823 to NE)

threatened by urban developments, recreational pressures and sand extraction. Protection is now afforded by the Ainsdale National Nature Reserve (461 ha), declared in 1965, and the adjacent Site of Special Scientific Interest (S.S.S.I.) in the Formby dunes (478 ha), both of which contain some woodland.

Woodlands are also important habitats in the Thurstaston Common with Royden Park S.S.S.I. (113 ha). These diverse estate plantations and recent birch and pine woods, which have regenerated naturally in heathland, are important nesting sites and roosts for over-wintering birds. They also contain badgers (*Meles meles*) which are very rare in Merseyside, and red squirrels (*Sciurus vulgaris*), which are also found in National Trust woodlands at Formby.

Probably the most important woods from the point of view of their intrinsic flora and fauna are those in the valleys of the Clatter and Dibbinsdale brooks near Bromborough (Fig. 8.5). These may be primary woodland sites, and a large area was designated a S.S.S.I. in 1979 (Plate 8.4). Two woods, one of which is crossed by a motorway, are designated Nature Reserves under the management of the Cheshire Conservation Trust. They contain typical native woodland species such as the golden saxifrage (*Chrysosplenium oppositifolium*) and dog's mercury (*Mercurialis perennis*). In North Merseyside, several estate woods at Croxteth, Ince Blundell and Crosby are known to have an interesting flora, and may also be modified primary woods, but these have not yet been afforded special conservation status.

Today, recreation is the most important single use for woods in Merseyside. Authorized public access is available to thirty-nine woods in Wirral and to seventy-two in North Merseyside. Recreation is largely in the form of walking, but horse, cycle and motorcycle riding are also found. There is access for vehicles to some woods in Knowsley Safari Park. Woods used for recreation are mainly in public or institutional ownership though some are found on golf courses, private housing estates and, more rarely, where public footpaths pass through private woods. Many were formerly estate woods (Plate 8.2) and a few occur in urban parks (Plate 8.5). They usually have only a few plant species in the field and shrub layers, but contain many exotic tree species. Unauthorized access (trespass) has been recorded as frequent in thirty-six woods in Wirral and one hundred and seven woods in North Merseyside. These woods are located close to residential areas or country roads.

A considerable number of woods are identified as having no obvious use, but clearly these woods all have potential uses unless they are derelict (Plate 8.6). Dereliction implies no management and the gradual destruction through pollution and vandalism of the trees in a wood, as for example Acorn Field Plantation near Kirkby Industrial Estate (Fig. 8.3).

Thus whilst woods continue to be used in traditional ways, their current importance lies in the enhanced perception of their amenity value and in the great increase in their use for recreation. This conflicts in part with the traditional uses, but of greater significance are the changes to the character of the woods which new uses may bring. These in turn give rise to a need for woodland management either to be introduced for the first time or to be changed in response to new uses.

Woodland today: natural changes

More than 80% of the woods surveyed on Merseyside contain large mature trees, but, for a variety of reasons, 30% had no regeneration recorded in the form of seedlings or saplings. However many woods do have a dense, if often patchy, understorey created by regenerating trees, and these will ensure a measure of continuity as older trees die. However, the character of the woodland is changing as only a few species are successful. Thus the English oak is regenerating in over 40% of North Merseyside woods, but the birch (in 22%) and beech (in 15%) are the only other large trees which are successful.

Plate 8.5 Mixed deciduous woodlands in Birkenhead Park. These small irregular woods were planted soon after the opening in 1847 of this the first civic park in England. They contain many exotic species and were planted on the hummocky spoil created by the excavation of a large lake. The elm (centre right) is affected by Dutch elm disease. Some replacement of trees has taken place (left). The woods have a grassy understorey and there is unrestricted access for walkers. Some tarred paths pass through the woods (G.R. 309 892 to E)

Plate 8.6 A derelict wood located in a recent council estate at Cantril Farm, between Croxteth and Knowsley estates. Though fenced, this predominantly oak woodland has suffered much vandalism and the deaths of many trees. There is however vigorous regrowth of sycamore saplings and coppice from some damaged trees (G.R. 425 936 to W)

Birch is particularly evident in the woods on sandstone ridges, and is forming dense new woods on heaths and mosslands and in woods where the canopy has been opened up. Pines are not generally successful except where they are colonizing heathland along with birches, but regular burning of such areas kills the pine seedlings whilst allowing the birch to coppice. The most successful tree, however, is the exotic sycamore which is regenerating, often in profusion, in half the woods in Merseyside. This fast-growing species is altering the overall composition of many woods, and as such may be regarded as a weed. Other exotics, such as the Turkey oak, have limited regeneration success, though greater than the native ash or elm.

Most of the mature woodlands contain dying or dead trees. The number of such trees has increased greatly during the past ten years through the increasing incidence of Dutch elm disease. Today many elms, especially the English elm, have died or are dying in the woodlands, but numerous trees are still unaffected, especially wych elms, and sucker regeneration from the base of many dying trees suggests that this species might survive. Little is known about the distributions and populations of rodents, seed eating birds and other animals which could affect the capacity of trees to regenerate. It is believed, however, that a marked increase in the number of grey squirrels (*Sciurus carolinensis*) has resulted in greater damage to young trees and seedlings and greater consumption of certain tree seeds.

The smaller native trees such as holly, hawthorn and elder regenerate freely in Merseyside woods, but are never very common. A few of the exotic shrubs are known to regenerate from seeds or root suckers, but many are of very local distribution and little importance overall. This cannot be said about the rhododendron however for, as elsewhere in western Britain, it has seeded freely, and forms a dense thicket understorey in many woods where it effectively excludes the field layer plants formerly growing there.

Woodland today: man-induced changes

Man brings changes to woodland through management, and through the ways he uses woods. Some of the most profound changes result from recreational use and in particular through trampling. This may destroy plants along paths, cause the compaction or, in wet weather, puddling of the surface soil, whilst less frequent use may alter floristic composition of the field layer. Changes are also induced by eutrophication along well-used paths. Such changes are best seen in boulder clay woods, whilst soil erosion may be started on thin soils of the sandstone ridge woods and on the steep slopes of valley woods. Horse riding and grazing are particularly damaging in woods, similarly affecting the soil and eliminating certain field and shrub layer species, preventing regeneration of trees and causing tree damage through bark stripping and rubbing.

Vandalism consists of damage to trees by fires lit at their bases, bark cutting and stripping, branch breaking and even illegal felling. Such damage often leads to the death of a tree, as it becomes more susceptible to disease and wind blow. Some vandalism may result from recreational activities such as rope swinging and tree climbing. Indeed it seems, not surprisingly, to be most common in woods within or near to urban areas, especially housing estates (Plate 8.5). Ten per cent of woods with recorded vandalism in North Merseyside can now be regarded as derelict.

Refuse dumping is not confined to the urban area (Table 8.2). It usually affects only a small part of a wood, but detracts from its amenity and recreational value. Old cars, drums, cans and bottles are common, and may be hazardous to people and animals. Biodegradable refuse is also commonly found, and, though this will eventually disappear, it can lead to the smothering of existing field layer plants, and encourage the establishment of weed species through eutrophication and the introduction of seeds and plants in the

TABLE 8.3 *Types of woodland management in Merseyside, 1974–1976*

Activity	Number of woods		
	Wirral	North Merseyside	Total
Thinning	5	13	18
Underplanting	4	2	6
Clear felling	3	1	4
Replanting	15	33	48
No management			
Mature woods	134	282	416
Derelict woods	9	9	18

Information for 202 woods of less than two hectares was not collected for North Merseyside.
Source: Roberts and Burnett (1976).

refuse. Stinging nettle (*Urtica dioica*) and goose grass (*Galium aparine*) are common associates of refuse in woods in Merseyside.

Other man-induced changes may result from management decisions. Felling and replanting with either a single species or different associated species, underplanting with a new species and drainage, especially on mosslands and some boulder clay woods, have all had an impact. Management in amenity woods may involve the removal and replacement of dead or dying trees. In Eastham Woods Country Park, for example, there has been some planting of new exotic and native trees and shrubs for both amenity enhancement and general replacement. The effects of all such changes are direct on the species composition of the wood, and will lead to changes in the field and shrub layers. Management that involves the removal of undesirable trees, such as the sycamore and birch, is not common.

Some of the major types of management are given in Table 8.3. Since 1976 woodland management has been introduced in Croxteth Country Park and in certain Local Authority-owned woods as those on Bidston Hill, but, despite the necessity for some degree of management to control natural and man-induced changes, very few woods in Merseyside receive such attention. Those that do are the larger estate woods which are managed by the Forestry Commission under the Dedication Scheme, the objectives of which were altered in 1974 to make forms of management other than for timber production acceptable. More recently the Small Woods Scheme, introduced in 1977 (Forestry Commission, 1978), was designed to encourage the restocking of small woods between one-quarter and ten hectares in area, but the effect of this measure and that of grants from the Countryside Commission in Merseyside cannot yet be assessed.

Woodland in the future

In the past the woodland has been protected in various ways. Most of it was planted on estates, and was retained by reason of its use for game, timber or amenity. In the twentieth century, however, many estates have been divided into smaller farm units, and the woods have become vulnerable to removal during agricultural or urban developments. Two legislative measures, Green Belts and Tree Preservation Orders, exist to protect woodland, but vary in their effectiveness.

The Green Belt has not yet been formally approved but at the time of writing the final plan was at the consultative stage (Chapter 7, p. 99). It almost surrounds the urban area, and covers 77% of the woods (Figs. 8.1 and 8.6). Although its main purpose is to restrict urban expansion, it could stifle improvements in the countryside even though it may be used more for recreational purposes (North West Joint Planning Team, 1973, p. 12). The majority of the woods outside the Green Belt are protected by Tree Preservation Orders (T.P.O.s) or are in the hands of Local Authorities, so that few woods have no explicit form of protection. T.P.O.s are served by the Local Planning Authority. It is an offence to damage or destroy designated trees without the Authority's consent, although exceptions are made for pylon and motorway construction. The effectiveness of T.P.O.s is questionable on two counts. They tend to stultify any management initiative, as the County Planning Officer recognizes for the open countryside and on the large estates, but suggests that alternative safeguards exist through consultation with the Forestry Commission with respect to Felling Licences. Furthermore, T.P.O.s do not seem to ensure the survival of a wood. On North Merseyside six woods under T.P.O.s have been fragmented and a further six decreased in area due to motorway development, while on the Wirral twenty-nine of the thirty-four woods added since 1954 due to fragmentation were originally covered by T.P.O.s.

There are no effective legislative measures to ensure the continued existence of woodlands, and yet they are a valuable resource in the County for they can be used for a variety of purposes. Their future lies not so much in the production of timber, or in shooting which is an exclusive activity, or in conservation as most of the woods are ecologically poor, but rather in their amenity and recreational potential. One aim of the County Council is to increase opportunities for countryside recreation, especially in areas accessible from the urban area, and Croxteth and Eastham Woods Country Parks are scheduled for further recreational development. The use made of existing facilities and the frequency of trespass suggest that woodland is successful in meeting many of the demands of outdoor recreation. However, silviculture management must be established to control natural and man-made changes which would lead otherwise to a decline in the value of the woodland and to its eventual clearance. Woodland owners need both practical and financial help with management, and, if this is done, then the woods will remain a valuable resource even to the extent of making an important contribution to local timber production.

The future for woods has been clearly laid down in the Merseyside Structure Plan. This envisages the retention and management of existing woods, and the planting of new woods in certain situations. Ten Heritage Landscapes where changes are to be minimized have been identified and include the estate lands at Knowsley, Rainford, Ince Blundell, Bold and Thornton Manor (Fig. 8.6). Protection of specific woods will also be extended if proposals are implemented for Local Nature Reserves in Croxteth Park and within the Ainsdale sand dunes, and a management scheme for Dibbinsdale valley includes proposals for three new Nature Reserves.

Though tree planting in the urban area has increased greatly in recent years, especially in inner city areas in programmes of the Inner City Partnership Scheme, few areas are large enough to be called woods. Yet there will be opportunities for more extensive planting of derelict land near railways and collieries, and special consideration is to be given to the restoration of landscapes on the North Wirral plain and along existing motorway corridors. Overall, policy aims to resist further losses of woods and to encourage the planting and better management of small woods. It needs to be pursued vigorously, for a combination of protection and management of woods is necessary if the quality and quantity of the woodland resource are to be maintained.

Chapter 9

THE EXPLOITATION OF MINERAL RESOURCES

D. K. CHESTER

The environmental issues

Minerals and their exploitation are an important aspect of the economic geography of Merseyside. Production has an annual value of over £30 m, and provides employment for more than 4000 people (Merseyside County Council, 1979E). Within Merseyside, there are minerals whose exploitation is of national importance. They include foundry moulding sand near Southport and glass sand which is extensively worked from an area lying to the east of Kirkby and to the north of St. Helens (Elton, 1973; Merseyside County Council, 1979E, 1980). However, the winning of minerals is as much an environmental issue as it is an economic one, for the legacy of abandoned workings means that both the North West Economic Planning Region in general and Merseyside in particular have high proportions of land officially classified as derelict, contributing to a poor image of the area and probably acting as a strong deterrent to new industrial development. In addition, much of the land currently being worked for minerals or used for the disposal of waste produced by mineral development falls outside the official definition of derelict land. Using a more comprehensive definition the Remote Sensing Unit of Aston University concluded in a survey carried out in 1974 that there were 3789 hectares of derelict and despoiled land, slightly over 11% of which was associated with past and present-day mineral working, a figure that rises to 31% in St. Helens Metropolitan Borough. At the same date official estimates suggested that only about 530 ha were derelict in the whole county (Merseyside County Council, 1979F).

Mineral extraction can directly affect the area from which it comes. In the case of moulding sand from the foreshore in the vicinity of Southport (Fig. 9.1) it has been known since 1911 that the commercial extraction of sand from beach environments may adversely affect the stability and protective functions of the foreshore, since the capacity of a beach to change in profile in response to marine processes makes it the optimal form of coastal defence. Furthermore, the foreshore at Southport has high amenity value, indirectly supporting much employment in the tourist industry. In this case the planning dilemma is clear: to provide a supply of a mineral of national importance while at the same time seeking to minimize short-term effects on amenity as extraction progresses and to prevent long-term coastal deterioration.

In the main area of extraction of glass sand (Fig. 9.1) the land between Kirkby and St. Helens is of Grade 1 agricultural potential, and, in spite of inevitable short-term disruption, the consensus view is that little or no long-term decline in fertility need occur (Elton, 1973). This is in part a consequence of the ease of working with the glass or silica sand lying beneath only about 0.3 m of topsoil (Taylor, 1967), but the diligence of the extraction companies, particularly Pilkington Brothers Ltd. of St. Helens, has also meant that an acceptable standard of land reclamation has been achieved. Indeed Elton's study of opencast reclamation concluded that farmers were able to find solutions to any temporary problems by adapting existing farming techniques and cropping patterns. The main environmental issue in relation to the working of silica sand lies elsewhere, and concerns the sterilization of silica sand deposits by other land uses. Taylor (1967) calculated that in 1966 some 20% of the known deposits of silica sand had been sterilized by urban and industrial development, making its future extraction impossible. Since the mid

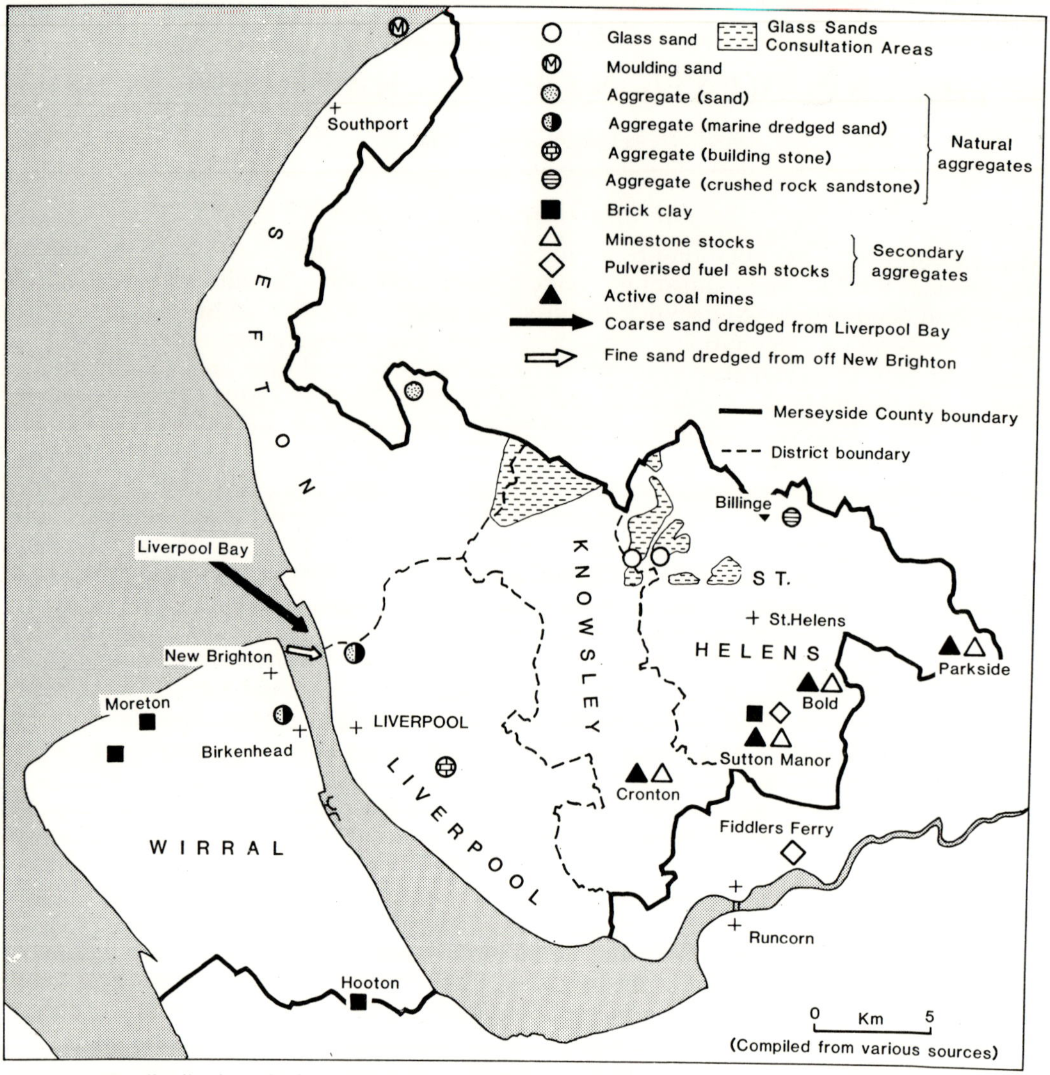

Fig. 9.1 The distribution of mineral extraction, 1980

nineteen-sixties, however, the position has improved. Pressure on these silica sand deposits is now less severe as a result of the partial substitution of sands from the Chelford area of Cheshire in certain types of glass. In addition, certain areas have been designated as Glass Sands Consultation Areas (Fig. 9.1). In these areas discussions take place between County planning officers and the companies to ensure that extraction is carried out before land is developed for other purposes (Merseyside County Council, 1979F, 1980). Unfortunately at present these Consultation Areas do not cover all known sources of potentially workable silica sand.

The coal industry, the oldest established major extractive industry in the County, is still the most important in terms of both employment and value of production in spite of major contraction over the last thirty years. It involves all the environmental problems already

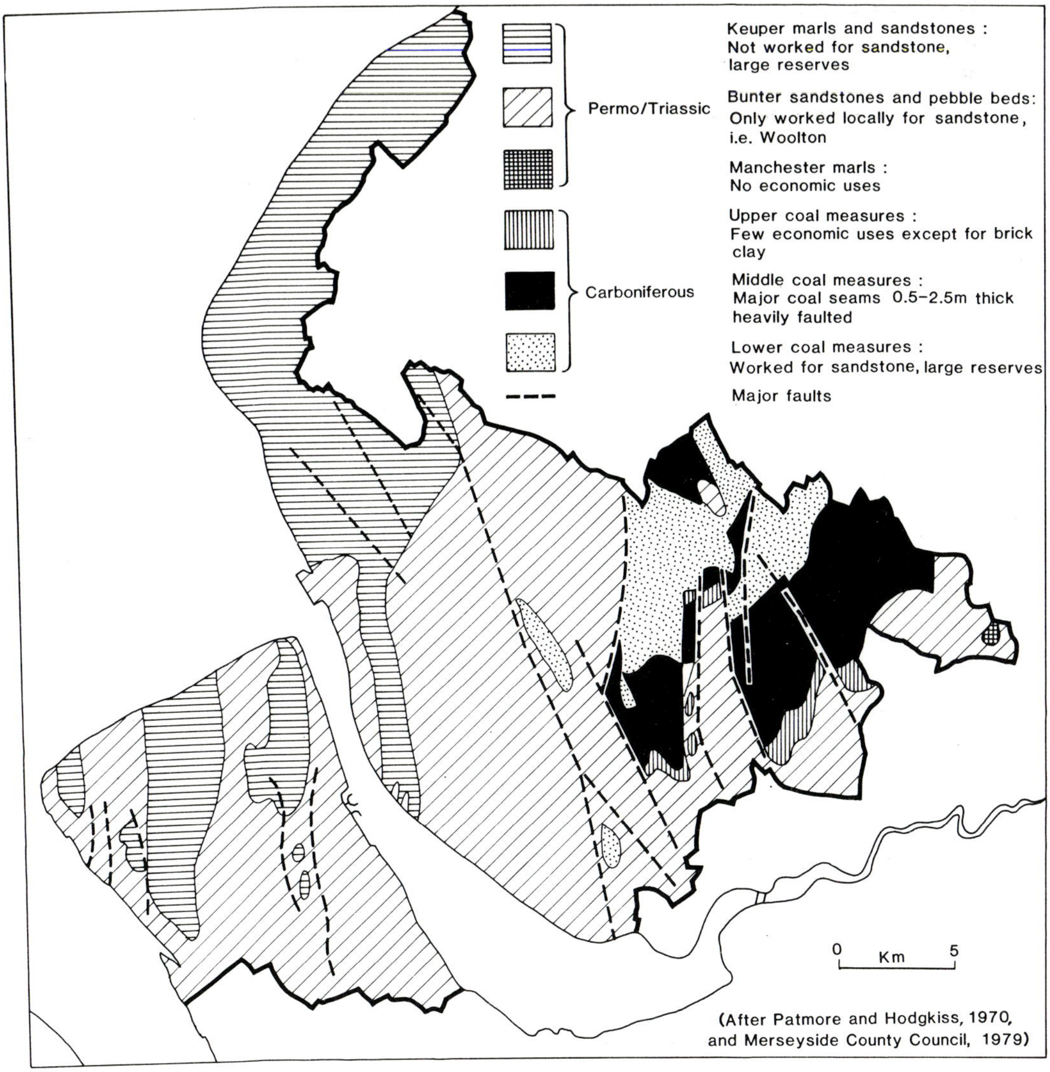

Fig. 9.2 Economic aspects of the solid geology of Merseyside

mentioned, including derelict land associated with both active and disused colliery spoil heaps, the sterilization of land of possible future use for opencast production, the conflicts that arise between active working and the amenity of local residents, and the difficulties faced by the Coal Board in reclaiming naturally infertile materials. These problems are heavily concentrated in the vicinity of St. Helens, where the carboniferous coal measures either crop out on the surface or occur at depth (Fig. 9.2). Statistics of derelict and despoiled land (Merseyside County Council, 1979E) show that 65% of mineral land dereliction is caused by the past and present extraction of coal, and 238 ha of these 278 ha occur within the St. Helens Metropolitan Borough. Surface subsidence caused by the settlement and/or collapse of old workings is an environmental problem confined to the coal mining areas of the County, notably in parts of St. Helens and Knowsley Districts.

In contrast to coal and industrial sands, the winning of construction minerals such as crushed rock, and sand and gravel is of purely local significance, and little if any is exported from Merseyside. These materials are collectively termed "aggregates", and together with brick-clay account for only about 7% of employment in the County's mineral industry and 6% of the annual value of production. Aggregates and brick-clay, however, have very different environmental impacts. Aggregates account for only about 6% of the area of derelict and despoiled land within Merseyside, whereas active and disused brick-clay workings comprise nearly 24%. These figures emphasize that the aggregates industry of Merseyside is of minimal environmental significance, and at the present time building sand is extracted from one site only, near Lydiate, and crushed rock (sandstone) for road construction from a single large quarry at Billinge (Fig. 9.1). The main impact of these workings is felt locally in noise, traffic generation and loss of visual amenity, but of wider significance is the fact that the site at Lydiate is located on Grade 1 agricultural land.

The problem with the derelict and despoiled land associated with past and present day brick clay working is not only the large area involved (101 ha in 1974), but also its location in just two areas of the County, Knowsley/St. Helens and Wirral (Fig. 9.1). This is the only major problem of dereliction caused by the working of minerals in Wirral, and in 1979 three sites were active (covering nearly 24 ha), together with one in St. Helens (covering about 10 ha). It is likely that much of this land will be at least partially restored by the operators under the stimulus of strict planning conditions. The land now abandoned, some 20 ha in Wirral and over 48 ha in Knowsley/St. Helens, requires a more positive approach to reinstatement.

Although the onshore winning of construction aggregates is of little importance within the county, offshore dredging from Liverpool Bay and off New Brighton has taken place for a number of years. Until 1973 both sand and gravel were landed, but increasingly costs of production and technical difficulties now mean that only sand is brought ashore (Mersey Sand Suppliers Ltd., personal communication 1981). Marine dredging is not thought to cause any serious environmental problems, the sand being replenished from further offshore, and dredging is known to benefit navigation (Merseyside County Council, 1979E). Offshore dredging is not under the control of the County Council, but is licensed by the Crown Estate Commissioners (Verney, 1976). The Commissioners ensure that there are no environmental objections to dredging proposals, in particular that fisheries are safeguarded, that navigation is not hindered and that coastal defences do not suffer. As a condition of being granted a licence, operators have to agree to an annual maximum tonnage and to pay a royalty on the volume of material landed. Due to this strict control the marine-dredged sector raises far fewer actual or potential environmental objections than its land-based equivalent.

The production of large quantities of waste by the deep mining of coal and by the burning of coal by thermal power stations not only creates formidable problems of long-term environmental blight, but also provides, somewhat paradoxically, a potential source of aggregate. The main types of "secondary aggregate" are colliery shale (minestone) and two forms of power station waste (pulverized fuel-ash and bottom/ash clinker). Large quantities of these materials are present within the County (Fig. 9.1), and stocks of minestone exceed 19 m tons (National Coal Board, personal communication 1981). There is only one large power station in the County, at Bold, but within the North West Economic Planning Region as a whole nearly one million tons is being produced each year (North West Aggregates Working Party, 1977), much of it near to the County boundary. The main use of secondary aggregate is as bulk-fill for road and other construction projects, although with processing these materials may be employed in the manufacture of synthetic building blocks and certain types of concrete (Verney, 1976).

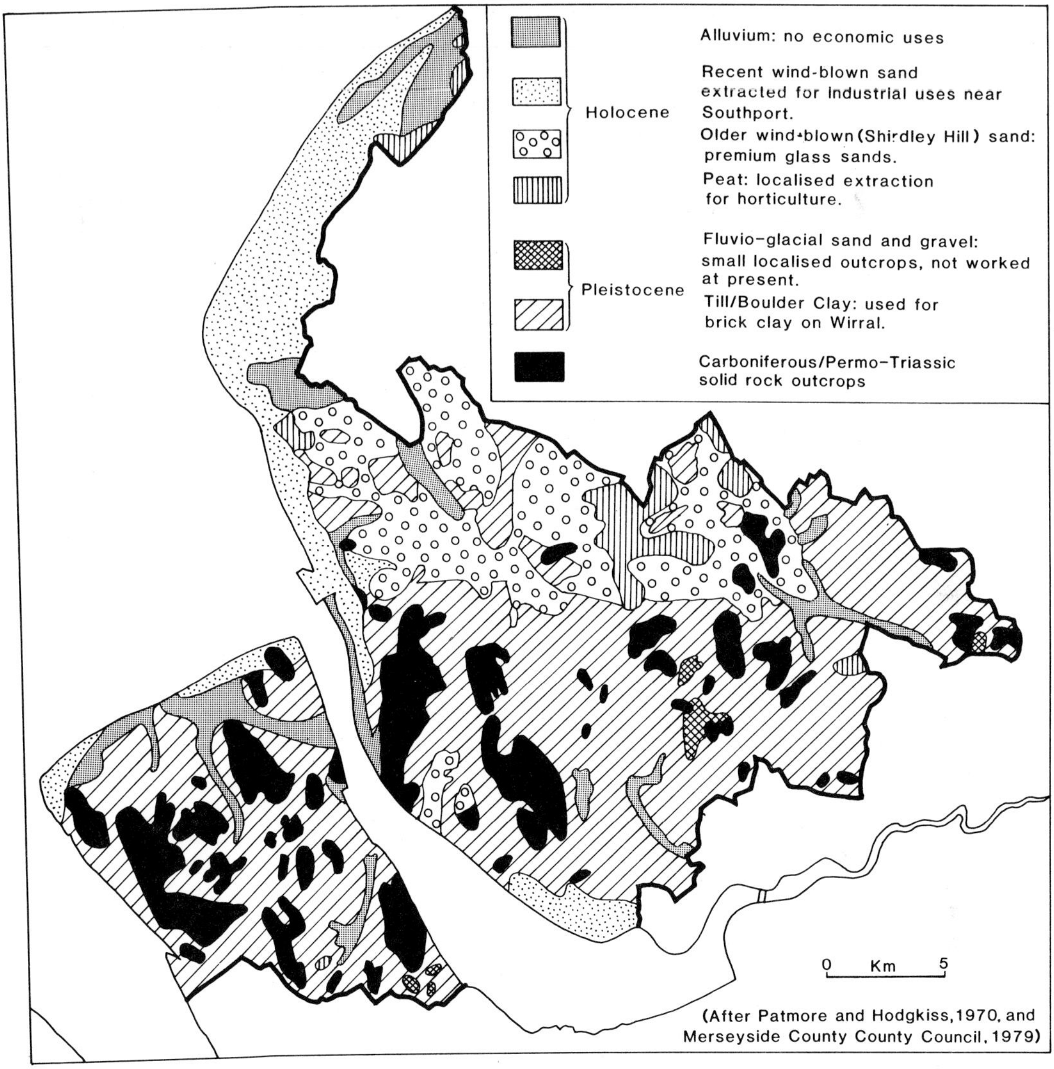

Fig. 9.3 Economic aspects of the drift geology of Merseyside

Unfortunately the rate at which new waste is being produced on Merseyside is many times greater than the rate at which it can be sold, and stockpiles are increasing. Even in the early nineteen-seventies, when sales of aggregate reached their all-time peak, only about 11% of minestone annually produced in the North-West Region was sold as aggregate, a figure falling to a mere 2% on Merseyside (North West Aggregates Working Party, 1977). Currently sales of minestone and power station waste products are negligible.

The resource base

The mere existence of a mineral, although a potential location for production, is not always an accurate guide to its exploitation. Even though a mineral deposit is known to exist within an area, its location in relation to markets, the present demand in these markets, its quality and volume and the availability of cost-effective mining or quarrying techniques may be such that no extraction takes place. For these reasons it is standard mining practice to classify deposits into "resources" and "reserves". Resources are deposits of minerals that are potentially usable, but require further evaluation to establish economic viability, whereas reserves are inventories of deposits that are capable of being exploited under current economic and technological conditions.

Figures 9.2 and 9.3, showing the economic geology of the county, are not, by themselves, a reliable guide to either resources or reserves. Deep-mined coal, for instance, has been evaluated in such detail by the National Coal Board that it is known that the four Merseyside collieries at Cronton, Sutton Manor, Bold and Parkside, will remain viable until beyond the turn of the century under prevailing market conditions and with existing technology (Merseyside County Council, 1977). Hence these deposits may be rightly classified as reserves. In contrast the drift geology (Fig. 9.3) has only been investigated in very broad outline, and the volumes of till (boulder clay) and fluvioglacial sand and gravel, usable or potentially usable as brick-clay and aggregate are not known, except in the vicinity of active workings. In contrast to many other important industrial areas of Britain, the Mineral Assessment Unit of the Institute of Geological Sciences has not at the time of writing made any detailed resource assessment of the deposits. The other minerals of Merseyside fall between these two extremes. Large, near-surface outcrops of coal are known to the east of the Boundary Fault (Fig. 9.2), both in Merseyside and beyond the County boundary. Overall these may be categorized as resources, but are only reserves in and near to sites of present and proposed opencast extraction, while a similar classification may be made of the silica (Shirdley Hill) sands and the outcrops of sandstone. Volumes of offshore sand and gravel are known to be vast, but many of these lie outside the range and depth of current economic dredging, and the only reserves are those that the producers have evaluated as viable under existing and projected market conditions and technology.

In the case of all the minerals being extracted on Merseyside, the definition of reserves is further constrained. Planning restrictions mean that deposits may only be worked in certain areas and that within these areas permission has been granted for extraction of only a specified quantity of the mineral, measured in tonnes. These deposits are termed "permitted reserves". The notion of permitted reserves is used by planners to resolve the conflict between the desire of mineral operators for new extraction and their duty to the community of steering "bad neighbour" land uses away from environmentally and amenity sensitive locations. On Merseyside there are many locations where minerals could be extracted, but only a small number of these will be granted planning permission at any given time. Thus, in the case of new sandstone quarrying, reserves are known to exist under high-grade agricultural land and to crop out as prominent ridges of high scenic value (e.g. Bidston Hill and Thurstaston Hill on Wirral), and these environmental constraints, together with the ready availability of large volumes of secondary aggregate, mean that there is a policy presumption against granting planning permission for this activity. Conversely the minerals industry, because of its importance to the national economy, has a well established right to some security of supply (Verney, 1976; Merseyside County Council, 1980), and the volume of permitted reserves has to be closely monitored so that new planning consents are granted as old workings become exhausted.

The cost of movement of materials both into and out of Merseyside provides a second constraint on the definition of reserves. Dredged sand from the Mersey could meet all the needs of the County for this raw material, but, because sand is relatively cheap to extract and fairly ubiquitous, transport costs to points of consumption make up a high proportion of total costs. It is uneconomic, therefore, to sell sand beyond a radius of about 22 km from Liverpool Docks (Mersey Sand Suppliers, personal communication, 1981). Beyond this

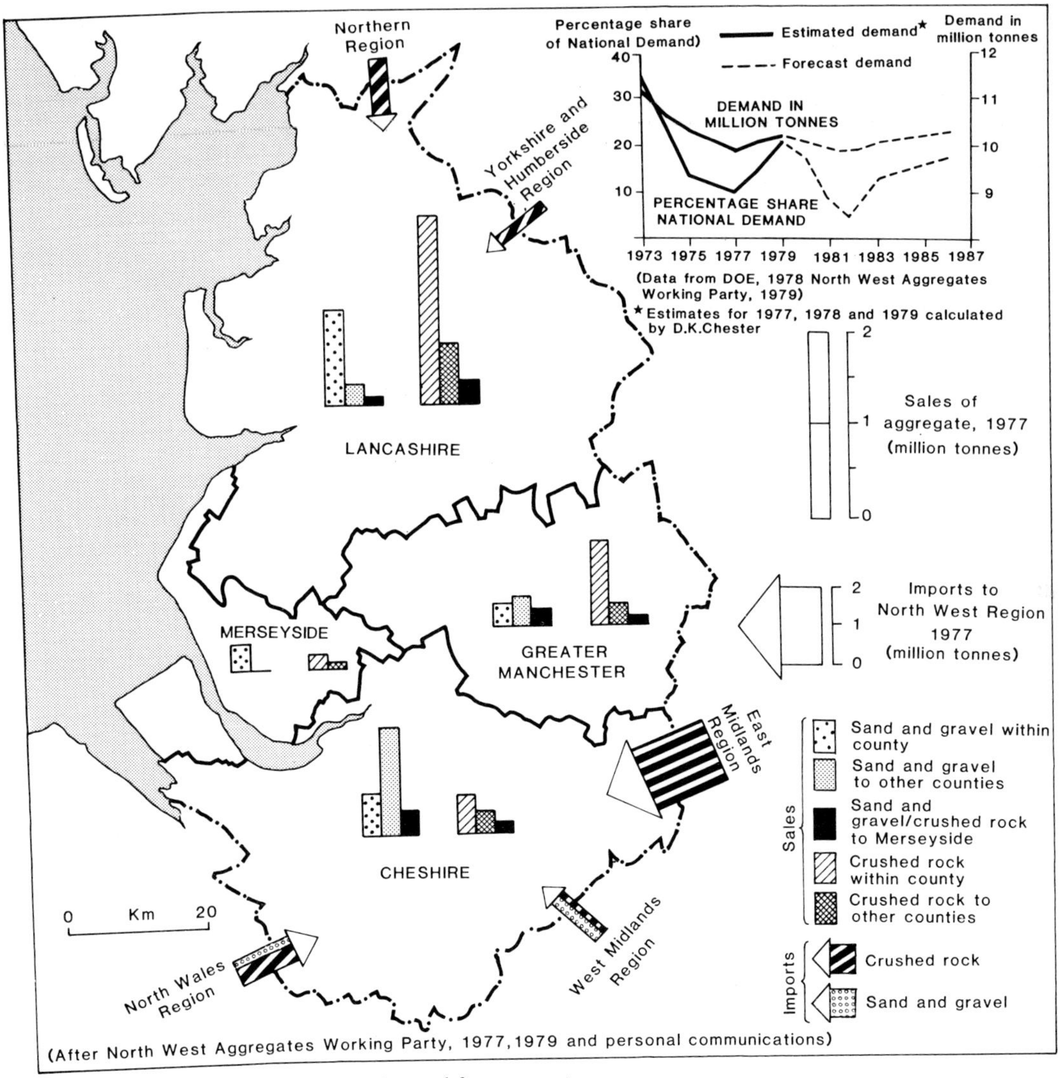

Fig. 9.4 Sales, imports and future demand for aggregates

distance sand from adjacent counties and from North Wales has a clear price advantage, and is imported in large quantities, while virtually nothing is exported in return (Fig. 9.4). Coal, in contrast, is found only in a relatively small number of locations, and is nearly ten times more expensive to produce than building sand. Although used in the main as a fuel in the power stations of North-West England, it is commonly both imported into and exported from the County (National Coal Board, personal communication, 1981). Construction aggregates have the lowest ratio of production costs to total costs (or lowest "intrinsic value") of the minerals produced on Merseyside, followed by clay, industrial sands and coal. Merseyside's stocks of coarse aggregate in the form of sandstone and waste materials are of poor quality, and are mainly used as bulk-fill and for non-critical building

TABLE 9.1 *The production of minerals in Merseyside and North West England, 1973/74–1979/80*

PRODUCTION (million tonnes)	1973/4	1977/8	1979/80	TRENDS
NATURAL DEPOSITS				
Clay (Merseyside)	0.30	0.16	—	Markets for building materials depressed.
Sand (Merseyside)	1.20	—	0.37	
Sandstone (Greater Manchester & Merseyside)	0.70	1.20	—	Markets on Merseyside more depressed than rest of region. Some closures of brick clay pits on Wirral.
Industrial Sand* (Lancashire & Merseyside)	0.50	0.31	—	Static or slightly falling demand. Relatively little being worked from Merseyside.
Coal (Merseyside)	1.80	—	2.32	Increased production from 1980. Depressed markets.
SECONDARY AGGREGATES				
Colliery Minestone* (N.W. Region)	0.22	0.33	—	Falling demand from construction sector. Increasing stock piles. Little being sold in 1981.
C.E.G.B. By-products* (N.W. Region)				
i. Pulverized fuel-ash	1.2	0.54	—	
ii. Bottom ash & clinker	0.25	0.22	—	

Note: *Separate figures for Merseyside not available.
Sources: Merseyside County Council, 1979F and 1980; North West Aggregates Working Party, 1977 and 1979; H.M.S.O., 1980; and personal communications.

specifications (Verney, 1976; Merseyside County Council, 1977). The total lack of high-quality coarse aggregate, either gravel or crushed rock, which is essential in certain road specifications and for concrete, necessitates the import of vast quantities from outside the County (Fig. 9.4). The majority of these imports are brought into Merseyside by road from adjacent counties, but long-distance movements by rail and by sea from as far away as Derbyshire and Gwynedd are also a feature of the pattern of supply (Department of the Environment, 1980). Not all these imports are for aggregate uses, and significant quantities of limestone are brought into the County for use in the chemical industry. Much larger volumes of this essential raw material are consumed by the chemical industries of Runcorn and Northwich in Cheshire. The poor quality of certain indigenous raw materials and competition from adjacent counties, therefore, severely limits the proportion of Merseyside's mineral resources that may be classified as reserves.

A third constraint on the concept of reserves occurs with the changing state of the market. Given that the definition of reserves involves the concept of exploitation under prevailing economic conditions, then changes in these conditions will bring about an alteration in the ratio of resources to reserves. At the present time markets for virtually all the minerals produced in Merseyside are either stagnant or declining (Table 9.1). In part this is due to the national economic depression, but it is also clear that the market shrinkage on Merseyside is both longer-term and more serious than that for either the United Kingdom as a whole or for the North-West Region. This decline, moreover, is most serious in those sectors where markets are essentially local and where the materials have a low intrinsic value. Hence production of sands from the Mersey has declined from about 6% of Great Britain's marine-dredged aggregate in 1973 to only about 2.5% in 1979 (Department of Environment, 1976; Mersey Sand Suppliers, personal communication 1981). Over a similar period clay production in Merseyside and Lancashire has remained constant at around 3% of national output, while output of industrial sands produced in the North-West Region has slightly increased its national share, but has declined both in absolute volume and relatively in Merseyside (H.M.S.O., 1980). The ratio of reserves to resources on Merseyside is much lower today than it was at the beginning of the nineteen-seventies.

Estimating future trends in the ratio of reserves to resources depends in part upon the willingness of the County Council to grant new planning permissions as existing sites become exhausted, so that the stock of permitted reserves is topped up, and also upon forward projections of the demand for mineral products from industry and construction. Policies for granting planning permissions have already been formulated and approved (Merseyside County Council, 1977; 1980), and these involve minimal controls over the future exploitation of minerals of national importance (i.e. industrial sands and coal), but fairly swingeing restrictions on future proposals to work minerals of more local significance (i.e. building sand, brick clay and sandstone) (Table 9.2). Production of industrial sands and coal will therefore be free to respond to national and regional demands for these products, and these will be the principal determinant of the ratio of reserves to resources. Restrictions on the working of building sand from inland sites will improve the prospects of the marine-dredged sector, and the future for marine dredging both in Merseyside and nationally is generally seen to be more favourable than in the recent past, as a result of tighter planning controls on land-based activities. Chillingworth (1980), however, sounds a cautionary note, and argues that in many parts of Britain land-won sand and gravel will probably still be cheaper, even taking into account costly environmental measures, due to increasing fuel and wharfages costs and the depletion of more easily worked marine deposits. This would mean for Merseyside the gradual penetration of markets traditionally supplied from marine dredging by land-won materials produced outside the County. Fortunately this is unlikely to apply, since the marine-dredged deposits of the Mersey and Liverpool Bay are known to be of high quality, plentiful and to occur fairly close to Liverpool Docks. The policy of severely restricting new sandstone workings should have the desired effect of improving the ratio of secondary aggregate reserves to resources, since secondary aggregate may be used as a substitute for poor quality crushed sandstone. The County will, nevertheless, still remain heavily dependent upon outside suppliers of high quality coarse concreting aggregates and industrial crushed rock such as limestone.

Projections of the demand for minerals are extremely difficult to make, since they depend upon the prospects and performance of user industries which are themselves subject to frequent and rapid changes in market circumstances, the relative strength of the local and national economy and the vicissitudes of political and corporate policies. A policy commitment, therefore, to massive industrial and urban renewal on Merseyside could favourably alter the prospects of the brick-clay and aggregates industries. Such schemes as the redevelopment of the Liverpool South Docks area may well act as a filip to these industries, but the general view within the industry is that the nineteen-eighties will be difficult years. Official forecasts (Fig. 9.4) suggest that even in 1987 the demand for aggregates in the North-West Region will not have reached the output recorded for 1975, itself thought at the time to be a very depressed year. Since the publication of this forecast

TABLE 9.2 *Planning proposals and policies for the working of minerals on Merseyside*

Industrial Sands	Building Sand	Brick Clay	Sandstone/ Secondary Aggregate	Coal*	
				Opencast	Deep-mined
i. Presumption against working in areas when deleterious to the environment and amenity of coastal areas. ii. Presumption against working when less than 50% to be used for special industrial uses. iii. To avoid sterilization of the Shirdley Hill (glass) sands. iv. Extraction of industrial sand will normally be allowed within consultation areas.	Presumption against planning permission for winning of sand from inland and coastal areas, due to the availability of marine dredged materials.	i. To seek code of practice to ensure restoration during working at existing and future sites of extraction. ii. Special consideration to be given to the needs of the brick clay industry in the Moreton area of Wirral and the Lea Green area of St. Helens.	Presumption against planning permission for sandstone quarrying, due to the availability of secondary aggregates.	i. To ensure that working is carried out in conjunction with the reclamation of derelict land. ii. Brick clay operators to be informed of opencast proposals with a view to the exploitation of brick clay within the area of working.	i. No planning control over extensions of working at Bold, Cronton and Sutton Manor. ii. Parkside subject to full planning control. Some control over waste disposal at Bold. iii. To avoid sterilization of coal bearing land. iv. Presumption against the winning of low grade coal from restored tips. v. To ensure the reclamation of disused tips. vi. To ensure the effective remedial treatment of subsidence (Coal Industry Act, 1975). vii. Make colliery waste disposal arrangements and ensure the landscaping of tips associated with active workings.

Note: *In consultation with the N.C.B. Sources: Merseyside County Council, 1977, 1979E and 1980.

in 1978 the position has further deteriorated, and on Merseyside the current depression in the industry is far more severe than in the North-West Region as a whole.

The prospects for the industrial sand and coal industries of the County are dependent upon national rather than local factors. Virtually all the output of industrial sand is used in the manufacture of steel (moulding sand) and glass (Shirdley Hill sand), and demands for these products are closely tied to the performance of the national economy. Since 80% of the coal produced by Merseyside's four collieries is used as a power station fuel (Merseyside County Council, 1977), the fortunes of this industry will clearly be primarily dependent upon the national demand for electricity. So far central government has not let short-term difficulties prejudice the long-term role envisaged for coal in energy planning, and the industry is still officially committed to the optimistic targets outlined in the 1974 *Plan for Coal*. Whether or not this policy will continue is impossible to predict, but it is certain that the nineteen-eighties will be a difficult decade for the coal industry. On Merseyside the situation is probably slightly better than in some other coalfields, as a result of the large volume of coal remaining to be worked at all four collieries.

Policies of environmental improvement

Policies that may be adopted to deal with the environmental issues discussed above are of three types. In the first place, policies may be formulated to tighten control over any new workings of a particular mineral by such measures as ensuring that land restoration takes place during and after extraction, by making presumptions against the winning of materials from environmentally and amenity sensitive locations, and by avoiding unnecessary sterilization of mineral-bearing land. All these approaches are used by Merseyside County Council (Table 9.2). Secondly, planning may be used as an instrument by which future demands for quarried products may assist in environmental improvement, rather than contributing to environmental deterioration. The policy of encouraging the use of secondary aggregate as a substitute for sandstone and the desire of the County to combine any new opencast coal working with the reclamation of derelict sites are examples of this type of planning initiative. The Opencast Executive currently plans to extract coal from a derelict site in the vicinity of St. Helens (National Coal Board, personal communication, 1981). A third area in which policy may assist environmental improvement is through measures designed to deal with the problems of inherited dereliction and blight caused by past mineral extraction. In spite of lip-service being paid to the ideal of derelict land restoration in virtually all Town and Country Planning statutes since 1947, little has been achieved until recently (Merseyside County Council, 1979F). Between 1974 and 1976, for instance, Merseyside planned to reclaim 44 ha of derelict land, not all of it caused by mineral extraction, but by 1976 only 7% of this programmed area had received treatment. This is a poor record when viewed in terms of both the scale of the inherited problem and the fact that additional land was becoming derelict over this three-year period.

It would be unfair to lay the blame for this state of affairs at the door of the County Planning Department, since several factors have combined to frustrate any effective response until recently. One difficulty has been unofficial "fly" tipping of waste on derelict sites. A lot of this waste is untreated and even toxic, making restoration more costly and narrowing the range of possible after-uses. The Aston University survey of derelict land in the County showed that 87% of excavations were used for tipping, much of it unofficial (Merseyside County Council, 1979F). Since this survey was carried out in 1974 the County Council has been given additional powers under the Control of Pollution Act, 1974, and may now license sites for tipping and impose planning conditions. Traditionally the deposition of colliery spoil has been excluded from full planning control, but this may now be partially controlled as a result of a change in planning law which allows the County

Planning Authority to take the initiative in landscaping and after-treatment of spoil-tips. A further constraint on the powers of the National Coal Board has followed the Coal Industry Act, 1975, and today the County is able, in consultation with the Coal Board, to ensure the effective remedial treatment of land subject to subsidence. By using these new powers the County may prevent much potential future dereliction in the coalfield area. This is most important because the projected life of the four Merseyside collieries is much greater than the amount of tipping space currently available (Merseyside County Council, 1979F), and it is probable that the involvement of the County will ensure an environmentally acceptable standard of waste disposal at any new sites.

Out of a total of about 423 ha of derelict and despoiled land associated with mineral working, only about 68% falls within the official definition used by the Department of the Environment. This remains a serious environmental problem because only land falling within the official definition is eligible for grant-aid from central government. Fortunately a relatively large number of sites in the coalfield area of the County are eligible for aid, and more than 12 disused waste tips are being reclaimed or have plans for reclamation in the near future (Merseyside County Council, 1977; 1980). At the present time there is little that the County Council can achieve to improve actively-used mineral land except by agreement with the producer companies.

Prospects for oil and gas

An exciting new development is the search for commercially viable reserves of oil and gas. A long-forgotten oil seepage near Formby was rediscovered in 1937, and small yet significant quantities were recovered before working ceased. Deep drilling failed at this time to locate any large oil pools (Shackleton, 1953). Over the last ten years there has been renewed interest in the possibility of finding oil and gas, and exploration is taking place on land, in Liverpool Bay and in the Irish Sea (Merseyside County Council, 1977; 1979E). Under the Petroleum (Production) Act, 1934, licences for land-based exploration are issued by the Department of Energy, whose policy is to inform the County of any that are granted. Licences to explore some 434 sq km have been issued, covering 70% of the land area of Merseyside (Merseyside County Council, 1980). It is the duty of licencees to consult planning authorities before they begin exploration, and they may also be required to apply for planning permission. The County Council is closely monitoring the progress of exploration so that it will be in a position to develop policies which will allow maximum economic benefit and at the same time will minimize environmental impact.

Once short- and medium-term problems of market stagnation are overcome the exploitation of minerals is likely to regain its position as an industry making a significant contribution to the economy of Merseyside. The character of this activity may change, but it seems probable that the strict application of planning controls will prevent many of the long-term problems of dereliction that have been the unfortunate legacy of the past.

Chapter 10

CONSERVING AND RENEWING THE BUILT ENVIRONMENT

DAVID MASSEY

The built environment of Merseyside displays in the 1980s the same "sharp areal definition" discerned by Wilfred Smith in his study of the urban structure of the metropolitan core city of Liverpool for the 1953 British Association "Scientific Survey of Merseyside". He considered this sharp definition was due to the "simplicity of the structure of the economy and the urban fabric arranged symmetrically around the river and fanwise about the focal central area of Liverpool" (Smith, 1953C, p. 199). The urban fabric was given its structure by four principal elements: the central area itself, the areas of the City's trading and industrial economy, its nineteenth-century residential areas and its twentieth-century suburbia "enveloping" the whole city. While the Merseyside area of the early 1950s expressed much of the structural simplicity of the core city, both its economy and its built environment reflected the modifications inherent in the size and complexity of the metropolitan scale. The metropolitan economy was more diversified, and its built environment could be seen to take the embryonic form of a "hub-and-spoke" configuration and to be punctuated by a fifth functional element, the smaller metropolitan town centres.

Changes in the three decades since Wilfred Smith's analysis have filled out and strengthened the distinctive features of the Merseyside metropolitan area. In the 1980s, however, planning policy is no longer directed as it was in the 1950s towards growth and outward expansion. Instead Merseyside faces the problems of metropolitan decline and severe limitations on public and private investment. Straitened circumstances have brought new attitudes to bear on the issues of obsolescence in the urban fabric. The distinctive qualities of the Victorian–Edwardian component of the built environment have also been reassessed in a more positive way. Whereas earlier policies looked towards the eventual clearance and redevelopment of all but a fragment of the country's pre-1979 urban stock, more recently there has been a growing appreciation that it represents an important resource and needs to be managed more selectively.

The strategy agreed in the Merseyside Structure Plan (Merseyside County Council, 1980) reflects these changed circumstances, attitudes and policies. It takes the approach of urban regeneration, that is of concentrating available investment in the existing built-up area, especially within those parts which have the most acute problems. It thus suggests an emphasis on the rehabilitation and improvement of the existing urban fabric, putting it to new use where practicable. Demolition is necessary only as a last resort or to make the most of special opportunities. Such an emphasis does not exclude new investment, rather it requires its application in different ways, towards repairs and maintenance, renovation and conversion, together with selective new buildings. Attitudes to conservation and renewal policies are of obvious general importance to each of the five principal elements in Merseyside's built environment noted above, but they hold a particular significance for three elements in which there is an especially strong inter-relationship between buildings and areas of historic and architectural importance and questions of neglect and disuse, redevelopment and new construction: the Liverpool central area, the nineteenth-century residential areas and the smaller metropolitan town centres.

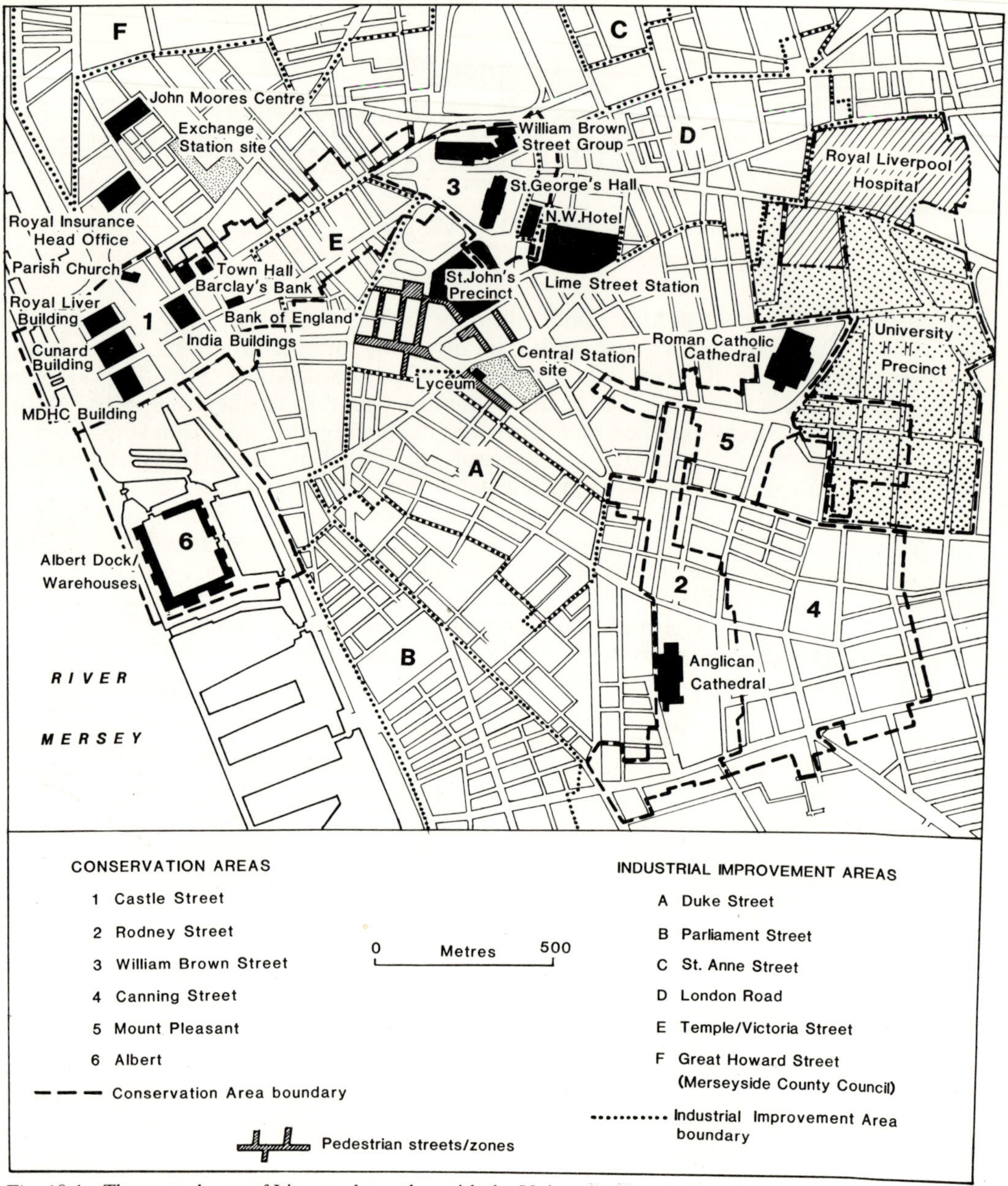

Fig. 10.1 The central area of Liverpool together with the University/Hospital Precinct and the Canning Street inner residential area (based upon the Ordnance Survey map with the permission of the Controller of Her Majesty's Stationery Office, Crown Copyright reserved)

The central area of Liverpool

Although perhaps the most easily identifiable single entity in the overall structure of Merseyside, the central area of Liverpool comprises a number of clearly distinct sections (Masser, 1970) (Fig. 10.1). At its heart are the tightly-defined office and shopping quarters; surrounding these are a number of rather more loosely-related marginal zones ranging from the civic and public buildings of St. George's Plateau to the mid-nineteenth

Plate 10.1 The Castle Street elevation of the Liverpool Branch of the Bank of England (Architect: C. R. Cockerell, 1845–1848) (photograph: Ian Qualtrough)

century Albert Dock and warehouses. Post-war planning and development activity was slow for the most part in the central area until the early 1960s, when in the aftermath of the application for the redevelopment of the St. John's Market, planning consultants were appointed to prepare comprehensive proposals for its future development. The ensuing "City Centre Plan" (City Centre Planning Group, 1965) was bold and controversial in its thinking, scale and content, providing a benchmark against which subsequent projects and proposals throughout the central area must be measured.

The business quarter lies at the core of the Liverpool's central area on the streets and sites of the medieval town, and contains a magnificent heritage of office buildings dating from the mid nineteenth century to the 1930s. It clusters around John Wood's classical Town Hall, with its sumptuous interiors, extending outwards only marginally to the Pier Head, whose three great Edwardian Imperial office blocks once provided a landmark for oceanic travellers. The centre's most noble office building, C. R. Cockerell's Bank of England branch "sombre, with impressive monumental dignity" (Hughes, 1964, p. 44), stands on Castle Street (Plate 10.1). Nearby, Peter Ellis' mid-Victorian Oriel Chambers, Water Street, and No. 16 Cook Street demonstrate this mid-Victorian architect's gifted handling of iron frame construction. Among the centre's inter-war buildings of distinction, H. J. Rowse's India Buildings with its interior arcade of shops and Barclay's (formerly Martin's) Bank stand on either side of Water Street.

Fortunately the 1965 City Centre Plan recognized the quality of this heritage, and paved the way for the designation of the Castle Street Conservation Area in 1968. It also encouraged redevelopment projects to be located elsewhere in the centre, for example in Old Hall Street, where the cool modernism of the JM Centre and the brown, boxy fortress of the Royal Insurance Head Office add contemporary buildings of character to the historic stock. A conservation policy does not exclude new building, and on Castle Street the Equity and Law Building shows how a modern office development can be inserted into a complex townscape. The Midland Bank branch office on the corner of Dale Street and Castle Street, on the other hand, is disastrously out of keeping with its setting. Elsewhere in the business quarter, considerable cleaning and restoration and conversion work has enabled many of its best buildings to be rediscovered and retained for modern usage. One of the most succesful examples of these rehabilitation works is that undertaken at the former Queen Insurance Building in Queen Avenue where listed buildings on Dale Street and Castle Street have been renovated together with an attractive pedestrian court of small shops. Jesse Hartley's Albert Dock and warehouses adjacent to the Pier Head present a conservation and renewal challenge of a different order and nature. Several ambitious and highly speculative projects for the buildings and water area have been put forward since the mid 1960s, although none has carried much conviction. Their future is still not settled, although it is hoped that the Merseyside Development Corporation will be able to take the practical action needed to preserve them and to attract appropriate new activities and private investment (Chapter 3).

Liverpool's central shopping quarter is highly concentrated into a compact area to the south-east of the business quarter. Its main spine is Church Street with extensions to Bold Street and Lord Street. Church Street, with several adjoining smaller streets and squares, and the lower part of Bold Street were pedestrianized in the mid 1970s as part of the implementation of the City Centre Plan, with care and attention being given to paving materials and design, to seating, planting and street lighting (see Fig. 6.3). An ingenious part of the whole scheme is the underground service access system to the Church Street shops and stores from ramps in the middle of the landscaped Roe Street/Hood Street Gyratory. Nearby, its tall chimney disguised as the "Beacon" complete with *de rigueur* revolving restaurant, the St. John's Precinct has added a new and potent symbol to this section of the Liverpool skyline. Its massive bulk, rather clinical finish and occasionally awkward interior arrangements do not, however, make it a wholly satisfactory addition to the built environment. Its more practical significance as Liverpool's single most important retail investment of the last thirty years, which also incorporates a hotel, two pubs, a dance hall and parking facilities together with its multi-storey shopping arcades and covered retail market, is the renewed emphasis it has given to the dominance of the Church Street quarter as the prime shopping centre of the Merseyside metropolitan area (Fig. 10.1).

Progress with implementing other aspects of the City Centre Plan outside the tightly-knit business and shopping quarters has been relatively uneven as changing attitudes and increasing scarcity of finance have modified the approaches thought desirable in the mid 1960s. The greatest amount of new building has taken place in the Strand/Paradise Street comprehensive development area. Here, in the midst of an uncompromisingly modern quarter of rather bleak, featureless slabs and blocks, of major roads and windswept upper-level walkways, lies one of the central area's greatest opportunities—a new public park is in the making. Progress is relatively slow, but it is clearly a chance for Liverpool to demonstrate its sense of style and verve. Elsewhere in the

Plate 10.2 St. George's Hall (Architect: H. L. Elmes, 1839–1847; building completed under the direction of C. R. Cockerell and R. Rawlinson). Like many other leading buildings in the central area, St. George's Hall has been cleaned in recent years; note also the refurbished and resurfaced forecourt to Lime Street (photograph: Ian Qualtrough)

central area other large-scale redevelopment projects have been slow to come to fruition or otherwise have failed to materialize, as for instance in the Moorfields/Temple/Victoria Street area. Here the mid 1960s approach of large scale redevelopment schemes has given way to a combination of Conservation Area and Commercial and Industrial Improvement Area designations to encourage the retention of the best of the Victorian and Edwardian offices and warehouses, to promote the refurbishment and adaptation of premises and to allow for smaller-scale new construction where funds can be attracted.

One major project, for a grandiose Civic and Social Centre in the now largely vacant, former Queen Square area, has been abandoned. Had it been built it would have provided a link between the Church Street shopping quarter and the city's most distinguished assembly of classical buildings—the College of Technology, the County Museum, the Picton Library, the Walker Art Gallery and the County Sessions House—strung along William Brown Street as a backcloth to Harvey Lonsdale Elmes' great Neo-Classical St. George's Hall (Plate 10.2). All that remains of the proposed link are the (largely-ignored) high level bridges for pedestrians from the St. John's Precinct and Williamson Square to the main rank of stops for outbound buses. Across from the St. George's Plateau group of buildings lies the peripheral London Road shopping area. It has suffered harshly in the last decade with competition from St. John's Precinct, from highway proposals including the hotly-contested Inner Motorway/Inner Ring Road and from changing bus routes and trading patterns. Although there is still a lively focus around the two department stores and open air market at Monument Place, much of the area presents a dismal picture of numerous empty and boarded shop frontages. It is difficult to know what to do in practical policy terms. One purposeful step has been to designate the shopping area together with the adjacent wholesaling quarter in and around Kempston Street as a Commercial and Industrial Improvement Area.

Two of the largest single sites for which major development schemes were envisaged, at Exchange and Central Stations, were released from their former railway uses by the opening of the Merseyrail underground "link". The late-nineteenth century Exchange Hotel still stands on Tithebarn Street, but the proposed office precinct for Government departments decentralized from Whitehall on the cleared site behind was cancelled in

1979. The Central Station site has been the subject of lengthy discussions over redevelopment proposals, most particularly in connection with their relationship to Thomas Harrison's Lyceum Club at the foot of Bold Street. The Lyceum has been saved from demolition through the intervention of the Secretary of State for the Environment, although it awaits renovation, and in early 1982 an indoor shopping precinct was nearing completion on the site of the former station.

The different experiences of the two station sites illustrate the deep complexities involved in policies for the built environment in a central area the size and nature of that of Liverpool, which functions as the hub of the Merseyside metropolitan area. On the one hand there is much scope and some demand for redevelopment and a need to conserve the best of the area's heritage of fine buildings and townscapes. On the other hand the new uses and massive funds required are not necessarily available; indeed they are in short supply. The consequence is that some buildings are demolished for redevelopment, but some sites remain vacant for years; elsewhere some new buildings are constructed; many older buildings have been cleaned and renovated, but not all have found new occupants; other buildings have gradually lost their onetime occupants, become empty and then perhaps are vandalized and derelict. In such circumstances difficult decisions have to be made about priorities, the scaling down of ambitions and about being opportunistic. The swings of change in national and local politics have not helped to provide a consistent framework for public policy decisions about central area activities and developments. And so, after the bold vision of the 1960s and the more limited approaches of the 1970s, perhaps the time has come for a thorough review of planning policies for Liverpool's central area. This would mean grasping some painful nettles, but would meet the very real need of providing realistic and integrated guidelines for making decisions about the future of the metropolitan hub in the uncertain and difficult years of the mid and late 1980s.

The residential areas

Merseyside possesses a considerable heritage of nineteenth- and early-twentieth-century housing which is mostly concentrated around Liverpool's central area and in the inner parts of Bootle, Birkenhead and Wallasey, Southport and St. Helens. Although it is often thought convenient to consider these older areas and their housing as single entities, "the inner city", for instance, it requires little enough acquaintance with either to appreciate that they are both far from being featureless, homogeneous elements in the built environment. The type and quality of the older housing stock, for instance, varies greatly from former shipowners' and merchants' mansions now converted into a number of rented flats or "bed-sits" to very ordinary, two-up and two-down terrace houses; from dwellings on the verge of being demolished through unfitness, to houses in good condition, renovated and improved to modern standards. Neighbourhoods in the inner residential areas also vary greatly between themselves: some areas retain the regular close-knit, patterned features of bye-law housing; others consist of somewhat larger houses, often with some garden space and mostly in multi-occupation; and yet others retain the character of a group of villas set apart on their own estate.

The residential environment does not just consist of houses, however, but includes parks, churches, schools, shops and other public buildings which range from libraries and health centres to cinemas converted to bingo clubs. A number of these different buildings and open spaces are of some quality, and add distinctiveness and character to their neighbourhoods. As the Merseyside Structure Plan suggests "unlike the newer outer estates, many parts of our inner areas possess major parks, green spaces and cultural assets to match the historic buildings in central areas" (Merseyside County Council, 1980, p. 143). A further differentiating factor is that the built environment of the inner residential

Plate 10.3 Conservation and rehabilitation in Percy Street (c. 1825–1830), described by Pevsner (1969, p. 186) as "the grandest street in the area" (photograph: Ian Qualtrough)

Plate 10.4 Princes Park: the entrance to the Park from Princes Boulevard (photograph: Ian Qualtrough)

areas is not all "old". In housing alone, the scale of demolition and rebuilding since 1919 has contributed its own characteristic building forms. The inter-war, walk-up tenements are to be found near the high-rise tower blocks of the 1960s and the semi-suburban terraces of the 1970s. This diversity also extends to the other elements of the residential environment. Here is a church built in a converted supermarket (St. Lawrence, Kirkdale); there is a modern superstore and parking lot built on cleared land (the Leo superstore, Park Road, Liverpool). A contemporary primary school of wood, brick and glass is set in its own grounds; acres of vacant, cleared land, some awaiting new uses, some now planted with shrubs, trees and grass lie next to small, new factory estates. Indeed far from being a featureless element in the built environment of Merseyside, the inner residential areas of the early 1980s more resemble a mosaic. The mosaic is clearly patterned, sometimes strikingly so; it is also changing as new pieces are added and old ones are amended.

Liverpool's Georgian "west end" quarter has been described by Pevsner (1969, pp. 178–9) as one of the finest in England. It is defined by a grid-iron pattern of residential streets and two squares, Abercromby Square and Falkner Square, lined with "sober and well-proportioned brick terraces". It also contains some distinguished Georgian churches, notably St. Bride, Percy Street, and St. Andrew, Rodney Street (the latter now sadly derelict), and other public buildings such as the Wellington Rooms (now the Irish Centre) and the Medical Institution on Mount Pleasant. Today buildings from more recent times and for different uses help shape the physical environment in new ways. They include two Cathedrals: the massive, red sandstone Anglican Cathedral, built over the first eight decades of this century, and the circular Roman Catholic Metropolitan Cathedral with its great lantern, built over five years in the mid 1960s. The University-Hospital precinct has become a significantly growing part of the "west end" since the 1950s and is now an important structural component of the urban fabric in its own right. The core of the Georgian residential area left after demolitions for University expansion and slum clearance is found in the group of streets immediately surrounding Canning Street and Catharine Street. Most of the houses are of brick, although some have stucco or stone frontages. Percy Street, however, is entirely of stone, and particularly fine as an example of the well-mannered Georgian street. The Canning Street area is Merseyside's leading example of housing rehabilitation combined with measures to protect and enhance buildings of architectural and historic importance. It has been both a Conservation Area and a (Housing) General Improvement Area since the early 1970s. Some two hundred or more houses have been renovated, mostly converted into flats by local housing associations with care being taken to keep the external details in character.

The "west end" was not large enough to accommodate the growing well-to-do classes of Merseyside in the mid nineteenth century. They created for themselves two new residential environments: the park surrounded by houses and the "villa estate". Merseyside contains two of England's earliest residential parks, Princes Park in Liverpool and the larger and more influential Birkenhead Park. Both Parks date from the 1840s, and owed their original designs to Sir Joseph Paxton. Each has its impressive main entrance: Princes Park through cast iron gates of a sun-burst design and Birkenhead Park through a monumental set of arches linking two lodges. The Parks are surrounded by a variety of houses, some obviously neglected, others well-maintained or rehabilitated, and others again converted to new uses, such as schools. The landscape of the Parks is romantic in style with ornamental lakes (one in Princes Park, two in Birkenhead Park) and islands, some mounded hillocks, and open spaces contrasting with more densely-planted areas. Each also contains gently curving paths for walking and a perimeter carriage way. Today the two Parks are both Conservation Areas, and contain numerous "listed" buildings of historic and architectural interest. Because of their age and to some extent their previous

Plate 10.5 The Rock Ferry By-Pass road and the Rock Park estate (laid out by Jonathan Bennison, 1836–1837), looking across to the River Mersey and the Liverpool shore beyond (photograph: Ian Qualtrough)

neglect and misuse, the landscapes and the buildings of the two great Merseyside Parks of the 1840s require continuing conservation and renovation to maintain them as a recreational and amenity resource for the urban population.

Liverpool went on to build a second generation (Sefton Park, Newsham Park and Stanley Park) of residential parks in the 1860s. However, another distinctive form of mid-nineteenth century residential environment also (quite unjustifiably) appropriated the title "park". More properly termed "villa estates", these consisted of rather select collections of large, detached and semi-detached houses set in their own gardens along tree-lined roads, and often had their own entrance gates and lodges, but lacked the essential open-space element of Birkenhead Park and Princes Park. They were often set somewhat apart from the built-up areas of their time, forming as it were "detached" elements of the Victorian residential environment. Liverpool's best known examples are Cressington Park and Grassendale Park with their riverside Promenade; across the Mersey they are complemented by Rock Park (which has been cut in two by the Rock Ferry By-Pass) with its Esplanade, and by nearby Egerton Park. Other examples include Sandfield Park, West Derby, which today has practically lost its separate identity, and Clifton Park in Birkenhead.

The third major component, spatially and numerically the most extensive, of the inner residential areas was described by Wilfred Smith as like "a great tide of terrace housing laid out row after row in sets of rectangular grids" (Smith, 1953C, p. 197). This Victorian and Edwardian flood of bricks and mortar was concentrated in but not limited to Liverpool. It spread northwards to Bootle and across the river to inner Birkenhead and south Wallasey, and constituted significant sections of St. Helens and its smaller related industrial towns. Thirty years later slum clearance in the 1960s and early 1970s had shattered the uniformity

Smith had observed in the early 1950s. The great tide has become a series of pools and shallows, some of which are larger than others; many are now relatively isolated, others are still linked together.

The process of fragmentation was slow at first, not least since the scale of the problem was so daunting. In Liverpool, which contained the bulk of Merseyside's older, unfit housing, and has seen the greater part of the physical changes relating to this component in the urban fabric, estimates in the mid 1950s indicated that 26 000 houses needed to be demolished, and a further 62 000 needed more or less extensive remedial treatment. In the first policy phase to the mid 1960s only 10 000 houses were demolished and little was done by way of repairs or improvement to the remainder, most of which continued to decay and to become potential candidates for demolition themselves. The City Council's approach of concentrating demolition on sites where there was an assured housing after-use resulted in a "piecemeal, scattered site clearance programme" (Muchnick, 1970, p. 30).

The second policy phase in the late 1960s and early 1970s saw renewed emphasis on clearance and development, but within a comprehensive framework. It produced a concerted programme to demolish the city's 33 000 worst slums over the period 1966–1971, and looked ahead to the demolition of the remaining 45 000 unsatisfactory dwellings over the subsequent twenty years. The pace and form of this change became both politically unpopular and hard to sustain in practice, so that by mid 1973 nearly 13 000 houses in the Stage I programme remained to be demolished. In fact the transition to a third policy phase was well under way. The new policy would abandon the mass clearance and redevelopment approach, and place emphasis on the rehabilitation of small groups of streets designated as General Improvement Areas under the Housing Act, 1969, and Housing Action Areas under the Housing Act, 1974.

After early experimentation in the Granby area and almost annual reassessments in the early 1970s, the new policy was spelled out in 1975 and 1976 in the establishment of a five-year housing renewal strategy. Among the particular features of the new phase were the continuing use of demolition (albeit on a much-diminished and highly-selective scale), the key role given to local housing associations to carry out much of the detailed work of rehabilitation and housing management (Thompson, 1977), and the declaration of three co-ordinated phases of Housing Action Areas over the period 1978 to 1982. Two phases of declarations had been made by early 1982, and, although early progress with treatment seemed promising, a dwindling supply of public sector financial resources makes it increasingly unlikely that the overall target of 25 000 dwellings improved will be reached in the original time span. In the meantime as the available resources are concentrated in the "priority" renewal areas, it is thought that the condition of older houses elsewhere in the "secondary" areas continues to decline.

As the underlying housing renewal dilemma for Liverpool begins to reappear, writ large it can be seen as the Merseyside housing renewal dilemma. Despite the efforts of the last three decades and the shattering of the great tide, the inner residential areas are still estimated to contain the great bulk of Merseyside's 100 000 unsatisfactory privately-owned dwellings in the early 1980s. They also contain substantial sections of unsatisfactory municipal housing, in particular the inter-war, walk-up blocks of tenement buildings, which also require treatment. "The [Merseyside Structure Plan's] urban regeneration strategy aims to improve or demolish all unsatisfactory council housing by 1986." (Merseyside County Council, 1980, p. 40). However, the County Council pointed out that existing rates of improvement would have to be doubled to almost 10 000 a year to achieve this target. If they were not, then decay would continue in the stock, and large-scale clearance projects would need once more to come to the fore. Much then rests on the level of resources available to the Metropolitan District Councils and, through the Housing

Plate 10.6 Cleared site (foreground) and rehabilitated , nineteenth-century terrace houses in Magdala Street, Liverpool 8 (photograph: Ian Qualtrough)

Corporation, to the local housing associations to carry out this task. A lack of resources almost certainly means that doubt is already being cast over the principal regeneration object of improving and replacing a substantial part of Merseyside's unsatisfactory housing. For the remainder of the once great tide of Merseyside's terrace houses the basic issue of the 1980s is starkly posed in the Structure Plan: "demolish or improve?"

The smaller town centres

The smaller town centres of Merseyside have been considerably strengthened as significant elements in the county's metropolitan structure during the last twenty years (Merseyside County Council, 1979B). In part this reflects some diminution in the position of Liverpool's central area, but to a greater extent it has been brought about by local action to develop a set of metropolitan sub-centres. Birkenhead, Bootle and St. Helens have each promoted the construction of large-scale, modern shopping precincts to renew and extend their largely nineteenth-century town centres.

Operating largely through its own individualistic and not uncontroversial municipal enterprise, Birkenhead (and latterly Wirral Metropolitan Borough Council) has built a substantial pedestrianized shopping centre and new Market in the Grange Precinct (Fig. 10.2). However, the new shopping focus is rather weakly linked along Argyle Street/Market Street with Hamilton Square, laid out by James Gillespie in the early nineteenth-century on lines reminiscent of Georgian Edinburgh, and now designated as a Conservation Area, its grand houses now mostly occupied by small offices (Plate 10.7). A similar form, although rather different nature, of municipal initiative has succeeded in developing the Stanley Road area of Bootle into a distinctive office sub-centre of metropolitan status in the last fifteen years (Chapter 5). This has been complemented in

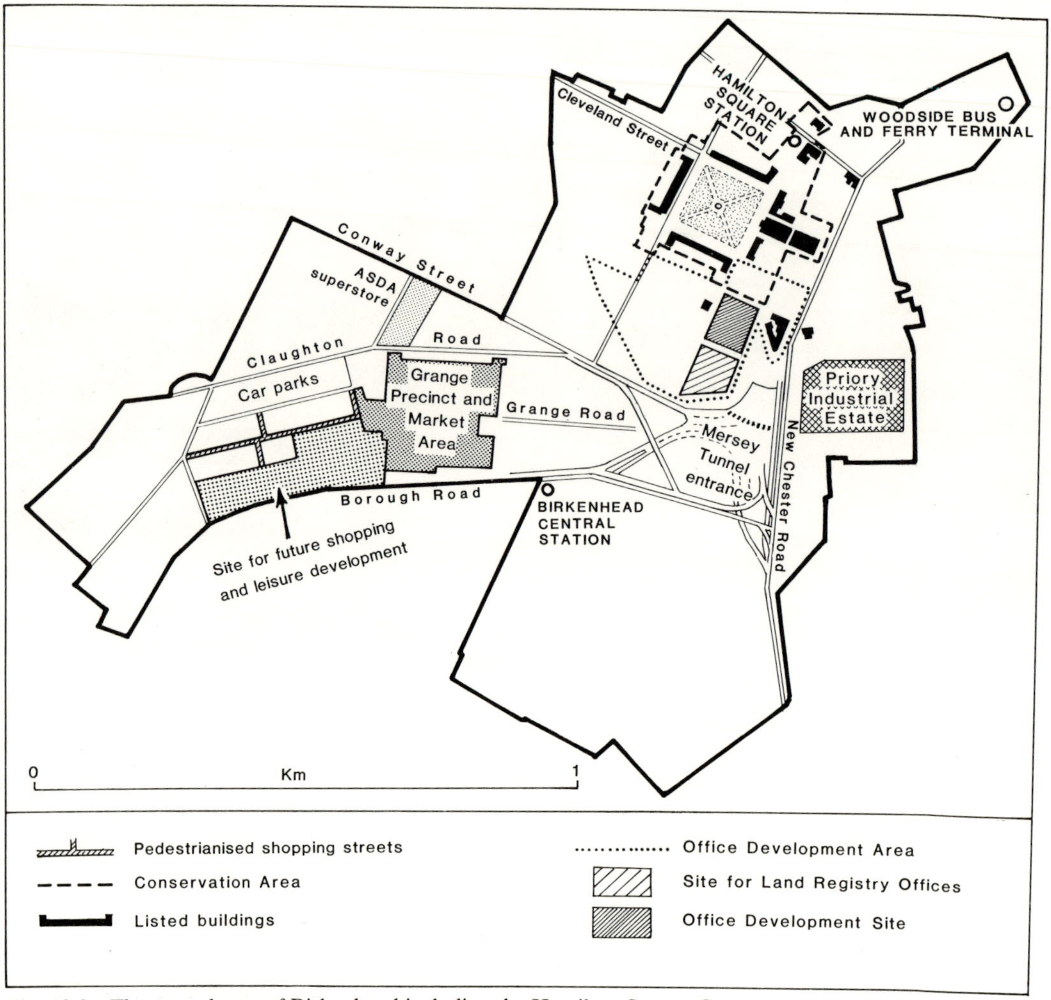

Fig. 10.2 The central area of Birkenhead including the Hamilton Square Conservation Area and the Grange Shopping Precinct and Market

the adjacent construction of a completely new pedestrianized shopping precinct at New Strand. In the once overwhelmingly Victorian town centre of St. Helens (Victoria Square, with the Town Hall and Gamble Institute, is St. Helens' town centre Conservation Area), the Tontine Market and two phases of the St. Mary's Precinct have been completed in the last ten years. The Precinct has diversified the range of retail outlets in St. Helens, and enhanced its general attractiveness to shoppers. Meanwhile, the Hardshaw Centre, across Church Street from St. Mary's is due to open in 1982, and will provide further shops and stores.

Southport, the second largest shopping centre in Merseyside, has taken a rather different approach. Its attractiveness is best expressed in the range and quality of its shopping facilities and as an entertainment and holiday centre. These characteristics are exemplified in the older-established, more specialist shops of Lord Street, a well-maintained and carefully-managed Conservation Area. Southport has consolidated its status as Merseyside's most attractive centre through good use of its existing building

Plate 10.7 Birkenhead: the eastern side of Hamilton Square (laid out by J. G. Graham, 1824–1825) and the Town Hall (Architect: C. O. Ellison & Co., 1883–1887) (photograph: Ian Qualtrough)

Plate 10.8 Wayfarers Arcade and part of the section of Lord Street, Southport lined by wrought iron and glass canopies to protect shoppers from inclement weather (photograph: Ian Qualtrough)

Plate 10.9 Brick-built, Georgian houses in Vicarage Place in the core of Prescot's Town Centre Conservation Area; note the use of traditional materials in the recently completed resurfacing scheme (photograph: Ian Qualtrough)

stock and a number of smaller and more scattered new shopping and office developments and conversions (Plate 10.8). Prescot town centre is not as large as Southport or Bootle, but it is one of the County's hidden and neglected assets (Plate 10.9). The almost complete survival of its medieval street and site pattern and a townscape now recognized as being of architectural and historic interest has brought public support for positive action to conserve its heritage elements and to bring new life to its derelict sites and disused buildings (Knowsley Metropolitan Borough, 1979). This includes re-establishing a weekly market, measures to attract trade and private investment and the rehabilitation of historic buildings and environmental improvements.

On the whole the smaller metropolitan town centres, not all of which are discussed above, stand to gain from the urban regeneration strategy. The main problems of their built environment in the 1980s are likely to be whether, as with the Liverpool central area, they can attract and retain the level of resources and variety of activities to support recent new investments. Related issues, where the conservation of architecturally and historically important buildings and areas are involved, include the more subtle but no less real threats of neglect through indifference and carelessness and inappropriate new building development.

Conclusions

This brief review of the changes in the built environment of Merseyside in the last thirty years has been highly selective in taking up the general theme of conservation and renewal and in limiting its discussion to three of the five principal components of the metropolitan spatial structure. Considerable changes have certainly taken place in attitudes towards conserving and renewing the built environment during this period, and if the hinge of this change can be discerned in the late 1960s, then it took the form of a radical re-appraisal and the choice of a new direction in the 1970s. In part the change came about through force of circumstances as resources for wholesale redevelopment became increasingly scarce. In addition, the detrimental consequences of continued outward development without compensating policies for the inner areas became vividly apparent. In part it also came about through wider changes in professional, political and public opinion which had both their national and their more particular, local aspects. The new attitude takes a more generally positive approach to Merseyside's urban fabric. It can be seen at work in policies for improving rather than rebuilding large parts of Liverpool's central area, in the selective rehabilitation emphasis in housing policies and in the designation of nearly sixty Conservation Areas throughout the County.

At a time when the pendulum of opinion has swung so far away from renewal and rebuilding towards conservation and improvement, however, it is important to stress that the two approaches are not (or ought not to be) mutually exclusive. They are inter-connected components within a wider complex of approaches to the continuing task of managing the built environment. Each generation sets its own balance between them. But if this balance is set towards one extreme or another, then, because of their inter-connectedness, experience has shown that sooner or later this over-emphasis will create a new set of environmental problems. This implies, for instance, that the current leaning towards conservation and improvement on Merseyside may lead to a neglect of new opportunities for the sake of clinging to a past stock which has served its purpose. It also gives rise to expectations that it is a low cost option; but if it is not supported by an appropriate level of funding, then the consequent growing neglect of repairs and maintenance will lead to a growing obsolescence to which the ultimate answer will be clearance and rebuilding. This dilemma is faced squarely in the assumptions and policies set out in the Metropolitan Structure Plan's urban regeneration strategy, which seeks to concentrate available new investment resources within the existing built-up areas, especially those in greatest need.

However, the strategy of urban regeneration is itself widely recognized as being in jeopardy, not least in its built environment elements, through a continuous shortage of financial resources. And if the County cannot generate and attract sufficient funds for this strategy, then the limited alternatives available present a very bleak future. Two of the three elements discussed above certainly face daunting prospects, and there are also problems for the two other major elements. The older areas of the County's trading and industrial economy, for instance, face conservation or renewal choices in relation to their built environment in the Docklands, in the industrial estates at Kirkby and Speke and in the smaller industrial settlements. The twentieth-century suburbs, the fifth major element, like their earlier counterparts, are by no means homogeneous in age, in character or in environmental quality. Some indeed, most particularly some of the post-war, outer municipal estates in Knowsley, Liverpool and Wirral, have severe problems by any score. These are demonstrated physically in their often unkempt and vandalized surroundings. They are demonstrated in policy terms in "hard-to-let" housing, in which nobody wants to live and which in time becomes a candidate for demolition. Of the other three elements, the Liverpool central area needs to attract a new, higher level and varied range of users and activities if it is to retain its metropolitan status and identity. The smaller metropolitan town centres may face an easier prospect, but they too have challenges to face in consolidating and retaining their attractiveness to support the extensive new investment of the 1960s and 1970s. Even the prospects of Merseyside's Heritage Areas are not without cause for concern, for, as the County Council has commented, although "the pattern of designation [of Conservation Areas] now leaves few gaps, on the other hand local authorities have not yet undertaken many schemes of positive enhancement, nor committed much investment . . ." (Merseyside County Council, 1980, p. 55). Elsewhere in the County the remaining older, inner terrace housing areas face perhaps the most difficult and widespread sort of problems.

Each of the five major elements of the built environment of Merseyside then faces particular challenges over the choices between conservation, renewal and new building within limited financial resources. That such a fundamental aspect of the regeneration strategy should be recognized as being at risk through a lack of finance before the ink was, as it were, already dry on the Structure Plan, must beg the key question of whether the strategy is going to work? If it is not, then, in terms rarely found in official documents, the Structure Plan Examining Panel concluded "the price to pay in terms of individual misery and social unrest and eventually even in cash terms will be horrifying". The regeneration strategy certainly provides a positive and realistic attitude towards the use and re-use of the built environment of Merseyside which seeks to avoid such apocalyptic eventualities, but its robustness and strength will certainly be tested to the full in the 1980s.

Chapter 11

THE DISTRIBUTION AND STRUCTURE OF POPULATION SINCE 1951

RICHARD LAWTON

During the late nineteenth century Liverpool's overcrowded residential areas were already losing population to suburbs of the incipient conurbation of Merseyside on both sides of the Mersey (Chapter 1). By 1911 a population of 1.17 million on Merseyside was spread over a wide area, and Liverpool's commuter hinterland extended over much of the present conurbation. However, the depression and the decline of the port and many of its traditional industries were reflected in a marked fall in the rate of population growth after the First World War, with a steady loss of population by migration especially to the Midlands and South East.

Within Merseyside massive inter-war local authority and private housing developments accelerated the physical expansion of the built-up area, permitting residential movement from the inner core to the rest of the conurbation and the outer suburban areas (Table 11.1). Thus, while 78.4% of the region's population lived in its four inner County Boroughs (Bootle, Liverpool, Birkenhead and Wallasey) in 1921, only 66.5% did so by 1951. Although relatively high natural growth, due to high birth rates, ensured continuing growth of population up to the late 1930s, even in the inner areas, rehousing policies produced substantial migrational gains in the suburban areas. Moreover, the relatively youthful age structure of these migrants meant substantial natural growth. Between 1921 and 1931 the areas beyond the inner core of Merseyside increased by an annual average 4300 (3100 due to migration) and between 1931 and 1951 by 8180 per year (6500 due to migration). These internal movements caused significant changes in distribution of population (see Fig. 1.2), and brought both marked contrasts in demographic and social structure within the region and also a longer and a more complex spatial pattern of journeys to work.

The social and economic factors underlying massive slum clearance and decanting of population in suburban and overspill housing schemes, the dispersal of industry to the periphery and the relative and, recently, absolute fall of jobs in the central areas, the decline of the region's economy and associated population migration have continued throughout the post-1945 period. While the reorganization of local government in 1974 and the lack of detailed results from the 1981 Census at the time of writing make comparison difficult, this chapter seeks to compare trends within the inner and outer parts of the conurbation and in the Merseyside region as a whole and to examine the main demographic causes and social effects within these areas.

Population trends, 1951–81

In the 1950s population growth in the Merseyside region slowed to a meagre 1400 persons per annum, due essentially to average yearly migrational losses of 5000 (Table 11.2). In a region which coincides fairly closely with the present Metropolitan County, together with the adjacent West Lancashire, Halton, and Ellesmere Port and Neston Districts with which it has close economic and demographic links, total population grew slowly; by 76 000 between 1951 and 1961, was virtually static in the 1960s, and fell sharply by 100 000 between 1971 and 1981 (Table 11.3). The main feature was the decline in the inner areas of the conurbation, especially in Liverpool whose population, with a pre-war peak of 867 000,

TABLE 11.1 *Population trends in Merseyside, 1921–1951*

	POPULATION 1921 ('000)	PERCENTAGE CHANGE per annum, 1921–31			POPULATION 1931 ('000)	PERCENTAGE CHANGE per annum, 1931–51			POPULATION 1951 ('000)
		Natural	Migration	Total		Natural	Migration	Total	
NORTH MERSEYSIDE	1079.6	+0.86	−0.35	+0.50	1168.0	+0.62	−0.41	+0.21	1207.5
Inner Core	896.9	+0.98	−0.57	+0.40	932.9	+0.67	−1.04	−0.37	859.9
Rest of Conurbation	35.4	+0.59	+0.78	+1.37	71.7	+1.07	+3.43	+4.50	138.6
Outer Area	147.3	+0.21	+0.72	+0.93	163.4	+0.15	+1.47	+1.62	209.0
SOUTH MERSEYSIDE	316.0	+0.70	+0.15	+0.85	342.1	+0.49	+0.10	+0.59	377.4
Inner Core	243.5	+0.64	−0.54	+0.10	249.9	+0.40	−0.52	−0.12	243.0
Rest of Conurbation	72.5	+0.92	+2.46	+3.38	92.2	+0.75	+1.77	+2.51	134.4
TOTAL CONURBATION	1395.6	+0.82	−0.24	+0.58	1510.0	+0.59	−0.30	+0.29	1584.9
Inner Core	1140.4	+0.90	−0.57	+0.34	1182.7	+0.61	−0.93	−0.32	1102.9
Rest of Conurbation and Outer Area	255.2	+0.46	+1.22	+1.69	327.3	+0.52	+1.99	+2.50	482.0
EAST MERSEYSIDE	58.5	+0.98	−0.88	+0.10	63.2	+1.68	−0.18	+1.50	72.6
MERSEYSIDE REGION	1454.1	+0.83	−0.27	+0.56	1573.2	+0.60	−0.29	+0.31	1657.5

NORTH MERSEYSIDE: Inner Core—Liverpool and Bootle C.B.s
Remainder of Conurbation—Crosby M.B.; Huyton with Roby and Litherland U.D.s.
Outer Area—Southport C.B.; Formby, Ormskirk, Prescot and Rainford U.D.s; West Lancashire and Whiston R.D.s.

SOUTH MERSEYSIDE: Inner Core—Birkenhead and Wallasey C.B.s;
Remainder—Bebington M.B.; Ellesmere Port, Hoylake, Neston and Wirral U.D.s.

EAST MERSEYSIDE: Outer Area—Widnes M.B.; Runcorn U.D.

The Inner Core and the Remainder comprise the Merseyside Conurbation as defined in the 1951 Census. Adjustments have been made in trends to take account of boundary changes.
Source: Ministry of Housing and Local Govt. "Liverpool Overspill and the Development of Merseyside" (TP2a, Oct., 1956).

TABLE 11.2 *Population trends in Merseyside, 1951–1971*

	POPULATION 1951 ('000)	PERCENTAGE CHANGE per annum, 1951–61			POPULATION 1961 ('000)	PERCENTAGE CHANGE per annum, 1961–71			POPULATION 1971 ('000)
		Natural	Migration	Total		Natural	Migration	Total	
CONURBATION									
Inner Merseyside	1109.8	+0.82	−1.13	−0.33	1073.7	+0.66	−2.10	−1.44	919.5
Rest of Conurbation	276.5	+0.68	+0.59	+1.24	310.7	+0.72	+0.46	+1.18	347.2
Outer Areas	410.4	+0.60	+1.31	+1.90	488.6	+0.72	+1.59	+2.30	601.7
MERSEYSIDE REGION	1796.7	+0.74	−0.31	+0.42	1873.0	+0.69	−0.71	−0.02	1868.4

The areas are as in Table 11.1, with the addition of St. Helens, Skelmersdale and Upholland to the Outer Areas. Kirkby (included in the Outer Areas) did not become an Urban District until 1958.

TABLE 11.3 *Population trends (estimated) in Merseyside Metropolitan County and adjacent districts, 1971–1981*

District	POPULATION 1971 ('000)	PERCENTAGE CHANGE per annum, 1971–81			POPULATION 1981 ('000)
		Natural	Migration	Total	
MERSEYSIDE CO.	1656.5	−0.06	−0.87	−0.91	1511.9
Knowsley	194.1	+0.61	−1.76	−1.15	173.0
Liverpool	610.3	−0.26	−1.53	−1.79	510.0
St. Helens	189.0	+0.30	−0.26	+0.04	189.8
Sefton	307.5	−0.11	−0.16	−0.27	299.7
Wirral	355.8	−0.11	−0.35	−0.47	339.5
OUTER AREAS	266.0	N.A.	N.A.	+1.54	310.3
Ellesmere Port and Neston	78.5	N.A.	N.A.	+0.38	81.5
Halton	95.9	N.A.	N.A.	+2.40	122.0
West Lancashire	91.6	N.A.	N.A.	+1.52	106.7
MERSEYSIDE REGION	1922.6	—	—	−0.54	1822.2

was 790 838 in 1951, but fell by 45 000, 135 000 and 100 000 in the three succeeding decades to 510 000 in 1981.

Liverpool's experience, typical of the inner conurbation as a whole, epitomizes the population and social problems of most large British cities. Peter Hall (1973) calculated that whereas in 1951 just over one million (70.6%) lived in the "core" of his Merseyside Standard Metropolitan Labour Area (S.M.L.A.), this had fallen to 970 000 (66.5%) by 1961 and in 1971 there were 150 000 fewer living in the core (59.2%). Although the workforce of the core rose slightly to a peak of half-a-million in 1961, this too had fallen by 20 000 in 1966. Thus the relative downward shift in the core in both jobs and population, 1951–61, gave way in the 1960s to an absolute decline in population, followed by an absolute fall in jobs from the late 1960s.

The Thompson Plan of 1944 (Thompson, 1945) envisaged the need for overspill of 258 000 from North Merseyside (183 000 from Liverpool and 35 000 from Bootle) and 67 000 from South Merseyside, of which two-thirds would move out into Lancashire and the rest to Cheshire. The Ministry of Housing and Local Government (1956) estimated that 130 000 persons would leave Liverpool for the rest of the region between 1951 and 1957 and up to another 40 000 between 1971 and 1981. The North-West Study (Department of Economic Affairs, 1965) forecast a total increase in Merseyside's population from 1.66 million in 1963 to 2.03 million in 1981, due largely to natural increase but assuming nil migrational loss. In the event losses from the region have been substantial: 133 526 between 1961 and 1971 and an estimated 145 000 from Merseyside County, 1971–81. Thus the population in the North-West Study's region was only 1.61 million in 1971 (not its 1963-based estimate of 1.86 million) and 1.56 million in 1981. The reasons are two-fold: first, substantial migrational losses of around one-quarter of a million between 1961 and 1981; secondly, the sharp decline, in accordance with the national trend, of natural growth since the mid 1960s.

High birth rates, though partially held in check by high mortality, have ensured a relatively high level of natural increase in Merseyside until recently. In the 1950s and 1960s crude death rate varied between 11.2 and 12.1 per thousand, close to the national average, though with substantial differences between the inner and outer areas. However, up to the mid 1960s birth rates were consistently higher than the national level, among the highest for any urban region of Britain (Department of Economic Affairs, 1965). In 1947, the peak of the post-war birth "bulge", Merseyside's crude birth rate was 25.7 per thousand, compared with 20.5 for England and Wales. The differential of 20–25%, which persisted up to 1962, was significant even allowing for the youthful population structure of the region. Birth rates tended to be higher in the inner areas, at some 4 per 1000 above the suburban rates in the 1950s, though outward migration reduced that to less than 1 per 1000 by 1962. Standardized birth rates, which allow for contrasts in age structure, show that in 1961 most local authorities in the Merseyside conurbation had high local/national ratios: for example 1.18 in Liverpool, 1.30 in Bootle and 1.11 in Birkenhead. They varied between 1.12 and 1.25 in both working- and middle-class overspill suburbs of the 1950s (Pickett, 1970A). Moreover, the general fertility rate (births as a proportion of women aged 15–49) was 13% above the national rate by 1962, due especially to the high age-specific fertility in the over-30s at 25% above national level. Among the reasons for such high fertility are the larger families among the substantial Roman Catholic population (many of Irish origin) and the relatively high proportion of lower socio-economic groups, associated with relatively large families, in many inner areas and local authority estates. Since one-third of Merseyside's workers was in these groups in 1961, the impact on total fertility was substantial.

By the mid 1960s the natural growth of Merseyside's population was slowing down. Mortality remained around the national average, but the ageing population structure of the inner areas was reflected in a mortality rate 13% above the general level. Births have declined throughout Merseyside, and, except in overspill areas, the ratios of the local adjusted rates to the national in the 1970s generally lie between 0.92 and 1.07 for Liverpool, 1.03 and 1.15 for St. Helens, are at or below 1.0 for Sefton and Wirral, and substantially above (1.15–1.29) only in Knowsley, though even these have fallen in recent years. Little natural growth, indeed a decline of over 3000 between 1975 and 1979, and continuing out-movement have produced substantial total losses in all Districts of Merseyside Metropolitan County in the past decade, except St. Helens which has remained virtually static (Table 11.3). Moreover, despite increases in the outer areas, especially in West Lancashire and Runcorn New Town, there has been a substantial migrational loss in the region as a whole.

The precise structure and direction of migrational movements in the 1970s cannot yet be determined. In the 1950s and 1960s the level of migration into Merseyside was limited, and was dominated by short-range movements within Merseyside and from adjacent parts of the North-West (Table 11.4). But small yet often socially significant longer range migrations from other regions of Britain and overseas continued to diversify the region's character. Pickett (1970B) noted that between 1951 and 1966 Merseyside lost population at an annual rate of around 0.2%. The migration fields outside Merseyside were dominated by South-Central Lancashire, Central Cheshire and North Wales. Links with the Midlands and South-East were mainly outwards, but traditional ties with Wales, Scotland and, especially, Ireland remained. The 1971 Census showed that only 9.7% of the conurbation's population had moved residence in the previous year and 30% in the previous five years, and a mere 2.1% and 5.3% respectively had come from outside Merseyside. The proportions for the larger Planning Sub-District were much the same, and in the previous year over 1000 had come from each of Scotland, Ireland and the New Commonwealth and 2610 from foreign countries. But the cumulative total of those born

TABLE 11.4 *Merseyside: Migration, 1970–1971 and 1966–1971*

	RESIDENTS MOVING IN 1970–71				RESIDENTS MOVING IN 1966–71			
	Merseyside Conurbation		Merseyside Sub-District		Merseyside Conurbation		Merseyside Sub-District	
ORIGIN OF RESIDENTS	No.	% of total	No.	% of total	No.	% of total	No.	% of total
Merseyside Conurbation	96 750	7.7			305 400	24.2		
Merseyside Sub-Dist.			146 440	8.3			454 870	26.0
SELNEC Conurbation	1 340	0.1	2 470	0.1	3 340	0.3	7 240	0.4
Rest of North West	9 650	0.8	40 010	2.3	21 070	1.7	107 220	6.1
Rest of Eng & Wales	9 550	0.8	14 620	0.8	26 810	2.1	42 660	2.4
Scotland	850	0.1	1 320	0.1	2 140	0.2	3 950	0.2
Ireland	840	0.1	1 030	0.1	2 670	0.2	3 340	0.2
New Commonwealth	1 010	0.1	1 320	0.1	3 480	0.3	4 640	0.3
Foreign	1 870	0.2	2 610	0.2	4 210	0.3	5 480	0.3
ALL AREAS	122 600	9.7	178 760	10.2	372 680	29.5	544 140	31.1
TOTAL POPULATION	1 262 467		1 750 245		1 262 467		1 750 295	

Source: Census of England and Wales, 1971; Migration Tables.

Persons moving residence in 1970–71 and 1966–71 who live in the Merseyside Conurbation and the Merseyside Planning Sub-District are shown by major areas of origin.

SELNEC: South-East Lancashire and North-East Cheshire, now largely the Metropolitan County of Greater Manchester.

outside England and Wales and living in the large towns of Merseyside was small: around 29 000 Irish (1.9%); 16 500 Scots (1.1%); about 20 000 Welsh (1.3%); only 3320 New Commonwealth (0.2%); and 10 430 foreigners (0.7%) (Table 11.4). Nevertheless some migrant groups, though small, are highly concentrated and significant in local population structures.

The changing population distribution

Since the 1950s the peripheral spread of jobs, housing and population on Merseyside has intensified, and inner area decline and continued out-migration have both exceeded expectations and also sharpened social contrasts in the region. Liverpool's strategy in the 1950s had three components: firstly an overspill of some 62 000 to local authority estates at Kirkby and Halewood; secondly overspill agreements with a number of nearby towns such as Widnes and Ellesmere Port and, later, the New Towns at Skelmersdale and Runcorn; third was the "voluntary" residential mobility to private housing developments in such areas as Formby, West Lancashire and Wirral.

The achievements in the first phase were substantial. There were 124 000 new dwellings in Merseyside as a whole, including 71 000 in the conurbation of which 70% were built by local authorities. Yet despite acceleration in the rate of house building, with 53 000 new homes between 1961 and 1966 of which 30 000 were in the outer areas, Liverpool still needed 78 000 dwellings in 1966 (nearly as many as in 1955). The Department of Economic Affairs (1965) estimated overspill needs to 1981 to be 256 000, with 70 000 each going to Skelmersdale (1961) and Runcorn (1964) New Towns. Falling birth rates and continuing out-migration reduced the mid 1960s forecasts of a population of over 2 million for Merseyside by the 1980s, though Merseyside County estimates of 1973 suggested 22 000 new houses would still be needed in 1986 when Merseyside's population might stabilize at a minimum at 1 595 000.

Between 1951 and 1961 population declined in all parts of the inner conurbation, though most of the 125 000 migrational loss was from Liverpool (Table 11.2). The older suburbs and outer areas, with the exceptions of St. Helens and Southport saw population increases, mainly due to migrational gain. The 1961 Census Conurbation (see Fig. 1.4) had a relatively high level of natural increase essentially due to high fertility. In 90% of Enumeration Districts (E.D.) in dockside and working class inner areas, fertility rates were above the national average, over 30% higher in two-thirds of them. In contrast, nearly half the E.D.s in older corporation estates and mixed residential areas around the edge of the conurbation had below-average fertility. Only in very rapidly expanding private residential outer areas, such as parts of Formby, was fertility significantly above average. Such marked variations in natural increase within Merseyside narrowed with the reduction in birth rates and in fertility differentials between social classes. Since the mid 1960s the widening gap between the declining population of the conurbation and the expanding outer areas has resulted mainly from residential migration.

Between 1961 and 1971 population fell in the four inner Boroughs and in most older suburbs, Huyton excepted, due in part to falling natural increase (except in Bootle and Huyton) but mainly to high net migrational losses (Table 11.2 and Fig. 11.1). A combination of migration and younger families, boosting natural increase, brought substantial increases in most outer areas. But there were falls in Prescot and St. Helens, due to a small net outward migration, and considerable net in-migration to Southport barely compensated for natural decrease in an ageing population. Kirkby's high natural increase was partly off-set by out-migration, a commentary on the worrying decline in jobs, the full impact of which was to be felt in the 1970s.

The consequences for the Metropolitan County may be seen in relatively low population densities in 1971 in those inner areas from which most old working-class housing was

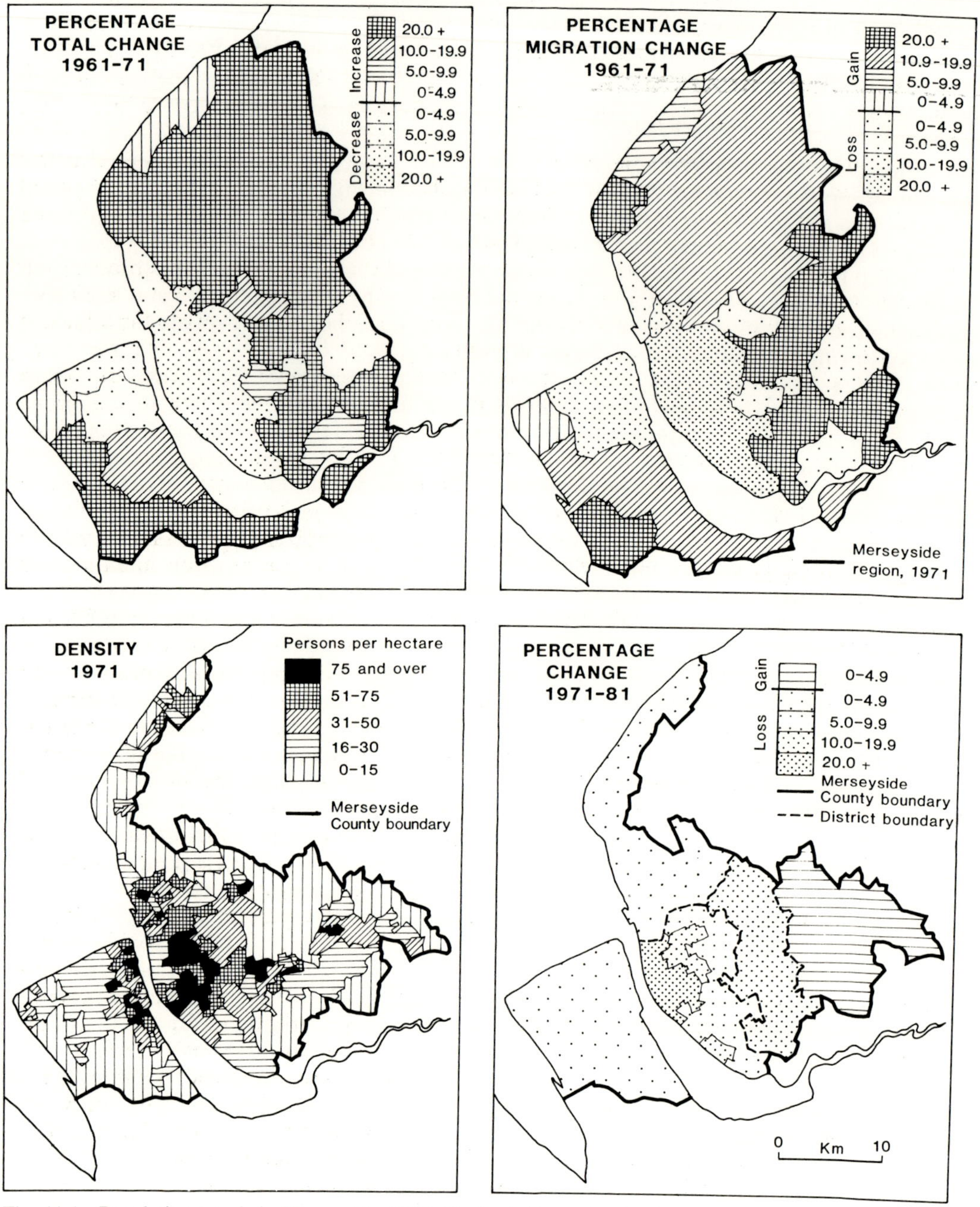

Fig. 11.1 Population trends in Merseyside, 1961–81: (top) % total and migration change 1961–71 for local authority areas in the Merseyside region (as defined in Table 11.1); (bottom) population density by Wards in Merseyside Metropolitan County, 1971, and population trend, 1971–81, by District and, for Liverpool Special Area only, by Ward

cleared in the 1960s. The highest densities are in an inner ring of late nineteenth- and early twentieth-century housing with substantial areas of multi-occupancy and of local authority high-rise renewal. They are also to be found in peripheral areas of post-war local authority overspill, such as Kirkby and parts of Whiston, with large families and high occupancy rates. While it is too early to assess the full effects of the demographic changes of the 1970s, the first results of the 1981 Census indicate a sharp fall in natural growth, due to fertility decline, and increased migrational losses from all Districts in the County (Table 11.3 and Fig. 11.1), but these have been particularly marked in the inner areas. In Liverpool Special Area (Supplement, Census 1981, CM 28/S) there has been a fall of 20.5%, some Wards losing over one-third of their population since the 1971 Census.

The 1971 Census residential migration tables showed that movement within Merseyside far exceeded the relatively modest longer-distance migration into Merseyside (Table 11.4). Around 90% of residents had not moved during 1970–71 in contrast to the adjacent Lancashire and Cheshire Districts where mobility was quite high. Over 50% of movers to those Districts came from outside, mainly from Merseyside and particularly from Liverpool, which also provided 39% of those moving to Knowsley and over 10% of those to St. Helens and Southport. Migration into the region from beyond the North-West, including most of the overseas migrants, went mainly to Liverpool.

These trends have had a marked effect on the population characteristics of various parts of the region. This can be illustrated from three contrasting types of area: an area of local authority overspill and New Town development such as Kirkby; an area of Merseyside's rapidly expanding areas of private residential development such as Formby; and an inner zone of population decline and social stress such as Toxteth.

In the 1950s the major overspill area was Kirkby, where population leapt from 3210 in 1951 to 52 139 in 1961. With 88% of its population housed by the local authority, it nevertheless had occupancy levels 40% above Liverpool's and 56% above Formby's, and in 1971 38% of Kirkby's households lived at over one person per room. High birth rates, 12% above national level in the 1950s, produced a youthful population. Despite the fall in standardized fertility since the mid 1960s to around national level, 11.4% of Kirkby's population in 1971 was under 5 (9.7% in Merseyside), and a staggering 24.1% was aged 5–14 (Merseyside 14.8%). The entry into the 1970s labour market of large numbers of often poorly qualified school-leavers has produced a major juvenile unemployment problem for this largely working-class community, and is reflected in migrational losses in the 1960s and 1970s as well as in high rates of youth unemployment.

As another means of easing Merseyside's population pressure, overspill agreements were contracted with Widnes, Burnley, Winsford and Ellesmere Port to provide 18 500 homes for 41 000 people between 1948 and 1981, though most have now gone to Skelmersdale and Runcorn New Towns. Ellesmere Port, whose booming industries depended greatly on commuter labour, had an overspill agreement with Liverpool for up to 20 000 people between 1958 and 1972, thereby helping the town's housing programme and giving it the considerable advantage of being placed in the Merseyside Development Area. In the event less than 10 000 were housed, but young families, with 60% of wives under 30 years and most with one or two children, contributed to a youthful population with a high rate of natural increase (Aspinall and Hudson, 1982, Chapter 11).

Formby, a classic example of a middle-class commuter suburb which housed Merseysiders from late Victorian times, doubled its population from 1951 to 23 501 in 1971, mainly by private residential migration. In 1961 39% of households were headed by persons of high socio-economic Class (Executive and Professional), with 47% in Class 3 (Skilled and Non-Manual Workers). A 1968 survey (Pickett, 1970B) showed that 31% of its population was under 15 and only 6% over 65. Moreover, although 25% of its population moved residence between 1965 and 1966, mainly by voluntary migration from Liverpool, the 1971 journey to work Census data show that most people still look to central Merseyside for employment.

The inner areas of the Conurbation have been mostly exporters of young families, leaving ageing people in ageing houses. Many such areas have a disproportionately large number of transient individuals and families, including immigrants and students. They have tended to become "rooming-house districts", as in Granby Ward, part of Toxteth, where in 1971 46% lived in privately rented accommodation (20% furnished), mainly in large sub-divided Victorian houses. Though total population fell by 37.5% between 1971 and 1981 there was partial redevelopment in the 1970s when local authority housing, accounting for 40% of dwellings, brought younger families back to the area. Characterized in the Liverpool Inner Area Study as an area of high unemployment, sickness and social malaise, Granby has been a problem area since the 1950s (Wilson and Womersley, 1977B, Chapter 12). With some 40% of its workforce in semi-skilled and unskilled categories, it has been badly hit by unemployment, especially among youths and the coloured population. The 1981 Census Liverpool Special Area Supplement shows that male and female economic activity is low (7% and 3% respectively below the city's level). The high proportion of under-five and school-age children is untypical of many inner areas, and the high proportion of one-person households (34%) contains a substantial number of pensioners living alone.

Population structure

These "snapshots" point to considerable local variety in both population and social structures within Merseyside. Until recently the higher birth rates in the older suburbs of the Conurbation and in adjacent industrial towns have produced a youthful population structure conducive to growth. Moreover, selective residential migration to new suburbs and overspill areas created a population with relatively large numbers of young married couples with young families. Such areas as Kirkby and Formby have high proportions of young people, whereas many declining inner areas and older suburbs have ageing populations.

In the 1960s Merseyside's age structure was similar to the national structure, though with a growing proportion of over-65s, particularly in the 1961 Census Conurbation (Table 11.5). In contrast the overspill areas had a marked increase of under-15s in the 1950s and early 1960s. Throughout the region there was a fall in the proportion of younger working-age population, somewhat mitigating the adverse unemployment rates. By 1971 fertility decline and residential mobility within Merseyside were reflected in a sharp reduction of 28 000 in the number of under-5s in inner Merseyside, though their numbers and those aged 5–14 increased in the rest of the region. Everywhere, however, the number and proportions of over-65s, many of whom lived in single-person households, increased substantially.

The dramatic changes of the 1970s have considerable implications for social and economic planning. Preliminary 1981 census figures and official 1979 based estimates for the Metropolitan County show a dramatic fall in Merseyside's under-5 and school-age populations of 43 600 and 65 000 respectively (Table 11.6). The impact has been particularly marked in parts of inner Liverpool, with serious consequences for schools (Chapter 13). Recent projections suggest a continuing fall in the school population in the 1980s. In contrast, the proportion aged over-65 continues to increase. While the population of working-age has remained remarkably constant, considerable pressure has been placed on the labour market at a time of declining job opportunities by the large numbers of school-leavers in the 1970s. Moreover, these pressures will carry through into the younger working-age groups (16–44) of the 1980s.

TABLE 11.5 *Population structure of Merseyside by age groups, 1951–1971*

Year	Total ('000)	0–4 No.	0–4 %	5–14 No.	5–14 %	15–44 No.	15–44 %	45–64 No.	45–64 %	65+ No.	65+ %
INNER MERSEYSIDE											
1951	1107.5	109.8	9.9	172.3	15.6	479.9	43.3	243.1	22.0	102.3	9.2
1961	1073.5	100.0	9.3	181.4	16.9	428.0	39.9	254.1	23.7	111.0	10.3
1971	919.5	72.4	7.9	158.2	17.2	349.8	38.0	222.0	24.1	117.5	12.8
SUBURBS											
1951	274.9	24.5	8.9	42.7	15.5	116.8	42.5	64.1	23.3	26.9	9.8
1961	310.7	27.7	8.9	51.8	16.7	120.9	38.9	77.9	25.1	32.5	10.5
1971	347.2	29.5	8.5	64.7	18.6	132.5	38.5	79.8	23.0	40.7	11.7
CONURBATION											
1951	1382.4	134.3	9.7	216.3	15.6	595.7	43.1	307.0	22.2	129.3	9.4
1961	1384.2	127.7	9.2	233.2	16.8	547.7	39.6	331.9	24.0	143.5	10.4
1971	1266.7	101.9	8.0	222.9	17.6	482.3	38.2	301.8	23.8	158.2	12.5
OUTER AREAS											
1951	405.6	34.7	8.6	57.1	14.1	169.9	41.9	98.8	24.4	43.6	10.7
1961	488.6	44.5	9.1	92.7	19.0	187.8	38.4	114.2	23.4	52.3	10.7
1971	601.7	55.3	9.2	110.4	18.3	238.2	39.6	131.9	21.9	65.9	11.0
MERSEYSIDE REGION											
1951	1788.0	169.0	9.5	273.4	15.3	766.6	42.9	406.0	22.7	172.9	9.7
1961	1872.8	172.2	9.2	325.9	17.4	735.5	39.2	446.1	23.8	195.8	10.4
1971	1868.4	157.2	8.4	333.3	17.8	720.5	38.6	433.7	23.2	224.1	12.0

The areas of the Conurbation and Merseyside region are as defined in Tables 11.1 and 11.2.

Population structure and mobility have affected many aspects of housing and household structure (Fig. 11.2). Despite major public housing programmes over the previous 25 years, the 1972 House Condition Survey estimated that only about 48% of Liverpool's housing stock was "fully fit", and 12% and 5% respectively unfit or suitable only for short term improvement. St. Helens too had relatively high figures of poor housing (23%). Moreover, 62% of Liverpool's 62 000 privately rented homes did not have exclusive use of hot water and an inside toilet. The spatial pattern of households lacking basic amenities is very much associated with the older privately-rented sector. However, overcrowding is not confined to the inner city, though the worst cases are still found there, but also reflects large families on recent local authority overspill estates, for example in Netherton, Belle Vale, Halewood, Kirkby and Woodchurch. The areas of predominant owner-occupation, particularly in north Sefton and west Wirral, have a high social status population with relative affluence and good housing conditions.

Household structure underlines one particularly significant aspect of demographic structure: the growing proportion of elderly households. In Merseyside County one- and two-person households of pensionable age form nearly one-quarter of all households. Moreover the proportions of pensioners living alone, mainly women, is now 14.7% of households, and in parts of Liverpool this rises to over 18%. Though there are substantial contrasts in the proportions between, for example, Knowsley with its youthful population and Sefton and Wirral's older populations, all areas have seen an increase in such single-person households. This is a major problem for the community and for medical and social services.

TABLE 11.6 *Population structure of Merseyside Metropolitan County by age groups, 1981 and (projected) 1991*

DISTRICT	YEAR	TOTAL RESIDENT	0–4 No.	0–4 %	5–15 No.	5–15 %	16–44 No.	16–44 %	45–64 (M) –59 (F) No.	45–64 (M) –59 (F) %	65+(M) 60+(F) No.	65+(M) 60+(F) %
KNOWSLEY	1981	173.0	12.3	7.1	32.7	18.9	74.2	42.9	33.2	19.2	20.8	12.0
	1991	*164.1*	*15.0*	*9.1*	*25.7*	*15.7*	*68.3*	*41.6*	*27.8*	*16.9*	*27.4*	*16.7*
LIVERPOOL	1981	503.7	29.2	5.8	79.6	15.8	200.5	39.8	100.7	20.0	93.2	18.5
	1991	*456.5*	*37.0*	*8.1*	*63.6*	*13.9*	*193.3*	*42.3*	*81.3*	*17.8*	*81.4*	*17.8*
ST. HELENS	1981	189.3	11.7	6.2	34.1	18.0	77.0	40.7	36.9	19.5	29.3	15.5
	1991	*185.1*	*16.7*	*9.0*	*26.0*	*14.0*	*80.9*	*43.7*	*34.8*	*18.8*	*26.7*	*14.4*
SEFTON	1981	298.2	16.7	5.6	50.1	16.8	116.6	39.1	60.8	20.4	54.3	18.2
	1991	*285.5*	*19.8*	*6.9*	*40.3*	*14.1*	*116.2*	*40.7*	*55.8*	*19.5*	*53.3*	*18.7*
WIRRAL	1981	339.0	20.3	6.0	56.3	16.6	132.5	39.1	66.8	19.7	63.0	18.6
	1991	*329.0*	*25.0*	*7.6*	*47.4*	*14.4*	*134.1*	*40.8*	*62.7*	*19.1*	*59.8*	*18.2*
MERSEYSIDE COUNTY	1981	1503.1	90.2	6.0	252.8	16.8	600.8	40.0	298.4	19.8	260.6	17.3
	1991	*1420.3*	*113.6*	*8.0*	*203.1*	*14.3*	*592.8*	*41.7*	*262.3*	*18.5*	*248.5*	*17.5*

The figures are 1979-based estimates. Population totals from the Preliminary Report of the 1981 Census give a population of 1 511 915 for the County and the following District populations: Knowsley—172 957; Liverpool—509 981; St Helens—189 759; Sefton—299 724; Wirral—339 494.

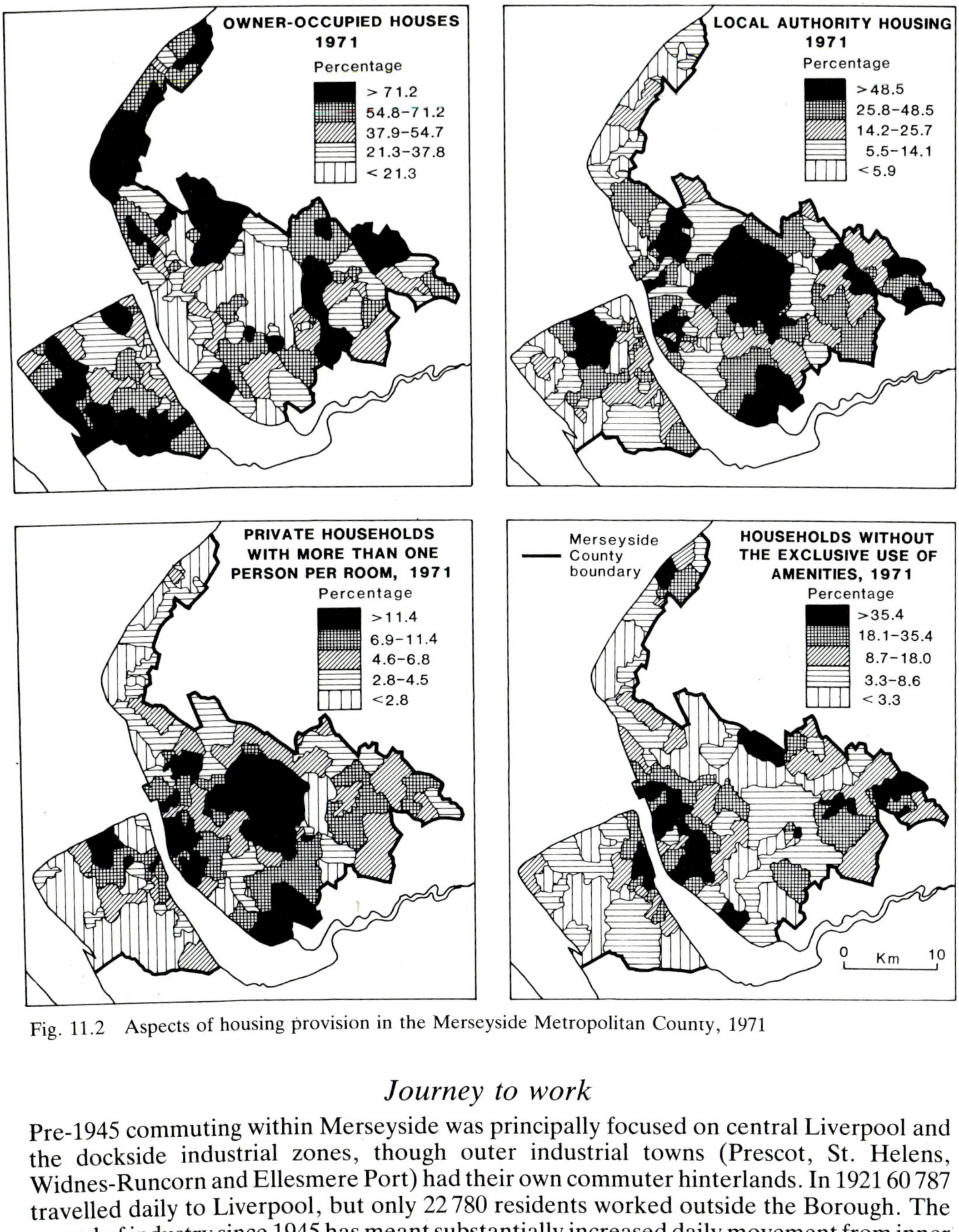

Fig. 11.2 Aspects of housing provision in the Merseyside Metropolitan County, 1971

Journey to work

Pre-1945 commuting within Merseyside was principally focused on central Liverpool and the dockside industrial zones, though outer industrial towns (Prescot, St. Helens, Widnes-Runcorn and Ellesmere Port) had their own commuter hinterlands. In 1921 60 787 travelled daily to Liverpool, but only 22 780 residents worked outside the Borough. The spread of industry since 1945 has meant substantially increased daily movement from inner areas to new industrial estates and major industrial complexes, such as those at Ellesmere Port, Port Sunlight and Kirkby, but residential migration from the inner conurbation has until recently maintained a strong centripetal flow. Thus while Central Liverpool absorbed

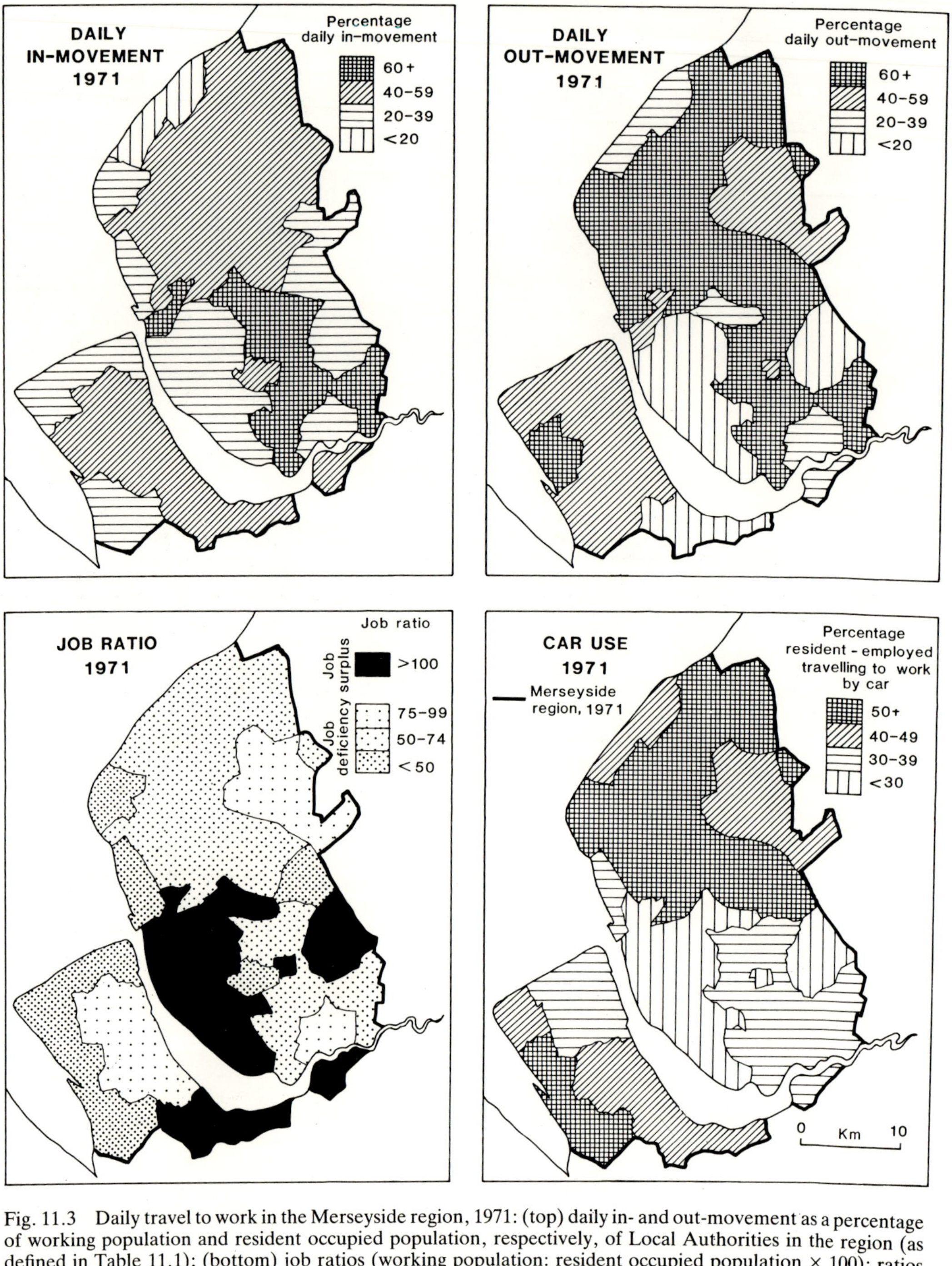

Fig. 11.3 Daily travel to work in the Merseyside region, 1971: (top) daily in- and out-movement as a percentage of working population and resident occupied population, respectively, of Local Authorities in the region (as defined in Table 11.1); (bottom) job ratios (working population: resident occupied population × 100); ratios above 100 indicate job surplus, and less than 100 job deficiency; car use: percentage of employed population who travel to work by car within and from the local authority areas in which they are resident

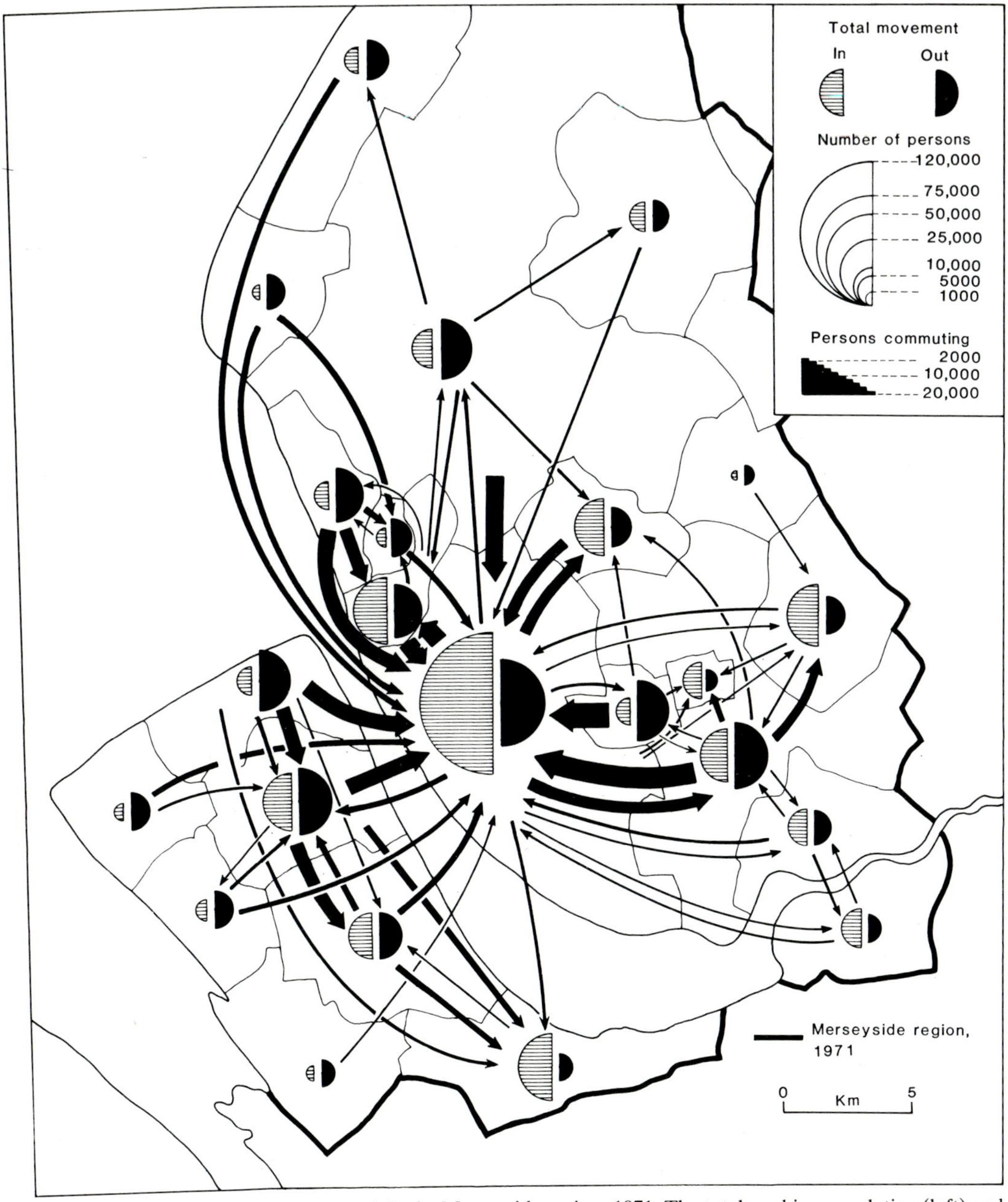

Fig. 11.4 Major daily journeys to work in the Merseyside region, 1971. The total working population (left) and resident working population (right) in each local authority area are indicated, together with all daily movements over 1000 between local authority areas

most of the 88 000 travelling to work in the Borough in 1951, the substantial increase to 119 080 by 1971 was spread among a larger number of workplaces in the city. Most inner Local Authorities, Birkenhead apart, had increased daily in-movement in the 1960s, but they experienced even greater increases in out-movement, a fact reflected in the falling ratio between employment and resident workers (the job ratio) (Fig. 11.3). Indeed, the largest increases in in-commuting between 1961 and 1971 were in peripheral areas such as

Kirkby, Ellesmere Port, Whiston and Runcorn, while even in mainly residential areas like West Lancashire, Ormskirk, Crosby and on Deeside there were relatively substantial increases in jobs and also in-movement. Nevertheless, the 1971 work journeys were still dominated by a relatively few job-surplus areas and by strong movements from periphery to centre (Fig. 11.4). But commuting to the conurbation centre, which in 1961 drew 157 000 workers from other parts of Liverpool and the Merseyside region, had fallen to 90 550 in 1971, and has been further reduced by job losses in the 1970s.

Mode of transport in work journeys is a commentary not only on the relation of residence to workplace, but also on the quality of public transport and on the varying levels of affluence within the region. One aspect, levels of car usage, is a useful indicator (Fig. 11.3). Lower levels of car usage by residents of Liverpool and other inner local authority areas reflect not only shorter journeys and better access to public transport, but also one of the lowest levels of car ownership in the country. In 1981 half Merseyside's households had no car (compared with 58% in 1971), ranging from 42% in more affluent Districts (Sefton and Wirral) to 62% in Liverpool. Although the economic problems of the 1970s have brought declining use of public transport since 1971, the high proportion of journeys to work by bus, over 40% in Bootle, Liverpool, Huyton and Kirkby and over one-third in Birkenhead, Wallasey, St. Helens and Whiston, underline their significance (Chapter 6). Moreover, the success of Merseyrail, which increased its daily passengers by 27% between 1977 and 1980 including an increase from 1200 to 30 000 per week on the Garston–Kirkby–Liverpool section, will undoubtedly be reflected in the 1981 Census Tables.

Conclusion

Population forecasts are notoriously liable to error. Nevertheless the forces which have led to a decline of Merseyside's population since the 1960s remain, and similar trends are likely to continue in the foreseeable future. The fertility decline of the 1970s, combined with net outward migration, have produced an ageing population with a lower growth potential than in the past. Recent (1979-based) estimates suggest a further fall of some 40–50 000 in Liverpool's population by 1991 (Table 11.6). A 40 000 reduction in the population of the other Districts (at rates between −2.5% and −5% over the decade) could produce a decline in the County's population of up to 90 000 (−6.5%). This is far below the most pessimistic forecast in the 1973 County estimates (1 595 000 by 1986), and it is now unlikely that the population of any District will increase, as was then expected for St. Helens, Sefton and Wirral.

While some of this loss may be due to higher migration to such peripheral districts as Halton and West Lancashire, the growth of these areas is also slowing. Clearly most of the decline is due to the marked fall in the numbers of young people resulting from a fall in birth rate. If the larger cohorts of the early 1960s produce families of the present size in the 1980s, the younger age-groups will increase, but not dramatically, and with a fall in the numbers of pensioners, except in Knowsley, the structure may stabilize.

This may bring some benefits. A lagging housing programme will have a sufficient number of dwellings, though renewal of some of the large stock of late nineteenth-century houses suggests a continuing need for 30 000 new dwellings by 1986. However, even with a reduction of 40–50 000 in people of working age by 1991, the possible loss of a further 60 000 jobs suggested in a recent report to the Merseyside Economic Development Committee in addition to the 60 000 lost between 1977 and 1981 will, if not compensated for by new jobs, exacerbate the unemployment problem. The balance between population and economic resources which has bedevilled Merseyside for most of this century is unlikely to be resolved in the immediate future.

Chapter 12

URBAN POVERTY, THE INNER CITY AND THE ECONOMY OF LIVERPOOL

ALAN CHAPE

This chapter is concerned with "urban poverty" and the "inner city" in Liverpool, and how these have been affected by the processes of industrial change and economic decline and by the responses of central and local government. Urban poverty has many aspects, including economic, social, environmental and even political (reflecting the lack of power and control of some groups), and can be broadly defined as a lack of access to a variety of markets or services covering areas such as housing, employment and education. It will also be used in this chapter as an umbrella term which embraces the related concepts of "deprivation", "disadvantage", "social malaise", "under-privilege" and "inequality". All of these concepts have been given more specific meanings linked to processes like the "culture of poverty" and "cycle of deprivation". Generally, however, they have become inter-changeable in the public mind since they leapt to the forefront of public policy in the 1960s.

The study of poverty, especially the emphasis on urban poverty, was advanced at that time under the "deprivation" banner. Poverty was considered to be a problem of people and families, and studies emphasized the internal pathology of deviant groups. This spawned theories like the "cycle of deprivation", which suggested that psychological handicaps and inadequacies of individuals and families were transmitted from one generation to the next. Deprived people were considered to reside in "small pockets", especially within the major cities, and this was reflected in the early anti-poverty urban-based initiatives. As the 1970s unfolded increasing attention was focused on the wider causes or structural influences which were sustaining urban poverty, especially the processes of industrial change and economic decline in the older industrial cities. The intensification of the national economic recession made it increasingly clear that such structural changes were fundamental, and the idea that poverty existed only in "small pockets" was increasingly discredited.

The inner city has entered the public consciousness as a term synonymous with a combination of bad housing conditions, vandalism, racial conflict, decaying infrastructure, vacant and high priced land, a declining economic base and high unemployment. There is no clear and consistent definition of the inner city, but in its spatial sense the term refers to the inner parts of the major conurbations (like Merseyside) which have been the scene of massive economic, social and physical changes in the post-war period. However, as the term "inner city" has become public currency, it has been increasingly questioned by many who claim that the concept is ill-defined and even misguided. Much of this critique is based on the twin propositions that most people who live in the inner city are neither poor nor deprived, and most poor and deprived people do not live in the inner city. This presupposes that the inner city can be spatially defined, a supposition which requires in turn a clear definition of the "inner city problem".

In this sense the inner city is an elusive term all too often defined for academic and other study in terms of data availability. This chapter will make no attempt to prejudge which part of Liverpool constitutes the inner city. The spatial frame of reference will be Liverpool generally—the City as an "inner city". The approach will be to highlight those areas of Liverpool which contain a concentration of urban problems. This then makes it possible to consider whether the spatial concentrations of such problems as unemployment merely reflect the greater representation of vulnerable groups in the area (e.g. the unskilled), or whether there is a significant "area" effect which transcends the presence of such groups. It also allows an assessment of the degree to which area-based initiatives by central and local governments are relevant to a wide range of urban problems, some of which are spatially concentrated (e.g. ethnic minorities and housing amenities) and some spatially dispersed (e.g. low incomes).

It is also important, whatever definition of the inner city is used, not to isolate the area from its regional, national and even international context. This avoids the trap of trying to explain inner city problems in terms of characteristics which are totally internal to such areas, for example, a supposed lack of skilled labour, the actions of local politicians and planners and the psychological and sociological propensities of the inhabitants (Massey, 1979). Nevertheless, while it is perfectly proper to set the inner city problem in a wider context, there is also a value in looking at the internal social and economic structure of Liverpool to promote a better understanding of the level and spatial pattern of some of the major dimensions of urban poverty.

Urban poverty as social malaise

The analysis of the spatial pattern of urban poverty emerged during the 1960s and early 1970s as an important element in many planning departments' work, especially in Liverpool, Newcastle, Glasgow and Southwark. The focus of the work was "social malaise" in the major cities, quantifying its existence and mapping the results to highlight the "worst" parts of these cities. Underpinning the approach were the theories of the Chicago school of urban economists and geographers, notably the techniques of Social Area Analysis developed in the 1950s as a tool for defining "natural" areas within cities. While the Chicago school theories do not have any great explanatory powers, the techniques associated with them are useful provided the emphasis is on identifying the differences between areas and not on ranking areas on a subjective "good" to "bad" basis. The techniques were first used by the Liverpool City Planning Department in 1968 with the publication of the study "Social Malaise in Liverpool" (Liverpool City Council, 1968). This involved collecting and analysing a wide range of demographic, social and economic data from the 1966 Census and from thirty-six local authority indicators which were said to reflect the presence of social malaise, e.g. job instability, crime, debtors and possession orders. The results were mapped and presented on a Ward basis, and these highlighted a small group of problem Wards chiefly located in and around the city centre with three outliers on the edge of the City at Dovecot, Gillmoss and Speke. Results from the study were used to define a number of "Priority Areas" which became the focus for special initiatives, such as the Vauxhall Community Development Project (1969), to combat urban poverty (see below, pp. 173–176).

The limitations of the Social Malaise Study quickly became evident (Webber, 1975, pp. 12–13). There was no conceptual base to the study so that malaise was defined according to the data available to the local authority. The techniques used, principal components analysis and linkage analysis, were only imperfectly understood. In addition by emphasizing a single aggregate measure of "need", the study failed to acknowledge the very different combinations of urban poverty indicators. Whatever its deficiencies, however, the study was important in two major respects. Dramatic differences between areas of the City were illustrated and presented at the politically-sensitive Ward level, although the technical nature of the study reduced its political impact. In addition the indicators used showed that many of the problems of the geographical inner city, as areas in and around the city centre, were also present in the geographical outer city, in the local

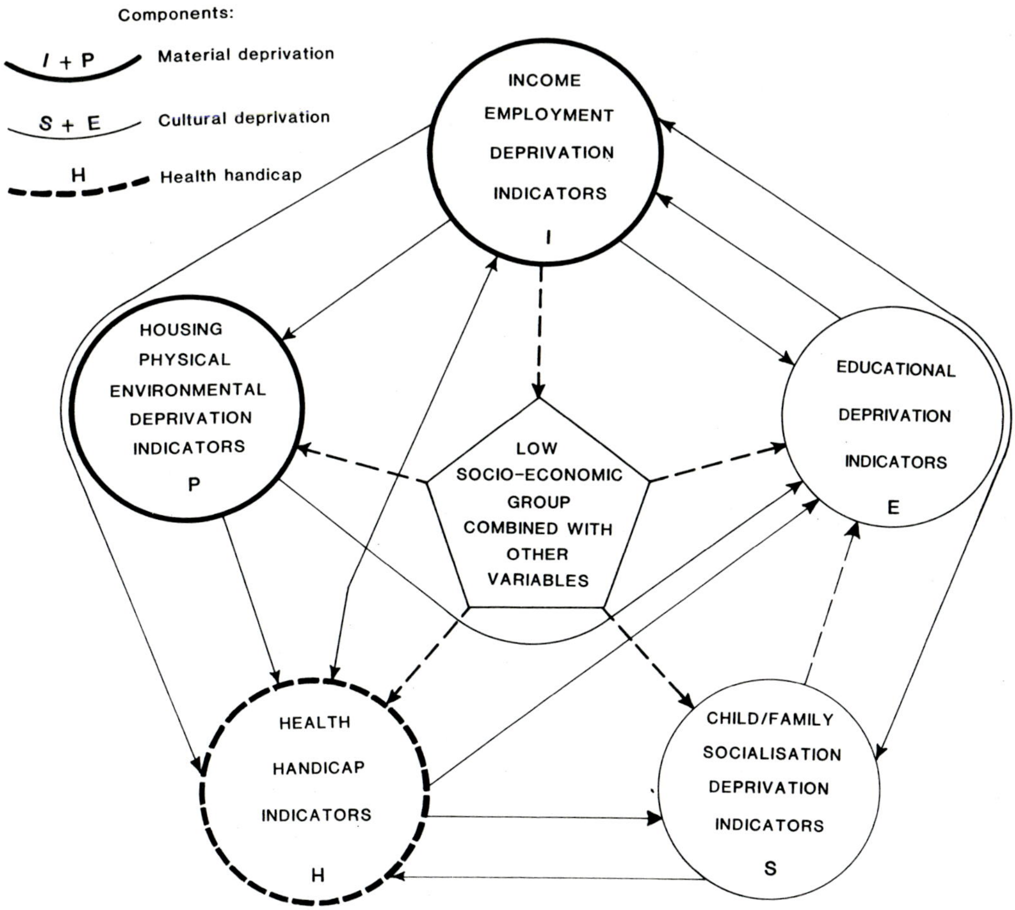

Fig. 12.1 A conceptual model of deprivation

authority estates of Dovecot, Gillmoss and Speke, and that there was no simple relationship between poor housing and the selected malaise indicators.

Refining the approach: The Social Area Study

Describing and understanding the levels and spatial pattern of urban poverty need to be supported by the development of a conceptual base. Following the 1968 Social Malaise Study this was an important element in the work of the Liverpool City Planning Department. The work involved a much deeper consideration of the indicators that should be used to represent urban "deprivation" ("malaise" was by then considered to be an offensive and inappropriate term), the relationships between them and how they influenced the social and spatial processes operating in a major urban area. Figure 12.1 summarizes the model that was eventually developed, and illustrates the potential linkages between the major components of deprivation. Using this conceptual base twenty non-census indicators were selected as being diagnostic of urban deprivation. However, because these indicators were thinly distributed throughout the City they could not be

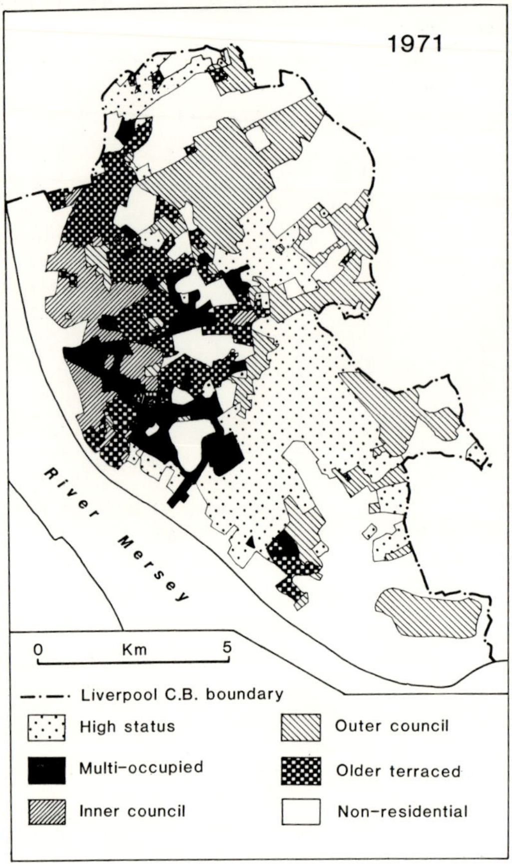

Fig. 12.2 Social Areas of Liverpool, 1971

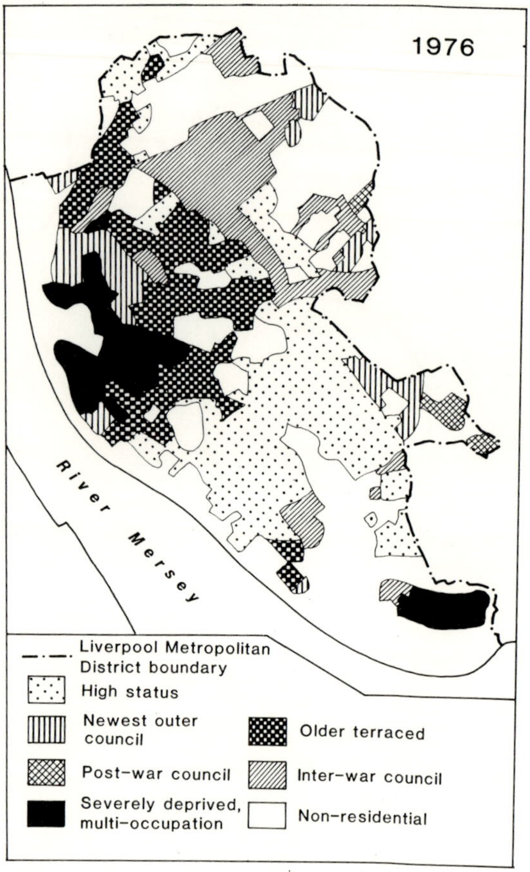

Fig. 12.3 Social Areas of Liverpool, 1976

used, by themselves, to generate any meaningful kind of area typology. For example, there were only 169 recorded cases of delinquency in Liverpool in 1971. Their spatial pattern was examined only after a description and interpretation of Liverpool's urban structure had been completed using the very rich body of data provided by the 1971 Census small-area statistics. The starting point for this work was that poverty or deprivation was connected with the distribution of wealth and income generally, and that many of the factors perpetuating and reinforcing area differences lay outside the poor areas. Thus poor and affluent areas had to be considered together.

In 1974 the Planning Research Applications Group (based at the Centre for Environmental Studies) was commissioned by the Liverpool City Council, Merseyside County Council and the Inner Area Study Consultants to provide a descriptive area typology of Liverpool, based on 1971 Census data and a range of non-census data collected by the City Council (Webber, 1975). This became known as the Liverpool Social Area Study. Broadly the Social Area Study found that the City could be classified into five different area types or Social Areas (Fig. 12.2). The Social Areas were described as follows:

TABLE 12.1 *Distribution of population, tenure and status by Social Areas, 1971 (figures are percentages of the City total)*

	High-status	Multi-occupied	Inner Council	Outer Council	Older terraced	City
Population	22	9	9	33	27	100
Tenure						
owner-occupied	51	8	1	11	29	100
council tenant	3	2	20	69	6	100
private unfurnished	17	14	3	6	60	100
private furnished	17	61	3	5	15	100
Socio-Economic Status						
professional/managerial	55	11	3	18	14	100
non-manual	37	12	4	27	21	100
skilled manual	17	8	6	38	31	100
semi-skilled	10	9	11	37	32	100
unskilled	4	6	24	35	31	100

Source: Wilson and Womersley (1977B).

- "High-status" areas—these were areas of mainly owner-occupied housing, and were subdivided into five different sub-areas or "clusters". They ranged from the very high-status areas found in the established parts of Calderstones to the new private housing on the eastern slopes of the Woolton Edge.
- "Multi-occupied and sharing" areas—in the main these provided furnished rented accommodation chiefly for young people. Again they were sub-divided into five clusters ranging from the low-status, dilapidated properties on Princes Avenue to the higher-status areas east of Sefton Park.
- "Inner Council" estates—these comprised mainly, though not exclusively, older blocks of flats. Three sub-areas were identified, all consisting of low-status Council areas chiefly differentiated by the size of their dwellings.
- "Outer Council" estates—these were mainly houses and newer blocks of flats. Eight different types of "Outer Council" estate were identified, differentiated by their socio-economic profiles and age of dwellings.
- "Older terraced" areas—these were mostly unfurnished, privately rented property, much of which lacked basic amenities like an internal W.C. Four sub-areas were identified, ranging from those in an advanced state of decay (where the majority of dwellings have been demolished since 1971) to areas transitional between the "older terraced" and "high-status" categories.

Table 12.1 summarizes some of the major characteristics of these Social Areas.

Urban poverty and the social areas

The Social Area Study was important because it allowed planners to manipulate a large mass of data within an emerging conceptual framework and to highlight the different combinations of urban poverty in terms of their spatial pattern, inter-relationships and linkages with wider societal processes. The Inner Council Social Area was characterized by its very depressed condition compared with the rest of the City, except for parts of the

Multi-occupied and Sharing Area. In virtually every respect life for many inner city council residents was "bad", whether this was measured by overcrowding, sickness, unemployment, level of skills or by non-census indicators such as delinquency and truancy. On only one indicator did these areas arguably "perform" well in 1971—one-third of their workers walked to work compared with one-sixth for the City generally. Unemployment was twice the City average, the unskilled 2.5 times, and overcrowding 3.5 times.

The Multi-occupied and Sharing Social Area was characterized by a relatively high-status population, combined with a high concentration of vulnerable minorities (normally associated with low-status areas). For some time these areas had been acting as reception points for groups entering the City, especially students and ethnic minorities. In 1971 this Social Area accommodated only 9% of the City's total population, but 45% of the New Commonwealth-born residents. Most people were renting furnished property, with some groups (the young, mobile, professional workers and students) using this as a temporary solution, while others (the elderly, those on low incomes and certain ethnic groups) regarded it as a permanent, if often unsatisfactory, home. In parts of this Social Area unemployment rates were equivalent to those pertaining in the Inner Council Social Area.

The Older terraced Social Area generally showed no more evidence of deprivation than the City generally. The exception was the poor quality of much of its housing stock, 62% of which lacked an internal W.C. Unemployment in 1971 was around the City average and overcrowding half the average.

The Outer Council Social Area was the largest, accommodating 33% of the City's total population in 1971. It also included some inner-area council estates which displayed social and economic characteristics more typical of the outer-area council estates. Any general picture of this Social Area would disguise the significant differences between the various types of estate, especially the established inter-war estates of Norris Green and Allerton and the most recent developments of Netherley/Belle Vale and Cantril Farm. Many of the post-war estates had high levels of unemployment and school absenteeism which were closely associated with indicators of low income (e.g. children in receipt of free school meals).

The High-status Social Area was characterized by few social problems and the absence of vulnerable groups such as single parent families, large families, sick and unemployed males and ethnic minorities. While this Social Area accommodated 22% of the City's population, it had over half the City's owner-occupied and professional/managerial households. Over three-fifths of workers had a degree or H.N.C., and car ownership was high. The journey to work was predominantly by car to service and government occupations in the city centre. Most of the migration into this Social Area was from outside the City.

Updating the approach and monitoring changes

The rich data base of the 1971 Census was the key to the Social Area Study. Unfortunately the cancellation of the 1976 Sample Census meant the updating of the approach and monitoring of changes had to be based on a range of non-Census indicators. These were selected to reflect the major components of the hypothetical model of deprivation outlined in Figure 12.1. While the model has deficiencies, one of the ways of examining its relevance is to collect indicators of the components which can then be tested using the techniques developed in the Social Area Study. Seventeen social indicators were selected, and used to produce area typologies for 1973 and 1976.

The Liverpool Social Area map for 1976 (Fig. 12.3) shows many similarities with the 1971 picture. Notwithstanding the similarities, however, there are significant differences.

TABLE 12.2 *Distribution of selected social indicators by Social Areas, 1976 (figures are percentages of the City total)*

	High-status	Low-cost housing	Newest Outer Council	Mainly Post-war Council	Mainly Inter-war Council	Deprived Council and Multi-Occupied Core	City
Population	25	30	3	11	19	12	100
Tenure							
owner-occupied	51	33	0	3	10	3	100
council tenant	8	8	6	23	35	20	100
private rented	21	61	1	2	4	11	100
Income/Employment							
long-term unemployment	9	27	4	16	18	26	100
free school meals	6	22	13	19	20	20	100
Health/Handicap							
infant mortality	15	31	8	12	12	21	100
elderly aged 75+	28	30	1	9	22	11	100
Educational							
school absenteeism	3	21	4	24	16	31	100

Source: Background Paper: "Deprivation Work and Social Area Analysis" (Liverpool Planning Department, 1980, Unpublished).

The severely deprived inner council estates and the "worst" parts of the multi-occupied and sharing areas have merged into one Social Area, which includes most of the outer area council estate at Speke. The Outer Council Social Area of 1971 has become three distinctive Social Areas, which distinguish between the inter-war and post-war council estates and the most recent council estates at Netherley and Cantril Farm. The "better" parts of the Multi-occupied and Sharing Areas have now merged with the mainly Older Terraced Housing Areas to create a new Low-cost Housing Social Area.

Table 12.2 summarizes some of the major characteristics of the 1976 Social Areas. One of the major findings of the 1976 analysis was the relatively poor position of much of the City's council housing areas similar to the "worst" parts of the multi-occupied core area on the fringe of the city centre. The Deprived Council and Multi-occupied Core Social Area, centred on Vauxhall, Abercromby, Granby and Brunswick, contained only 12% of the City's population, but accommodated 26% of all long-term unemployment, 20% of all children receiving free school meals and 31% of all school absenteeism. In addition the Mainly Post-war Council and Newest outer Council Social Areas were characterized by a disproportionate incidence of a range of social indicators (Table 12.2). Conversely the Mainly Inter-war Council Social Area was relatively less deprived, as was the Low-cost Housing Social Area.

Urban poverty, unemployment and the Liverpool economy

The common deficiency of the work on the Social Malaise Study, the Social Area Study and on updating the social indicators is the lack of a clear link with the processes of industrial change and economic decline. Poverty, deprivation or malaise is now better described but not necessarily more clearly understood. A better understanding requires a greater appreciation of the role played by industrial changes and economic decline. These processes are not new to the Liverpool economy; they have been more or less continuous for much of this century. It is these processes which have been an important underlying influence in the level and spatial pattern of urban poverty in Liverpool, and have given rise to conditions such as unemployment, job instability, low pay, poor housing conditions and environmental dereliction. An important indicator of the scale of industrial change and economic decline in Liverpool is the changing level of the City's employment between 1971 and 1981. The number of jobs declined by 26% overall during the period; construction jobs declined by 53%, manufacturing jobs by 38% and service jobs by 18%. In all cases these rates of decline were significantly greater than for Great Britain generally (Chapter 2). Job losses resulting from the fall in traffic in the Port of Liverpool have been further accelerated by investments designed to modernize the Port and increase its capital intensiveness (Chapter 3). The Port's decline has led in turn to a loss of jobs in other parts of the local economy associated with the City's maritime trade—railways, haulage, insurance and banking. It has also had a serious effect upon the inner council estates fronting the docks whose traditional source of employment was mainly unskilled labour in the Port or in related activities.

The process of de-industrialization is most pronounced in Liverpool's manufacturing industries, which lost 38% of their jobs between 1971 and 1981. One study (Massey and Meegan, 1978) is particularly important in the present context, because it focused on the industrial restructuring process within the major cities and within an industry (electrical, electronics and aerospace) which is particularly prominent in Liverpool. This study showed that while 34% of this industry's employment was located in the cities of Birmingham, Liverpool, London and Manchester, these sustained 84% of the total job losses. Within this industry the observed restructuring process and resultant job loss were considered to be essential to their continuing success, and were a response to three main pressures: over-capacity and resulting high costs; the need to expand and to reap scale economies; and the need to retain and secure market standing. If such restructuring is necessary and inevitable why did the city-based plants fare so badly? In the case of the electrical, electronics and aerospace industry this reflected the heavy preponderance of firms with over-capacity, outdated capital equipment or premises and a tendency for city-based plants to be more labour intensive. The pressures to restructure emanated from national and international forces which resulted in the elimination of unprofitable or low profit plants, mainly located in the major cities. In addition 89% of the jobs lost to the cities were lost to the economy as a whole, while only 11% moved to other areas.

Another important aspect of the industrial restructuring process is the relationship between the different components of industrial change (especially employment) and the spatial pattern of job losses or growth (Lloyd, 1979). Studies of Inner and Outer Merseyside's manufacturing industry have highlighted a number of important aspects of industrial change (Lloyd, 1979, and Dicken and Lloyd, 1978). These areas are defined in Figure 12.4. Between 1966 and 1975 manufacturing industries in Inner Merseyside suffered a net loss of 18 291 manual jobs. The main contribution to their job loss came from plant closures, of which closures 46.2% were single-plant firms and 53.8% multi-plant firms, although no closures occurred among the area's largest plants (500 or more workers). This contrasts markedly with the post-1975 period which has witnessed several major plant closures in Liverpool's manufacturing sector, notably Tate and Lyle, Meccano, British Leyland and Dunlop. In addition to the high level of factory closures the other key component of change in Inner Merseyside was the *in situ* shrinkage of employment in the surviving plants (Chapters 2 and 4). This accounted for a net loss of

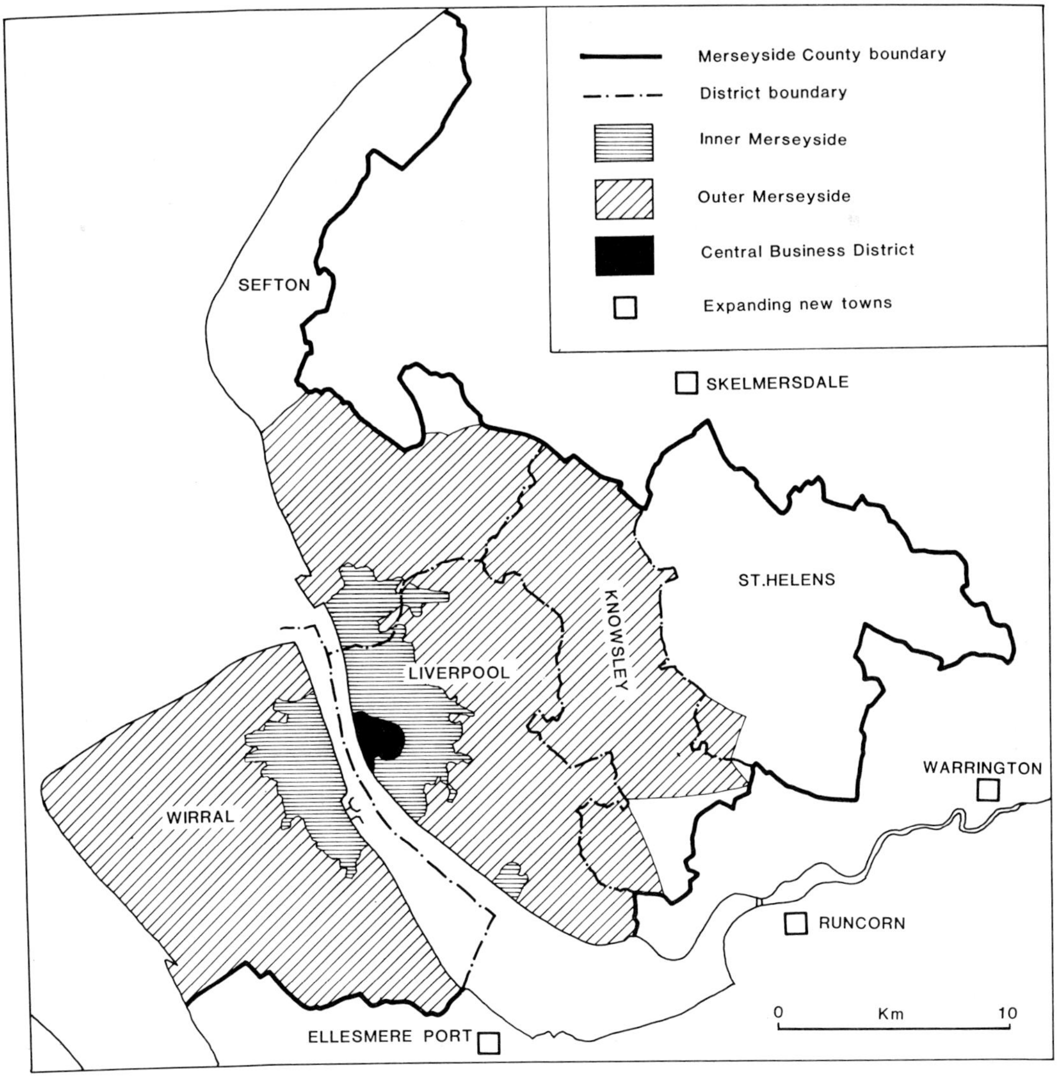

Fig. 12.4 Inner and Outer Merseyside

9167 jobs of which 88.5% were concentrated in multi-plant firms. At the same time there was a net increase in jobs in the Outer City of over 25 000, largely accounted for by increases associated with incoming firms and new firms locating in suburban Merseyside. Undoubtedly the range and level of Development Area incentives available to new and existing firms in Outer Merseyside played a part in this growth, and these incentives contributed to the general preference of new or incoming firms for suburban locations. The size, structure and corporate control of firms has been another major influence on employment in the manufacturing sector of the Liverpool and Merseyside economy. An increasing proportion of workers were employed in multi-plant firms, and there was an even more dramatic increase in the proportion of the workforce employed in plants controlled from outside Merseyside. Within Liverpool itself large firms (1000 or more employees) accounted for 59% of all manufacturing jobs, and as few as 32 firms employed over 70% of the City's manufacturing workforce in 1977 (Liverpool City Council, 1981, pp. 5–6). Only one of the City's twenty largest manufacturing employers was locally based and controlled. In essence, therefore, many of the decisions of vital importance to the future viability of Liverpool's and Inner Merseyside's manufacturing base will rest with corporate organizations whose centres of power lie outside the local area, and even outside the country.

While service employment generally declined throughout the 1970s its share of total employment rose because of the greater rate of decline of the City's manufacturing employment (Chapter 5). Only one service industry, Public Administration, experienced any growth between 1971 and 1981, although even in this sector employment has been declining from 1977 onwards. By 1977 public sector employment accounted for 33% of all the City's jobs and nearly half of all the service employment (Liverpool City Council, 1980E, p. 44, and 1981, p. 5). Almost one-third of all public sector employment in 1977 was provided by the Liverpool City Council (32 681 jobs). Since 1976 the number of jobs provided by the City Council has also been declining.

The City's declining manufacturing and service employment has been matched by a rising trend of unemployment throughout the 1970s (see Fig. 2.2). In 1971 the unemployment rate for the Liverpool Travel-to-work Area was around 5%. By 1981 this had risen to over 18%. This increase in unemployment closely reflected the fortunes of the national economy, but was accentuated in Liverpool by the relationship between the types of work that were declining and the skills of those seeking work. Between 1966 and 1971, for example, the number of jobs declined faster than the number of residents for all types of work except that of a supervisory, professional and managerial nature. The differences between the rates of change were greatest for the "worst" jobs. Personal service workers, semi-skilled and unskilled workers were placed in an increasingly difficult job situation over this five-year period (Liverpool City Council, 1977, p. 22). This meant that many semi-skilled and unskilled workers had to seek employment in the new growth areas outside the City. This option was certainly available to those workers who lived towards the City's outskirts and in the new council estates. It was less available for the semi-skilled and unskilled resident in the inner areas because travel to and beyond the City boundary was both difficult and costly. In 1975 commuting costs facing residents of inner Liverpool seeking work in the new employment centres of Ellesmere Port, Runcorn and Halewood accounted for between 10% and 15% of the net wage of a manual worker (Nabarro, 1980). The proportion was considerably higher for unskilled workers, and also involved on average 10 hours of travelling. Such costs effectively acted to circumscribe the job search area for the unskilled inner-area worker. The trends evident between 1966 and 1971 have, if anything, been continued throughout the 1970s, the major difference being that unemployment has increased dramatically.

The Social Area Study (Webber, 1975, p. 103) showed that the unemployment rate for the Inner Council Social Area was over 18% in 1971. This highlights another important feature of unemployment in Liverpool, notably its uneven distribution between Social Areas and its uneven incidence within these areas between different socio-economic groups. Table 12.3 illustrates this for 1971. Within each of the five 1971 Social Areas the highest unemployment rates generally occurred in the lowest-status groups, especially unskilled manual workers. But an unskilled worker in the High-status Social Area, while being more likely to be unemployed than other groups in that area, was much more likely to be in employment than an unskilled worker residing in the Inner Council Social Area. The Social Area Study revealed that unemployment in Liverpool was related not only to socio-economic status (generally higher amongst unskilled workers) but also to area and

TABLE 12.3 *Unemployment by occupational status and Social Area, Liverpool, 1971 (figures are percentages of the group who were unemployed)*

	High status	Multi-occupied	Inner Council	Outer Council	Older terraced	Liverpool	England and Wales
Professional & managerial	1.9	5.1	6.8	3.8	2.0	2.8	1.8
Non-manual	1.6	5.4	9.1	5.3	4.8	4.1	2.2
Skilled manual	4.3	14.9	13.1	6.9	7.6	7.8	4.0
Semi-skilled manual	3.7	13.1	17.3	8.9	8.5	9.6	4.0
Unskilled manual	6.7	11.0	27.6	15.8	13.8	18.4	9.1

Source: Webber (1975), pp. 102–103.
Note: The measure of unemployment used is the total number of workers economically active (male and female) but not in employment as a proportion of all economically active workers.

type of housing (residents of the inner council areas generally fared worse than other areas).

The concentration of unskilled and unemployed workers into certain areas of the City has been confirmed by later surveys, e.g. National Dwelling and Housing Survey, 1977/78. It prompts the question of why such concentration occurs, and how it affects the job chances of the residents concerned? What seems to happen is that unskilled and unemployed labour is concentrated into the areas of least desirable housing through a combination of low wages, low income and administrative selection. It has been maintained that two further processes then operate. Firstly, the flow of job information to individuals living in the area is reduced since the bulk of job placements arise from prior contact with friends or neighbours who are in employment. Secondly, the "slum" image of these areas gives rise to active discrimination by certain employers against residents, the no-one-from-Liverpool-8-need-apply syndrome (Webber 1975, p. 33).

The spatial pattern of unemployment in Liverpool highlights how certain areas are characterized by greater concentration of unemployment. The spatial pattern of long-term unemployment (fifty-two weeks or more) for 1973 to 1976 (Fig. 12.5) shows that while the highest rates were concentrated in and around the city centre in the Inner Council and Multi-occupied Social Areas, the next highest were located not only in the inner parts of the City but also in many of the Outer Council estates. Again therefore the pattern of urban poverty does not conform to any simple concept of the geographical inner city.

The governmental response and future policy directions

Special programmes for tackling the problem of urban poverty have been implemented in Liverpool from 1968 onwards. They began with the launching of the Urban Aid Programme in 1968, and were followed by the Vauxhall Community Development Project in 1969, the Brunswick Neighbourhood Project in 1971 and the Inner Areas Study in 1972 (Fig. 12.6). This first wave of programmes was characterized by limited resources, a concentration on a restricted number of small areas and an experimental flavour which placed them outside the mainstream of major services (Chape, 1978). The programmes were widely criticized, and there was increasing pressure, especially from authorities like Liverpool, for programmes that would address themselves to the root causes of urban poverty. This led to the publication of the Labour Government's 1977 White Paper "Policy for the Inner Cities". The White Paper proposed not only an increased allocation of resources to the inner cities, including a tilting of the Government's Rate Support Grant in

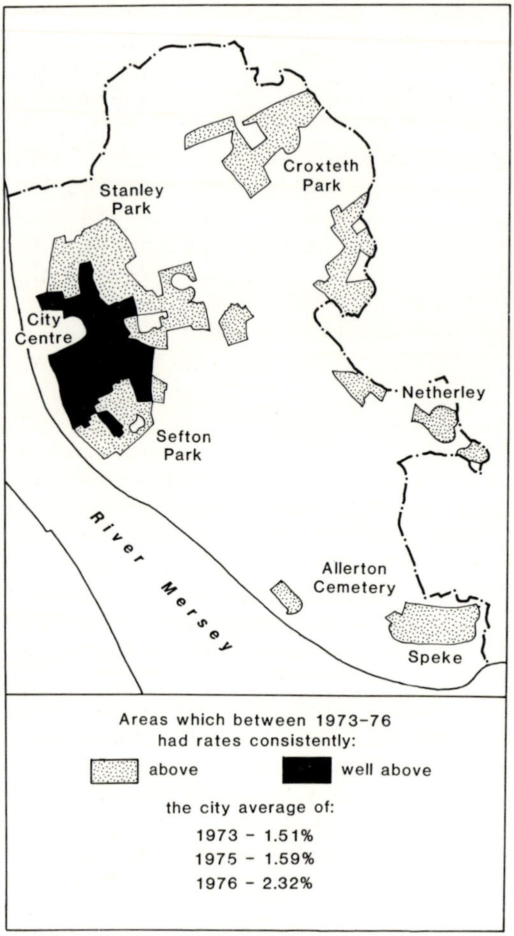

Fig. 12.5 Long-term unemployment, 1973–1976

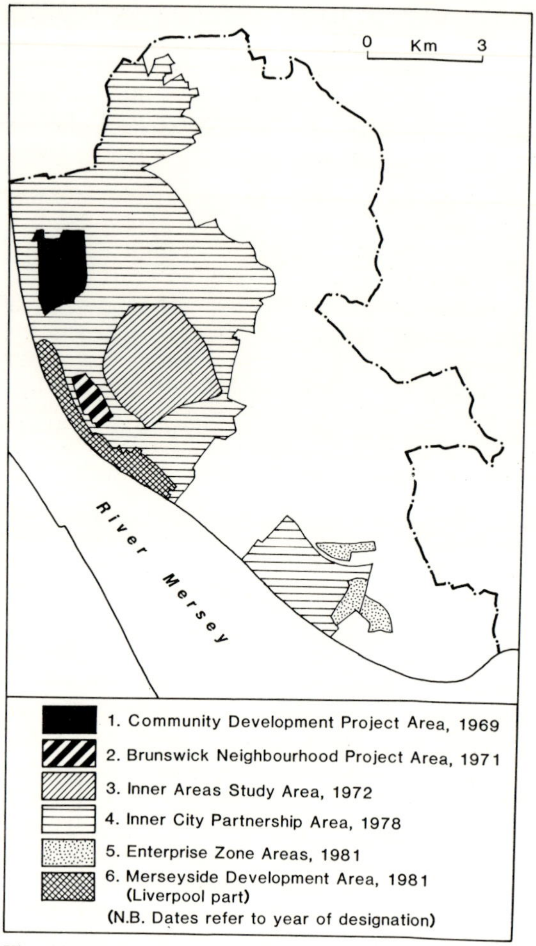

Fig. 12.6 Special Areas of Liverpool, 1969–1981

their favour, but also that explicit priority should be given to achieving the goal of economic regeneration. In addition special machinery was created to link central and local government in the areas of greatest need, the Inner City Partnerships.

The over-riding concern with the economic regeneration of the inner cities was an important development in governmental thinking. It was a response to the sudden and previously unanticipated crisis in the manufacturing sector of British cities and the dramatic rise in unemployment which occurred after 1974. In the Liverpool Travel-to-work area, for example, unemployment rose from 6.2% in 1974 to 11.1% in 1976. The crisis in the cities' manufacturing industries had developed from the mid 1960s, and began to affect all the major conurbations, including those like the South-East and West Midlands, previously regarded as impregnably prosperous. Placing the emphasis on economic regeneration represented a fundamentally different approach from the earlier anti-poverty programmes which began by focussing on social deprivation and developed thereafter a preoccupation with local administration and management. In Liverpool the outcome of the 1977 White Paper was the establishment of the Liverpool Inner City Partnership in 1978 (Fig. 12.6).

The present Government has generally endorsed the Partnership initiative, but has modified the approach through "tilting" resources away from cities like Liverpool by adjusting the Rate Support Grant, although the level of "special" funding through the Urban Programme has been maintained. In addition it has designated further special areas in Liverpool: the Merseyside Development Area, to be administered by the Merseyside Development Corporation, and the Speke Enterprise Zones. It has established a Public Land Register to prevent "land hoarding" by the City Council and other public authorities.

The problem now facing a city such as Liverpool is that the rising tide of the national and local economic crisis is threatening to "drown" these initiatives by sweeping away the premise on which they are based—that the economic recession would be relatively short-lived, and that national revival would float even the most badly affected areas "off the rocks". A view has also developed, however, that even if the national economy does revive there is no guarantee that this, by itself, will regenerate inner city areas. A radical review is now needed of the role and future of older industrial cities. At present, notwithstanding the Heseltine initiative, the Government seems to be placing its faith in some form of spontaneous regeneration process, with the public sector playing a minimum enabling role. It is difficult to envisage the form such a regeneration process would take, especially if it is to be based on private entrepreneurs with a belief in and commitment to inner cities. A revival of the City's manufacturing industry and the fortunes of the Port seems remote given present trends and the continuing process of industrial restructuring. In addition Liverpool's service sector is very dependent on public expenditure and the prosperity of the Port, neither of which can be expected to increase in the immediate future.

Clearly the problem of urban poverty is now being redefined by circumstances and events. Increasing attention needs to be paid to the problems of youth and long-term unemployment, race relations and ways of securing greater public involvement. These are all problems which require significant increases in public resources, of both money and jobs not only to sustain public provision but also to stimulate private and voluntary community initiatives. What is also required is a different view of the inner city. In Liverpool this has now been administratively defined as the Inner City Partnership Area which embraces half of the City's total population. By 1981 this area accommodated 253 154 people out of a total population of 510 306 (1981 Census Preliminary Results). The defined area was largely based on three of the areas identified by the Social Area Study—the Inner Council, Multi-occupied and Sharing and Older-terraced Social Areas of the 1971 typology (Chape, 1978). However, it excludes, for example, most of the Outer Council Social Area which has been highlighted in this chapter as suffering from a wide range of urban poverty measures. As presently conceived the spatial frame of reference for inner city policy is too narrow. The whole concept needs to be reappraised, and applied on a conurbation-wide level to facilitate a better integration of economic, social and environmental programmes.

It is not possible in a chapter of this scope to consider in any detail what would be the appropriate governmental response to Liverpool's urban poverty and declining economy. The riots in the summer of 1981, however, are a grim warning of the thin veneer of public acquiescence as the City's economic crisis continues to create substantial groups of people who exist "outside of society", or are excluded on economic or other grounds from participating fully in the life of the City. Massive injections of resources have taken place, but they have not stemmed the rising tide of a national economic recession. The future of Liverpool as a viable economic and social entity is now dependent upon the realization that a completely different perspective needs to be developed about the economies of the older industrial areas. Job protection, job creation and job improvement will have to become the over-riding criteria, linked to the pressing social and environmental needs of the City—its poor housing conditions, deficient recreational facilities, vacant and derelict land, declining transport system and hard pressed educational services. In addition the City will have to be protected by Central Government from the ravages of a continuing national economic crisis and industrial restructuring by large and multi-plant firms.

Chapter 13

SCHOOLS AND POPULATION CHANGE IN LIVERPOOL

PETER J. B. BROWN and STEPHEN S. FERGUSON

In recent years, attacks on public expenditure have frequently included reference to the savings which could be effected as the number of pupils in schools declines in accordance with the demographic trend. This argument, based upon the assumption that the education system expands and contracts in line with pupil numbers, has a strong appeal to those who seek to limit government expenditure. However, the strength of its logic requires closer scrutiny and an understanding of the educational, political and organizational dimensions which impinge upon the educational system. An opportunity for undertaking such an examination is provided in Liverpool, a city which has experienced population decline and falling pupil numbers over a far longer period than that indicated by the overall national pattern. In this respect an examination of Liverpool's response to the declining school population over that period may serve to highlight some of the factors and issues associated with educational planning which either confirm or refute the logic of relating declining pupil numbers to a reduction in cost.

Demographic decline from the 1930s to the 1970s

The population of the area that is now Merseyside reached its peak in 1961 (Chapter 11), but with the exception of the immediate post war period, Liverpool has experienced almost continuous depopulation since the 1930s. The census of 1931 recorded a total Liverpool population of 856 072, although other sources suggest that the peak came in 1935 at 867 350 (Fig. 13.1). Subsequent censuses have charted the progressive decline in numbers, with the 1981 figure of 510 306 indicating a fall of 40.4% over the fifty-year period since 1931.

An overall fall in population affects the prosperity of an area and its rate income, but an immediate impact on the education system is felt through the associated decline in the school-age population which the system is required to accommodate. With something of a lag, the school population is related to the number of births recorded, which is itself a function of the birth rate. Figure 13.1 illustrates how the annually recorded births and total population in Liverpool have varied in the years between 1930 and 1980. From this it can be deduced that these five decades have witnessed both a substantial overall decline and short term fluctuations in child population. The unprecedented and continuous decline in births recorded in Liverpool was particularly significant during the recent period from 1962 to 1977. The scale of this decline is underlined when expressed in round numbers: from a total of 16 479 births in 1962 to only 6166 in 1977, a fall of 62.6%.

This fall can be explained in part by the large-scale migration out of the city that took place during this period. The loss of population had the effect of accentuating the impact of the concurrent fall in the birth rate, as can be seen in Figure 13.2 in which both the annual birth rate and number of births for the years 1960 to 1980 are plotted, and the points representing the birth rate and the number of children born in 1960 coincide. Had the population of the city remained constant at the 1960 level, the sets of plotted points would have continued to coincide. However, the decrease in the number of children born was much more pronounced than that displayed by the underlying birth rate trend, reflecting the significant movement of population out of the city throughout this period. Since, in

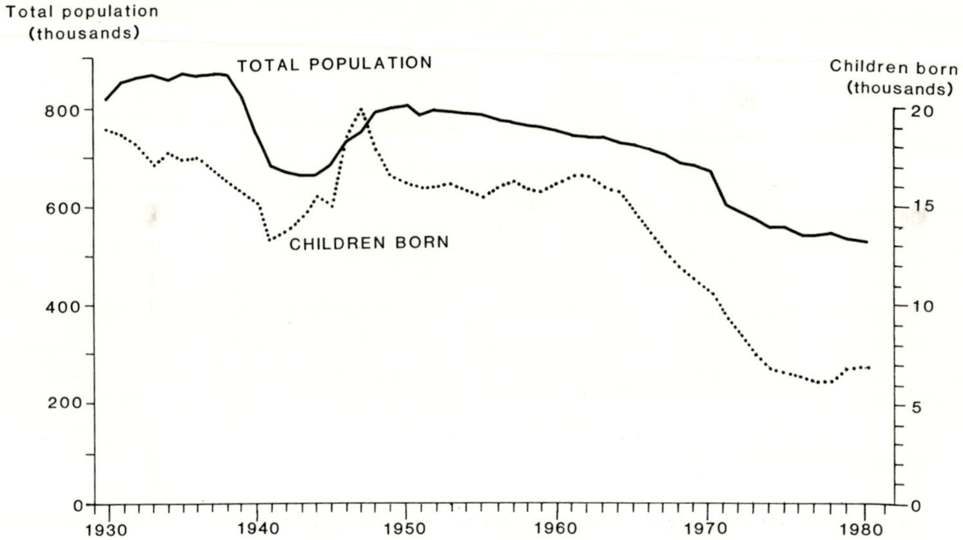

Fig. 13.1 Total population and number of children born to residents of Liverpool, 1930–1980

addition, the city was losing women of childbearing age at a greater than average rate (Liverpool City Council, 1977), this had a further adverse effect on the level of school population, as school-age children as well as the new-born were emigrating with their families.

The city-wide view of a falling child population masks important local variations within the city caused by the local pattern of population movement, much of which was a result of political decisions to clear property designated as "slums" and to provide new housing on the periphery of the city. Although this internal migration has had a significant effect on school provision over the last twenty years, as will be discussed later, even as early as 1948 the Director of Education was anticipating a decline of some 45% in the population of parts of the inner city, while the population in some of the peripheral housing estates was forecast to rise by more than 200% (Magnay, 1948). The Director's Development Plan for 1948 took into account these variations, and outlined specific plans for the closure of some schools and the opening of others.

The context for decline: changing education policy

The response of the Local Education Authority (L.E.A.) to both the demographic trend and migration has been complicated, however, by the need to respond to parallel political decisions of both central and local government which have taken place throughout the period. These decisions have affected the nature of the school system itself, and have often been expansionary in character. For example, the 1944 Education Act placed a responsibility on L.E.A.s to phase out the former all-age elementary schools. Liverpool initially opted for a tripartite grammar/technical/modern school system, and adapted existing schools and built new ones to accommodate the new school types. Then in the mid 1950s the further reorganization of those schools was debated, and there began a piecemeal shift towards the establishment of comprehensive schools. The process of change-over, with all its building implications, was virtually complete in 1976 in the maintained sector, but in contrast the Roman Catholic sector remains selective at the time

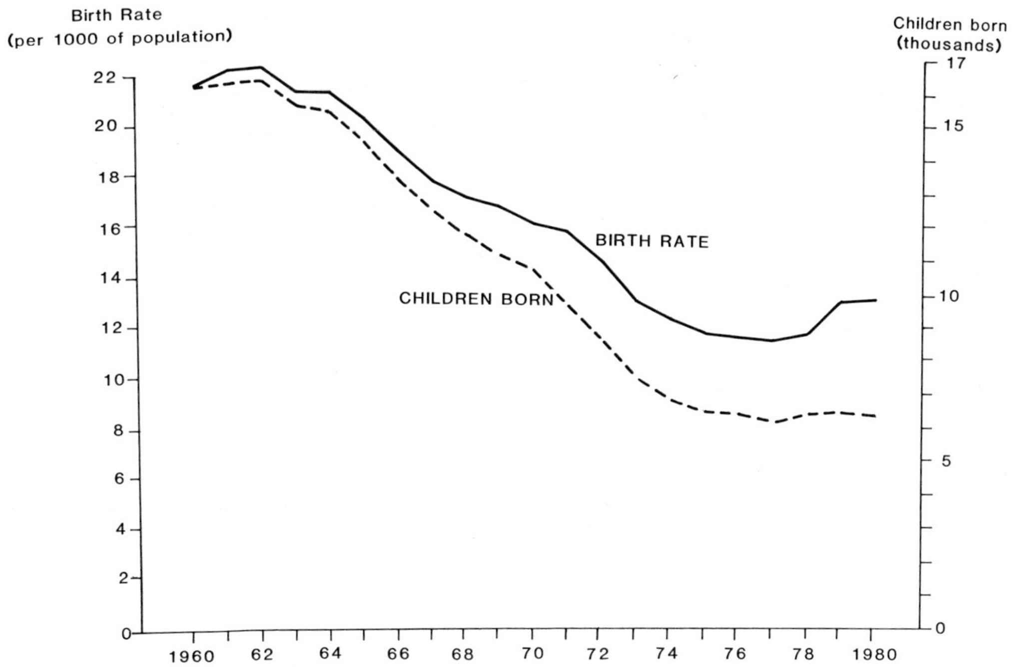

Fig. 13.2 Birth rate and number of children born to residents of Liverpool, 1960–1980

of writing (1981). The 1944 Act and subsequent regulations also imposed upon authorities new standards for school buildings and sites, and to meet these there was a gradual phasing out of inadequate buildings and the acquisition of new land.

Other national initiatives and decisions have affected the local response to the fall in child population. In the early 1960s and 1970s, for example, the modernization and construction of new schools featured in unemployment relief programmes. Similarly, in the early 1970s further new school construction was generated by the release of loan sanctions to permit the replacement of pre-1903 school buildings. As matters of national policy, pre-school nursery provision was expanded, and the school leaving age was raised by one year to sixteen years. Liverpool has also benefitted from the Urban Aid Programme and, more recently, from the Inner City Partnership arrangements which have impinged upon education by making available funds for its development, though in some instances extra resources have been released at short notice without sufficient time to enable the expenditure to be fitted into longer-term strategies. Over a period of years, Liverpool's shift from the tripartite to the comprehensive system permitted a simultaneous rationalization of secondary school provision and the achievement of a more equitable spatial distribution of facilities. However, the gestation period for some politically-inspired projects can be very long indeed, and can easily exceed six years in the case of new school programming, planning and construction. Over such a period of time, demographic change can continue apace, and new political decisions may well diminish the validity of earlier proposals. Liverpool is not the only authority to have built a new school to find the catchment area depopulated as a result of planning and housing decisions inspired by national and local changes in political direction and policy. It is clear that the planning of a response to the decline in child population has taken place within a constantly shifting field which has been subject to simultaneous pressures for both the expansion and contraction of education facility provision.

Given the policies adopted both nationally and locally for the development of the education system, it is not surprising that Liverpool's expenditure per pupil increased during the 1960s at a faster rate than inflation. The growth in resource allocation reflected decisions based upon the relative worth of education as an investment and assessments of the qualitative needs of the education system. Indeed the prevailing wisdom of the 1960s, again at the national as well as local level, was that an increased per capita investment in education was an indispensible condition for the achievement of greater equality of opportunity and national economic prosperity. This goes a long way towards explaining why, for some considerable time, the overall fall in pupil numbers in Liverpool was not perceived to be a problem. On the contrary, the decline was judged to be fortuitous in as much as it was felt that many schools and classes in the city had long been unacceptably overcrowded, and the reduction in intake was viewed as a means of reducing the crush.

The problem of school size and capacity

The "capacity" of individual schools and therefore the capacity of the school system is initially based upon the maximum number of pupils which the Department of Education and Science (D.E.S.) considers to be appropriate for the premises. Once the capacity is designated, however, the actual number accommodated in the school can be allowed to rise to an upper limit beyond which approval from the Secretary of State is required. The determination of the actual numbers which can be accommodated is frequently decided less by the formal regulations than by subjective and qualitative judgements about whether a school is "under-used" or, alternatively, "generously" provided with rooms for libraries, individual pupil study-rooms, resource rooms, staff accommodation and rooms in which community activities can be conducted. Similar judgements apply when a school is considered to be "full". Is a school full because the accommodation of additional pupils would require that non-teaching space would have to be relinquished? Can a full school accommodate more pupils through the provision of mobile classrooms in the school grounds? Even when a figure is established to represent capacity it is impossible to ensure that a school rigidly adheres to its designated capacity while it is subject to demographic and market demand forces beyond its control. These subjective judgements make it equally impossible to look back upon the 1960s and 1970s and conclude with certainty the degree to which Liverpool schools were either "over-crowded" or "under-used".

In the 1960s admission areas for county primary schools were introduced. This administrative device was designed to ensure that there would be an equitable distribution of demand for school places across the city. This was achieved by matching each school to an admission area which contained the appropriate number of school-age children. Such a system worked well as long as there was a good match between designated school capacity and stability of demand for school places in the admission area. In this sense it was successful in limiting the maximum demand pressure on each school. However, when the school population in individual areas fell and the supply of places exceeded the demand, pupils were able to cross admission area boundaries. Thus, a popular school in an area of pupil depopulation drew pupils from beyond its boundaries (Masser and Ferguson, 1977). In the final stages of reorganization of county secondary schools in Liverpool in the 1970s, the admission area principle was again employed to determine the catchments from which most schools would draw their pupils. However, the poaching problem was not solved at the secondary level either, and those schools perceived by parents to have a high prestige experienced excessive demand while adjacent, less popular comprehensives were depleted.

TABLE 13.1 *Distribution of primary school or department size in Liverpool, 1960, 1974 and 1981*

Department or School Size Range	1960	1974	1980
721+	1	—	—
661–720	2	—	—
601–660	3	—	—
541–600	2	3	—
481–540	10	4	—
421–480	12	12	6
361–420	23	12	8
301–360	55	26	13
241–300	66	51	35
181–240	75	63	57
121–180	41	67	88
61–120	17	30	48
1–60	—	—	4
Number of Schools or Departments	307	268	261
Number of Pupils	84 154	62 915	47 640
Mean Size	274	235	182

Matching capacity and demand

Dependent as it is upon such a wide range of subjective factors and political judgements, it is unlikely that the designated capacity of the school system will closely match the pupil population trend. This is clearly borne out in Liverpool where, although the primary school age population fell by 43% between 1960 and 1980, the number of primary schools or departments only decreased by some 15% over the same period (Table 13.1). It is evident that this net change in the school stock conceals the total amount of change in the system, as throughout the period some schools were closed or amalgamated while new ones were built. Nevertheless, the extent of the fall in pupil population was such that the average number of children accommodated in each of the remaining individual units decreased significantly from 274 to 182, a fall of almost exactly one-third. This decrease reflected a marked shift in the distribution of the sizes of individual primary schools and departments. In 1960 almost 40% of schools or departments accommodated over 300 pupils, but in 1980 only 10% catered for more than this number (Fig. 13.3).

Most of the net reduction in the number of primary school units took place before 1974. This year is singled out as it marked the point at which the city broke from the tradition of majority political control, and began a lengthy phase of shifting minority government, characterized by an inconsistent political direction of education policy. Indeed it is notable that it has been in the years since 1974, when the effects of the decline in the birth rate and child population have been at their most acute, that there seems to have been a marked slow-down in the rate of decline in the number of primary schools. Between 1960 and 1974 the primary age pupil population fell by 25% and number of school units by 13%, but

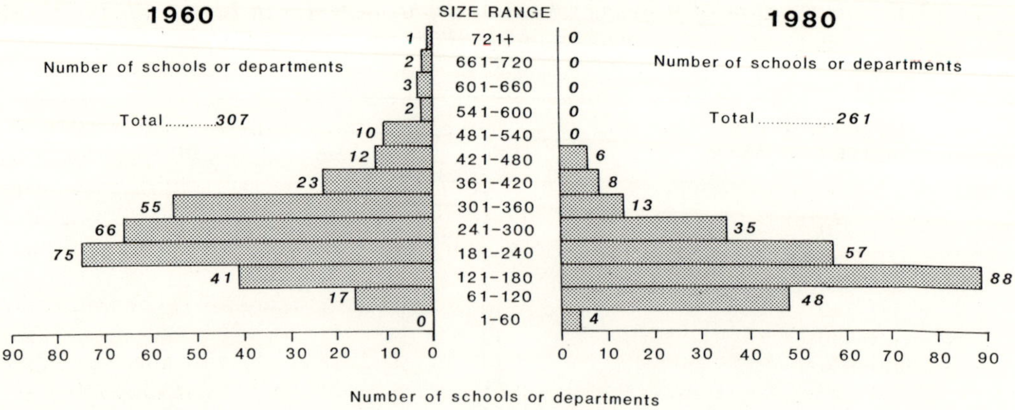

Fig. 13.3 Distribution of primary school or department sizes, Liverpool, 1960 and 1980

between 1974 and 1980 pupils dropped by another 24% and school units by only 3%. Much of the net reduction which took place in the 1960s was the result of the efforts directed towards the withdrawal of out-of-date buildings, referred to above, to which the reduction in capacity was in many ways coincidental.

The lack of decisive policies to bring the supply of primary school places more into line with the reduced pupil population was clearly influenced by the ambiguity surrounding the number of pupils who could be accommodated within the system. However, it is also true that there was a distinct lack of political will to address the problem. In many ways this was not at all surprising, since the effect of continuing to maintain schools as pupil population declined was to improve the per capita provision of space for each pupil and to reduce class sizes and pupil/teacher ratios, for all of which there had been both national and local enthusiasm. One further consequence of the lack of determined policy on school closure or amalgamation was to increase the unit cost of education, because costs such as heating, lighting, maintenance and rates are related to the number of premises in use rather than to the number of pupils served. Thus, the unit costs of education, already rising as a result of national and locally generated developments, were further increased by the running expenses of the system.

Since approximately 60% of the costs of operating a school are earmarked for staffing, most significant savings can be achieved through a reduction in staff. Local authorities are limited in their ability to shed staff both by the legislation which regulates redundancy agreements and by the contractual arrangements which exist between them and their teachers. Making staff redundant could lead to substantial compensation payments, while at the same time mobilizing the articulate and politically aware teaching profession. It is unlikely, therefore, that the enforced redundancy of teachers would ever be a politically attractive course of action at either local or national level.

The changing circumstances of the 1970s

As long as the level of central government support for local services was maintained, the increased unit costs of the system did not present a critical problem for Liverpool. From the mid 1970s, however, circumstances changed. In response to the declining state of the economy, the central government campaign for cuts in public expenditure gathered momentum. This campaign also coincided with a perceptible shift of public support away from education. A significant marker of this movement was a speech by Prime Minister Callaghan at Ruskin College in October, 1976, in which he cast doubt on the value-for-money being obtained from the education service. The impact was all the greater since it was virtually unheard of for a Prime Minister to make pronouncements on education policy. Local authorities now found themselves in a new and more hostile environment. Revenue expenditure was to be reduced, but the duties and responsibilities of the authorities were to remain the same. Furthermore, the capital building programmes of the 1960s, initiated in response to national pressure, had significantly increased the financial burden of local authorities. At the same time not only was public expenditure to be cut, but local authorities were to be the major agents of that cut. They were being urged to take the initiative in cutting their own services, while being asked to evaluate these same services in terms of value-for-money.

With staffing costs accounting for some 60% of Liverpool's revenue expenditure devoted to education, it was inevitable that savings would have to be made in that area. Lacking the political will to pursue a staff redundancy policy and thereby incur the wrath of the teachers' associations, Liverpool began a policy of restricting the recruitment of staff. An indication of the severity of contraction is provided by the substantial reduction in the number of new teachers recruited from training institutions, which fell from 755 in 1973/4 to approximately 170 in 1977/8. When the redeployment scheme agreed between the Authority and local branches of the teachers' associations failed to produce any significant movement of staff between schools, the Authority introduced a programme of early retirement. The net effect of the reduction in recruitment, early retirement and natural wastage did eventually enable savings to be made in the budget, but the educational price paid for this policy was to threaten the range of subjects offered in many schools. Headteachers of both primary and secondary schools were forced to evaluate the curriculum and opportunities offered to pupils and to make difficult decisions about which of a choice of teaching posts was to be replaced. A one-for-one replacement of staff was a diminishing luxury. For City Councillors the political risks attached to this policy were balanced by the political gains which were expected to arise from the considerable financial savings and reduction in the local rate demand consequent upon lower staffing costs.

One of the solutions to declining staffing and the attrition of the curriculum was to

TABLE 13.2 *Number and mean size of primary schools or departments by type of school in Liverpool, 1960, 1974 and 1980*

	Number of Schools or Departments (Mean Size)		
School or Department Type	1960	1974	1980
County Primary	158 (277)	148 (238)	140 (196)
Church of England (Aided)	20 (170)	13 (203)	13 (164)
Church of England (Controlled)	15 (207)	11 (168)	13 (140)
Roman Catholic (Aided)	113 (297)	95 (239)	94 (189)
Hebrew	1 (281)	1 (473)	1 (452)
Totals	307 (274)	268 (235)	261 (182)
Total Number of Pupils	84 154	62 915	47 640

Source: Department of Education and Science Form 7 (schools), compiled by City of Liverpool Education Department.

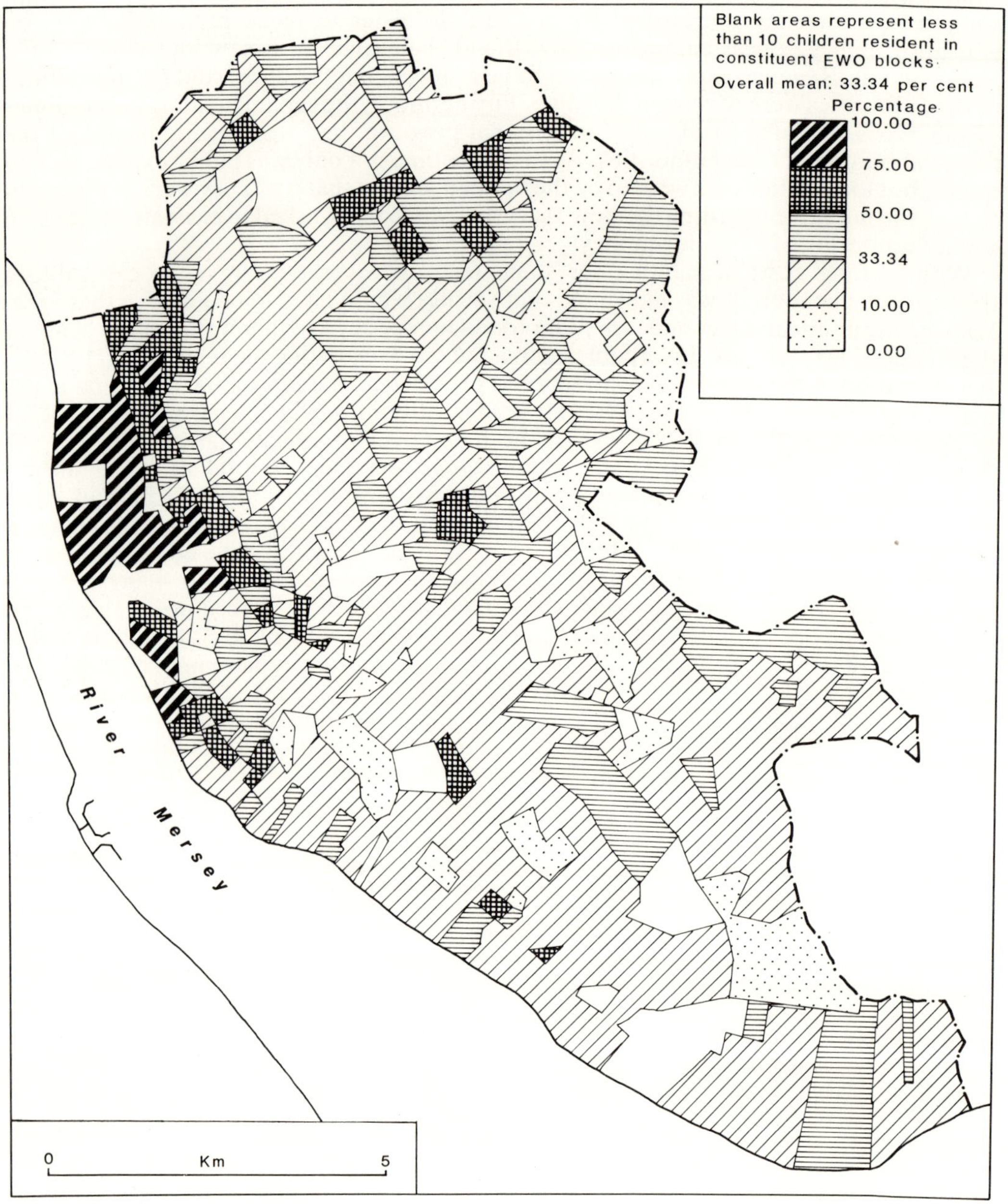

Fig. 13.4 Primary school children (aged 4–10) attending Roman Catholic schools or departments as a percentage of the total primary school age population, Liverpool, 1980

accelerate the policy of school amalgamation and closure. This would increase the size of individual schools and thereby increase the range of curricular opportunities. This argument was advanced in Liverpool, and was strongly reinforced by D.E.S. circulars, sponsored research, reports from Her Majesty's Inspectors and public statements by Secretaries of State. Although the apparent educational justifications for pursuing an amalgamation and closure policy were seen to be convincing, the statutory power to close schools lies with the Local Authority, and in Liverpool there did not exist a sufficiently strong political will to carry through a significant number of closures. As noted earlier, the pace of closure and amalgamation from 1974 was much slower than in previous years.

An additional dimension: the voluntary sector

At this point it is perhaps appropriate to describe some of the features of the educational system in Liverpool which go some way towards accounting for the apparently low level of commitment to a policy which simplistic logic suggested was essential. First of all, it is important to recognize that educational planning problems in Liverpool are made more difficult by the size of the voluntary school sector. Approximately one-third of the school population in the city is Roman Catholic, and educated in Roman Catholic voluntary schools. This is a larger proportion of voluntary school pupils than is found in any other city in England and Wales. In addition there is a small but significant Church of England sector (Table 13.2). The Local Education Authority is responsible for paying the salaries and a major proportion of the operating costs of all voluntary schools and not only of those in the Catholic sector. Yet voluntary schools are autonomous, and managed by separate denominational education authorities.

Roman Catholic children are not evenly distributed among all parts of the city (Fig. 13.4; see below for a description of the spatial units employed). Although the large scale slum clearance and rehousing programmes of the 1960s resulted in the migration of many Catholic families from their traditional locations in the northern inner parts of the city, the present day distribution remains remarkably similar to that which prevailed in 1948 (Magnay, 1948). The 1960s also witnessed the major school building programme to accommodate secondary pupils in the "new" grammar and modern schools, some of which were located in the outer estates to which the former inner city residents were encouraged to move. However, since then the birth rate among Roman Catholic families has fallen even more rapidly than that of the non-Catholic population, and there is now a very large surplus of places in Catholic secondary schools.

The size of the voluntary school sector in Liverpool suggests that it would need to feature in any move towards a reduction in school expenditure. It is possible for a local authority to follow a statutorily-defined procedure if it should decide to terminate its support for such schools. However, the likely political repercussions of such a decision, in a city with a voluntary sector the size of Liverpool's, render that course of direct action improbable. Instead the Authority has adopted the less controversial approach of encouraging and cajoling the church authorities to undertake a review of their own provision. It is no surprise that this has brought little progress towards the achievement of economies. The political difficulties within the voluntary sector in many ways parallel those in the local authority, and are no less involved. Despite three attempts since 1975 to reorganize its secondary school system in line with pupil enrolment, the Roman Catholic Authority in Liverpool had failed to alter a single secondary school by the end of 1981. During the same period only two Roman Catholic primary schools have been amalgamated. Furthermore, the size of the secondary sector has actually increased during this period as the national government policy of phasing out Direct Grant schools resulted in three Roman Catholic schools opting to join the voluntary sector rather than becoming independent. The same process led the Church of England voluntary sector to increase by one secondary school.

Liverpool's political response

Proposals for the closure of county schools in Liverpool have also proved to be extremely contentious. Different schemes put forward by the Director of Education and by other interested parties have been variously rejected by Working Parties, Education Committees and City Council (Ferguson and Brown, 1979). The reasons for a distinct lack of conviction in following through such proposals can be ascribed largely to the minority political control of the City Council which has shifted uneasily between Liberal and Labour control since 1974. Proposals have also been subject to political factors at the national level. Since 1976 two schemes which represented compromises of interests within the City Council were rejected or modified by Secretaries of State: the first by Shirley Williams on the eve of the 1979 General Election and the second by Sir Keith Joseph in the wake of the 1981 summer riots. The closures which have taken place have not had a significant impact on average school size in the city, either in the primary or secondary sector. Although the curricular benefits of school closure schemes have been frequently cited by protagonists, opposition from parents and community groups has been sufficient to block many of the plans. School closure or amalgamation is seen by many interests to be the removal of a local service, often from areas where, due to depopulation, there has already been a retreat of other services and jobs. Primary schools, which over the years have established strong parent and community links as a means of improving the educational environment for children, have now found those same interests defending them from closure proposals. The notable instances where objections have not been significant have been those where headteachers, teaching staff, and the school governors supported the amalgamations, and where, in addition, the City has been able to direct Urban Aid and Inner City Partnership funds into the improvement of the premises into which displaced pupils will be moving. Objections to closure or amalgamation proposals at the secondary level have reflected, if not re-enacted, the comprehensive reorganization battles waged from the late 1950s to the early 1970s. The arguments advanced then concerning the "quality of education", "equality of opportunity", "elitism" and "parental choice" are all now being applied to proposals for restructuring the secondary system.

Anticipating the uncertainty in the political environment which was to accompany any attempt to close or amalgamate schools, the City Council established a "Reorganization and Development Working Party" which first met in 1977. The intention was that this Working Party, whose membership included teachers, councillors and representatives from Catholic and non-Catholic parents' associations, would provide both a forum for debate and a mechanism for co-ordinating consultation. Its operation proved otherwise. The disagreements which emerged within it replicated the divisions which existed within the Education Committee and City Council itself. The Working Party failed to agree upon any guidelines which could be applied consistently in order to bring about a programme of school closures. Indeed, its one firm resolution, stipulating what it called "the desirable minimum sizes of primary schools" and which might have been used as a criterion upon which to generate proposals, was vitiated by the rider that local social circumstances could secure the retention of a school which fell below the agreed desirable minima.

In the period from the establishment of the Working Party to the end of 1980, political decisions had been made to close two very small secondary schools and to reduce the form-entry of others, and then spread the available pupils more evenly among the remaining schools. Five small primary schools were amalgamated into two larger units, while pairs of junior and infant departments were merged to create combined junior and infant schools. The scale of these actions is minute when contrasted with the Director of Education's own assessment of the problem. In 1976 he estimated that 91 primary schools or departments were substantially below the "desirable minimum size".

This apparent difficulty in reducing the number of school places in Liverpool is an indication of the profoundly political and contentious character of this planning process (Ferguson and Brown, 1979). It is this key feature of the process which tends to ensure that decision making will remain incremental in scale and effect. The local electoral process itself, with annual elections of one-third of the councillors, makes politicians reluctant to undertake a city-wide review of school provision which might provoke widespread hostility among the electorate. Seven years of minority government in the City Council has ensured, if nothing else has, that Councillors are particularly sensitive to the threat of being unseated. The shifting control has also disrupted the continuity of experience, knowledge and policy. Since 1974 there have been three different Chairmen of the Education Committee, and the tenure of each has been broken by changes in political party control.

The quest for a rational basis for decision making

Given the extreme political sensitivity of these issues there has been a search among educational planners in the City for indicators which might lead to politically acceptable solutions. On the one hand, officers are under pressure to find measures which will produce financial savings, but on the other hand they are well aware of the need to produce proposals which will be politically acceptable. Given this high degree of sensitivity there has been a diligent search for data which can be accepted as uncontentious. Population data and demographic trends are looked to as providing such a base. They have also been used to calculate unit costs, an index which can have credibility in political discussions.

The planning of school provision stretches the readily-available data beyond its limits. The decennial census is inadequate since there are only four to five years between birth and the start of schooling. In addition, the clustering of age groups in the census tables masks potentially important trends in births which may occur within the enumerated age groups, and in any event the age-group cohorts are not especially relevant to school planning needs. Liverpool has sought to overcome these limitations by making use of the population data collected and recorded by Education Welfare Officers (E.W.O.s) in the course of their duties. One part of an E.W.O.'s work is to ensure school attendance by pupils, and this requires them to know the location of pre-school children and the schools to which parents intend to send them. To preserve anonymity these data are aggregated to some 580 spatial units which are referred to as "blocks". The blocks aggregate in turn to primary school admission areas.

The E.W.O. blocks thus provide a useful set of areal units with which to assess future school demand, and the present authors have been closely associated with the Authority in undertaking an annual analysis of these data. When the block data are presented in map form they illustrate not only the variation in the rate of child population decline in different parts of the city, but also reveal quite clearly that decline is not restricted to the inner city. They further indicate how the task of planning future school provision in those areas traditionally associated with a falling population is complicated by their juxtaposition to areas of new housing in which marked short-term increases in child numbers are being experienced. The data reveal a considerable spatial complexity which to a great extent undermines the clearer guidance sought from what might have been seen as supposedly clear and uncontentious data.

Figure 13.5 illustrates the percentage change in the number of children of primary school age over the five year period, 1976–1980. This map and Figure 13.4 above are based upon

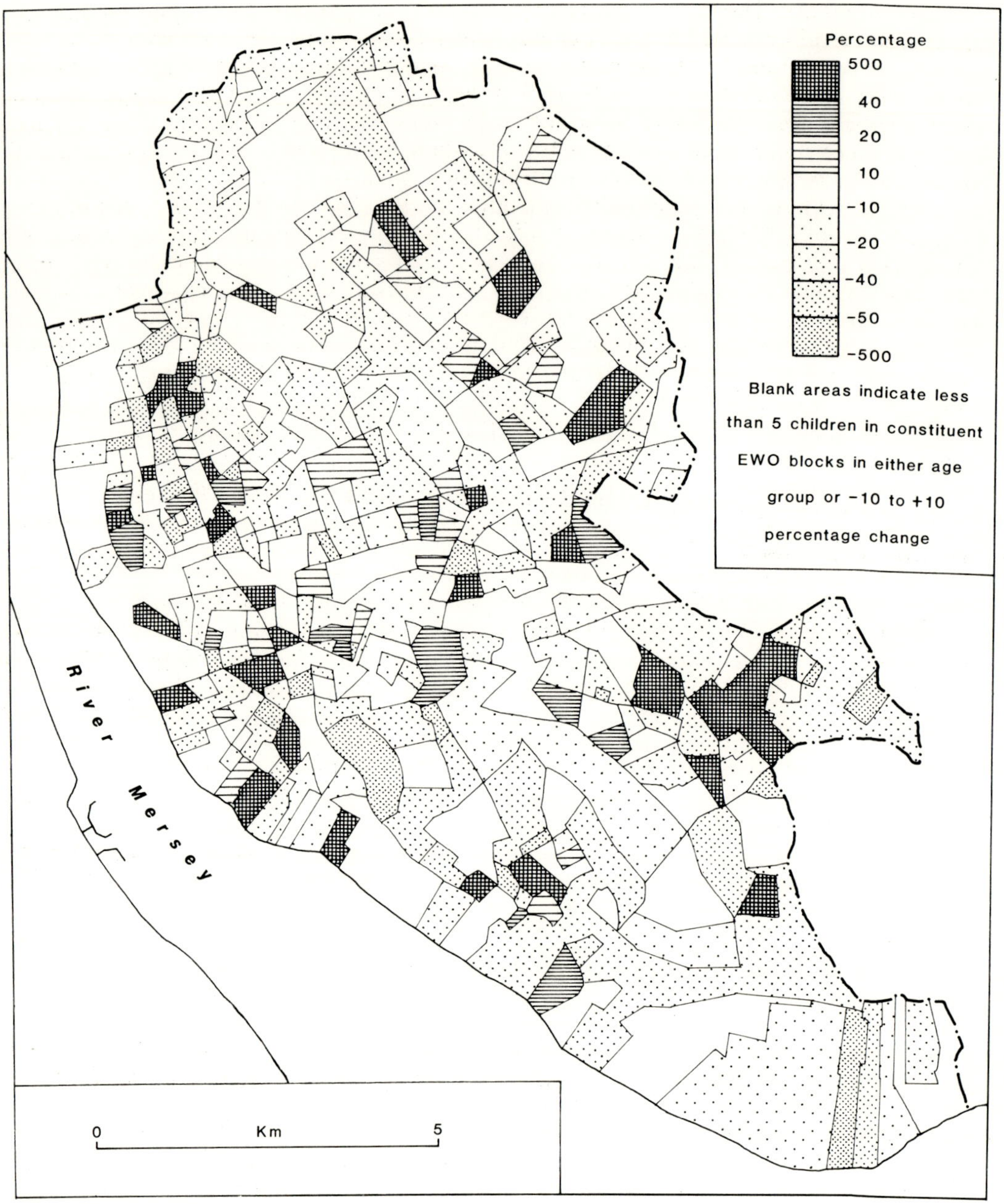

Fig. 13.5 Percentage change in numbers of primary school children (aged 4–10) in Liverpool, 1976–1980

E.W.O. block data, and contiguous blocks have been aggregated when they share the same data characteristics. The shading convention adopted in the map has been chosen to highlight those aggregated areas which have experienced a substantial increase or decrease in child numbers. Those areas which experienced a change of between plus or minus 10% have been left blank, while those experiencing a loss of more than 50% have been shaded with a dense stipple. Caution should be exercised in interpreting the map as children are not evenly distributed within each block or aggregated area. In addition some blocks are very sparsely populated, and these can be conveniently illustrated with reference to the "blank" area at the southern edge of the city where the airport is located and to the similar areas in the northeast which are predominantly open parkland.

During the five-year period, 1976 to 1980, the number of 4 to 10 year olds in the city declined from 57 103 to 47 040, an overall fall of 17.6%. Yet the most striking feature of the map is the incidence of high rates of increase in excess of 40% in some inner city areas. In most cases this can be attributed to major new housing developments which have taken place in areas cleared of housing in earlier years. In other areas it reflects the completion of a more modest scale of housing improvement and rehabilitation. The map also identifies areas experiencing a relatively large proportional decline. Although most of the blocks sustaining a loss in excess of 50% are found, as might be expected, in the inner city areas and in particular in the area to the north of the city centre, there are substantial areas in the outer parts of the city in which a similar order of decline has taken place, notably in the extreme south where Speke is located to the east of the airport. Decline has also been critical on the large but relatively isolated estate at Netherley, some 5 km north of Speke. Yet on this particular housing estate, built during the 1960s and early 1970s, four new primary schools and one ten-form entry comprehensive school (1500 plus sixth form capacity) were provided, all of which are now operating at less than capacity.

The patchwork pattern of child population changes illustrates the difficulties faced by the Education Authority in deciding upon an appropriate level of school provision to meet not only the immediate needs, but also those which can be expected in the foreseeable future. Larger school units will, of course, take pupils from a larger number of blocks, thereby averaging out the variations between individual blocks. Yet, at the primary school level this process is limited by the distance which pupils are expected to travel to school. Although the Education Act requires local authorities to provide free transport to pupils who live more than 3 miles from their school (2 miles for pupils under the age of 8), such distances are not the limiting factor in most urban areas. A more important criterion of catchment area size for primary schools will be what parents consider to be "acceptable". At the secondary level, the extension of parental choice and the ability of pupils to travel long distances by public transport have tended to diminish the value of small-area population projections in secondary school planning.

Concluding comments

Experience seems to suggest that small-area population projections are not the lodestones to provide the uncontentious base sought by administrators to identify schools for closure or amalgamation, but they can have a useful diagnostic role. Given the uncertainties of determining optimum school size and the difficulties in predicting patterns of family mobility within the city, small-area population projections have tended to be used to study the likely future enrolment trends for a school which has been brought to the attention of the Education Committee for reasons other than its small size. This is likely to occur if, for example, the school requires major building works, a head teacher has retired or the enrolment has declined to a point where there are manifest gaps in the curriculum provision. Political decisions about allocating extra resources to that school then have to be made, and it is here that the population trends relating to its immediate catchment area can be invoked to provide additional evidence.

Demographers might find it strange that population data are relegated to such a confirmatory and subsidiary role in the planning of school provision. Nevertheless, this practice reflects political reality. The planning of school provision is a highly political exercise, and, in the sensitive environment of a city experiencing acute population and economic decline, it is inevitable that politicians will shy away from initiating unpopular actions. To single out a school for closure or amalgamation on demographic grounds alone has simply not proven to be politically feasible.

Acknowledgements

The authors wish to acknowledge the considerable assistance given to them by officers of the Liverpool Education Authority and in particular by Mr. R. Osborne and Mr. J. Glover. Nevertheless the views expressed, together with any errors, omissions or other shortcomings, must remain the responsibility of the authors.

REFERENCES

AGRICULTURAL DEVELOPMENT AND ADVISORY SERVICE (1969) *Report to accompany Sheet 100, Merseyside* (Ministry of Agriculture, Fisheries and Food)

ASPINALL, P. J. and D. M. HUDSON (1982) *Ellesmere Port, The making of an industrial borough* (Morten)

BERRY, P. M. (1980) *An evaluation of woodland on North Merseyside* (Ph.D. thesis, University of Liverpool)

BEST, R. H. and A. G. CAMPION (1970) Regional conversions of agricultural land to urban use in England and Wales, 1945–1967, *Transactions of the Institute of British Geographers*, 49, pp. 15–32

BURDETT, P. P. (1777) *A survey of the County Palatine of Chester*

CAMERON, C. G. (ed.) (1980) *The future of the British conurbations. Policies and prescriptions for change* (Longman)

CHAPE, A. (1978) *The inner city partnership: its background and approach in Liverpool*, in Planning and Transport Research and Computation, *Structure and regional planning practice and local planning practice*, pp. 118–33

CHILLINGWORTH, P. C. H. (1980) Marine sand and gravel. Prospects for the future, *Quarry Management and Products*, 7 (4), pp. 93–95

CITY CENTRE PLANNING GROUP (1965) *Liverpool City Centre Plan.*

COLEMAN, A. (1976) Is planning really necessary? *Geographical Journal*, 142 (3), pp. 411–37

COLEMAN, A. (1978) *Completion dates of Second Land Utilization Survey, Merseyside* (Report to Merseyside County Council)

COLEMAN, A. and K. R. A. MAGGS (1968) *Land Use Survey Handbook* (Second Land Use Survey)

COLEMAN, A. H. (1979) *Fares and ticketing policies in Merseyside* (M.P.T.E. unpublished paper)

COLLINS, W. G. (1975A) *Survey of Natural Environments in the Metropolitan County of Merseyside* (Report to Merseyside County Council; Remote Sensing Unit, University of Aston)

COLLINS, W. G. (1975B) *Derelict and despoiled land survey of the Metropolitan County of Merseyside* (Report to Merseyside County Council; Remote Sensing Unit, University of Aston)

DANIELS, P. W. and A. M. WARNES (1980) *Movement in cities* (Methuen)

DANSON, M. W., W. F. LEVER and J. F. MALCOLM (1980) The Inner-city employment problem in Great Britain, 1952–76: a shift-share approach, *Urban Studies*, 17 (2), pp. 192–210

DEPARTMENT OF ECONOMIC AFFAIRS (1965) *The problems of Merseyside* (H.M.S.O.)

DEPARTMENT OF EMPLOYMENT (1976) *Annual Census of Employment* (H.M.S.O.)

DEPARTMENT OF INDUSTRY (1980) *Guide to regional industrial policy changes July 1979 to August 1982*

DEPARTMENT OF THE ENVIRONMENT (1974) *Bus demonstration project: Summary report, 6: Formby*

DEPARTMENT OF THE ENVIRONMENT (1975) *Survey of derelict and despoiled land in England, 1974* (H.M.S.O. for Regional and Countryside Directorate of the Department of the Environment)

DEPARTMENT OF THE ENVIRONMENT (1976) *Production of aggregates in Great Britain, 1973–1974* (H.M.S.O.)

DEPARTMENT OF THE ENVIRONMENT (1977A) *Inner area studies: Liverpool, Birmingham and Lambeth. Summaries of consultants' final reports.* (H.M.S.O.)

DEPARTMENT OF THE ENVIRONMENT (1977B) *Change or decay. Final report of the Liverpool Inner Area Study* (H.M.S.O.)

DEPARTMENT OF THE ENVIRONMENT (1980) *Regional aggregates working parties—collation of the results of the 1977 survey*

DEPARTMENT OF THE ENVIRONMENT (1981) *Merseyside* (Press Release, 9th October)

DICKEN, P. and P. E. LLOYD (1978) Inner metropolitan industrial change, enterprise, structures and policy issues: case studies of Manchester and Merseyside, *Regional Studies*, 12 (2), pp. 181–97

ELLIOTT, G. (1973) *Field systems of North-west England*, in A. R. H. Baker and R. A. Butlin (eds.), *Studies of field systems in the British Isles* (C.U.P.), pp. 42–92

ELTON, C. J. (1973) *The impact of opencast mining on farming practices and patterns in S. Lancashire* (M.A. thesis, University of Liverpool)

FERGUSON, S. S. and P. J. B. BROWN (1979) *Issues related to decision making in the planning of inner city primary school provision under conditions of declining enrolment: an English example* (University of Liverpool, Department of Civic Design, Working Paper 12)

FORESTRY COMMISSION (1978) *Managing small woodlands* (Booklet 46)

FURNESS, R. R. and S. J. KING (1973) *Soils in Cheshire II—Sheet SJ37, Ellesmere Port* (Soil Survey Record No. 17)

GREENWOOD, C. (1819) *Map of the County Palatine of Chester*

GRESSWELL, R. K. (1953) *Sandy shores in South Lancashire* (Liverpool University Press)

HALL, B. R. and C. J. FOLLAND (1967) *The soils of the South West Lancashire coastal plain* (Memoir of the Soil Survey of Great Britain)

HALL, B. R. and C. J. FOLLAND (1970) *Soils of Lancashire* (Soil Survey of Great Britain, Bulletin No. 5)

HALL, P. et al. (1973) *The containment of urban England: Vol. I. Urban and metropolitan growth processes* (P.E.P. and Allen and Unwin)

HALSALL, D. A. (1978) Rapid transit on Merseyside, *Area*, 10 (2), pp. 212–16

H.M.S.O. (1977) *Policy for the inner cities* (Cmnd. 6845)

H.M.S.O. (1979) *Industry Act, 1972, Annual Report, 1978–79* (HC 204)

H.M.S.O (1980) *United Kingdom mineral statistics, 1979*

HUGHES, Q. (1969) *Liverpool* (City Buildings Series, Studio Vista)

HYDE, F. E. (1971) *Liverpool and the Mersey: an Economic History of a port* (David and Charles)

JACKSON, H. C. (1979) The decline of the sand lizard, *Lacerta agilis L.*, population on the sand dunes of the Merseyside coast, England, *Biological Conservation*, 16 (3), pp. 177–93

KEEBLE, D. E. (1980) Industrial decline, regional policy and the urban-rural manufacturing shift in the U.K., *Environment and Planning* A, 12 (8), pp. 945–62

KINSEY, J. (1980) *The economic impact of the Port of Liverpool on the economy of Merseyside* (Report to the Leverhulme Trust; School of Business Studies, University of Liverpool)

KNOWSLEY METROPOLITAN BOROUGH COUNCIL (1979) *Prescot Town Centre: Action Area Local Plan, Draft Written Statement*

KNOWSLEY METROPOLITAN BOROUGH COUNCIL (1980) *The Prescot town trail*

LAWTON, R. (1964) *Liverpool and the Tropics*, in R. W. Steel and R. M. Prothero (eds.), *Geographers and the Tropics: Liverpool essays* (Longman) pp. 349–75

LAWTON, R. (1970) *Conclusion*, in Lawton and Cunningham, op. cit., pp. 484–96

LAWTON, R. and C. M. CUNNINGHAM (1970) *Merseyside: social and economic studies* (Longman)

LAWLESS, P. (1981) *Britain's inner cities: problems and policies* (Harper and Row)

LAXTON, P. (1981) Liverpool in 1801: a manuscript return for the first national census, *Transactions Historic Society of Lancashire and Cheshire*, 130, pp. 73–113

LISTER, P. H. (1982) *Public sector factory building programmes within Merseyside Metropolitan County* (Report to Merseyside County Council)

LISTER, P. H. (forthcoming) *Regional policies and industrial development on Merseyside 1930–1960)*, in B. L. Anderson and P. J. Stoney (eds.) *Commerce, industry and transport: studies in economic change on Merseyside* (Liverpool University Press)

LIVERPOOL CITY COUNCIL (1968) *Social Malaise in Liverpool: Interim report on social problems and their distribution*

LIVERPOOL CITY COUNCIL (1972) *South Docks, principles of re-development*

LIVERPOOL CITY COUNCIL (1977) *City in Transition: A review of urban trends in Liverpool 1961–76 and their future implications*

LIVERPOOL CITY COUNCIL (1978) *Availability of land for industrial development* (CPO/50/78)

LIVERPOOL CITY COUNCIL (1979) *City of Liverpool: Improvement Areas declared under the Inner Urban Areas Act, 1978*

LIVERPOOL CITY COUNCIL (1980A) *Shopping: Trends and Opportunities* (City Planning Department)

LIVERPOOL CITY COUNCIL (1980B) *The Economy: Distributive Trades Statement* (City Planning Department)

LIVERPOOL CITY COUNCIL (1980C) *The Economy: Service Industries Statement* (City Planning Department)

LIVERPOOL CITY COUNCIL (1980D) *The Economy: Office Development Statement* (City Planning Department)

LIVERPOOL CITY COUNCIL (1980E) *City Centre Offices: Trends and Opportunities* (City Planning Department)

LIVERPOOL CITY COUNCIL (1980F) *Liverpool: Planning information digest* (City Planning Department)

LIVERPOOL CITY COUNCIL (1981) *Local economic trends and future prospects* (City Planning Department)

LIVERPOOL HERITAGE BUREAU (1978) *Buildings of Liverpool* (Liverpool City Planning Department)

LIVERPOOL HERITAGE BUREAU (1979) *Liverpool Conservation Areas* (Liverpool City Planning Department)

LIVERPOOL INNER CITY PARTNERSHIP COMMITTEE (1978) *Liverpool Inner City Partnership Programme, 1979–82*

LIVERPOOL INNER CITY PARTNERSHIP COMMITTEE (1980) *Liverpool Inner City Partnership Programme, 1980–83*

LIVERPOOL POLYTECHNIC (1978) *The City Centre Shopper* (Business Research Centre)

LLOYD, P. E. (1969) *The impact of Development Area Policies on Merseyside, 1949–1967*, in Lawton and Cunningham, op. cit., pp. 374–410

LLOYD, P. E. (1979) The components of industrial change for Merseyside Inner Area, 1966–75, *Urban Studies*, 16 (1), pp. 45–60

MCDOWELL, D. M. (1973) Liverpool Bay: a better site than Maplin?, *Surveyor*, 16, pp. 13–15

MAGNAY, H. S. (1948) *City of Liverpool: development plan for education* (Liverpool City Council)

MANPOWER RESEARCH GROUP (1981) *Review of the economy and employment* (University of Warwick)

MASSER, F. I. (1970) *The analysis and prediction of physical change in the central area of Liverpool*, in Lawton and Cunningham, op. cit., pp. 450–83

MASSER, F. I. and S. S. FERGUSON (1977) *Spatial issues in school admission policy within Liverpool* (University of Liverpool, Department of Civic Design, Working Paper 5)

MASSEY, D. (1979) In what sense à regional problem?, *Regional Studies*, 13 (2), pp. 233–43

MASSEY, D. and R. MEEGAN (1978) Industrial Restructuring Versus the Cities, *Urban Studies*, 15 (3), pp. 273–88

MERSEY BARRAGE PANEL (1981) *A Mersey Barrage: a focus for the future of Merseyside?* (Merseyside Enterprise Forum)

MERSEY AND WEAVER RIVER AUTHORITY (1972) *Altmouth Pumping Station*

MERSEYSIDE COUNTY COUNCIL (1975A) *Merseyside Structure Plan; Draft Report of Survey: Housing*

MERSEYSIDE COUNTY COUNCIL (1975B) *Merseyside Structure Plan; Stage One Report*

MERSEYSIDE COUNTY COUNCIL (1976A) *A strategic policy for the South Docks*

MERSEYSIDE COUNTY COUNCIL (1976B) *Targets for Merseyside in the 1980s* (County Planning Department)

MERSEYSIDE COUNTY COUNCIL (1976C) *Transport policies and programme, 1977/78*

MERSEYSIDE COUNTY COUNCIL (1976D) *Merseyside Structure Plan: Draft Report. Natural Resources.* Chapter 4, *Woodland*

MERSEYSIDE COUNTY COUNCIL (1977) *Draft policy for the use of open land-mineral working* (Report CPO/80/77)

MERSEYSIDE COUNTY COUNCIL (1978) *Economic development programme and employment policies for Merseyside* (CPO/36/78)

MERSEYSIDE COUNTY COUNCIL (1979A–G) *Merseyside Structure Plan; Reports of Survey: A—The economy, B— Shopping, C—Tourism, D—Population, E—Natural resources, F—Environmental pollution and condition of land, G—Land resources*

MERSEYSIDE COUNTY COUNCIL (1980) *Merseyside Structure Plan: Written Statement*

MERSEYSIDE COUNTY COUNCIL (1981A) *The Merseyside economy: performance and prospects to 1986* (County Planning Department)

MERSEYSIDE COUNTY COUNCIL (1981B) *Merseyside Industrial Monitor* (County Planning Department)

MERSEYSIDE COUNTY COUNCIL (1981C) *Transport policies and programme, 1982/83*

MERSEYSIDE COUNTY COUNCIL (1981D). *Information leaflet, 1981–82*

MERSEYSIDE COUNTY COUNCIL (1982) *Croxteth Country Park—A Woodland Management Plan*

MERSEYSIDE ENTERPRISE FORUM (1980) *Chips with everything or technology with a human face*

MERSEYSIDE PASSENGER TRANSPORT AUTHORITY AND EXECUTIVE (1972) *A Transport Plan for Merseyside*

MERSEYSIDE PASSENGER TRANSPORT EXECUTIVE (1981) *The Merseyrail Projects: A monitoring report*

MINISTRY OF AGRICULTURE, FISHERIES AND FOOD (1966) *Agricultural land classification* (Agricultural Land Service, Technical report No. 11)

MINISTRY OF AGRICULTURE, FISHERIES AND FOOD (1967) *Horticulture in Britain, Part I, Vegetables* (H.M.S.O.)

MINISTRY OF AGRICULTURE, FISHERIES AND FOOD (1969) *Asparagus* (Technical Bulletin, No. 60)

MINISTRY OF AGRICULTURE, FISHERIES AND FOOD (1974) *Merseyside Metropolitan County: agricultural facts and figures*

MINISTRY OF AGRICULTURE, FISHERIES AND FOOD (1981) *Agricultural Land Classification report for selected estuarine sites in North-West England and Clwyd* (Resource Planning Group, Land and Water Service)

MINISTRY OF HOUSING AND LOCAL GOVERNMENT (1956) *Liverpool overspill and the development of Merseyside* (TP2a)

MOUNTFIELD, S. (1965) *Western gateway. A history of the Mersey Docks and Harbour Board* (Liverpool University Press)

MUCHNICK, D. M. (1970) *Urban renewal in Liverpool: a study of the politics of redevelopment* (Bell and Sons)

NABARRO, R. (1980) *The impact on workers from the inner city of Liverpool's economic decline* in A. Evans and D. Eversley (eds.) *The inner city: employment and industry* (Heinemann), pp. 294–322

NORTH WEST AGGREGATES WORKING PARTY (1977) *A survey of aggregates supply and demand in the North West Region. Interim report*

NORTH WEST ECONOMIC PLANNING COUNCIL (1978) *Land for agriculture in the North West*

NORTH WEST JOINT PLANNING TEAM (1973) *Strategic Plan for the North West.* Technical Paper No. 7, *Regional open land*

NORTH WEST JOINT PLANNING TEAM (1974) *Strategic Plan for the North West* (H.M.S.O.)

PATMORE, J. A. (1970) *The Mersey crossing*, in Patmore and Hodgkiss, op. cit., pp. 52–53

PATMORE, J. A. and A. G. HODGKISS (eds.) (1970) *Merseyside in Maps* (Longman)

PAUL, A. H. (1980) Vanishing railways and the urban scene: the case of Liverpool, *Geography*, 65 (2), pp. 119–24

PETERKEN, G. F. (1974) A method of assessing woodland flora for conservation using indicator species, *Biological Conservation*, 6 (3), pp. 239–45

PEVSNER, N. (1969) *Lancashire: Vol. 1—The industrial and commercial South* (The Buildings of England Series, Penguin)

PEVSNER, N. and E. HUBBARD (1971) *Cheshire* (The Buildings of England Series, Penguin)

PICKETT, K. (1970A) *Merseyside's population and social structure*, in Lawton and Cunningham, op. cit., pp. 72–107

PICKETT, K. (1970B) *Migration in the Merseyside area*, in Lawton and Cunningham, op. cit., pp. 108–348

POUNCE, R. J. (1981) *Industrial movement in the United Kingdom, 1966–75* (Department of Industry)

PRUS-CHACINSKI, M. and W. B. HARRIS (1963) Standards for lowland drainage and flood alleviation and drainage of peatlands, with special reference to the Crossens Scheme, *Proc. Inst. Civil Engineers*, 24, pp. 177–206

ROBERTS, J. (1974) *The distribution and vegetation composition of woodland on the Wirral Peninsula* (Ph.D. thesis, University of Liverpool)

ROBERTS, J. (1975) *Woodland on the Wirral Peninsula* (Report to Merseyside County Council; University of Liverpool)

ROBERTS, J. and P. M. BURNETT (1976) *Woodland in Merseyside* (Consultancy Report to Merseyside County Council)

SALT, J. (1967) The impact of Ford and Vauxhall plants on the employment situation of Merseyside, 1962–65, *Tijdschrift voor Economische en Sociale Geografie*, 58 (3), pp. 255–64

SHACKLETON, R. M. (1953) *Geology*, in Smith, op. cit., pp. 19–37

SMITH, D. M. (1969) *Industrial Britain: The North West* (David and Charles)

SMITH, W. (1953A) *A scientific survey of Merseyside* (Liverpool University Press)

SMITH, W. (1953B) *Merseyside and the Merseyside District*, in Smith, op. cit. pp. 1–18

SMITH, W. (1953C) *The urban structure of Liverpool*, in Smith, op. cit., pp. 188–99

SMITH, W. (1953D) *The agricultural geography*, in Smith, op. cit., pp. 289–99

STEEL, R. W. (1970) *Preface*, in Lawton and Cunningham, op. cit., pp. vi–viii

STRUTHERS, W. A. K. and C. B. WILLIAMSON (1979) Local economic development. Integrated policy planning and implementation in Merseyside, *Town Planning Review*, 50 (2), pp. 164–83

SWALLOW, K. W. (1981) Merseyside Transport, 1969–1981, *Omnibus Magazine*, July/August, pp. 87–89

TAYLOR, J. A. (1952) The relation of crop distribution to the drift pattern of south-west Lancashire, *Transactions of the Institute of British Geographers*, 18, pp. 77–91

TAYLOR, J. A. (1967) *The Shirdley Hill sands*, in R. W. Steel and R. Lawton (eds.), *Liverpool essays in geography*, (Longman), pp. 441–61

THOMPSON, A. (1977) *The role of Housing Associations in major urban areas: a case study of Merseyside Improved Houses* (University of Birmingham)

THOMPSON, F. L. (1945) *Merseyside Plan, 1945* (H.M.S.O.)

TRIST, E. L. (1974) *The structural presence of the post-industrial society*, in N. Cross, D. Elliott and P. Roy (eds.), *Man-made futures* (Hutchinson in association with Open University Press), pp. 107–17

VERNEY, R. (1976) *Aggregates: the way ahead. Report of the Advisory Committee on Aggregates* (H.M.S.O. for Department of the Environment)

VICK, C. M. and J. F. HANDLEY (1977) Lime and fertilizer use in the maintenance of turf in urban parks and open spaces, *Parks and Recreation*, October, pp. 39–48

WEBBER, R. J. (1975) *Liverpool Social Area Study 1971 Data: Final Report* (Planning Research Applications Group, Technical Papers TP14)

WILLIAMS, A. F. (1977) *'Crossroads': the new accessibility of the West Midlands*, in F. Joyce (ed.) *Metropolitan development and change. The West Midlands: a policy review* (Gower), pp. 367–92

WILSON, H. and L. WOMERSLEY (1977A) *Change or decay: Final report of the Liverpool Inner Area Study* (H.M.S.O.)

WILSON, H. and L. WOMERSLEY (1977B) *Inner Area Study. Liverpool: social area analysis* (Department of the Environment, 1AS/L1/22)

WU, L and A. D. BRADSHAW (1972) Aerial pollution and the rapid evolution of copper tolerance, *Nature*, V. 238 (5360), pp. 167–69

YATES, W. (1786) *The County Palatine of Lancaster. Surveyed by Willm Yates*

INDEX